D1483341

THE ROYAL GEORGE

H.R.H. THE DUKE OF CAMBRIDGE

THE
ROYAL GEORGE
1819-1904

The Life of H.R.H. Prince George
Duke of Cambridge

by GILES ST. AUBYN

New York : Alfred · A · Knopf
1964

L. C. catalog card number: 64-12317

THIS IS A BORZOI BOOK,
PUBLISHED BY ALFRED A. KNOPF, INC.

FIRST AMERICAN EDITION

THIS BOOK IS DEDICATED TO THE MEMORY OF

MRS. MARY NAYLER,

WHO FOR MANY YEARS HELPED ME WITH

MY WRITING AND WHO ASSISTED

WITH THIS BIOGRAPHY, WHICH SHE

DID NOT LIVE TO SEE FINISHED.

PREFACE

THE BIOGRAPHER in his choice of a victim is confronted with a dilemma. Either he writes about famous people of whom little new can be said, or he selects a lesser-known person, the subject of a mass of unpublished documents, who nevertheless is too obscure to catch the public's fancy. How well known the Duke of Cambridge is today is difficult to tell, but of three things I am certain. First, as Commander-in-Chief of the Victorian Army for thirty-nine years he occupied the centre of the political stage at one of the greatest moments in our history. Second, the material for his life and times, much of it unpublished, is important, extensive, and exciting. Third, the Duke enjoyed a fascinating and momentous life. It is customary, I know, to leave such extravagant claims to the publisher, it not being thought proper in an author to advertise his wares, but having stumbled on a historical treasure trove, I am anxious to share my discovery. Merely because the Duke of Cambridge is no longer a household name, I hope it will not be thought that this biography is only of interest to scholars.

To prevent this study of the Duke from becoming a two-volume work like its predecessors, I have purposely omitted much which the official lives included. For example, I have said little of the Duke's travels, of his German relations, of his staff, of his concern with colonial wars, of his correspondence with the commanders-in-chief in India, or of his interest in a number of military matters, which, however absorbing they might have been in the Victorian Age, have lost something of their relevance in the mid-twentieth century. Besides intentional omissions, there are gaps which proceed from ignorance rather than choice. Despite an overwhelming mass of evidence, parts of H.R.H.'s life escape the biographer's trawl. While it is possible to discover from the Duke's diary the exact time he left Gloucester House for the War Office on the morning of November 12, 1884, and with whom he dined on September 7, 1901, it is not possible to find out where he first met his wife. When the story becomes disjointed, the charitable reader will I hope assume that the evidence is wanting rather than the author.

I am deeply indebted to Her Majesty the Queen for permission to use the Royal Archives at Windsor. I owe the loan of the FitzGeorge papers to the kindness of Princess Galitzine and Brigadier Balfour. For leave to study Lord Wolseley's letters at the Royal United Service Institution, the Cardwell papers at the Public Record Office, and various nineteenth-century political collections in the British Museum, I must gratefully acknowledge the permission of the authorities concerned. Whoever has worked at any of these institutions, or in the Library and Archives at Windsor, or in the War Office, will know how much help, patience, and knowledge are ungrudgingly bestowed on researchers.

I should like to thank Mr. James Pope-Hennessy, Mr. Michael Howard, Mr. Peter Townend, and the Reverend Charles Tomkins, who, after reading the book in manuscript, made many valuable suggestions and helped me to avoid some serious errors of fact, judgement, and style. Finally, I owe an immense amount to Miss Rosemary Stopford, who helped in countless ways, and who contrived to translate an illegible draft into a faultless typescript.

GILES ST. AUBYN

St. Tudwal's Island
1963

CONTENTS

ILLUSTRATIONS

Frontispiece

H.R.H. The Duke of Cambridge

Following page 176

A SIMPLIFIED FAMILY TREE OF

THE DUKE OF CAMBRIDGE'S RELATIONS

*Except for Augustus FitzGeorge and Francis Teck, who never
married, all the Princess Royal's generation had issue.*

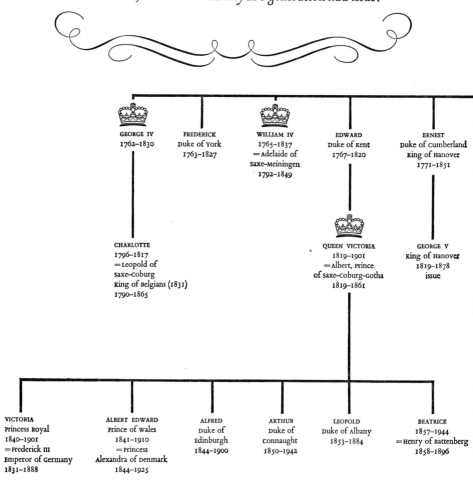

GEORGE IV
1762–1830

FREDERICK
Duke of York
1763–1827

WILLIAM IV
1765–1837
= Adelaide of
Saxe-Meiningen
1792–1849

EDWARD
Duke of Kent
1767–1820

ERNEST
Duke of Cumberland
King of Hanover
1771–1851

CHARLOTTE
1796–1817
= Leopold of
Saxe-Coburg
King of Belgians (1831)
1790–1865

QUEEN VICTORIA
1819–1901
= Albert, Prince
of Saxe-Coburg-Gotha
1819–1861

GEORGE V
King of Hanover
1819–1878
issue

VICTORIA
Princess Royal
1840–1901
= Frederick III
Emperor of Germany
1831–1888

ALBERT EDWARD
Prince of Wales
1841–1910
= Princess
Alexandra of Denmark
1844–1925

ALFRED
Duke of
Edinburgh
1844–1900

ARTHUR
Duke of
Connaught
1850–1942

LEOPOLD
Duke of Albany
1853–1884

BEATRICE
1857–1944
= Henry of Battenberg
1858–1896

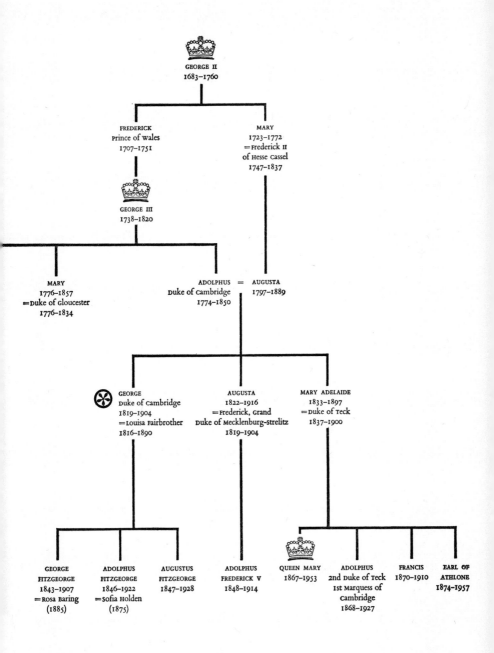

GEORGE II
1683–1760

FREDERICK
Prince of wales
1707–1751

MARY
1723–1772
=Frederick II
of Hesse Cassel
1747–1837

GEORGE III
1738–1820

MARY
1776–1857
=Duke of Gloucester
1776–1834

ADOLPHUS = AUGUSTA
Duke of cambridge   1797–1889
1774–1850

GEORGE
Duke of cambridge
1819–1904
=Louisa Fairbrother
1816–1890

AUGUSTA
1822–1916
=Frederick, Grand
Duke of Mecklenburg-strelitz
1819–1904

MARY ADELAIDE
1833–1897
=Duke of Teck
1837–1900

GEORGE
FITZGEORGE
1843–1907
=Rosa Baring
(1885)

ADOLPHUS
FITZGEORGE
1846–1922
=sofia Holden
(1875)

AUGUSTUS
FITZGEORGE
1847–1928

ADOLPHUS
FREDERICK V
1848–1914

QUEEN MARY
1867–1953

ADOLPHUS
2nd Duke of Teck
1st Marquess of
cambridge
1868–1927

FRANCIS
1870–1910

EARL OF
ATHLONE
1874–1957

THE ROYAL GEORGE

THE superior characters (n) in the text refer to notes of bibliographical or scholarly interest (chiefly source identifications), which are indicated by page and line at the back of the book.

A Prince in the Making

THE SONS of King George III were disconcertingly reluctant to marry. Moreover, they were disposed to
regard as unattractive alliances which their advisers assured them were alluring. Some even indulged in the delights of matrimony without incurring its legal liabilities.
Consequently it was not until the fifty-ninth year of his
father's reign that Adolphus, Duke of Cambridge, the
favourite son of the King and a young man unblemished
by scandal, produced a boy whom the law could recognize
as a Prince of the Blood Royal. In honour of his grandfather, the child was christened George. Before the birth
of his cousin, Princess Victoria, the infant Prince was heir
presumptive to the throne.

Prince Adolphus was born in 1774 and in 1801 was
created Duke of Cambridge. The title had originally been
bestowed upon four of the sons of James II, all of whom died
in infancy. It was revived by Queen Anne for the Prince
Electoral of Hanover, later King George II, and became
merged in the Crown when he ascended the throne.[n]
Prince Adolphus played a gallant part in the Revolutionary
War. In 1794 he was captured by the French in Flanders
but contrived to escape unrecognized. One of his staff officers spoke as highly of his amiability as of his courage,
and described him as having "a countenance beaming with
benevolence and goodwill towards all."[n] In the following
year he was wounded, ordered back to England, and after

a few months sent to Hanover, a part of Germany he knew well since he had been educated at the University of Göttingen with his brothers, Ernest and Augustus. On Napoleon's annexation of the Electorate, the Duke retired to England, but when in 1813 the Emperor was compelled to withdraw, Adolphus was sent to Hanover once more as commander of its army. At the Congress of Vienna the Electorate was raised to a kingdom and the Duke was appointed its Governor General.

The death in 1817 of Princess Charlotte, the only child of the Prince Regent, and the wife of Prince Leopold of Saxe-Coburg, made it urgently necessary for the Duke to marry if the Hanoverian line was to be preserved. On November 5, the anniversary of a great deliverance, Princess Charlotte had given birth to a stillborn son. Early next morning she herself was dead, exhausted by protracted labour and weakened by dieting and bleeding. The Royal Dukes, conscious of their duty to their country, and not unmindful of the prospect of marriage settlements, began to look about for wives. Unfortunately they were scarcely attractive suitors. Their mistresses, their natural children, their formidable debts, and their advancing years, were defects which might be considered overwhelming by any but the most despondent of princesses. The Duke of Cambridge alone was unscarred by scandal and still comparatively young.

The Duke of Clarence commissioned the Duke of Cambridge to explore the German courts to find him a bride. Soon Adolphus began sending his brother back glowing descriptions of the wit, beauty, and charm of Princess Augusta, daughter of Frederick, Landgrave of Hesse-Cassel. The Duke of Clarence was greatly amused by these letters. "By Heavens!" he said. "He's in love with her himself. I'll write and tell him to take her, bless him!"" The wedding accordingly took place at the castle of Hesse-Cassel on May 7, 1818, and was subsequently also solemnized in England.

4

In March 1819, at the palace in Hanover, the Duchess was confined with a child, which, if it survived the attention of her medical advisers, would become the only lawful descendant of George III. So important an event needed to be observed by witnesses of undisputed integrity. Among others, the Duke of Clarence was present. Scrupulous precautions were taken to ensure that all was in order, and that no grounds could be entertained for alleging that anything spurious had taken place. Henry Rose, Envoy Extraordinary at the Court of Berlin, reported the details to Castlereagh, then Foreign Secretary.

Having been apprised by His Royal Highness the Duke of Cambridge at a quarter before one o'clock of the morning of Friday the twenty-sixth day of March in the year of Our Lord one thousand eight hundred and nineteen that Her Royal Highness the Duchess of Cambridge's labour pains had commenced, we repaired forthwith to the room adjoining to that in which Her Royal Highness was to be delivered, in Cambridge House in the City of Hanover, the door between these two rooms remaining open during the whole of our attendance; having been previously informed by His Royal Highness that Her Royal Highness would be confined in Her Bedroom up one pair of stairs, and that free access must remain from that room to Her Dressing room immediately contiguous to it, and these rooms having been previously shewn to one of us, the Right Honourable George Henry Rose, the seal of the said Right Honourable George Henry Rose was affixed so as to close it, upon the outside of the outward door of the dressing room under the directions of His Royal Highness, the Duke of Cambridge, who locked the door and gave the key of it to the said Right Honourable George Henry Rose, so that no communication with the bedroom could take place from without, but under Our eyes, we remaining in the room adjoining to the bedroom, and through which all persons entering that bedroom must pass; sharp labour continued until ten minutes past

5

two o'clock of the morning aforesaid, when Her Royal Highness the Duchess of Cambridge was safely delivered of a male child, whose sex we determined by actual inspection."

The boy was christened on May 11, in Hanover, according to the rites of the Church of England. He was called George William Frederick Charles. Royalty are disposed to be prodigal with Christian names and for a Prince of the Blood to possess so few was to be sent almost naked into the world, but as most of his relations bore at least one of these names they forgave the parsimony. The Prince Regent, represented at the ceremony by the Duke of Clarence, and the Duke of Clarence, represented by the Earl of Mayo, were the child's godfathers.

Prince George was fortunate in his parents. His father was by far the most agreeable of all the King's sons, although, considering his heredity, his eccentricity bordered on the disturbing. Wellington, in a moment of exasperation, told Mrs. Arbuthnot that Adolphus was "as mad as Bedlam."" As a young man he read widely, was interested in science, loved music, and proved himself an industrious and efficient soldier. He played the violin expertly and had an impressive voice: invariably audible if not inevitably melodious. Many of his friends were scholars, musicians, and artists, who shared his tastes. In the Victorian Age he appeared a pleasant survival of the eighteenth century, courteous, cultivated, and robustly religious, displaying the charm of that vanished era without betraying its vices.

Sir Charles Bagot met the Duke of Cambridge at Brussels in 1825 and found him volubly affable. "Yesterday," he wrote to a friend, "I dined with His Lowland Majesty to meet the Duke of a place called Cambridge somewhere in the English fens, where they teach arithmetic. This Duke, with his Duchess and Dukelings, set out for England this morning. He is just the same good-humoured rattle that he always was, and she, I think, is a very personable body for a Princess."" Other people, however, found the Duke's explosions of goodwill overwhelming. Lady Lyttelton met him at Windsor in 1839, while she was in waiting on Queen Victoria, and described the encounter in her letters.

> . . . The Cambridges arrived yesterday, and enriched our dancing evening. Queen's headache quite gone, luckily, for it requires a sound head to listen to the Duke . . . I was so *bestürmt* with questions, one hundred in a breath, close to my eye, by the Duke on his first arrival that I was fairly bewildered, and answered, "Yes, Ma'am." After dinner, during the dancing, he came and sat by me, and to be sure how he did shout and cross-examine! but he never wants any answer, so it don't matter. "Where do you *habitually* reside, Ma'am? Oh, Hagley, you *did* live there. I see, I see—your son lately married—how long? a few months? I understand. *Now* where do you mean to live? At Richmond for the winter? Oh, I see! Where have you been since your son's marriage? Leamington? Why Leamington? Oh, your brother—I understand! Your brother, Captain Spencer! I remember—I perfectly recollect. A naval man, I believe. Yes, I saw him in 1825 at your father's in the Isle of Wight. Yes, yes, I know—Frederick Spencer, to be sure! *Your* father-in-law, Mr. Poyntz? No, surely not so, Ma'am. Oh, his father-in-law? Oh, I see, I see," and so on for half an hour. I was quite out of breath with listening, and could hardly stick in a word in answer here and there, and all as loud as a very sonorous voice can reach . . .

When the Duke left Windsor it was like the silence of night after a battle.

> . . . The Cambridges are gone, and the Castle is still as death, for want of the Duke. Think of his asking *me* if I had "any commands" to town? Think if I had told him I wanted a small parcel carried! He shouted on to the last, singing the quadrilles while they danced, and "God save the Queen" while we dined, rather than be silent . . ."

7

Wherever the Duke went he spoke so loud and inces-
santly that it was impossible to be unaware of his presence.
He had, moreover, inherited his father's trick of repeating
everything three times: a habit described by Horace Wal-
pole as "triptology." He often thought aloud, sometimes
with disquieting candour. The stories of his absent-minded
comments in church are legion: some are even true. Like
the sayings of Dr. Spooner, the authorized version is very
much shorter than the Apocrypha. That he shouted "en-
core" after a preacher had delivered himself of a particularly eloquent peroration is too improbable to be believed,
but the following reminiscences are authentic. The Duke
of Cambridge "constantly attended the Sunday Morning
Services at St. Paul's, Knightsbridge, in the time of the
Rev. W. J. E. Bennett, and occasionally was pleased to express in an audible tone his approbation of the proceedings,
and his opinion of the sermon. I remember on one occasion
when the officiating clergyman pronounced the exhorta-
tion—'Let us pray'—the Duke bravely responded from
his pew:

" 'Aye, to be sure; why not? let us pray, let us pray, let
us pray!'

"On another occasion, while the commandments were
being read I heard him remark—

" 'Steal! no, of course not; mustn't steal, mustn't steal,
mustn't steal.'

"At the opera, this eccentric habit betrayed itself in a
still more marked and frequent way. I remember once hearing him all across the house, exclaim, as he moved his
opera-glass round the circles—

" 'Why, I declare there are not half a dozen pretty girls
in the house; not half a dozen, not half a dozen, not half
a dozen.'

"One night when a young pupil of Molique's, a mere boy,
was playing in the orchestra from his master's desk, the
Duke, who was very observant and also had a keen ear for

8

music, struck by his precocity, sent between the acts for the boy to come up to his box, which was opposite ours, and taking him on his knee entered into a lively conversation with him, the Duke's share in the dialogue being heard pretty well all over the house. All that generation of the Royal Family were in the habit of talking in what we will call a *cursory* way, employing expletives rather expressive than choice."[n]

Toward the end of his life the Duke became increasingly deaf, so he decided to move from the gallery of the church at Kew, which he frequently attended, into a pew near the pulpit. Close by were some local schoolboys and every Sunday he counted them. If any were missing he would lean over the pew and say to the schoolmaster: "Simpson, there are two or three boys not here today." "They are ill, Your Royal Highness," Simpson would reply. "Send to my house for soup for them," was the welcome answer. During a very dry summer, the vicar read the prayer for rain; at the close the Duke joined fervently in the "Amen," adding, in exactly the same tone of voice, "but we shan't get it till the wind changes." One Sunday, during the reading of the offertory sentences, when the words "Behold, the half of my goods I give to the poor" were read, His Royal Highness astonished his fellow-worshippers by exclaiming: "No, no, I can't do that; a half is too much for any man, but I have no objection to a tenth." Again, on hearing the text "for we brought nothing into the world, neither may we carry anything out," he ejaculated: "True, true—too many calls upon us for that."[n]

Such stories of eccentricity present a distorted portrait of the Duke, for he was a very ordinary person, little inclined to stand on his dignity, friendly to all and admired for his integrity. He showed scant regard for pomp and officialdom. When he was taken to visit a cricket match on Upper Club at Eton, he broke away from the escorting provost, preferring to be shown round by a small boy of his acquaintance." It was because he so little resembled the common conception of a Royal Duke that he was so much better liked than his brothers.

Although Prince George owed many Hanoverian characteristics to his father, his mother was the more profound influence on his life. The Duchess died at the age of ninety-two. She survived her husband by forty years and lived long enough to congratulate her son on the anniversary of half a century's service in the British Army. Like Prince Adolphus, she was a great-grandchild of King George II. Without being especially clever or highly educated, she was interested in politics, enjoyed music, loved the theatre, and read widely. She had been brought up in the traditions of the eighteenth century and was wholeheartedly conservative. Her dignified and somewhat austere manner was lightened by flashes of humour. Those who remembered her only in old age thought her forbidding and terrifying. Queen Mary never felt wholly at ease with her querulous grandmother, although Ella Taylor, a lady-in-waiting who knew the Duchess from earlier days, described her as "a Duck of a Duchess. I never met with anyone with whom it is so easy to get on . . ." Princess Augusta spoke to the last with a strong, guttural, German accent and never became entirely reconciled to English ways.

"The Duchess of Cambridge," wrote her daughter's biographer, "was a handsome, stately lady somewhat above the average height of women . . . When in repose her face wore rather a severe expression, but directly she spoke her countenance lighted up and a charming smile at once betrayed the gentle nature within . . . Dignified in bearing and manner, as became a great lady brought up in the sentiments of the *ancien régime,* the Duchess was invariably kind and gracious to those about her. . . . Punctuality was a strong point with Her Royal Highness, and she never allowed the carriage to be kept waiting longer than was necessary. Method and regularity were seen in every department, and it would have been difficult to find a household better ordered. . . . Her Royal Highness had much ability, and was a good conversationalist, while her keen sense of fun and humour made her a most delightful companion . . . The Duchess was a thorough musician, possessing a beautiful soprano voice, and greatly enjoyed the opera. She was also warmly interested in politics; she was a frequent attendant at the debates in the House of Lords, and never missed reading her daily paper."[20]

The early years of Prince George's life were spent with his parents in Hanover. While still very young, he caught scarlet fever and the doctors despaired of his life. His father was at dinner when a message was sent to him that the Prince appeared to be dying. The Duke, in a frenzy of agitation, seized some Steinberger, a Rhine wine which he particularly relished, and rushed to the sickroom. Heedless of all protests, he forced the child to drink a glass. From that moment the boy revived and the fever abated. For many years Steinberger was always drunk on Prince George's birthday to commemorate this marvellous recovery.

Prince George, having been saved from fever, only narrowly escaped being murdered. His first tutor, the Rev. Henry Harvey, finding his task too arduous, employed a Mr. Welsh as his assistant. From the first, Welsh proved eccentric, but nobody actually suspected him of madness until he was discovered one night kneeling by the Prince's bedside, armed with a knife, exclaiming loudly that he had been called upon to cut the child's throat and "send him straight to heaven."[21] Fortunately he was overheard and overpowered before being able to fulfil his pious intention. Harvey's selection of a tutor was a poor testimony to his discernment, and in 1828 he was replaced by the Rev. John Ryle Wood, who took charge of the Prince for the next eight years.

Wood was a strong, upright man, severe in his judgments and a strict disciplinarian. He believed in leaving little to chance. His pupil's work and leisure were minutely supervised, yet he entirely won the confidence of the Prince, who later referred to him as "my beloved preceptor." Wood subsequently became chaplain to Queen Adelaide and a canon of Worcester Cathedral. His old pupil never forgot him. When the Kaiser visited England in 1874, Prince George, then Duke of Cambridge and Officer Commanding-in-Chief of the British Army, gave an official banquet to welcome the German Emperor. The Prince of Wales and all the foremost generals in England were invited. Among these eminent guests was Canon Wood, a little out of place in so glittering an array of military men, his clerical dress somewhat drab in that flurry of gold, silver, and scarlet, but very proud to have been invited. When Wood died, Prince George recalled in his diary the many years they had known each other and the fervour of their friendship.

> 8 November 1886. Heard today of the death of my dear old friend and tutor, Mr. Wood, after a very painful and somewhat protracted illness. He died early this morning. He is a friend of fifty-eight years' standing, and was very dear and good to me.

Wood encouraged his pupil to keep a journal, which, with some interruptions, H.R.H. continued to the last year of his life. The early volumes are a mixture of pious observations, evidently dictated, or at least suggested, by the master, and comments which could only have come from the boy.

> I fidgeted on my chair whilst learning my lesson, until coming to the edge without knowing it, I slipt off and fell to the ground pulling the chair over me and causing it to give me a hard blow on the head.
> I cried for an orange! How silly. I think it must have been my third or fourth Birthday which I last celebrated and not my *ninth!*
> I told a lie, saying that I had not spoken to anyone, when I had spoken to the upholsterer. I tried, when found out by Mr. Wood, to explain away my falsehood, arguing and equiv-

ocating, pretending that I did not know *when* he meant. Oh! that I could leave off lying and shuffling. It always gets me into trouble—is so unlike a gentleman and so wicked.

When the Duke of Clarence ascended the throne as William IV, he decided that his nephew should be brought up in England. The boy's parents seem to have been allowed no choice in the matter. So in 1830, at the age of eleven, Prince George, under Mr. Wood's care, set out from Hanover for Windsor. What prompted the decision is a matter of conjecture, but Queen Adelaide loved children and, having lost her own in infancy, may well have encouraged her husband in his belief that the boy should live with them.

Both the Duchess and her son found the separation painful. "Since I love you so unutterably my good George," she wrote to him, "I do not like a single day to pass without my having written you at least a few words." Her very first letter to him, dated August 9, 1830, showed her despair on losing him.

My precious George,—These are the first words I have to address to you by the help of pen and paper, since it is the first time we have ever been separated. Did I not, my angel boy, well keep my promise to you to make the parting very quick and short? God grant that you have not grieved too much, and had no return of your severe bad headache, for then you would have sadly needed poor Mama, who knows her George so well and knows best what he needs and likes. Ah! could I but hasten to you every two hours to exchange a couple of words! But that happy time the good God will soon restore to us! Be of bright and good courage, we shall soon meet again. Already three days have passed in which we have not seen each other, thus one slips away after the other, and before long the bright day of our happy reunion will shine for us. . . . You must write to me very fully—all details, my dear good George! Also how you like your

13

new home—all, all, everything. I want to know! No secrets from me. *Make* plenty of time to write, it is my only consolation . . ."

To leave home and to live with the King was a daunting experience for so young a boy. His mother warned him to be "respectful" to his uncle, "but not shy and nervous, which makes you appear quiet and formal." She advised him to be "very open and confiding with the Queen," and to "tell everything and all that you wish, very openly and frankly." The Duchess's confidence in Queen Adelaide was justified, for she soon became devoted to her nephew, who ever remembered her with gratitude and affection.

The Queen had a gift for entertaining children. It gave her a chance to escape for a time from the formality of regal life and to be entirely natural. Prince George of Cumberland, later the blind King of Hanover, spent much of his youth in her charge, but the royal residences at Windsor and Brighton were poor places in which to bring up children, and the gaiety of court life was blighted by the King's outbursts. His marriage had begun unpromisingly; he was thirty years older than his bride, and had scarcely troubled to conceal from her that he proposed to marry out of a sense of duty and for money. Moreover, there were times when William IV seemed to have inherited his father's insanity. In 1828, according to Princess Lieven, he became violent and had to be put in a strait-jacket." At George IV's funeral, instead of walking solemnly behind the coffin and making some gesture of grief, the new King waved and smiled at the congregation, and excitedly shook hands with several of his friends. He behaved at his brother's funeral with an exultation he had not displayed at his own wedding. Indeed, some of his observations were so startling that the Duke of Cumberland at one time contemplated having him put under restraint and ascending the throne himself.

Queen Adelaide acquired a certain skill in humouring her husband's outbursts and repairing the wreckage of his

witless indiscretions. But tact was often insufficient to re-
strain him and her sheltered life and her natural timidity
and diffidence left her without resources to weather the
storms. The Queen distrusted anything unfamiliar, and her
husband's unpredictable temperament introduced the very
uncertainty into her existence which she always strove to
avoid. So scared was she of innovation that when she first
took up residence at Windsor, she had the gas cut off, despite the fact that George IV had only just installed it in the
castle.

One of the principal reasons given for taking Prince
George from his family was that it was essential for him to
be given an English education. Queen Adelaide, however,
although she lived in England for many years, always remained very much a foreigner. From the first, she regarded
Prince George as her "special property," and he took the
place of the children she longed to have. On March 27, 1831,
she wrote: "The birthday and death day of my first child
was very much softened for me by the possession of Georgy,
for he is a consolation for my loss in this world.""

William IV was himself extremely fond of his nephews
and niece, but the Duchess of Kent was determined that
Princess Victoria should have nothing to do with the court.
She was very jealous of any rival authority to her own, and
she refused to permit her daughter to associate with the
King's natural children. This virtually deprived the Princess
of the company of her uncle and aunt, since they were surrounded by FitzClarences wherever they went. The King
felt the rebuff deeply, for he was of a generous, friendly,
and hospitable nature. When the court was in residence at
the Royal Pavilion, Brighton, he used to send to the principal
hotels to ask for the visitors' books. If he saw the name of
anyone he knew, or had ever met, an invitation to dinner
followed. Mr. Leveson Gower, describing his life as a schoolboy at Brighton, wrote: "We saw a great deal of the royal
cousins, Prince George of Hanover [the Duke of Cumberland's son] and Prince George of Cambridge. They were

put under the care of their Uncle the King in order that they might be brought up with English surroundings, and were staying with him at the Pavilion. We liked them both; they played with us at our school, and we were often summoned to the Pavilion to play with them. We were delighted with the King, who was very kind to us, and told us sailors' stories, sometimes rather coarse ones, which amused us very much."

Prince George preferred Windsor to the Royal Pavilion. "We can make little use of the hounds," he complained in his diary on November 3, 1834, "and this adds to the disagreeableness of Brighton." Later in life he discussed the days of William IV with Lord James of Hereford, a fellow guest at Sandringham. William IV, he recalled, "was a most determined fellow. Of course he used absurdly strong language, but was a good King for all that. He used to post from Brighton to London and return the same evening, to have a row with his Ministers . . . He would tell me what he had said and done in London with great satisfaction.""

As a boy, Prince George lived at the centre of political excitements and intrigues. At the time of the Reform Bill agitation, he was riding in the Queen's carriage when it was attacked by a mob and he was slightly injured by a stone." As an old man, he retained a somewhat confused recollection of the defiant courage of his much-hated uncle, the Duke of Cumberland. Lady Geraldine Somerset, lady-in-waiting to Prince George's mother, whose diary is a prolific source of information about the whole Cambridge family, records that "the Duke told us à propos of our evening here [St. James's Palace] yesterday, he had been discussing with Sir Charles Wyke the various scenes they had witnessed in this house! The Duke remembered coming as a child, to lunch with his cousin, George of Cumberland, in the room we dined in last night, and the Duke of Cumberland making at the same time an early dinner of it, because he was going down to the House of Lords for the debate on Catholic

Emancipation. [Was it not rather the Reform Bill?] He was then at the height of his unpopularity, the whole courtyard and street *crammed* with ill-conditioned people awaiting him, everyone *implored* him not to go out and expose himself to their insults, perhaps ill treatment! Nothing would dissuade him, and he *rode* boldly down through them all to the House of Lords! yelled at and hooted all the way!! He had pluck enough for anything!"[n]

Life at Windsor was more placid than at St. James's. After the long hours of study under Mr. Wood's vigilant eye, Eton boys would be invited to the castle to amuse the Prince. Miss Clitherow, a friend of Queen Adelaide's, saw him "at gymnastics with half a dozen young nobility from Eton, who came once a week to play with him."[n] On his sixteenth birthday, thirteen Eton boys went out hunting with him. The Prince was a sensitive, nervous child, not over-endowed with Hanoverian bravado, and his diary is full of self-criticism on the subject. Evidently Mr. Wood was caustic about cowardice and bestowed on his pupil the sort of common-sense advice which unimaginative people suppose sufficient to dispel irrational fears. "The day before yesterday," admitted Prince George in his diary on August 14, 1834, "I went out shooting for the first time, had three shots, but, as might be expected, killed nothing. I, however, at first behaved very ill indeed, and was quite alarmed lest the gun should kick, and therefore lost many good opportunities of firing. I feel dreadfully ashamed of what I have done, and have made up my mind to try to get the better of every kind of useless fear."

Again on July 24, 1835, there is a characteristic entry. "I regret to say that my conduct yesterday morning was such as to cause Mr. Wood to order me to breakfast in my own room. After he had had a long and very kind conversation with me relative to my conduct, particularly about my riding, and had said that Papa and Mama were so very anxious about me, I said, 'That is my look out!' an expres-

sion which is anything but proper on such an occasion."
Even in the company of two of his Eton companions, the
young Prince was unable to conceal his terror of a frisky
horse. "Yesterday," he noted with regret, on March 9, 1832,
"two Eton boys came to see me. Their names were Ward
and Compton. We rode together and then played at hockey.
During the ride I am afraid I showed some marks of
cowardice. I do hope this will soon be over."
Despite moments of fear and panic, he grew to enjoy
riding and hunting, and became so knowledgeable about his
mounts that, many years later, an astonished cavalry officer
declared: "The Commander-in-Chief knows as much about
horses as any veterinary surgeon." Although the society in
which he moved preferred chasing foxes to pursuing culture, he was permitted to indulge his inherited love of
music. In his youth he played the piano and organ skilfully,
but on joining the Army he gave up performing for fear of
being thought effeminate.

Early in 1834 Prince George returned home to Hanover
for the christening of his younger sister, Princess Mary
Adelaide, later Duchess of Teck and mother of Queen Mary.
His other sister, Princess Augusta, who was to marry the
Grand Duke of Mecklenburg-Strelitz, was born in 1822, and
being a girl had been permitted to live with her parents in
Germany. Prince George's diary during this visit was only
passingly concerned with the great event which occa-
sioned it.

10 January 1834. Yesterday evening the christening of
Mary took place. A most solemn and beautiful ceremony
and the service was well performed by Mr. W[ood]. The
little baby did not cry at all. I signed my name as witness.

A fortnight later a great ball was given to celebrate Princess Mary's birth. All her brother remarked about it was:
"The Hanoverians are great eaters of supper."

The Hanover visit was no holiday. Mr. Wood had not accompanied his pupil merely to conduct the baptismal service. Work went on as usual, as did the *contretemps* between the Prince and his tutor.

25 January. Though I got up late yesterday I did my lessons after breakfast as usual. First some Cicero to construe, and then I did my German . . .

6 February. Yesterday I fear some more bad behaviour showed itself. I have not remembered so many bad days following so soon after each other for some time . . . I was violent, hasty, and indeed might almost say did everything that was wrong. I shall however to-day give myself the greatest pains to behave well.

9 February. Did not behave very well in the morning, but better afterwards. A constant desire to chatter which always brings me into trouble.

19 February. Last night I got rather a disagreeable letter from England. The Queen writes me word that I am to return soon after Papa's birthday, probably therefore in a fortnight.

1 March. Another month gone by. Have I been diligent enough, or behaved in it as I ought? I fear that but too often I have not. Chattering is one of my chief faults.

4 March. My most glaring fault now is that I desire to argue with everybody, and then after all I generally am in the wrong. I must now however make up my mind to conquer it.

12 March. Mr. Wood was very angry with me in the morning for my always standing near the stove. He said it was very wrong because Mama as well as he himself had so often told me of it, and on my saying I could not help it, he explained to me the necessity of my conquering myself, because if I could not do it in trifles, I should not be able to do it in much greater things.

13 March. Yesterday I again fell into that bad fault of mine to form hasty opinions and speak hastily rather than

first thinking them over in my mind, and saying my ideas quietly. I am then generally obliged to retract them, which will become a very unfortunate thing hereafter. I must really take great pains to avoid this.

Prince George returned to England in April 1834, and soon began an arduous course of preparation for his Confirmation. His mother, who came over for the ceremony, wrote proudly to her father, the Landgrave of Hesse-Cassel, telling him that her son had been examined by Dr. Blomfield, Bishop of London, who "was very pleased and even astonished, and said to others he wished that all young candidates for Confirmation could pass as well as George did."[n] Possibly this tribute was somewhat exaggerated. Mothers are quick to seize on such compliments, and bishops of an established Church seldom go out of their way to insult the Sovereign's relations.

The Queen herself examined the boy.

30 March 1835. I understand from Mr. Wood that it is the Queen's intention to-day to examine me in the thirty-nine Articles and other branches of scriptural instruction relative to my Confirmation. I feel rather nervous, particularly as Lord and Lady Howe have asked to be present likewise, and I only hope it will go off well.

31 March. I am happy to say that my examination went off very fairly yesterday, and I hope and think that the Queen and Lady Howe, who were present, were satisfied. Once or twice my attention failed for a few minutes, but I soon recovered it. The whole lasted about two hours and a half, and I must confess that at the end of that time I was very tired.

Prince George was given little opportunity to take Confirmation anything but earnestly, and fortunately the zeal of his instructors, far from producing the opposite consequence to that intended, as sometimes happens, was triumphantly rewarded.

> 8 August. The solemn day is come and my Confirmation is to take place this day. May God give me grace to enter upon it with proper feelings, and may He enable me to give all my attention to the ceremony before me, and not to those vain forms of this world which are as nothing, when compared with Eternity.
>
> 9 August. I am delighted to say that my Confirmation yesterday went off remarkably well, and I thank God that I am now admitted among His real disciples. May He this day give me grace to enable me to receive the Sacrament worthily, and may I henceforth behave in such a manner as to prove that I have attended to and duly appreciated the good advice the Archbishop gave me.
>
> 10 August. Yesterday morning I received for the first time the most comfortable Sacrament of the Body and Blood of Christ. God be praised that I am now admitted into the number of His people, but I trust also that I am admitted worthily, and that I have made such good resolutions as to be able to abide by them. I think that the whole Ceremony of the Lord's Supper is a most solemn one, and one that ought not to be entered upon without preparation.

The Duchess of Cambridge, during her visit, hoped to persuade the King to let her take Prince George back to Hanover, but, for the moment, her pleading was overruled. "I am afraid," she wrote to her father, "I shall not be allowed to bring him away with me; the King, alas! will not yet part with him . . ." The prospect of his mother's return to Germany depressed the Prince exceedingly.

> 25 August 1835. The nearer Thursday is approaching the more I feel the misery I shall have to endure at parting, and I only pray to God that it may not be of long duration,

and that we shall soon meet again in health and happiness. I now begin to feel that very natural desire of entering once more the house of my Parents.

28 August. Yesterday I regret to say I was obliged to take leave of my most beloved and respected Mother, and of my two darling sisters. God grant that I may soon—yes very soon—see them again. This prayer is very short, but it is most true and fervent, and nothing would give me more real satisfaction than to see it accomplished. . . .

Prince George's prayer was answered sooner than he could reasonably have expected. The very next year it was decided that he should return to Hanover. Nor was that all. Mr. Wood was to become Chaplain to the Queen, and Colonel Cornwall was appointed in his place as a military governor. The Prince, and Colonel Cornwall, left England on July 21, 1836. The Duke of Wellington had been consulted by the King about his nephew's military education, and this arrangement was in part the consequence of his advice. Although Prince George was naturally delighted to be reunited with his family, he left England with mingled feelings of pleasure and pain. "I love this country dearly," he wrote while still at Windsor, "and I shall be very sorry to have to leave it for long!" Moreover, he dreaded parting with his "beloved preceptor," for despite his severity, Mr. Wood, as the Prince said, "has ever been my friend in all circumstances."

Notwithstanding Mr. Wood's departure, Prince George's routine in Hanover was still partly academic.

3 February 1837. My days here in Hanover are spent on the whole very quietly. In the morning from seven thirty till one p.m. occupied with my studies. Then I generally ride in the School till three, and then I have another lesson till dinner-time. We dine at four thirty, and in the evening I either go to the play, the concert or some party. Three

times a week I have a music lesson in the evening. Wednesdays and Saturdays I have more time for myself.

While in Hanover, the Prince met many German royalty, most of them in some way related, part of the time he travelled, there were balls, and occasionally he hunted and went shooting. But far more important than any of these activities was the start of his military career. It is true that since the age of nine he had been a colonel in the Hanoverian Guards, but the position, as might be imagined, was honorary. It was not until he reached the age of seventeen that he was expected to perform any martial duties, and these were no more arduous than mounting guard. He took a great pride in his work and loved to drill his men in front of his parents' summer residence. He described his first guard duty as one of the happiest days of his life, "for I, for the first time, felt as if I was really a soldier."

Late in June 1837, Prince George received news of the King's death from Mr. Wood and in response to the suggestion contained in the letter he instantly set out for England, travelling day and night with Colonel Cornwall. "My dearest Prince," ran the letter, "God's will be done! Our dear lamented King expired this morning at twelve minutes after two—calm, resigned, happy and without a struggle. The transition from life to death was so easy as to be almost imperceptible to those who stood by and solaced His Majesty's last moments. He had been gradually sinking during the whole day. Towards night the near approach of death, of which he himself was quite conscious, became more evident. He remained, however, sitting in his dressing-room till one o'clock, when he was moved into his sitting-room, where, in consequence of his extreme weakness, a small bed had been prepared for him. On this the dear King was laid, the Queen, as she had done for hours before, continuing on her knees by his side, gently rubbing his hands and striving thus to restore the rapidly departing warmth.

Under these circumstances, with his hand within those of the Queen, our beloved King calmly breathed his last, the Archbishop, who had been summoned a few minutes previously, pronouncing a prayer as his spirit returned unto God who gave it. Our lamented Sovereign's dearest friends could not have desired a happier, easier death. May the Almighty grant that it may be blessed to him and to ourselves.

"The poor Queen remained some time on her knees in prayer by the bedside. She then went to her room, and slept for some hours. She got up, however, soon after eight to receive Lord Conyngham, who with the Archbishop had been to announce the sad event to the Princess Victoria. . . .

"Of our dear Queen's conduct throughout the trials which she has undergone, few persons can speak with composure. Dr. Chambers, a perfect stranger, can mention neither the name of the King nor the Queen without tears. . . .

"On the immediate effect of this great loss of one who was with so much sincerity a father and benefactor and friend to you, my dear Prince, for so many years, as regards your plans and those of the Duke, it would be almost presumption in me to speculate. But I should be much to blame, if I did not inform you of the opinion which Sir Herbert Taylor has just expressed, that you ought to lose no time in hastening to this country, to be present when the last sad offices are performed to our departed King. It is probable that your own affectionate heart has anticipated this suggestion of public duty, and that the Duke and Duchess, even if necessity should detain His Royal Highness in Hanover, will have already proposed to you to come over. . . ."[n]

When the Prince reached Windsor he found the Queen Dowager more composed than he had expected, and indeed it must be admitted that the loss was not without consolation, for her marriage had been beset with troubles, and there had been agonizing moments of trial. In after-years, the memory of her husband, hallowed by discriminating forgetfulness, gave Queen Adelaide greater happiness than she had ever enjoyed during the King's lifetime, for he was a monarch bursting with ill-conceived enthusiasms, and, at best, an unpredictable companion.

The funeral over, the whole Cambridge family were obliged to leave Hanover, a kingdom in which the Salic Law prevailed. On the accession of Queen Victoria to the English throne, the Duke of Cumberland became King of Hanover and the position Prince George's father had held since 1815 became superfluous.

> 12 July 1837. The death of our poor dear King, besides the sorrow we all feel for his personal loss, is in another way a most severe blow to us all, particularly to my own family, for by his death and the accession of Queen Victoria, the kingdom of Hanover is separated from the Crown of Great Britain, and my father is therefore removed from the Government of that country, where he has lived for these twenty-four years, and where we have all been born . . . Alas! our connection with it is now suddenly broken off: for though we are still, and by God's blessings ever shall remain Princes of Hanover, yet we shall live for the most part in this country. My Uncle the Duke of Cumberland has now become king of that country, and my cousin Princess Victoria is Queen of England. I am thus nearly allied in blood to two great and happy families that are governing two happy and prosperous nations.

On returning to England, the family took up residence at Cambridge House, Piccadilly, now the Naval and Military Club (the "In and Out"); and at Cambridge Cottage, Kew, a building of some forty rooms, which they regarded as a country retreat. In the spring of 1838 Prince George was introduced to the London season, the first of the new reign. He was not altogether convinced of its delights. On May 28 he observed in his diary: "I am now quite a gay young man, leading a regular London life, in a quiet sort of way nevertheless. Really, pleasure sometimes becomes quite a business . . ." The Queen watched her cousin's social life with concern. She spoke to Melbourne "of George Cambridge's being somewhat in the hands of the fashionable ladies; Lord Melbourne said his (George's) age was a very awkward one, and that he remembered it well himself; that living only for amusement in London was very tiresome, if you had no pursuits besides.'" H.R.H. was wholly sceptical about a fancy-dress ball he attended, finding that "there were a great many most extraordinary and, at the same time, vulgar looking people present, who had on the very oddest costumes I ever saw." The Queen's Drawing Rooms displeased him. He refers to one at which there were over two thousand people present, among whom "there was a considerable collection of ugly ones." Even a ball at Buckingham Palace, which he admitted was "magnificent," had gone on too long, and by four o'clock in the morning "almost everybody was gone before the Queen retired." Prince George opened the ball with Her Majesty, and "thought she danced really very nicely, and seemed to be very much amused."

The coronation provided the climax of a dazzling and fatiguing summer. Prince George, a tireless if not profuse diarist, evidently felt so great an occasion required an expansive technique. His account of the ceremony reveals a royal eye for detail, and one can visualize him taking in the scene with an intense Hanoverian stare; the unyielding gaze of one accustomed to being looked at and determined on revenge.

28 June 1838. To-day was a very busy day for all of us, and at the same time a most important one for the Country at large. Queen Victoria was crowned Queen of England. God grant that her reign may be happy to herself, and glorious to the nation . . . At a very early hour of the morning people began to assemble along the streets through which

the procession was to pass, and the carriages rolled to the Abbey. At seven, the troops and the police made their appearance . . . My sister, Miss Kerr, Colonel Cornwall and myself started from hence at a little before nine, when we drove down to St. James's Palace . . . and then we all went together down to the Abbey. The effect on entering was magnificent. The Cathedral was already quite full and looked most imposing. On the right of the Throne were the Peers, on the left the Peeresses, and in front the House of Commons. To the back of the Throne was the Orchestra, and all the rest of the places were filled by the public. We were close to the Altar, and opposite to us were the Bishops. Just above us was the Queen's private box, and above the Bishops were the boxes for the foreign Ambassadors and Ministers. In our box, which was exceedingly small, besides our party, the three Duchesses and their respective attendants, were the Duke of Nemours, the Duke of Coburg, the Duke of Nassau (who had just arrived), Prince Christian of Glücksburg, the Princess of Hohenlohe, daughter of the Duchess of Kent, and the Prince of Leiningen. The Queen arrived a little before twelve, and the ceremony was conducted in the usual manner and without any remarkable occurrence. The Archbishop of Canterbury performed the Service, assisted by the Sub-Dean. The Bishop of London preached a most beautiful and appropriate sermon. The Queen, I think, looked less well than usual, but on the whole was very graceful and dignified . . . The ceremony lasted till near four. Before it was quite over, the party with which I went started off for Cambridge House, where we arrived without the least difficulty. We here had time to take our luncheon comfortably, and had to wait two hours before the procession came past. It was exceedingly beautiful and indeed I think one of the finest parts of the spectacle. All the foreign Ambassadors, the various members of the Royal family, the Queen's attendants, and at last the Queen herself, had a most imposing effect. Some of the foreigners had most beautiful equipages, and of the Royal carriages I think my father's were the handsomest. My parents did not return till after six . . . After dinner I walked all over London to see the illuminations, which were quite beautiful. At eleven there were some splendid fireworks, in the Green Park and also in Hyde Park. We, of course, saw the former. Soon after twelve, I went to a great full dress ball, given by the Duke of Wellington, and did not get to bed till near three o'clock.

Owing to insufficient rehearsal, the ceremony in the Abbey was not without awkward incidents. The coronation ring had been designed to fit the Queen's little finger, but the Archbishop, insisting on precedent, forced it on the fourth finger: an agonizing procedure. During the homage Lord Rolle, an old man of eighty-eight, slipped and fell on the steps of the throne. A foreign visitor was assured that the roll was intentional, seeing that his Lordship's family held their title on condition that they performed this acrobatic feat at every coronation. Toward the end of the service, the Bishop of Bath and Wells turned over two pages at once without noticing and told the Queen that the service was over. She consequently retired to Edward the Confessor's Chapel. After prolonged consultation, she was summoned back. The first thing the Queen did on her return to Buckingham Palace was to give her poodle, "Dash," a bath.

The London season was only a brief interlude in Prince George's military career, and at the end of the summer of 1838 he was sent to join the military garrison at Gibraltar. He set sail from Falmouth on September 24 with Colonel Cornwall in attendance. As he was a poor sailor even in calm weather, he spent the early part of the voyage in his cabin. At length the ship reached Portugal, where the Prince, much to his relief, was able to spend a few days ashore. Part of the time was occupied visiting the battlefields of the Peninsular War. At Caldas he stayed in an inn which was "very uncomfortable, and the animals of every description, such as bugs, fleas, flies, etc. were so bad, that I did not undress at all, but lay down in my clothes."

While in the country, he paid an informal visit to the King and Queen at the Palace of the Necessidades. He had determined to travel incognito, under the name of Lord Culloden, and was most aggravated to find that, owing to some misunderstanding, a state carriage with an escort had been sent to collect him from the consulate, where he was staying. The Queen of Portugal was near confinement, and for this, or for other reasons, hardly spoke a word. The King, however, was pleasantly conversational and "exceedingly good-natured," but "unfortunately has his hair so long he looks almost more like a woman than a man."

From Lisbon the "Royal George," as his contemporaries dubbed the young prince, sailed direct to Gibraltar, where the Governor, Sir Alexander Woodford, a soldier who had distinguished himself in the Peninsular Campaign and at Waterloo, ordered a ceremonial reception.

9 October 1838. At about seven a.m. Colonel Bridgeman, military secretary to the General, came off in a boat to ask at what hour I should wish to land, and we then settled to do so at eight o'clock. The General wished that I should come on shore in uniform, and so I put on my regimentals, and at eight a boat came off for me with Mr. Morret, the Governor's Aide-de-camp. When we landed there was a Guard of Honour of the 33rd Regiment to receive me and several of the principal officers of the Garrison. The Governor's carriage was waiting for me, and I got in with Colonel Cornwall and drove to the Convent, where I was very kindly received by Sir Alexander and Lady Woodford. I breakfasted with them, and then the General took me to my quarters. . . . I dined in the evening at the Convent, where there was a large dinner, and I was introduced to several people, which is not the most amusing thing in the world.

Prince George contrived to conceal how bored he was by the restricted social life of Gibraltar, although Colonel Cornwall was sometimes hard pressed to invent or discover amusements for him. In a letter he wrote to the Duke, the Colonel refers to "the ennui and consequent depression of spirits to which the Prince I regret to say is liable." However, the gallant officer was not utterly at a loss. "I have succeeded in procuring a Piano Forte." Music was to provide a diversion to relieve the tedium of garrison life. Wherever the Prince went, he was followed by "Nelson," a black retriever, who swam in the sea at every opportunity and who slept in his master's bedroom. While based on Gibraltar, H.R.H. made a number of short journeys to Granada, Tangier, Cadiz, and Seville. But most of his time was spent in parades, drills, and guard mounting, occasional hunting and shooting of a meagre kind, and frequent receptions and dinners in which the same small circle of officers and their wives met at each other's tables and exchanged trivial gossip. A severe attack of measles, during which he lost almost all his hair, provided a rare, if unwelcome, change from this monotonous routine.

The Duke received news of his son's progress not only from Colonel Cornwall but also from General Woodford, and all reports were gratifying. "My dearest George," wrote the Duke on October 24, 1838, "We were all delighted the day before yesterday at the receipt of your letter from Gibraltar, which contained the welcome information that you had not suffered at all on your passage from Lisbon and that this time you really had enjoyed your voyage by sea. I was also very glad to hear that you were pleased with the house that General Woodford had got ready for you, and that you felt sensible of the attention he and Lady Woodford have shown you on your arrival. Sir Alexander writes me word that he is delighted at the manner in which you had received the officers of the Garrison when they were presented to you, and that every one was pleased with you. This I mention to you, my dearest George, in the hope that this will encourage you to go on as you have begun. You are now beginning your military career, and I do not doubt that with proper application you will soon learn your duty under so experienced an officer as Sir Alexander Woodford. By your being placed on his Staff, you have the great advantage of being employed in any way in which he thinks is best for you, and which would not be the case if you were attached exclusively to one Regiment. During the time you are learning the Regimental duties, you will of necessity be commanded by officers who are of an inferior rank to the one you hold in the Army, and of course you will be bound to obey them."

The Duke's letters were full of good advice. Just before Christmas he warned his son of the danger of officers interfering in politics. "In my opinion," his father told him in a letter dated December 22, 1838, "no soldier or sailor should have anything to do with politics. His duty is to obey the orders he receives from his superiors, be they Tories or be they Whigs." A soldier, he maintained, should keep his political opinions to himself, and certainly in a garrison there could be no obligation to divulge them." It was a temptation Prince George never wholly resisted. Later in his career he constantly professed an impartiality he never quite achieved. Fervently believing that he was personally above faction, as in theory the Commander-in-Chief was bound to be, he nevertheless used language which betrayed his Tory principles. Conservatism was so ingrained in his nature that he grew to identify it with constitutional propriety.

In April 1839, Prince George left Gibraltar for a tour of the Mediterranean. He had been exceedingly popular with the garrison and Sir Alexander was able to report most favourably on him to the Government. "It is very gratifying to me," he wrote in an official dispatch, "to be able to add that Prince George has entered upon all the duties assigned to him in the most exemplary manner. H.R.H.'s conduct throughout has been highly praiseworthy; the quickness of his perception and taste for the profession give a fair promise of his becoming a distinguished officer in the service."

After visits to Malta, Corfu, and Athens, H.R.H. returned to England in November 1839. It was rumoured that the whole purpose of his going abroad was to avoid being forced into marriage with the Queen. Within three months of her coronation he left for Gibraltar, and only returned home a little before her marriage to Prince Albert. Lord Melbourne is said to have spoken to the Queen suggesting the cancellation of Prince George's appointment. When she asked him whether her cousin wished to go, the Prime Minister replied: "He is very distressed at the idea of leaving his parents—and friends—Ma'am!" Certainly Prince George betrayed relief at the news of the Queen's engagement. In his diary he wrote on December 15, 1839: "After dinner Papa got a letter from the young Queen, in which she announces her Marriage with Prince Albert of Coburg. Nothing could have given me greater pleasure than this intelligence." His congratulations are so enthusiastic that the Queen noted in her journal on December 18: "George quite different towards me, much less reserved, and evidently happy to be clear of me."

Rumour needs scant nourishment and gossips can make a meal of a morsel. Tongues had begun wagging when it was noticed that the Queen at court balls nearly always started dancing with her Cambridge cousin: a fact which a casual acquaintance with rules of precedence would have shown to be inevitable rather than significant. For a time the Duchess of Kent favoured a match. Prince Albert, who watched all intrigues with personal concern, reported to his father that the Duchess of Kent "is always full of complaints against her daughter, which she repeats to the horrible Royal Family, who use them for their own ends; at present she is said to have taken George Cambridge under her wing." It was his opinion that "cross-currents of cabal and intrigue run in every direction," united only in opposition to the Coburgs: "the stud farm of Europe," as Bismarck once described the family." In her diary the Queen records on June 13, 1838: "Spoke of George [the conversation was with Lord Melbourne] who I said I did not like—though had nothing to say for himself and was particularly stiff with me; but that I believed his parents teased him about me, and that Ma got into the Duke and Duchess's favour, by saying she would promote a match between us; all which Lord Melbourne thought very likely." The Duchess was eager that Prince George should be invited to Windsor. "I then spoke with Lord Melbourne," wrote the Queen on September 8, 1838, "about the Cambridges, and about George, and if I ought to ask him to stay, which Ma hinted at." Melbourne was rather disparaging about the family. According to the same diary entry he told the Queen that the Cambridges were foolish people. " 'The Duke is the foolishest man I ever saw'; all which, God knows! is most true . . ." Again on October 17, 1839, the Queen mentions a discussion with Lord Melbourne on the subject of her cousin. "Lord M. talks of their wishing George for me; 'It was clear *he* did not wish it,' said Lord M., 'by his distant manner'; and I said I never could have thought of taking him—ugly and disagreeable as he was." On October 23 she refers to him as "an odious boy," and when Lord Melbourne pointed out what a success he had been at Gibraltar, he was told that Prince Albert "disliked him very much."

The Queen was often the victim of sudden and substantial prejudices and at least one of her objections to Prince George was manifestly perverse, for she listed among his shortcomings the accusation that he was "ugly." Contemporary verdicts agree that he was strikingly handsome. As the Queen grew older and more inclined to charity, she revised her opinion: indeed her early hostility towards her cousin may have been expressed so vehemently in order to disguise an affection she was anxious to conceal, or to fortify a change of heart. Toward the end of her life Ponsonby, her

33

private secretary, remarked on her "great affection" for the Commander-in-Chief. "It was noticeable at a drawing room when she came into the ante-room where the royal parties were assembled, she would single him out for a word of conversation before turning round and proceeding to the Throne Room.""

On February 10, 1840, the Queen's wedding day, Prince George was in the highest spirits. "The Queen," he records in his diary, in an entry quoted in the official lives, "was married at the Chapel Royal at twelve in the day, and we all attended in State, and walked in procession from the State Apartments to the Church. After the Ceremony there was a great breakfast at Buckingham Palace to which we went, and then the young couple went to Windsor, where they were to stay till yesterday and then return to town. We, the family, went to dine with the Queen Dowager and after-wards I walked out for a short time to see the illuminations, which was exceedingly good fun, there being an immense crowd of people in the streets! I concluded this long day by going to a full dress party at the Duchess of Sutherland's, which was a very handsome thing altogether."

On the Queen's wedding day Prince George met his own future wife. His diary for the year 1840 is now lost, as are several volumes covering this period of his life, but a subsequent entry enables us to fix the date of the meeting precisely. "10 February 1899. This is the anniversary of my first acquaintance with my dearest wife Louisa, also the anniversary of the Queen's Wedding fifty-nine years ago." As Louisa was an actress, it seems unlikely that they met either at the wedding service itself or at the ensuing royal festivities. It is more probable that they saw each other for the first time at the Duchess of Sutherland's ball, although the newspapers of the time make no mention of Louisa in what appear to be complete lists of guests.

Even before he met his future wife, Prince George made no secret of his views about marriage. He believed, reasonably enough, that "arranged marriages were doomed to failure." He asserted that he would wed whom he pleased, if necessary in defiance of the Royal Marriage Act of 1772, which, among other provisions, made the consent of the King and Parliament necessary for the marriage of princes under twenty-five. He was ready to devote himself unsparingly to the service of his country, but his private life he maintained was his own. Although the political advantages of various possible alliances were urged upon him, he remained obstinately unconvinced of the wisdom of marrying some princess whom he did not love.

Louisa was the ninth child and fifth daughter of John Fairbrother, a partner in a family printing firm in Bow Street, where she was born and lived. She took to the stage in 1830 and acted at Drury Lane, the Lyceum, and Covent Garden Theatre. She was a woman of classic beauty and elegance, an accomplished actress, and a graceful dancer. Moreover, in private life she possessed captivating charm and was an admirable conversationalist.*

There is a tradition that Louisa's father was bitterly opposed to her going on the stage, believing the theatre to be a disreputable calling. He told her that actresses were wanton women. She did not attempt to deny that some of them were, but simply observed that he had not as yet contemplated abandoning his own profession merely because there were villainous printers.

The marriage did not take place until January 8, 1847. As later there was a controversy about this date, it is necessary to examine the evidence supporting it. In a letter Prince George wrote Louisa on January 8, 1851, he talks of "writing *on the day itself*. . . . You alone know love, or *ought* to know, how blessed and happy I feel that *this day* (four years) made you my own and me yours . . ." Moreover, the records of St. John's Church, Clerkenwell, despite some inaccuracies, establish that the marriage was solemnized there on January 8, 1847, by the rector, Doctor Hughes. (A letter written to Louisa, begging for money, mentions in passing the fact that she was married by this clergyman.) No less a person than King Edward VII thought the date incorrect and the entry in the register false. The King detected three errors in the records, but the inference he drew from the discovery was invalid. Sir Almeric Fitz-Roy tells the story in his memoirs.

"Sheppard [H.R.H.'s official biographer] was very anxious to verify the time and place of the Duke's marriage, which he had always understood, from the old Duchess of Cambridge, took place on the eve of his departure for the Crimea, but he had never been able to trace it, when one day in a train he overheard some men talking of the Duke; he interrupted them with the remark that he was intimately associated with events in the Duke's life, and they might therefore perhaps think it as well to be cautious in what they said. One of them thanked him and replied that they looked upon the Duke as a public character about whom they might talk as they liked, but in fact they were discussing the subject of his marriage; upon which Sheppard told them of his anxiety to obtain information about it. 'Oh,' said one of the men, 'I can tell you where it took place, as I have seen the register at St. John's, Clerkenwell.' Sheppard accordingly paid a visit to the church, and there, sure enough, was an entry purporting to be the register of the Duke's marriage; but the date given was 1847, and he noted with surprise that the Duke's signature was entered as George Cambridge. A few days after he acquainted the King with what he had seen who expressed a strong desire to look at the register. Sheppard obtained it from the Vicar and submitted it to His Majesty, who, with that extraordinary precision he has in matters of personal detail, at once exclaimed, 'There are three errors in this. In the first place, the Duke never signed himself as George Cambridge —one was his name and the other his title; and, in the second place, he never was at [Clerkenwell] in his life; and thirdly, his father's names are given inaccurately.' Whether these inaccuracies, taken with a date so much at variance with the Duchess of Cambridge's statement on the subject, suggest that the register is a bogus one, Sheppard cannot determine.'"

After Prince George's death in 1904, Lady Geraldine Somerset discussed the marriage date with Sheppard, then Sub-Dean of the Chapels Royal. She made a note of the conversation in her diary on July 30, 1904.

"He also showed me a most *incomprehensible* mystification!! At the time of Mrs. FitzGeorge's death fourteen years ago, when the Duke was as fresh as ever he was, and his memory far better than that of most men of twenty-five! one evening the Sub-Dean was spending alone with the Duke speaking of her and his past life and he told him he married her the night before he started for the Crimea to give her a better position with the status of a wife in case it should ill befall him in war." Lady Geraldine goes on to say that Prince George's sons now "declare that he married her in 1847!! at St. John's Church Clerkenwell. The Sub-Dean wrote to the vicar to ask for a copy of the Register and the vicar sent him it and he showed it to me!! All duly *entered: his* signature George Cambridge! and hers Louisa Fairbrother! witnessed by her sister. It passes understanding and is impossible to believe! The vicar incidentally says the Duke's signature is in a small, 'apparently faint hand.' Now this is so *very* unlike the Duke!!! If he did the thing at all he was the last man to dream of disguising his hand and to my mind it is the clue to make one believe the register is a false one! Why should the Duke speaking openly of his past with the Sub-Dean volunteer to tell him this version of his marriage? If it were not true how could he with his fabulous memory be mistaken on such a point? . . . It is of profound mystification and I am *convinced* the true story of the marriage is before the Crimea."

Prince George's family consisted of three sons. The eldest, George FitzGeorge, was born on August 27, 1843. The next child, Adolphus, was born on January 30, 1846, and the youngest, Augustus, on June 12, 1847. There were two other children who lived with the family: Louisa Katherine, and Charles Manners Sutton. Louisa was born on March 22, probably in 1839, and Charles on August 5, three years before. If the years of these births are given correctly, Louisa and Charles were born before Prince George met his wife. All that is certain is that Mrs. FitzGeorge was Louisa's mother: a letter signed "your affectionate daughter Louisa" is among her papers. Charles also was in all probability Louisa's son. She left him most of her property in her will: a document in which his surname is significantly given as Fairbrother. The Duchess of Cambridge presented George, Adolphus, and Augustus with five thousand pounds each," and saw a good deal of them at St. James's, but she gave Charles nothing and there is no record of their ever meeting. When in 1869 Adolphus was travelling as the Duke of Edinburgh's A.D.C. in the East, he asked his father what he should say to the Duke if they happened to meet Charles, who was then a soldier serving in India. H.R.H. was "rather at a loss what to say" and advised Adolphus to use his good judgment, "and whilst not offending Charley you need not say more to the Duke than is absolutely necessary to explain matters." A month later he wrote again: "If you see Charley be very kind and affectionate to him and do not on any account give him any offence. If you are asked who he is, of course you must say he is your half-brother."" When in 1875 there was trouble over Adolphus's marriage and his mother declined to attend the wedding, he wrote to her: "Of course as you refused I have not asked Charles." It is improbable that Prince George was Charles's father, as Prince George was only seventeen at the time of Charles's birth. Moreover, in many of his letters to Louisa H.R.H. refers to George as "our eldest boy."

Although Prince George and Louisa postponed the marriage ceremony until 1847, they regarded themselves as man and wife long before that—as is apparent both from the existence of their family and from a sentence in a travel diary Louisa kept in 1844. "I hope," she says, "I shall see my dear George waiting for me, tomorrow night. I hope to God to be in his arms and when once there, I care for naught else, bless you for tonight my dear husband."

What Queen Victoria thought of her cousin's marriage is largely a matter of conjecture, for she did not commit her views to paper. Obviously, she strongly disapproved of the match. Her fondness for the theatre hardly extended to welcoming actresses as members of the family. Besides, she was unlikely to look with favour on any arrangement in which neither her opinion nor her consent had been sought. Publicly she pretended to be ignorant of the marriage, and Louisa was never invited, or even mentioned, on official occasions. The Queen, indeed, went further, and kept up this pretence in her private life and with her own relations. When George FitzGeorge was sent back to England by Wolseley, with the news of the victory of Tel-el-Kebir (1882), he took the dispatches to the Queen at Balmoral. She was exceedingly curious to see him and noticed a strong family likeness, but never a word passed to suggest that they were in any way connected. She told the Duke of Connaught in a letter: "We had Major FitzGeorge here from Saturday to Monday. Of course I made not the slightest allusion to his being Uncle George's son. He is very gentlemanlike and unassuming."

There is a tradition in the FitzGeorge family that the Queen finally relented and agreed to meet Louisa. The encounter, it is alleged, lasted two hours instead of the few minutes originally proposed. It was followed by many more such visits and even by a grudging admission that Mrs. FitzGeorge was so enchanting that H.R.H.'s marriage was justified." Neither the Queen nor the Duke refer to any such meetings in their diaries. Moreover, on January 12, 1890, the day Louisa died, the Duke noted: "I received a most affectionate letter from Her Majesty which I highly appreciate, and which would have been such a joy to my beloved one had she known the fact." Presumably this implies that the Queen had at long last relented and was prepared, now that Louisa was dead, to admit that she had existed.

Louisa lived in a house given her by Prince George, Number 6, Queen Street, Mayfair; and later she had a place in the country, Cambridge Lodge, Horley. As Mrs. Fitz-George, she lived her own life with her own friends, and in her company her husband entered another world. It was a commonplace world, inhabited by very ordinary people, including Louisa's old theatrical friends. To H.R.H. it was a happy escape from the confined splendours of royal life, and he was enchanted by the snug, bourgeois comforts of the little house in Queen Street.

To what extent Louisa was accepted by Prince George's own family is difficult to decide. She was at least known to her father-in-law. Writing to her husband in 1848, she mentions that she saw Prince Adolphus on Constitution Hill, and "he kissed his hand to me for no person was near." There is no evidence that the Duchess of Cambridge ever saw Louisa; indeed, all we do know is that she was mistaken about the date of her son's marriage. There is a story that while Princess Mary, Prince George's youngest sister, was driving in Hyde Park, her lady-in-waiting suddenly exclaimed: "Why! There's Mrs. FitzGeorge." "Where?" asked the Princess excitedly. "Which is she? I have never yet seen her."

If the marriage was frowned on by his own family, it was very popular with most Englishmen. An old soldier's widow, who had been housekeeper at the Horse Guards, summed up popular feeling. "Ah, well," she said, "he loved a fine woman and he married her and stuck to her, and said he would rather be buried with her in Kensal Green than with his own family in the royal vaults at Windsor."

Prince George was exceedingly sensitive about Louisa's position and there are many stories of the vigour of his resentment when he imagined that his wife had been insulted. A young Prince of Mecklenburg was reputed to have been flung bodily into Piccadilly for showing disrespect to Mrs. FitzGeorge. Even the Kaiser William I, it is said, was not spared. Ignoring the marriage, he kept proposing alliances with German princesses. Finally Prince George lost his temper. "His wealth of invective nearly paralysed the Emperor. In bluntest terms he described Germans in general, Prussians in particular, and Teutonic princesses in detail. No gentleman, he stormed, would ever advise another to desert a lady to whom he had pledged his word in the sight of God and man." Prince William, later Emperor William II, fared little better than his grandfather, although he at least attempted, somewhat clumsily, to be courteous. When he was visiting London in 1885, he inquired after Mrs. FitzGeorge's health, adding that if it would gratify her he might find time to visit her. "I am afraid, Willie," was the crushing reply, "that my wife will not be able to spare the time to see you. She only sees friends. But I will mention that you asked after her.""

The Profession of Arms

IN 1840 Prince George was attached as Lieutenant-Colonel to the 12th Lancers. His new duties took him no further afield than Brighton. Two years later he was gazetted Colonel of the 17th Lancers and sent to Leeds to command the regiment. Here he was engaged in his first action: he fought against the inhabitants of the town. The magistrates obsequiously thanked him for his assistance in suppressing riots. It was during these years with the Lancers that H.R.H. acquired his detailed knowledge of cavalry.

While serving with the Lancers, Prince George became the innocent victim of a most unfortunate scandal, the details of which Greville records in his *Memoirs*, not without a suspicion of sanctimonious relish. The story went that Prince George had fallen in love with Lady Augusta Somerset, a daughter of the Duke of Beaufort, and that she was about to have his child. It was alleged that both the Prince and the Duke agreed upon a belated marriage but that the Queen refused her consent.

"This story with many trifling variations has been in all the newspapers and been circulated with incredible success not only all over England but over the Continent also. The whole is false from beginning to end, except that He did flirt with her and She with him last year at Kew, where she was staying while her Father was abroad—flirtation such as is continually going on without any serious result between half the youths and girls in London." A formal contradiction

42

of the rumour was published in *The Times,* but Greville doubted it would succeed, since "the appetite for scandal is so general and insatiable, there is such a disposition to believe such stories and such reluctance to renounce a belief once entertained, that it is very improbable that what has been done can be entirely undone, and this calumny will affect the Lady more or less as long as She lives. Though it is totally false that she was ever with child, and P. George certainly never thought of marrying her, it is probably true enough that She behaved with very little prudence, delicacy or reserve, for she is a very ill-behaved girl, ready for anything that her caprice or passions excite her to do. Fortunately He is a very timid unenterprising youth, not unwilling to amuse himself but by no means inclined to incur any serious risks, as he has abundantly shown on other occasions. His vanity prompts him to make love to the Ladies whom he meets in his country quarters, and as Princes are scarce his blood royal generally finds easy access to rural and provincial Beauties. But when he finds these affairs growing serious and the objects of his admiration evince an embarrassing alacrity to meet his flame with corresponding ardour, I am told that he usually gets alarmed and backs out with much more prudence than gallantry."

The matter might have ended there, had the Queen not declared that she knew the story was true. Her habit of believing scandal without troubling about evidence had already led to tragic consequences. As Greville justly observed: "It is really incredible that after the Flora Hastings' affair and the deplorable catastrophe in which it ended, the Queen should not have shrunk instinctively from anything like another such scandal. Anybody would imagine that after the grievous wrong she had done to one woman She would have been especially cautious never to run the least risk of doing the same to any other; but between the prudery of Albert and her own love of gossip and exceeding arrogance and heartlessness this tracasserie arose."

The Duchess of Cambridge, possibly quite unaware of the gossip, took Lady Augusta with her on a visit to Windsor. Soon after, the Queen, in a violent outburst, told the Duchess of Gloucester, "that she knew the stories about Lady Augusta were all true and that She was only brought there for the purpose of getting rid of the scandal, and that it was very wrong of the Duchess of Cambridge to have brought her, with a great deal more in the same strain. The Duchess of Gloucester told her that this was a very serious charge not only against the girl but against the Duchess of Cambridge herself, and asked her if She intended that she should tell the latter what the Queen had said. The Queen said She did." Prince George's parents were furious when the charge was made known to them.

"Both the Duke and Duchess of Cambridge immediately took the matter up in the warmest manner and one of them wrote to the Queen, complaining of such an imputation having been cast on both the girl and on them, and that H.M. could not suppose they would either bring her, if She had not been innocent, into Her Majesty's presence, or allow her to continue at Kew as the associate of their own daughter. The Duke of Cambridge said that he considered himself bound to protect and defend her as much as if he were her Father. To this expostulation a very unsatisfactory answer came from Albert, in which he said that "as Prince George had given his word of honour that the story was untrue, He supposed they must believe that it was so." This letter by no means satisfied the Duke of Cambridge, and still less the Duke of Beaufort, who was by this time made acquainted with what had occurred and who was not at all disposed to submit to such an indignity. The Duke of Beaufort wrote to Sir Robert Peel on the subject, expressing what he felt and announcing his determination to demand an audience of the Queen. Peel endeavoured to pacify him, and represented to him that he would gain nothing by an audience, as the Queen would infallibly say nothing and bow him out, just as she formerly did Lord Hastings. The Duke, however, desired Peel to communicate with the Queen on the subject and to let her know what his feelings were. But the Duke of Wellington (who is always appealed to on these occasions) told the Beauforts Peel was so afraid of the Queen he did not think he would venture to speak to her. Peel, however, had some communication with her and, after a great many pourparlers and much negotiation amongst them all, Peel wrote a letter to the Duke of Beaufort (or to the D. of Cambridge, I forget which) in which he said that the Queen had desired him to say she was now entirely satisfied and she begged there might be no further discussion on the subject.

"This is a tolerably correct account of the incident as the Duchess of Beaufort told it to me yesterday. They are however boiling with resentment and indignation, and anxious to show their sentiments, if they only knew how."⁾

In 1843 Prince George was sent to command the garrison of Corfu, where he remained until 1845. Louisa, who at the time of his departure was about to have a child, felt she was being deserted. She never quite appreciated the need for her husband to obey orders. In a letter written on August 27, 1854, while H.R.H. was at Varna waiting to embark for the Crimea, he recalled the night he left for Corfu. "This day, or rather night, eleven years, our dear child Georgy, our eldest boy was born. Well do I recollect that dreadful, that painful night, when I was on the point of departure and left you in the middle of your misery." Next door to H.R.H.'s residence in the Citadel stood the Artillery House, occupied by Colonel Gordon, "a dull, heavy, common-looking Scotchman," whose son, the General, was to become a national hero, and whom Prince George in later days remembered well as a small boy.⁾

Lord Seaton, High Commissioner of the Ionian Islands, who had been Sir John Moore's secretary in the Peninsula, reported "to the Duke of Wellington, Commander-in-Chief of the Army, that Prince George had by his exertions and his unremitting attentions to the discipline of the troops under his immediate command, effected a great improvement in the several Corps, both as to their general conduct and appearance under arms."[n]

At the age of twenty-seven, H.R.H. was promoted to Major General and sent to Ireland, first in command of the troops at Limerick and in April of the following year, 1847, of the Dublin District, a position he held until 1852. Although he took his duties seriously enough, they were not so demanding as to prevent him spending considerable periods on leave in England, from whence he conducted the business of his command by post. In 1848, however, he remained nearly the whole year in Ireland, because, as in most countries of Europe, revolution threatened. H.R.H. followed events in Germany with a personal interest, and was disposed to blame its rulers for precipitating unrest by opposing all reform. "The news from Germany," he wrote to his mother on March 15, "is at this time not pleasant, and unfortunately the Princes are now forced to do what they would have done very much better to have yielded voluntarily long ago. I am not at all for giving way in everything, and in the way it is now being done, certainly not, but to set oneself sharply against all changes that time brings—that does not do at all, and causes much eventual misfortune."[n]

In Ireland, revolution seemed probable, but despite the fact that people were arming themselves, Prince George believed no serious outbreak would occur, and he maintained that if one did, the troops would prove "faithful, true and good." One reason trouble was averted was the successful arrest of William O'Brien, a most dangerous Irish rebel. H.R.H. in a letter to his mother described his own part in the event. O'Brien was recognized "in a village called Thurles and seized, which was effected without the slightest trouble. Thereupon he was brought here to my quarters under an escort of police. It was at two a.m. in the night of Saturday and Sunday. Everyone here was in

bed. I alone was sitting up. Suddenly I heard a violent
knocking and ringing of the bell. All my servants sleep at
the other end of the house and they heard nothing. I did
not want to wake them, and as no one came I went myself
to the door and opened it. Imagine my astonishment at seeing a number of constables, all armed, with the information
that it was Smith O'Brien standing before my house. I
could not believe my ears. I admitted the A.D.C. and shut
the door, as I would not let Smith O'Brien himself in (although the stupid newspapers say I had a long interview
with him, in which there is not one word of truth). I should
have much liked to see him, but I thought it would have a
bad effect and therefore I let it alone, of which now I am
doubly glad. I then sent the fellow and his escort to the
prison, where he is now happily confined. I myself then
quickly got my horse and rode off to Phoenix Park to announce the fact to the Lord-Lieutenant who also was in
bed, and whom I had some trouble in getting at, as his
people likewise never heard my knocking. Jim [Macdonald,
H.R.H.'s equerry] told me he never saw a man so quiet and
collected in so critical a position. He is prepared for everything, and says he did not succeed because it was six weeks
too early, that had he had those six weeks longer the whole
country would have followed him. Well, Heaven be praised
we have got him and everything is quite quiet. . . ."[n]

The Prince was not happy in Ireland. Writing from
Windsor, he described England as "a charming country,"
and added, "would that I could get some appointment that
would keep me on this side of the water." In another letter
he speaks of a "sort of oppression which rests upon me in
that unfortunate country."[n] He grew increasingly unsettled,
hankered after politics, and was so critical and outspoken
on military matters that he ran into trouble. Despite official
rebukes, he remained unrepentant. "The real fact is," he
wrote to a friend, "a General Officer should make a point
of saying *nothing* and he will always be well thought of.
But that is not my system, and, in spite of annoyance and

rebuff, I shall continue to say what I think and shall freely give my opinion.'" There can be little doubt that throughout his life he remained as good as his word. Even when he became Commander-in-Chief, H.R.H. felt himself free to criticize the Government, whose servant he found it difficult to believe himself to be. His opposition to the army reforms of Mr. Gladstone's party were so vigorous and unrestrained that the Queen, who sympathized with his views but felt that they should be more reticently expressed, administered a tactful rebuke. In a letter written from Osborne, July 24, 1871, she warned him to be "very careful in conversation lest opinions which you express may, perhaps in a distorted manner, be quoted by persons who do infinite harm in society by retailing gossip. It is to be remembered that a conversation is hardly ever repeated exactly as it takes place. Party feeling at this moment is unfortunately very bitter. People who feel strongly . . . and who may consider that you have not been fairly treated, are only too ready to catch any expression of yours which may confirm this view, forgetting that by reporting what you may have said . . . they are doing you a great mischief, and are giving a handle to those who wish to affirm that you are not acting cordially with the Government.'"

The Queen and Prince Albert paid one of their rare visits to Ireland in 1849 and H.R.H. was responsible for all the military arrangements. The visit was a flawless success. Prince George delightedly informed his mother that "the grace and favour and affection for me shown by the Queen and at the same time the friendly and hearty tone of Albert, were such that I can only be flattered. . . . My efforts and military arrangements are very fully appreciated here, as the Queen herself proved by expressing it to me on every occasion . . . Lord Clarendon and Sir George Grey also very expressly told me it would have been impossible to have made better dispositions than I had done, and that the

Queen had specially imparted to them her very great satisfaction with all I had done, and how she felt 'greatly indebted to me for the manner in which I had conducted everything, which had greatly added to the comfort and pleasure she had experienced during her visit to Dublin.' . . . Albert also was very friendly and made me the finest compliments upon my military knowledge, which is a fresh proof that he is kindly disposed towards me. And he said to others he had never seen prettier manoeuvres and that the troops were magnificent under my leadership. It certainly all went extraordinarily favourably, not a mistake was made, not an escort, not a guard of honour was faulty, and the troops of every arm behaved excellently and did their utmost. The enthusiasm of the people it is impossible to express in words, and it is impossible any longer to doubt that Irishmen are at heart thoroughly Royalistically inclined, if only the agitators would leave them in peace. . . ."[n]

During the preparations for the Queen's visit, Prince George made a decision of the greatest importance to his career, for he turned down a somewhat mysterious invitation to become Regent of Hanover. He explained his reasons for so doing in a document dated April 1849, in which he argued that, despite the fact that he had been born in Hanover, he had been educated in England and had acquired the habits and outlook of an English prince. He believed it would be folly to exchange a secure position and great prospects for the uncertainty of German politics." Although almost wholly German by birth, he had come to love England more than anywhere else. "I can perfectly understand," he wrote to a friend who had just returned from abroad, "your feelings on landing in dear old England after so long an absence, as I have experienced them myself on several occasions. The fact is however one likes seeing foreign countries and however amused and interested one is in seeing the various customs and habits of others, still upon returning to England one feels that everything here is so very superior to what one has seen that one is doubly proud of being an Englishman and of belonging to a nation that has such a country to live in."[n]

On hearing that his father was ill, Prince George came over to England in June 1850. (It was after visiting the Duke, at Cambridge House, that the Queen was attacked by Lieutenant Pate, late of the 10th Hussars.) On June 30, the day Sir Robert Peel fell from his horse and received injuries from which he died, the Duke had a violent stomach attack which left him exhausted and feeble. Prince George's diary records his father's gradual decline.

> 3 July. My father continues much the same, but without any material improvement. The gloom cast over London by Sir Robert Peel's death overpowers everything. 5 July. My father to-day not so well, and the medical men not satisfied. Great debility . . . 6 July. My dear father was moved on a sofa into his sitting room for a few hours. This, however, rather exhausted him. 7 July. Dr. Bright saw my father to-day and evidently had a very bad opinion of him. . . . Towards night my father, who had been progressing favourably and tranquilly during the day, grew much worse quite suddenly and about eleven o'clock the medical men did not think that it could last much longer. By help of stimulants, however, he got better, after one o'clock, and towards morning was so considerably better that the pulse had regained its composure and firmness, and his mind which had been very languid, had quite regained its energy. We sat up all night with him—and a fearful night it was. . . . After one o'clock, he seemed to get more quiet and better and we moved him on to the sofa and he rallied wonderfully and got quite himself again, very collected in thought. 8 July. At about seven all things were so much improved, and he appeared going on so well altogether, that I went to Gloucester House to carry the better tidings to my dear Aunt [the Duchess of Gloucester]. We sent for Watson.

I called Dr. Bright myself. They came immediately and were astonished at the rally that had been made. . . . The dear Duchess of Gloucester came at eight, and took me to Buckingham Palace, when I saw the Queen, who was most anxious and much affected. Returned to Cambridge House and went to see my father, who spoke kindly to me and blessed me. Went down to dine. At nine fifty I received a message to say I was wanted immediately. I rushed up without a moment's delay, but ere I got there all was over. My dear Father had expired quite unexpectedly and most calmly and quietly. . . . My poor mother had just gone out of the room. Suddenly he opened his eyes wide, uttered a faint exclamation and fell back lifeless without a struggle. . . . I have lost the best of fathers, the most sincere and kindest of friends. May we meet again in Heaven. After all was over we had prayers by the bedside of the dead, which was the only consolation left to us. . . . This is the most fearful blow that has ever come upon me.

Princess Augusta, who in 1843 had married the son and heir of the Grand Duke of Mecklenburg-Strelitz, and consequently spent most of her life abroad, travelled night and day to reach her father before he died. She arrived seven hours after all was over, and sank down by his bedside, sobbing: "Too late, too late!" During the Duke's last days her sister, Princess Mary, spent many hours at Cambridge House. "I feel so grateful to God," she wrote, "that I was permitted to be with him during his illness. . . . The last day I never left him for he liked to have me with him, when Mama was for a moment called away, to fan him and to bathe his temples with eau-de-Cologne; and then he would press my hand and whisper, 'charming,' 'Dear.' The same evening all was over, and the spirit had returned to God who gave it. His will be done.'"

The Duke was buried at Kew Church, which he had so often attended, and the funeral over, his son returned to London in an agony of grief. "I cannot tell you," he wrote to

Louisa, "how miserable I am. Every minute makes me more
so and I feel that I have lost the dearest and best *friend* not
alone Father that I possessed on Earth. My only prayer is
that I may meet him again in Heaven. Bless my dear children. May they at my last end have as much cause to be
grateful to me, as I have to be so to him."

On Prince George's succeeding to the Dukedom, the question arose of a parliamentary grant. Prince Adolphus left
his children less than £30,000 between them, a sum which
in his circle amounted to destitution. If the Government
did not come to the rescue, they would be left royal pau-
pers." Lord John Russell proposed an allowance for Prince
George of £10,000 a year, but the Queen, taking up the
cudgels on her cousin's behalf, declared this sum insufficient and proposed £12,000." Prince Albert then sent for
various ministers, ostensibly to sound their opinions; in fact
in the hope of gaining their support of the larger allowance.
Sir James Graham, an austere economist, told the Prince
Consort, "that there might be some danger in allowing the
Duke to have the £12,000 rather than a smaller amount
now and the hope of an increase on a marriage." If the
Duke's eventual income were to depend on his choice of a
wife, the Queen would be given a powerful means of in-
fluencing such a decision. Moreover, Sir James feared that
"the religious part of the House" might well attack Prince
George's moral character, since his "connexion with an actress or dancer, and his having several children of her, was
very notorious." Prince Albert, who some years before had
suspected that his brother Prince Ernest of Saxe-Coburg
was being led astray by Prince George," appreciated the
force of his argument, but replied that it would be better
to show confidence in H.R.H., and "to lay hold of his affection and gratitude." Seizing the opportunity thus offered,
the Prince Consort brought up the whole matter with the
Duke. He told him "he might consider the point [the larger
allowance] as gained" and took the chance "to hint at the

fear entertained on account of his relations with that woman, but said at the same time that Victoria had the fullest confidence in his never bringing dishonour on the Royal Family by making a disgraceful marriage. George was embarrassed but made the strongest professions of regard for his position, and gratitude for our exertions to help him."" Considering that the Duke was already married to Louisa, his embarrassment, under the circumstances, was understandable. As predicted, the House of Commons voted him an allowance of £12,000 a year, and his sisters £3,000 a year each; an arrangement which H.R.H. described in his diary on July 20, 1850, as "very satisfactory at the present time."

On his mother's birthday, July 25, 1850, the Duke took his seat in the House of Lords, sponsored by the Duke of Wellington and the Duke of Beaufort. Prince George had a great regard for Wellington, and this was almost the last occasion on which he saw him, for two years later the great Duke died suddenly, at Walmer. The Queen wrote to her cousin from Balmoral, September 22, 1852, deploring her personal loss. "My dear George, You will, I know, join in the grief of the whole nation at the loss of that great and immortal man, whom it has been my privilege, I may truly say, to have known intimately. The dear old Duke's loss is an irreparable one in every sense of the word, and one cannot realize at all the possibility of his being no longer amongst us, or think of *England without him*.""

On November 18, the day of the funeral at St. Paul's Cathedral, H.R.H. was given command of the troops and made responsible for most of the arrangements of the procession. By a strange chance, his father had supervised Nelson's funeral. In his diary he wrote: "Up and dressed by six fifteen and out by a quarter before seven. Though most unpromising in the morning, it turned out a most beautiful day. I had the entire command and responsibility as regards the troops. Everything went off to perfection and without an accident. The masses of people enormous: their conduct dignified and admirable in the extreme. . . . Got home safe and sound, though a good deal tired, by five thirty." Princess Mary came up from Kew to watch the ceremony from the Duchess of Gloucester's house in Park Lane. She was full of admiration for her brother's arrangements. "From the balcony we saw the military part of the procession pass soon after eight o'clock. Infantry, artillery, and cavalry, all looked so magnificent! and George, commanding them, *so* well! that there was a sort of melancholy pleasure in seeing them march slowly by, while the bands played funeral marches by some of the *old* composers. They were chosen by Albert, and were very appropriate."⁷¹ The Queen on the evening of the funeral wrote to congratulate the Duke for his part in the ceremony. "It was a most touching and impressive sight," she concluded, "which never can be forgotten, may *his* example ever live in *our* hearts, Dear great Duke. I cannot yet believe it was *him* who was borne with all his country and honours and all his nation's tears—to the grave! Albert says the ceremony in the Cathedral was most affecting."⁷²

Wellington's death made it necessary to appoint a new Commander-in-Chief. His own view, expressed in 1850, had been that the Prince Consort should succeed him. The Queen seriously considered the idea, for no choice in her eyes could be wiser, but Prince Albert himself rejected it, rightly judging it would be bitterly resented. He saved the Prime Minister, Lord Derby, possible embarrassment by telling him at once that he did not himself wish for the appointment. Lord Derby next suggested the Duke of Cambridge, but the proposal was rejected. He was only thirty-three at the time and his rank of Major General was regarded as insufficient to qualify him for the post. Moreover, to promote him over the heads of senior officers would cause intense ill-feeling. Despite the desirability of having a royal Commander-in-Chief—a proposal originally advocated by Wellington and wholeheartedly endorsed by the Queen

—it was finally decided that the Duke was too junior in the Army, too young, and that "he would have carried no weight with the public" at a moment when, as Prince Albert foresaw, "many attacks on the Army, which have been sleeping on account of the Duke, will now be forthcoming."" Another possible candidate was FitzRoy Somerset, later Lord Raglan. Greville thought he would have been a very popular choice, and was inclined to attribute the eventual appointment of Lord Hardinge to court favouritism.

Lord Hardinge, even if he did owe his promotion to the Queen, was an admirable choice. He was gazetted as General Commanding-in-Chief, a lesser title than his predecessor's, and a formal recognition of the unique position Wellington had held. Hardinge had purchased a commission in 1804, had stood by Sir John Moore when he received his fatal wound at Corunna, and was himself injured at Ligny so badly that his hand had to be amputated. In 1820 he became a Member of Parliament in the unreformed House of Commons, in 1828 he was appointed Secretary at War,* and in 1844 was sent to India as Governor General, to replace his brother-in-law, Lord Ellenborough. Eight years later he re-entered Parliament and was appointed Master General of the Ordnance, a post which he only held for a few months. He at once discovered that there were only some fifty cannons fit for service in the entire country, the most recent of which had been made before Waterloo, so he persuaded the Government to manufacture three hundred guns and two hundred ammunition wagons, without which the Crimean expedition would have been disastrously hampered." His military and parliamentary experience, combined with his administrative ability,

---

* Originally the Secretary at War was Military Secretary to the Commander-in-Chief, but in 1704 the civilian Head of the War Department assumed the title. The post was absorbed in 1854 in that of Secretary for War, and was formally abolished in 1863. The Secretary for War was a Secretary of State with wider powers and responsibilities than those exercised by the Secretary at War.

energy, and common sense, were qualities well suited to the office he now held.

Although the Duke of Cambridge was rejected as Wellington's successor, he had earlier in the year been appointed Inspector General of Cavalry, a position which he retained until he was given a command in the field during the Crimean War. His new duties placed him at the centre of military and political affairs, and by requiring him to live in London ended his weary separation from Louisa which had caused them both such grief. Moreover, he had grown to rely upon her judgment and he missed being able to consult her immediately. "There are so many things going on," he wrote on September 22, 1850, "in which I want advice, that I am quite at a loss without you, my dearest beast."

Since the Duke wrote to Louisa every day that they were separated, a considerable part of his correspondence refers to his longing to be reunited. Louisa was a more erratic writer than her husband, but her theme was the same. Life, he constantly assured her, was never the same or so happy without her. Again and again he tells her how much he loves her, how he longs to "press her to his heart," and how his affections are given to her alone: the word "alone" sometimes being underlined as many as three times. She, in reply, longs to "lie in his arms," to see "his dear old face again," and to have "a good cuddle." "Ah! my beast, my own darling George," she wrote in an undated letter—signed "Your affectionate wife, Louisa Cambridge"—"I shall be so glad to see your dear face again and to lie in your arms and to be pressed to your heart where I have lain for so many years, so many happy years, and you darling have often said how intensely happy and blessed you have been in mine, and that you would not change wives with anybody, for that you loved me with all your heart and soul—praise be to God that it is so."

When the Duke went away to shoot, or to stay at country houses, Louisa pined for his return, and such visits some-

times provoked quarrels. "How I wish I was with you," she once wrote from Brighton, "paying visits. There is nothing I dislike more than your remaining away so long. I most sincerely hope soon all secrecy will be at an end, and then I shall be rewarded for my patience, and you must say I have behaved well upon that point. Oh George what a beast you are! I do not think I can continue to love you dearest . . . I hate these separations, to me they are detestable."
"Believe me, my own love," the Duke assured her, "that had I my own way, I *never* should leave you even for a day, but there are little duties that one must do now and then, and these you my love are the first to acknowledge in your heart, however much they may bore and annoy you at the moment." In another letter he admits that "he does not object now and then to a shooting expedition," but he adds consolingly, "I am always far more pleased when it is over, and I can get back to you my dearest wife."

When the Duke was away, Louisa was inclined to grow suspicious. She hints in many of her letters that there must be somebody else in the background, and her misgivings were not without substance. She admitted that she had a jealous nature but attributed it to "excess of love." "I think dearest," she wrote, "I ought to be a little angry with you. You left London without having a cuddle. I do not think that was very kind of you. I suppose you were reserving yourself *for your friends.*" It seemed in vain that her husband assured her, "I like nothing so much as to tell you how much and how devotedly I love you, and you *alone,* for you and the children are all in all to me."

The Duke never forgot anniversaries, and many of his letters to Louisa reminded her of them. The day of their wedding was never allowed to pass unnoticed. "My own Louly," he wrote on the fourth anniversary, "my dearest wife, need I assure you how I thought of you on awaking this morning, and how I wished you were by my side? Need I assure you dearest, that my love for you now is greater, if possible, than it ever was? I love you better dearest than

57

anything on earth, than life itself." Later in the same year, 1851, when he was visiting Germany, he wrote on October 15, from Hanover, a characteristic letter, full of love and longing for Louisa.

Hanover, 15 October 1851

My own Louly, My dearest Wife,

I have but a free moment to myself today dearest, but I must just send you one line love to tell you, that I think my calculations are correct, that I intend to start from hence on Friday and hope to be with you, my dearest beast, my darling love, in the night from the Saturday to the Sunday. There is a charm in that thought dearest, which to me is perfectly delicious and so I am sure dearest it is also to you. I feel confident of this not only because I know it, but also because you say so in your dear letters. So my darling you may expect me and I hope as I said in my last that you will leave the street door unlocked and will let me find a lamp in the passage, to creep up into my own Louly's, my dear wife's arms. Oh! God how I long to press you to my heart, that heart, which beats only for you. I have bought some beautiful pocket handkerchiefs for you. And now my letter must go by the post, so God Almighty bless you love, and our dear children. That I may soon press you to my heart, is the fervent prayer of

Your most loving and affectionate husband,

George

While the Duke was serving in Dublin, Louisa paid him occasional visits, but separations were long and frequent. After he began working in London in 1852, he saw her almost every day, although the duties of Inspector General of Cavalry were more demanding than those of the Dublin command. The Army in 1852 was in urgent need of reform, having been absurdly neglected ever since Waterloo. "If unreadiness for hostilities," wrote Fortescue, the great his-torian of the British Army, "be any furtherance of the cause of peace, then assuredly the English cannot be blamed for leaving the experiment untried. After every great war in our history we have treated the Army as if it would never be needed again. Marlborough's troops marched from victory to victory, and returned to be cursed as the plagues of the nation. Thousands of officers and tens of thousands of men were turned adrift." When in 1914 Britain declared war on Germany, the War Minister said of his Cabinet colleagues: "They at least have courage, they pit themselves without any army against the greatest military power in Europe." The mania of the Government for economy after 1815 led them to consider military problems exclusively from the point of view of the Exchequer, and to pursue, in Fortescue's phrase, "the time-hallowed policy of striving to purchase a good Army for the price of a bad one."

Ever since the days of Cromwell, the military have been looked upon with suspicion. After the restoration of Charles II, such troops as he retained were a source of bitter controversy, and James II, by filling regiments with Catholics, increased ill-feeling. The Whigs—the tradition was inherited by many nineteenth-century Liberals—regarded professional soldiers as dangerous reactionaries, ever ready to fight in defence of despotism. They declared that the Militia was the surest protection of English liberties, recruited as it was from volunteers; unpaid, untrained, and probably unusable in a serious emergency. Indeed, military ineffectiveness, rather than the fact that it consisted of ordinary citizens doing part-time service, constituted the best conceivable guarantee that it would never overthrow a government. Nor, of course, would it have repulsed an enemy. When members voted for reductions of military estimates, they persuaded themselves that the Army could always be expanded as necessary in times of emergency: an utterly false premise. "A shocking waste of blood and treasure was involved in the improvisation of forces to meet each crisis as it arose." Even if we lose the opening engagements of a war, it was argued, we always win the last battle. Moreover, the sea is England's best defence against a foreign foe, and the Navy may always be relied on to ward off invasion. Standing armies were characteristic of continental states, as was the absence of that "freedom in speech and action which every Englishman claims as his birthright. Why, therefore, should parliament both hazard the loss of these benefits and exhaust the national treasure by maintaining a Standing Army as a defence *at home*, when the Navy, as the first, and the Militia as the second line of defence, were not shown to be unable to secure our shores?"' It was such arguments as these which encouraged otherwise responsible statesmen to disregard the Army in peacetime, to reduce its establishments, to deprive it of weapons, to ill-treat its officers, and to neglect its men. Then, when inevitable disaster followed in time of war as the direct result of their own incompetence, their own ignorant interference, and their own inveterate frugality, they complacently heaped abuse on the commanders in the field. Soldiers soon learned what to expect. Kipling was to express their feelings in a caustic couplet:

It's Tommy this, an' Tommy that, an' "Chuck 'im out, the brute!"
But it's "Saviour of 'is country," when the guns begin to shoot.

So little regard was shown for the military profession that convicts were given the choice of enlistment or jail.

Despite the defects of army organization revealed in the war against France, little was done after 1815 to improve its administration. Business was conducted by thirteen different departments, not to mention several boards and commissions, virtually independent and mutually jealous. Nearly all communication was in writing. Florence Nightingale, who knew something of the inertia of the War Office, described it as "a very slow office, an enormously expensive office, a not very efficient office, and one in which the Minister's intentions [she was writing to Sidney Herbert] can be entirely negatived by all his sub-departments, and those of each of the sub-departments by every other."

To escape the notice of hostile politicians, troops were hidden away in distant parts of the Empire, and had little opportunity for effective military training in such scattered detachments. Battalions abroad were seldom relieved. To be posted was to start a life sentence. Soldiers in distant stations soon became part of the landscape, married, grew vegetables, mounted a few guards, and if an inspecting general threatened—a rare disaster—polished their drill and their uniforms. The Army, in Prince Albert's phrase, was "a mere aggregate of battalions." There were no manoeuvres, no wagon train, no divisional organization. Except for officers who had taken part in the French war, nobody had seen a larger collection of men than a brigade. Wellington fought hard to retain even the nucleus of the transport system he had built up in the Peninsula, but Parliament swept it away. No staff existed accustomed to deal with the three arms. Sir Thomas Picton was popularly supposed to have shot the last commissariat officer for incompetence."

Attempts were made to blame Wellington for the deficiencies of the Army, despite the fact that he spent much of his time denouncing reductions. "The Government," he once complained, "will not, they dare not, look our difficulties in the face and provide for them." In 1847, much to his annoyance, part of a confidential letter he wrote to Sir John Burgoyne was published in the newspapers. In it he described his fruitless attempts to induce the Government to improve the country's defences. There was not the means, he maintained, to resist an invasion anywhere along the south coast. This disclosure provoked Cobden and the Radicals to deny the need for military expenditure and to ridicule the Duke for proposing it. Even so perceptive a statesman as Peel shared the views of the

Manchester economists. "We should best consult the true interests of the country," he told the Commons, "by husbanding our resources in time of peace and—instead of a lavish expenditure on all the means of defence—by placing some trust in the latent and dormant energies of the nation . . . to defy the menaces of any foreign power."[n]

Such was the condition of the Army and such the climate of political opinion when the Duke of Cambridge was appointed Inspector General of Cavalry. The Duke's name is not ordinarily associated with reform. Toward the end of his career as Commander-in-Chief he became increasingly conservative and his obstruction and opposition to change became notorious. It would, however, be wrong to imagine that the proposals he resisted were invariably enlightened: many were inspired by ill-conceived notions of economy. In 1852 he was only thirty-three, and was every bit as anxious as Lord Hardinge to fit the Army for war. So vigorous and even ruthless were they in their efforts that Sir George Brown, "who cordially hated all change whether good or bad," resigned his appointment as Adjutant General. The departure of this martinet from the Horse Guards was not greatly regretted by those, and they were many, who found his insistence on the letter of Army regulations oppressive.

In the brief period between the death of the Duke of Wellington and the beginning of the Crimean War, many improvements were made, "largely due to the energy and administrative ability displayed by a young member of the Royal Family . . . An energetic, tall, slim young man, a crack shot and keen hard rider to hounds, a young officer who had taken pains to perfect himself in every branch of his profession, and was impatient of inefficiency in any form."[n] In the first year of office the Duke produced four important memoranda, which between them exposed the deficiencies of the service. The first was entitled "Observations on the Organization of the British Army at Home" (December 1852), which was followed by "The Organiza-

tion of British Infantry" (January 1853). Next he produced
a paper on "The Organization of British Cavalry" (October
1853), and he concluded his survey with a document on
"The Age of General Officers" (December 1853). These
memoranda were the result of considerable experience, informed common sense, and a passionate regard for the
interests of the Army. The Queen and Prince Consort read
them with concern. "My paper," wrote the Duke to Louisa
on January 14, 1853, "was well received by the Prince and
he has asked me for a copy of it which looks well. They are
very full here [Windsor Castle] of the defences and what
ought to be done, and I am in great hopes that something
really will be done at last."

The Duke's memorandum on the state of the Army constituted a distressing revelation of military unpreparedness,
which was soon to be further exposed by the events of the
Crimean War. It insisted on the need for divisional organization, and proposed annual manoeuvres of all three arms
to give officers and men experience which they could not
gain in their regiments. H.R.H. predicted that there would
be chaos at the start of a war unless this were done. "It will
no doubt be generally admitted," he wrote, "that no army
can be considered as in a proper state to take the field, however good its component parts may be, unless it has some
organization on a more extended scale than the mere formation of regiments and batteries, in fact, unless a brigade
and division system be introduced, which is to be found in
every continental army. The British Army alone is . . . not
at present subject to any such organization, the result of
which must be inevitably that, however excellent the regimental system existing in it may be, and which no doubt
cannot be surpassed, still the confusion and uncertainty on
the first outbreak of a war or an attack from without would
be most lamentably and seriously felt."

The Duke's memorandum on the retirement age of senior
officers revealed an astonishing state of affairs. "We have
hardly," he reported, "a single general officer in our service

who has not attained or will shortly attain his sixtieth year. It must be admitted that this is far too advanced a period of life to *commence* upon the arduous duties of active military command . . . A system of retirement must sooner or later be adopted." He recommended that this should take place compulsorily after fifty years' service, and then "younger men could be brought forward in the vigour of life and physically capable of filling satisfactorily the higher grades of the Service." Wolseley, writing to the Duke from Dongola on December 11, 1884, told him: "When I was a very young man I was brought into intimate relations with generals and staff officers of high position, who were absolutely useless, many of them worn out old gentlemen, as brave as lions, but whom physical infirmities alone prevented from being more than an encumbrance to the Army they served." The Duke himself was only thirty-four when he wrote so incisively on the need to retire elderly generals. His youth gave him a certain detachment, but when in 1895 the question of his own retirement at the age of seventy-six was raised, he insisted that he still felt perfectly equal to the performance of his duties.

One practical result of all this paper work was the decision in 1853 to hold large-scale manoeuvres. The novelty of the "Camp of Exercise" held at Chobham excited great interest in the newspapers. *The Times* devoted many columns to describing the military operations in "the wilds of Surrey." Unfortunately it was a particularly wet summer and the troops were exposed to fearful discomforts. *Punch* declared that the Camp established that the Army "could not only stand fire but also stand water." The manoeuvres certainly proved how necessary they were. Exceedingly few soldiers had the remotest conception of military tactics, and some regarded "the whole damned thing as a waste of time." Distracted staff officers were kept busy searching for lost units, or persuading over-zealous commanders that they were attacking their own side. " 'This Army,' remarked an officer in the Royal Artillery with angry exasperation, 'is a shambles.' "" Shortly afterwards the Government agreed to purchase nine thousand acres of Hampshire moorland—the present Aldershot—to improve future manoeuvres, little anticipating that in the following year the Army would be engaged, in earnest, on the heights of Sebastopol.

The Crimean Command

EARLY in 1854 the Crimean War broke out, and the price of the neglect and apathy of successive governments was to be paid in blood. The Army's administrative system, such as it was, collapsed under the strain, and British troops endured sufferings intensely provoking because evidently avoidable. In February the Guards Division sailed for Malta in a holiday mood. A series of farewell banquets constituted the most energetic preparation of an otherwise leisurely departure.

At first H.R.H. was uncertain whether he would be given a command in the field, but on February 16 he was able to write in his diary: "At 2.30 the Duke of Newcastle [Secretary of State for War*] came, who announced to me my good fortune in being appointed to a Division in the expeditionary force. Overjoyed at this news. Communicated it to all my friends." At the age of thirty-five, he had been given the First Division, consisting of Guards and Highlanders. The Supreme Commander of the Expeditionary Force was Lord Raglan. Under him were four Infantry Generals: H.R.H., commanding the First Division, Sir De Lacy Evans the Second Division, Sir Richard England the Third Division, and Sir George Brown the Light Division. The Duke's Division consisted of two brigades. The First, commanded by General Bentinck, was composed of the Third Battalion

---

* See note on page 55.

Grenadiers, the First Battalion of the Coldstream Guards, and the First Battalion of the Fusilier Guards. The Second Brigade was commanded by Sir Colin Campbell and consisted of the 42nd, 79th, and 93rd Highlanders. All the other infantry divisions were given to Peninsular veterans, some over seventy, none under sixty.

The decision to give the Duke a command was partly a consequence of the Queen's advocacy. In her diary she wrote on February 13: "George came to see Albert (and I afterwards went to see him) in a great state about his going with the troops, and having a command, about which, between the danger of placing him in too responsible a position, and his being so high in rank, a hitch seems to have arisen. He said he would feel himself disgraced, were he not allowed to go. We agreed with him and promised to do all we could." "My heart," her entry concluded, "is not in this unsatisfactory War."

The instant he received definite news of his appointment, the Duke wrote to Louisa. "Knowing as you do," he told her, "that I thought my military reputation was at stake if I did not go out with the First Division, you will easily conceive how much I have been gratified at hearing today officially that I am to have the First Division . . . To leave you is *almost* death to me, but with God's blessing I shall get back all safe, and then if I have done any good I am a made man and my military career is really open to me. I am sure you will feel this as I do."

Louisa, to whom the separation was to be almost unendurable, was at least delighted at the fulfilment of her husband's ambition, and wrote him a letter quoting a most favourable newspaper article.

18 February 1854

My Darling,

I have copied this article out of the Papers, it is charming. "The Appointment of the Duke of Cambridge to a divisional command has excited much satisfaction among military circles, by whom he is greatly esteemed. Though an extremely young Major General, there are very few of his Military grade, though double his years, who can approach him in a thorough knowledge of his profession in every department down to the minutest details. Those who have had the pleasure of serving under him in garrisons will readily and strongly bear testimony to his extraordinary activity, zeal and devotion to the service, as well as to his quickness, clearness, dexterity in handling troops and marvellous memory." Just write a line to say you are pleased. I am delighted.

> Your loving wife,
> Louisa

Before leaving England, the Duke left a sealed letter with his mother, only to be opened if he was killed in the war. In it he took a last farewell of her, and told her what he said he could not and would not disclose verbally, or except in the event of his death, that he had *married* Louisa. He begged her to think of him with affection, and to look after his three dear boys, for nobody else he knew would take a loving interest in them. Although he had done all in his power to leave them independent, her protection would help them in the world. He asked for her forgiveness, and hoped that his last letter would perhaps explain much which might have seemed strange to her.

Instead of sailing with his division for the East, the Duke, at the special request of Napoleon III, accompanied Lord Raglan to Paris to discuss the coming campaign with the Emperor. He stayed at the Embassy with Lord Cowley, and Louisa, her son Augustus, and her sister Georgina put up at the Hôtel de Londres. The Ambassador was doubtless somewhat surprised that his royal guest spent so little time under his roof; and the Duke, for his part, must have found it increasingly difficult to invent plausible excuses for leaving the Embassy. Some days he visited his wife before breakfast, and at other times late at night, when Georgina's presence was a little frustrating, for, as Louisa later complained, it made it "hard to have a cuddle."

The Duke was impressed by the Emperor, and he did not fail to observe the charm of the Empress, who, he grudgingly admitted, "is certainly very handsome." On April 12 there was a great review; but most of the time was spent in detailed military discussions. In his diary the Duke comments on April 13: "The Emperor is most interesting. He is extremely judicious in his remarks." Napoleon strongly supported an idea, initially proposed by Francis Joseph, that the Duke should travel to Constantinople by way of Vienna, where he would be in time to attend the Emperor's wedding. The British Government, anxious to seize any opportunity to persuade the Austrians to join the war, endorsed the plan. Taking leave of Lord Raglan, who travelled directly to join the expedition, the Duke on April 18 left Paris for Vienna. There was a more important farewell to be taken. "Went to the Hôtel de Londres to say goodbye to dearest Louisa, having fully made up my mind to start for Vienna that evening. The parting was a fearful moment and I shall never forget it as long as I live, and I confess had I known what it would have been before, I am doubtful whether I should have been so anxious to have gone on this expedition. But the die was cast and it must be done and so at six o'clock I kissed the boy, my dear child Augustus, and then Louisa, and was off." Two days later he wrote to his wife from Prague. "Dearest love, if you knew how I suffered when taking leave of you. Oh! darling, to look at your face, and dear Augustus's, and then to think how long I should probably not see it again, was the most painful moment of my life." On reaching Vienna on April 22, he wrote a further letter full of despair and misery. "Ah! My dearest dear Louly, I feel daily, hourly more and more how impossible it is for me to live or exist without you. You are all in all to me and life is positively not bearable when it is spent away from you. A short absence is a most serious annoyance, but a long one is intolerable. I shall set all my will to work to get near you love, be it by arranging for you to come out to join me, or be it for me to return to you." On his way to Vienna, his sister Augusta, the Grand Duchess of Mecklenburg-Strelitz, met him at the station at Dresden. "She said," concluded the Duke's letter, "she would consider it a duty and a sacred trust to look after and befriend our dear boys should anything occur to me."

The Duke's conversations with Napoleon, and his appearances in public, helped recommend the English alliance to the French nation, both countries being more accustomed to regard each other as enemies than allies. The Foreign Secretary, Lord Clarendon, wrote on April 15 to congratulate H.R.H. on the success of his mission. "I consider that the visit of Your Royal Highness to Paris has been a great political success as it has given the French people an opportunity of publicly ratifying the policy of the Emperor, while on the other hand His Majesty will be more confirmed in that policy and more bound to the English alliance by receiving such unmistakable proofs of the advantage he derives from it at home. Permit me to add, Sir, that much of this good effect is due to Your Royal Highness individually, to your personal bearing and courtesy, and to the manner in which you appear to have satisfied all classes.'" But delighted as was Lord Clarendon, and he was in an unrivalled position to judge the importance and success of the visit, it did not commend itself to the British press, which ignorantly condemned the Duke for dallying in the French capital, allegedly for his own entertainment, instead of hurrying to the war. *Punch,* at the end of April, published a cartoon representing Hector (Mr. Punch) chiding Paris (H.R.H.) for not hastening to the East. The Duke in fact joined his division at Constantinople over a month before it embarked for Varna, and four months before it set foot in the Crimea. Such unjust and inept attacks encouraged H.R.H. to form a rather embittered view of newspapers.

The journey from France was very disagreeable. Although only April it was exceedingly hot, and the Duke travelled "in the worst possible carriage," in which he was "completely shaken to pieces." The mission to Vienna was even more important than the visit to Paris, for Napoleon was already an ally, whereas Austria had yet to be won over. "Lord Clarendon," observed the Queen in her diary on March 6, "agreed with us in the great importance of George going to Vienna, which is desired by the Emperor of Austria, and which both from a military and political point of view, is most important." H.R.H. stayed with Lord Westmorland, the Ambassador, and was well rehearsed for his encounters with Francis Joseph. Their first meeting took place on April 23. "After breakfast at eleven a.m. was received in state by the Emperor. He is a young man, full of life and energy, and appears also full of talent. He conversed long on the important topics of the day, and all that he said was most just and true and, as far as it went, satisfactory. I congratulated him, on the part of the Queen, on his approaching marriage. As this was my first interview with him, I did not wish to press him too much, but I am confident his intentions are with us." The following day he attended the Emperor's wedding, and before leaving Vienna had "a most interesting talk" with Metternich. His daily letters to Louisa told her his most confidential news, for he trusted her with all his secrets. He complained that he was obliged to pay visits to countless Austrian royalty, "which is a great plague here with a family of *twenty* Archdukes." But H.R.H. regarded the visit he received from the veteran Marshal Radetzky as "a real honour and happiness," and he described him as "a delightful old man of eighty-nine, as fresh as ever, full of energy and life." In another letter, written three days later, dated April 30, he speaks of Francis Joseph as "a charming young man of great ability," and says that his discussions were more successful than he expected, for Austria was clearly favourable to England, but proposed to "wait till they think it judicious to join us."

Lord Clarendon again wrote to congratulate H.R.H. "It would have been impossible," he declared, "for any experienced diplomatist to have conducted matters with more judgement and ability." The Queen, Prince Albert, and the Government were "greatly pleased" with the Duke's dispatches. The Foreign Secretary told Lord Westmorland, with whom he had no need to be obsequious, that the Government were intensely "gratified by the reception given to the Duke of Cambridge," who they considered had performed his mission "admirably."" So did the Queen. "I am anxious," she wrote on May 3, "to express to you our pleasure and satisfaction at the manner in which you acquitted yourself of your delicate mission at Vienna. We and the Government think your letters most interesting, and the news they contained very important."

The Duke left Vienna on May 1, and after a brief visit to his old quarters in Corfu, reached Constantinople on the tenth. On the day of his arrival he met the Sultan, and was received in an audience he described as "neither long nor interesting." "I cannot say," he admits in his diary, "I was very favourably impressed by his appearance or manner. In fact he seemed to me to be a most miserable creature." The Sultan arranged for the Duke to stay in apartments in the palace of Ferez, "very nicely furnished for the sort of thing, but inconvenient to me from its great distance from the troops." Before the day was out, H.R.H. had visited the Ambassador, Lord Stratford de Redcliffe, with whom he had a long conversation. Wherever he went "he was most enthusiastically received by the troops," whom he found in "the best of health and spirits."

While at Constantinople, the Duke was tireless in his efforts to drill his division, so much so that some of his more lethargic officers regretted he had not been detained longer in Paris and Vienna. "The Duke of Cambridge," wrote a colonel under his command, "is full of zeal. We are out every morning at seven o'clock and either march into the country or have a field day in camp. The Duke is a capital fellow, nothing escapes him, and some of the mounted gentlemen have brushed up very much."" Prince Edward of

Saxe-Weimar, writing to the Queen, said: "George is very popular both with the officers and men." Nevertheless, his excessive enthusiasm for field days, essential as they doubtless were, put a considerable strain on the soldiers under him. "Our life," wrote one of them, "is not an idle one . . . Our royal chief is far too fond of field days, and keeps us out five hours under arms so that we return pretty well knocked up while the day is yet young."

The Duke with his division embarked for Varna on June 13 and landed the following day amid heavy rain and thunder. The town struck him as "a most miserable place and the fortifications very poor." As he became better acquainted with this part of Bulgaria, he liked it even less. "The town of Varna," he told Louisa, in a letter written on June 18, "is a most wretched place. The most miserable village in Ireland or Germany is better than this place, which is full of squalor, filth and disease . . . The fact is this country is really not worth fighting for, and the people less so. The sooner we can get out of it the better." He blamed Lord Stratford de Redcliffe for involving England in a war on behalf of an utterly worthless ally.

Soon cholera broke out at Varna, particularly among the Grenadier Guards, and the hospitals became overcrowded. "We are doing everything we can for them, but it is most distressing and the men are a good deal frightened." Toward the end of June, the Duke himself developed a fever. Besides suffering from stomach spasms, he became crippled by gout. Throughout much of August he was in great pain, and only able to move about on crutches. Lord Raglan lent him his coach so that he might visit the camp. The summer heat was fearful and he longed to be home. He told Louisa in a letter of August 4 that it was too late in the year to land in the Crimea. By the end of the month it was known at Varna that a landing was in fact to be made, and the Duke feared that he might not be well enough to take part in the expedition. However, he recovered sufficiently to join the fleet anchored off Varna Bay. Writing to his wife on September 4, he told her that the transports were on the point of sailing, "I presume for Sebastopol." "If God in his mercy spare me," he concluded the letter, "I shall have had enough and more than enough of soldiering, and the rest of my days shall be devoted to making my dearest wife happy and to looking after our children."

The Crimean expedition was decided upon by politicians who ignored both the inherent difficulties of the undertaking and the advice of their own generals. Raglan warned the Duke of Newcastle that he doubted it would be possible to winter in Russia, and was told for his pains that the Crimean climate was "one of the mildest and finest in the world." Against such invincible ignorance there was no hope of sense prevailing. Without a proper base, without land transport, without ambulances, without winter clothing, and without even maps, the Army was launched against one of the strongest fortresses in Europe. It was an insane enterprise.

The Duke was utterly opposed to an expedition so late in the year, but, as he observed in his diary on August 8, "public opinion in England is to be satisfied at any hazard, and so the attempt is to be made." In the letter he wrote Louisa on board ship at Varna, he told her of a conversation he had had with Saint-Arnaud, Commander of the French Army. Saint-Arnaud was very much amazed at finding so many people against the expedition, "amongst others myself, and said it was very odd and he could not make it out. I told him I believed the whole of his Army was against it and he acknowledged this to be the case." Louisa agreed with her husband that the attack on Sebastopol was rash in the extreme, and rightly foresaw that if things went wrong "all blame would be thrown upon the Chief [Lord Raglan] the Ministers of course creeping out of the affair."[n]

After several delays, the huge fleet of transports and warships set sail on September 7. "Got under weigh for the great expedition. It was a lovely morning and everything looked propitious. At about twelve all were fairly off and certainly it was a most magnificent sight." Five days later the coast north of Sebastopol was reached, but landing was delayed until three o'clock on the morning of the fourteenth. The day before disembarking, the Duke wrote to Louisa describing the voyage and a conference which nearly ended the invasion. "I must just scribble a line to you my dearest wife to prove to you that amidst the bustle and confusion of the moment, I am thinking of you, my soul, my life, and of our dear, dear, little children . . . We heard that there had been a conference at sea, that Marshal St. Arnaud was very ill," and that his generals "had handed in a protest against the expedition." But Lord Raglan, believing that the allies were far too committed to withdraw, persuaded the French to go on with the landing. "Of course I do not know more than anybody else so am all in the dark."

Some despondency was caused when it appeared that disembarkation was to take place within close range of Russian guns. It was with relief that it was discovered that what at first had appeared to be formidable batteries were, after all, only windmills. The landing was carried out successfully, although it rained heavily the first night. "If opposed we should have had a very tough job of it," was the Duke's comment. "To me it was quite marvellous why the landing was not opposed, for it was a tremendous confusion. Though the infantry landed very fast, hardly any artillery and no cavalry whatever were landed the first day." As the baggage was also left on the transports, the Duke had to sleep under a gun carriage, and the letter describing that wet and restless night was written sitting on the ground. Fortunately, as not a Russian was seen, "all went off to perfection," except that the Navy refused to bring their ships near enough inshore, and consequently the soldiers had a long wade through deep water.

From the moment of disembarkation, the Army began to suffer for the improvidence of the Government in failing to provide a Land Transport Corps. Indeed, the House of

Commons had deliberately destroyed the last vestige of a wagon train. The English nearly always forget the lessons of war the instant peace is signed, and the constancy with which the same mistakes are repeated proves how faithful we have ever been to this astounding practice. Already at Varna the want of horses had been seriously felt, and the Duke on June 20 complained in his journal: "The difficulty of moving or getting anything is very great and the commissariat extremely bad and helpless in every respect. It is difficult to see how we are able to move at all." Writing from Constantinople on June 20, he told Louisa, who loyally affected to take a professional interest in military matters, "the want of horses is dreadful, and where they are to be got I cannot tell . . . The stores are in a sadly confused way and many of the most important things have not arrived."

After repeated delays, for which English staff work was largely responsible, the allied armies began their march on Sebastopol, and on September 20 engaged the Russians at the battle of the Alma. It was an extremely confused engagement. Sir George Brown, a stickler for the drill book, was driven almost to distraction when it proved impossible to scramble through vineyards, to ford the Alma, and to ascend the steep slopes on the further side, as if still on the barrack square. Groups of men, from different regiments and even divisions, got so mixed up that they offered their services to any officer prepared to accept them.

Lord Raglan's strategy was not unduly elaborate. He simply launched a frontal attack on the strongly entrenched Russian positions holding the heights of the Alma. The Duke's rather vague instruction was to advance in support of the Light Division, which was on the extreme left of the British line and which had been ordered to cross the river Alma and capture the enemy guns in the Great Redoubt. This apparently simple plan was complicated by the nature of the ground to be crossed, and the great strength of the Russian defences.

The Light Division, under devastating fire, crossed the river, gained the heights, and stormed the batteries; but the Russians brought up reinforcements and drove them out. The casualties of the Light Division were very heavy, their formation was broken, and some regiments retreated in disorder. The Duke, only too aware of the responsibility of having the Brigade of Guards under his command, and lacking clear orders what to do, was agitated and bewildered. His progress was consequently hesitant, and more than once he had to be urged to hurry. At one moment he is said to have considered retiring, but was prevented from doing so by Sir Colin Campbell. "No Sir, British troops never do that, nor ever shall while I can prevent it."*

At long last, with the Guards Brigade on the right and the Highlanders on the left, the First Division began its attack, moving with splendid precision in unbroken lines, as if on parade. Halfway up the hill, the Fusilier Guards in the centre were thrown temporarily into confusion by some retreating remnants of the Light Division, but the advance continued, and after a withering volley of rifle fire, the Russians were driven from their position at the point of the bayonet. The day was won. Soon after, a Russian general, with both legs shot off, was found dying near the crest of the hill. So amazed was he by the courage of British soldiers that he begged to see the officer who had led them to victory. The Duke, on hearing of the request, hurried to the scene. *"Mais je veux voir le Général,"* exclaimed the wounded man, *"pas ce jeune homme-çi."*

Louisa was staying in Brighton when she first heard news of the battle. She spent two wretched, sleepless nights, thinking of her husband and praying for his safety. "Ah! George," she wrote to him on October 4, "if it has pleased the Almighty to bring you out of all those dangers that have encompassed you, the *first* thing we will do when we meet shall be to thank our Almighty Father for his great mercy towards us . . . I dreamt of you one night. You walked into some room where I was, you looked so pale. I spoke to you, you leant your head upon my shoulder and after some little time lifted up your hand and showed you had lost the tops of your fingers. I kissed them, you smiled and I know nothing more." So long as his heart was the same, she assured him, she would not care if he was disfigured.

Two days after the battle, while Louisa anxiously waited for news, her husband found time to describe it for her. The engagement, he told her, began at seven o'clock in the morning. The village of Alma was in flames when Sir George Brown's division crossed the river and began to attack. They were hard pressed and soon in confusion. "I was ordered up to support." While advancing through the vineyards and crossing the river, "the Division was exposed to a most murderous fire of grape." The Light Division was falling back. "The moment was an awful one. I had merely time to ask Sir Colin Campbell, a very fine old soldier, what was to be done. He said the only salvation is to go on ahead and he called to me 'put yourself at the head of the Division and lead them right up to the Battery.' I followed his advice." After the Russians retreated from the Redoubts, "we then and there halted and, Lord Raglan coming up, the whole line cheered from right to left. I think to me it was the proudest and noblest moment of my life. Everybody rushed up to me, seized me by the hand and congratulated me. I could not help it but cried like a child . . . I feel I owe all to the excellent advice of Sir Colin Campbell, who behaved admirably and had a horse shot under him. Finally I firmly believe that the First Division carried the day and the whole army admit it. How often have my words to you my love come across me, when I used to joke to say, that I should like some day to see in the papers 'The Division led by the D. of C. now came gallantly forward and the day was gained.' This has now I flatter myself literally taken place . . . Yesterday we spent in riding over the ground, collecting killed and wounded both Russian and English, and burying the dead. This was an awful sight and I shall never forget the horror of it as long as I live."

The Duke had confronted fire unflinchingly; mounted general officers were always dangerously exposed and provided select and conspicuous targets. But, although heedless of his own life, he was almost too careful of the safety of the troops he commanded, and was reluctant to commit them to action. It was a most amiable failing but not one shared by the world's great generals. "Dogs! Will ye live for ever?" was how Frederick the Great addressed his hesitant troops. The Duke, however, was neither hardened against remorse nor, if he could avoid it, prepared to accept its pangs. Lacking initiative, fearful of committing himself, and inclined to be over-anxious, he was not a skilled commander in the field. Indeed, it would have required exceptional military genius to have overcome the disadvantages of his youth and his inexperience of war. But H.R.H., although seldom consulted, was not without strategic insight. He pressed for a *coup-de-main* against Sebastopol immediately after the Alma, which Russian historians later agreed would probably have succeeded. Three weeks before Gortchakoff tried to raise the siege by attacking the rear of the British lines, H.R.H. anticipated the possibility of such a move, and begged Lord Raglan, unavailingly, to strengthen the position.

The congratulations he received for his part in the battle, in which, in fact, he had been jostled into victory, were somewhat extravagant. His son George, writing from school, attributed the success entirely to his father's efforts. "I am very glad," he wrote, "to hear that you escaped unhurt and were the cause of the battle being won. I hope that you will not be hurt in besieging the fort of Sebastopol. I wish that you would tell me how to spell it. I think that you had better be quick about taking Sebastopol as the winter is beginning." Mrs. FitzGeorge's congratulations were scarcely more restrained. "To think," said Louisa, writing on October 14, "that you should with the Light Division have had to bear the brunt of the battle, for it appears that had your Division hesitated the English army would have been cut to pieces.

Ah! My love how well I can conceive your feelings of pride and triumph. It must have been a proud moment for you and God knows from the innermost recesses of my heart I congratulate you my own dearest George. . . . What you have often said in joke is now a reality and almost your own words."

Grateful as Louisa was for her daily letter, she chaffed to join her husband in the Crimea, and to see what was happening for herself. Lord Errol, who commanded the 60th Rifles, was accompanied throughout the campaign by his wife and her French maid. Indeed, her ladyship's tent was pitched directly behind the Duke's. It was very small, so Lady Errol slept on the ground and her husband occupied the bed. But it was generally known that she was with the Army, and Louisa thought it was a precedent to follow. "Other people," she told H.R.H., "have their wives out, agreeable or otherwise to the authorities, and I am determined that if you do not join me, or I you, I shall make some arrangements for myself. As to your thinking for one moment that I am to continue to lead this lonely life, this dull monotonous existence, *I will not do it upon my soul*. If you have the great love you profess for me, you will not make any excuses. If you can live in discomfort so can I." It was a constant theme of her letters that she must be allowed to come out. "I promise you," she writes, "I will not be troublesome. You never shall feel that I am in the way. How I envy all that are near you, and I who love you the most, and am most beloved, cannot share what your servants are allowed, the pleasure of being near you." Lady Errol is alluded to frequently. "You tell me Lady Errol is the only person who has been permitted to follow her husband, and that on account of his being mad. If he is so, why is he allowed to remain in the Army?'"

The Duke, eager as he was to be reunited with Louisa, knew that a camp was no place for a woman. He promised her he would return home or send for her the moment he moved into regular quarters. "As regards my own individual feelings and wishes," he assured her, "I cannot tell you how dreadfully I miss you every hour of the day and how I long to see your dear old face again." As for Lady Errol, it is true she came out, but "all from Lord Raglan downwards agree in thinking that it is very, very wrong.""

Louisa was not to be silenced by talk of the hardships of campaigning. "No discomfort can be so great," she told her husband, "as that of being separated from you." Only when he was sent to Corfu had they been parted for more than a month. "I know dearest that I am most wretched and miserable *without* you and had I my way I would leave England and join my own dear husband. Oh! George, do you suppose that I would not rather put up with every sort of inconvenience and discomfort than be separated from you." As the weeks went by, she became less submissive. "If you will not send for me I shall leave England and go to the East. I cannot bear it any longer. One day is so like the other, work, read and drive and see no person scarcely. It is beyond everything miserable." She even suggested that she should cut off her hair and dress as a private soldier. "I could pass as a friend of yours. I think I could manage to disguise very well and be always *near* you." In the same letter, she described her utter loneliness. ". . . About six o'clock I cannot help feeling very low spirited, it is your usual hour love for coming home, but alas no dear beast makes his appearance and we get on as well as we can, and then at night when I go to my room, ah! how lonely and deserted it appears. It breaks my heart to think that you are no longer there to press me to your heart and bless me before going to sleep. Oh! George dear George what misery would I not undergo for your sake, you my darling husband who I love better than any creature in the world and without whom I should not care to live. I really sometimes can scarcely tell how I can go on without seeing you, you are so necessary to my existence, for I have given to you every feeling of affection, of love, of adoration, my whole heart is entirely yours, and should the war last long I *must* see you, I *will* see you, let what may come.'"

Although the Duke discouraged the idea of Louisa joining him, he held out hopes that he might himself return home. He thought it improbable that the Army could winter in the Crimea. "To remain here," he wrote on October 3, "would be awful and quite impossible I should think, for as it is one can get nothing to eat but what is supplied by the ships . . . Should it please God to spare me I am fully determined to go home, for I am dreadfully tired and sick of this sort of life, which is a desperately hard one, and for my part love I have had quite, quite enough of it."

Despite the approach of winter, the prospect of the arrival of further Russian reinforcements, and the almost hourly strengthening of Sebastopol's fortifications, valuable time was wasted and nothing whatever was done. Lord Wolseley, writing to H.R.H. in 1892, after a visit to the Crimean battlefields, said: "I have always thought . . . we should have taken the works, then just begun, on the South side at the Malakoff . . . We unfortunately halted to wait for our siege guns to be landed to knock down works that did not exist upon our first arrival, and which were actually built during the time we squandered in landing guns.'"

As the weeks passed, the Duke became more and more exhausted. Nearly every night there was some alarm, and the noise of gunfire was incessant. On October 12, he confided to Louisa his intention of returning home. He hoped that Sebastopol would be taken, the troops re-embarked for Constantinople, and he would be free to hurry back. "My darling, I cannot tell you how miserable I feel and how I long for the end of this dreadful campaign, for I am thoroughly worn out with fatigue and so are we all, and the misfortune is that we see little or no progress made . . . As to our holding this country I conceive that to be madness and unprofitable. This is the opinion of all, but we dread our Government insisting upon it, and our Chief possibly thinking it necessary to obey. Should this be so I for one shall do *my utmost to get home* and think it cannot well be refused me. . . . If it pleases God to spare me upon the taking of Sebastopol home I go, either with the army if we are all to go, or by myself, if the rest must remain, which for their sakes poor fellows I trust may not be the case, for there is not one of them who does not require thorough rest and reorganization both bodily and militarily." The gay, picnic mood in which the expedition began had given way to despair. "War is indeed a fearful thing," wrote the Duke to Louisa on October 31. "And the more I see it the more dreadful it appears."

If Louisa had reason to be distressed by her husband's hardships and depression of spirit, he was made uneasy for his part by references in her letters to suspicions and jealousies, inflamed in part by anonymous communications. "I am so sorry to tell you I have had several anonymous letters respecting you and your intrigue. If I could prove it, not that I have taken the least step in the matter, God! how I should hate you." "You know I am a jealous person and I must confess it gives me great pain, for I love you dearly George and I cannot understand why all these allusions should be made. I cannot suppose you would prove inconstant or false to me." "Dearest child," came the reassuring reply, "I cannot imagine who annoys you with anonymous letters but of this you may rest assured, that the accusations against me of which you speak are infamous, and wholly and entirely unfounded, that I swear to you.'"

The anonymous letters continued and Louisa was made wretched by them. "You must feel," she wrote on June 27, 1854, "that accusations like these make me very unhappy, I having thought you truth and honesty itself, and flattered myself that when you pressed my hand at the altar so fervently at the words 'until Death do us part' that nothing could force you to break that Oath . . . I now ask you (and much, very much will depend upon your replies) have you ever directly or indirectly supplied her [a Mrs.

Burton] with money, visited her unknown to me, been criminally known to her, or taken liberties with her, or she with you?" Louisa required a separate answer to each question, "as though you were standing in the presence of your God."

The Duke's repeated affirmations of innocence, which were, in fact, something less than candid, left his wife none the less disturbed by shadows of doubt. Unfortunately he had occasionally lied to her, and had been discovered doing so, which, naturally enough, reduced his credit. On October 25 she wrote: "There is one thing I trust you will never do again, that is to tell me a *falsehood*. I have no wish to prevent your going where you please, but I should soon have a thorough contempt for a person that did so often. You must remember after I found you out in the first, you promised you would not do so again, how you kept that promise you well know." Such deceits were not forgotten, for a year later Louisa again referred to them. "Had you not twice told me little stories I should never for one moment have thought you could deceive me and in my heart I do not think you would, for I am sure dearest love that you are a good and dear husband and love your dear wife with all your heart and soul." But this confidence was not always sustained, and a letter from the Duke to his wife, written on November 21, 1855, after he had returned from the Crimea, showed how offended he claimed to be by her suspicions. "I found your letter here," he told her from Paris, "and I confess to you dearest I am quite *broken hearted*. Is it credible that you my wife, my love, can write to me your dear husband, such a *cruel*, such a dreadful letter, and that after having known me for nearly sixteen years, after having had the greatest confidence and trust in me, and knowing that I have ever been the most true, faithful and devoted husband, and that the first and great object of my life has been to make my wife happy, as she has ever made me so . . . As there is a God in heaven I swear to you that I am a good and faithful husband." But these expressions of doubt and questioning were rare, compared with Louisa's constant protestations of devotion and love.

For the Duke in the Crimea, the entire world of Queen Street was little more than a momentary escape, a dream soon enough shattered by the war around him. After the Alma the allies advanced to Balaclava, a convenient base for the siege of Sebastopol. On October 25, the Russians made a sudden, surprise attack. The First Division was not engaged, but the Duke records in his diary what happened that eventful day, having, soon after the charge of the Light Brigade, received accounts from survivors. "The first thing this morning we heard heavy firing towards Balaclava and I immediately rode off to see what had happened. It was soon evident that it was a serious attack on the part of the whole Russian Army on Balaclava, as the enemy was seen in heavy masses of Infantry and Cavalry with a good deal of Artillery before the village of Kemara. An order came for the First Division to march to Balaclava. On reaching the telegraph in our rear we were horrified to see that the Russians had attacked and carried all the fortified points occupied by the Turks, who had fled in the most shameful manner without hardly firing a shot and leaving the guns in the hand of the enemy. At that moment heavy bodies of Russian Cavalry were pressing them and coming into the plain just below us. It was then that the Heavy Brigade of Cavalry, admirably led by General Scarlett, attacked the Russians, the Greys leading in splendid style, and though far outnumbered they cut through and entirely defeated the enemy who fled in wild disorder leaving vast numbers of dead on the field. We then continued our march and reached Balaclava where we found that the enemy's cavalry had attempted to enter the town, but were repulsed by the 93rd Highlanders in line, the Turks again shamefully running away. General Cathcart moved down with a Brigade towards the mounds held by the Turks . . .

I moved to the left to connect Cathcart with Balaclava and support him if necessary. The Russians held the further mounds and there we stood all day looking at one another. Meanwhile a fearful disaster occurred. Our light Cavalry was by some mistaken order directed to charge the enemy. The order was in writing and rather a vague one. Unfortunately it was carried by Captain Nolan, the first man almost who was killed. He made such offensive remarks both to Lords Lucan and Cardigan, that though doubtful what was intended and foreseeing what would happen, they allowed the orders thus given to be carried out. The Light Cavalry advanced right into the head of the Russian army. A battery of ten guns was to their front and batteries raked them on both flanks. Into this destruction they rode nearly two miles ahead of any support. Most nobly did they behave and a more gallant act never was done, though at the same time an utterly useless and senseless one. They rode right over the guns, took them all, cut down the gunners, but could not bring them away as they were completely surrounded. The Brigade returned destroyed. Only one hundred and eighty-nine men mustered on their return. I personally escaped the horrors of this fearful sight and I am grateful that I did. There lay our noble fellows all amongst the enemy and we could not go forward to assist them. Oh, it was heartbreaking . . . Miserable and dejected we returned to our quarters after dark."

After the failure of the attack on Balaclava, the Russians on November 5 made another attempt to surprise the allied camp, attacking at five thirty in the morning in drizzling rain and dense fog. The fiercest fighting at the battle of Inkerman centred round a position known as the Sandbag Battery. For a time it was held by the 41st and 49th Regiments, who, heavily outnumbered, were eventually forced to retire. The Guards were then ordered to retake the position. The attack was made with bayonets and the Russians were put to flight. But soon reinforcements arrived and the enemy re-formed. With reckless bravery, and outnumbering the defenders five to one, the Tsar's troops at length recaptured the position. When the Guards eventually retired, H.R.H. galloped in front of them and ordered them to stand firm and fire, but their ammunition was exhausted. The Duke was surrounded by the enemy in the midst of a hailstorm of bullets and shells. His horse "Wideawake" was shot in the leg, and he had to use his orderly's mount. A ball passed through his sleeve but only grazed his hand, as it was deflected by a pair of gold buttons containing his sister's hair. His A.D.C.s, Captain Clifton and Major Macdonald, both lost horses under them, and indeed so conspicuous were mounted officers that, of seventeen commanders on Inkerman Ridge, six were killed and only two escaped without wounds. At one period of the battle, the Duke entirely lost the Brigade of Guards, and was driven almost to distraction. With a nonchalance which did little to dispel H.R.H.'s anxiety and irritation, a young officer cheerfully reassured him: "The Guards, Sir, will be sure to turn up."[n]

Although the Russians were repulsed at Inkerman, it was an expensive victory. At the close of the action British soldiers lay on the ground utterly exhausted and hardly able to speak. Nobody escaped the general feeling of depression and discouragement. Lord Raglan was advised to evacuate the Crimea, and officers openly discussed sending in their papers and going home. Lord George Paget actually gave up his command and returned to England. Few in the Crimea blamed him, but the Queen was so outraged by his conduct that he bowed before her displeasure and returned to winter on the heights of Sebastopol.

"The Duke of Cambridge," according to a letter from the Crimea, "behaved uncommonly gallantly at Inkerman. No private soldier or officer behaved better than he did that day. He was the only man who looked after our interests. He is one of the best hearted men going. Nobody I think could have made himself much more popular than he did amongst us."[n] The Duke of Newcastle, writing to Lord

87

Raglan, told him how delighted the Queen was to read the favourable account in his despatches of the conduct of her cousin. "Her Majesty has received with feelings of no ordinary pleasure your Lordship's report of the manner in which His Royal Highness the Duke of Cambridge distinguished himself. That one of the illustrious members of Her Royal House should be associated with the toils and glories of such an Army is to the Queen a source of pride and congratulation."[n]

H.R.H. was undoubtedly a great favourite with the men. A sergeant in the 63rd Regiment wrote: "No officer was more truly beloved by the Army than was the Duke, from his constant attention to their welfare, his identity with them in their dangers and sufferings, and his ready acquiescence in anything likely to add to their comforts."[n] The Prince of Wales, after the war was over, discussed the campaign with Sergeant Major Edwards, and asked him who was the favourite general with the soldiers. "The Duke of Cambridge," was the reply. "He was what we called our number one. He took great care of his men—and was very brave—in fact I used to think he was too brave and exposed himself too much."[n]

Two days after Inkerman, Dr. Gibson ordered H.R.H. to rest. In a letter written to the Countess of Westmorland on November 30, the Duke speaks of "having been very ill with dysentery and typhoid fever."[n] He was moreover worn out by camp life, overwhelmed by the anxieties of command, and "quite unequal to work." Consequently he was sent aboard H.M.S. *Retribution*, at anchor off Balaclava. "I am dreadfully out of spirits," he wrote in his diary on November 10, "and cannot at all recover myself." The day he left camp, he wrote to Louisa: "I am worn out with fatigue and anxiety and am really completely done." He described the battle, compared with which he assured her "the Alma was a joke," and told her of the fearful English losses. "Broken-hearted with sorrow and fatigue, though grateful to God for his providential mercy, I returned to camp with my handful of men." He could not see how the war would ever be won. "We shall always beat the Russians when we meet, but our army is diminishing while their army is continually reinforced." He ended by saying how disheartened he felt, and that he was determined to get home as soon as he could possibly do so "with honour." In another letter, written ten days later, he told Louisa: "I have got a sort of ague which is very disagreeable, being at times extremely cold, at others equally hot, and then my nerves, which as you know are never of the best, are quite shaken and everything fidgets me and puts me out."

For one suffering from battle fatigue, H.M.S. *Retribution* was the worst possible place to have chosen to rest. On November 14 it barely survived the storm which destroyed so many ships off Balaclava, and which wreaked such havoc in the Army encampment. Tents were scattered in all directions, barrels bounded along "like cricket balls," trees were uprooted by the hurricane, and many ships, loaded with everything that was most needed, were dashed to bits on the rocks.

The storm broke at five o'clock in the morning and a thunderbolt struck *Retribution*. At first, those on board thought it was a Russian shell. "I prayed to God to forgive my sins," the Duke told his wife, "and was quite prepared to die." According to one account, H.R.H. grasped a steward's hand, and bewailing his fate, moaned: "Oh! Is it come to this? Oh! We shall be lost." Several gossips and some newspapers reported that the Duke had gone out of his mind as a result of the war and the gale. "I suppose you are aware," wrote Richard Cobden to a friend, "that the poor Duke of Cambridge lost his head at the last battle. I mean the little reason that was in it . . . The Slaughter of his Guards drove him mad. He showed the usual courage of his family, but the excitement was too great for him."" Angered by accounts in the English papers of his having gone out of his mind, and after reading in the *Daily News* a story of his alleged quarrels with Lord Raglan, H.R.H.

hastened to assure Louisa: "I am quite as sane, if not more so, than the writers of these abominable aspersions."

After the storm, H.R.H. wrote a letter, addressed to all his immediate family, in which he described his deliverance from shipwreck. "God's gracious and protecting hand has once again spared me, and I have been saved from a most awful calamity . . . The Morning of the 14th, a most fearful gale set in, and so suddenly that in about an hour's time there was no possibility of getting away. There we lay outside the harbour with quantities of ships all around us, which of course increased the danger. It began about six in the morning, and continued to increase momentarily in violence. The other ships and transports were dragging their anchors and passing us in rapid succession, some so close that we thought they must have been upon us, in which case we must have gone with them. These poor creatures drove on the coast, which was of perpendicular rock, and in a moment all perished, the ships regularly breaking or blowing up. At ten o'clock our rudder was carried away and there we were perfectly at the mercy of wind and waves. Our Captain, Drummond, a fine fellow, behaved most nobly, and by his coolness, courage and determination, certainly saved us under God's blessing. He threw all his heavy guns overboard, and all his shot, and kept her up to her anchor by the steam. We had three anchors down. At twelve, however, two of these anchors went and we had then only one left, and this one saved us . . . At two a thunderbolt came down and struck the ship. We thought at first it was a Russian shell . . . and then there came a tremendous shower of hail . . . I being unwell at the time lay in my cot all day, it was in fact impossible to sit up, and the decks were streaming with the water which was coming in every moment. The men brought us in accounts every now and then how things were going and by their countenances one could see how ill they thought of it. Tho' I did not give up all hope, I confess I thought all was lost and was fully prepared to die, I prayed for you all and thought much of dear home. Had the last anchor gone I had made up my mind to go on deck, prepared to try to swim with the rest, but I suspect that not many of us would have had a chance . . ."[n]

The experience of the storm, "worse than even the most fearful action," did nothing to improve H.R.H.'s health and spirits, and so he decided to go on leave to Constantinople. "Lord Raglan," he told Louisa, "sent me a very good natured message to say that he hoped I would not go about much at Constantinople as otherwise disagreeable remarks might be made, though he, for his part, thought my going there quite natural." Even in Balaclava Bay H.R.H. had thought it wise to keep to his cabin so as to prevent comments "as to my not being with the troops." What troubled the Duke far more than his fever was that he had grown utterly weary of war. He had witnessed it "in all its horror, and a most dreadful thing it is. The more I see of it the more I think it would be well if it could be avoided."[n]

Before H.R.H. left for Constantinople, he was visited on board H.M.S. *Retribution* by Prince Edward of Saxe-Weimar, who wrote to the Queen after seeing him, giving her an account of his health. "I went a few days after the storm to see him on board, his nerves of course were not in a better condition after the storm than before it, he had also a little fever or ague upon him but was otherwise well. He has now gone to Constantinople. There are plenty of ill natured people who make remarks about his going, although I firmly believe it was necessary for his health, but he was indiscreet in not disguising his joy at going away from this in no way enviable abode. George showed a great deal of courage and sangfroid, but he lost his head, he did not know what to do at the critical moment and the responsibility was too much for him; he is popular, amiable and kind, but has no decision whatever, and has certainly not shown the talents of a general which had been expected of him."[n]

From Constantinople, the Duke wrote to Louisa, telling her he was still afflicted with fever and sick of the "dreadful

war, which has fairly worn out my nerves and spirits. I feel
an altered man, twenty years at least older than I was." If
he were free, he told her, to follow his own inclinations, he
would immediately return to England, but she must not
depend upon his coming home. His health had improved
and he could not appear to desert the troops. "I shall do all
in my power to get home to you my wife, my life, my all,
but I must not do so at the expense of my *honour* and this
I know you will yourself admit."" On December 27 H.R.H.
was examined by a medical board and ordered home on
sick leave. Three days later he remarked in his diary: "I
received a significant letter from the Queen as to my return to the Crimea, which put me out a good deal. 'I hope,'
it ran, 'you will be back in the Crimea by this time. Forgive
my telling you frankly that I hope you will not let your
low spirits and desponding feelings be known to others;
you cannot think how ill natured people are here, and I can
assure you that the Clubs have not been slow in circulating
the most shameful lies about you. It is for this reason that I,
as your true friend and affectionate cousin, wish to *caution*
you for the future not to let your very natural feelings be
known and observed by others. To your own relations of
course this is another thing. Your kindness to all around
you and your thoughtfulness for the poor wounded has
touched and gratified all.' "" On the same day the Queen
recorded in her diary: "A letter from George, saying that as
he could not shake off the fever, and the Doctor said he was
not fit for a Winter campaign, he had asked Lord Raglan to
come home on sick leave. We were horrified as I am sure
this will have the very worst effect!" In the end, at the suggestion of Lord Stratford, he decided to go to Malta, either
to recover sufficiently to return to the Crimea or to negotiate
his return to England.

Before leaving Constantinople, he visited the hospital at
Scutari, accompanied by Lady Stratford, and was shown
round by Florence Nightingale, "a most unaffected nice
looking person." "I was very well satisfied with all that I saw

there," he wrote in his diary on December 29, the day of the visit, "and think they really have done as much as they possibly could to make it comfortable. However it was a sad sight. Such a fearful number of sick and wounded men, many in the very last stages of disease." Miss Nightingale herself later in life recalled this visit. "What makes 'George' popular is this kind of thing. In going round the Scutari Hospitals at their worst time with me he recognized a sergeant of the Guards (he has a royal memory, always a good passport of popularity) who had had at least one-third of his body shot away, and said to him with a great oath, calling him by his christian and surname, 'Aren't you dead Yet?' The man said to me afterwards, 'Sa feelin' o' 'Is Royal 'Ighness wasn't it m'm?' with tears in his eyes. George's manner is very popular, his oaths are popular, with the army. And he is certainly the best man, both of business and of nature, at the Horse Guards: that, even I admit. And there is no man I should like to see in his place.'" The Duke ever after this visit supported Florence Nightingale, although complaints about "The Queen of Scutari" were often enough made to him. "It is a pity," ran one, "that the Army should be dictated to by a young lady who has not lived in the first Society." Her reluctance to go through proper military channels, and her preference for direct contact with civilians at home, although essential if anything was to be effected, enraged the officers she ignored."

The Duke left for Malta on January 3, 1855, and in the last letter he wrote Louisa from Constantinople, dated two days earlier, he told her he was broken-hearted about "the shameful lies that have been circulated about me." Some suggested he had behaved badly at Inkerman. Others complained of his taking sick leave, entirely ignoring the fact that a medical board had passed him unfit. "Now love, I have received such a host of letters praying me on no account to think of coming home, that I confess I have been quite perplexed and staggered . . . I will tell you in the strictest confidence what I have decided to do by the advice of Lord Stratford himself, who really has behaved most generously and kindly to me. I shall go to *Malta*."

In Malta the Duke stayed at a small family hotel, and much of his time was spent in writing letters home negotiating his return, "never dreaming of the extraordinary excitement that would be caused in England by the return of any officer from the Crimea." "I got quantities of letters," he told Louisa, "from the Queen, my mother and aunt: all begging and praying me not to think of coming home. Even you, quite against your own interest and inclination, give the same advice. The fact is I am not ill enough to be in bed, nor do I look ill, but my whole nervous system has had a great shake from continued anxiety." He told Louisa he was going to send strong letters to the Queen and his mother, although "if I return, it is not impossible I shall be banished to Kew for a time." Three days later, on January 10, he wrote again. "I have sent a very firm reply to the Queen to say that she could hardly expect my return [to the Crimea] after having passed a Medical Board, and that though I hoped to improve greatly here, it would be with a view of returning to England, as I could not go through a winter campaign . . . To my mother I have written a very long letter and entered into full particulars, I have told her all, that I was unhappy there, that everything was going to the dogs, that nobody was listened to and that it broke one's heart to see it . . . Thank God that I had a good and *honourable* cause for getting away on the very natural plea of health." This was the first letter in which the Duke admitted that his difficulties as a general contributed to his desire to return home. "I told you from the first we ought not to have gone to the Crimea, we knew nothing of what we were doing and were not prepared for it. How right I have been. From first to last nothing but blunders have been committed, and now . . . us poor devils out here who have worked like slaves, have fought for the honour of the country, are to be made to pay for the follies and mistakes of the Government." Despite H.R.H.'s friendship and loyalty to "the Chief," he confessed that some of the Crimean follies were of his making. "Poor dear Lord Raglan he is an honourable man and gallant to a fault, but he is no *General* and those about him are not, and the whole thing is such utter and hopeless confusion, that I thank my stars I am well out of it and don't want to be mixed up with it again for the world, for he will not listen to us . . . Oh! it is so awful and breaks one's heart. You can now easily understand why I was so anxious to have so good an excuse to escape as that of health, which is *real* and *not put on,* that I can swear to you. Had I thought that I could have saved a man of those fine noble fellows, I would willingly have stayed with them . . . It has quite broken down both my spirit and my heart." The letter concluded by insisting that Louisa must not repeat one word he had said in criticism of Lord Raglan.

In another letter, written on January 16, he defended Raglan against ignorant press criticism. "The fault lies with those who sent out the expedition inadequately prepared for so great an enterprise." He again referred to newspaper rumours that he had quarrelled with the "Chief," and although he objected to their tone, he admitted that they were partly true.

H.R.H.'s correspondence with his mother was similarly filled with hatred of war and despair at casualties. "I am now dejected in mind and body and overwhelmed with our dreadful losses." "I am completely worn out with fatigue and anxiety of mind and want of rest. I have not had my things off my back for weeks." He complained of the difficulties of being a general. "Lord Raglan is an excellent man certainly but I admit I do not think he is up to the job and is not the man to be in command of an army . . . Lord R. is too reserved, he does not reveal his views to anyone and we generals are not treated by him as we should be in our position. . . . He listens to no one and gives no information . . . I am making all these observations to

95

you, dear Mother, but they should not and must not go further . . . Please, please not a word of all this to any living soul. . . . Of course if I went home I should put it all down to my health needing rest through the winter which indeed it does . . . As to my nerves it is better not to say too much about them, so I am writing this for *you* alone, so that you really may understand me and not be upset on my account. I must put everything down to the fatigues and the fever, and this is the absolute truth, for you have no idea how many of us are in the same condition, all broken down . . . England is so unjust . . . Once this War is over for my part I shall *never* serve again, that I swear by God."

The letter which finally overcame the Duchess's resistance to her son's return home was written on January 7. It was an indignant epistle. "And now at last I must open my heart to you, dearest Mother, because I cannot hide my indignation at all this from you. It is possible then that you, my family and friends, wish to bury me with this wretched expedition so lamentably undertaken, and which, as you all realize by now, cannot and will not succeed . . . ? God knows I was not commanding it but I did all in my power to defend and uphold England's honour . . . If I could save the Army I would stay until I went to my grave, but I cannot help them because nobody listens to me . . . He [Raglan] is an upright and honourable man and that is all you can say about him, but as a general he is a *nonentity* . . . Sleepless nights, hard, continuous work, all so exhausted my nerves that if I had stayed any longer I should have had a nervous fever; I was already well on the way to it . . . Now that I am ill and finished they [the Queen, Prince Albert, etc.] will not even grant me what every poor soldier finally obtains, because hundreds of officers and men are being sent home sick . . . Look at Evans, Cardigan and all the many others. They have all gone home, but I mustn't go because I am the Duke of Cambridge and as such must personally make good the mistakes of Albert and the Government. A thousand thanks, but I shall not lend myself to this . . . What do I care about Albert and the Duke of Newcastle? They can explain their own mistakes but they won't have me die as a victim, that I swear." If he returned to the war, he argued, the Army would think his illness a fraud. He was determined to come home, but he must be supported by his own family. "If you and Aunt [the Duchess of Gloucester] welcome me kindly then *everything* will be alright, and the Queen, Albert and the Prime Minister can say what they like. Why doesn't he [the Prince Consort] come himself and have a try? He wouldn't stay *twenty-four hours* I know, the fine gentleman . . . I always said it was no use going to the Crimea and who was right? I was insulted for it and now look at things. All good soldiers are on my side and would go through fire and water for me. That is my sole satisfaction . . . Just let me come back quietly, I am only returning to recuperate and not to *amuse* myself, for none can think of doing so in these sad days. But I repeat, I must and will have rest and I shall only find it in England. The ridiculous rumours that I have become insane are all humbug, but if they want to drive me into an asylum then let them send me back to the Crimea because that will really finish me." The Duke thought that the opposition of the court and the Government to his return was "so that I cannot say anything at all (which however was never in any way my intention) and to sacrifice me, so to speak, for their mistakes and blunders . . . I must ask you, dearest Mama, to stand by me with the Queen.""

In a letter to Lord Raglan, the Queen explained her objections to the Duke's return. "The Queen has been much grieved to hear that the Duke of Cambridge has asked for *sick leave,* and means to come home; she fears the effect of his leaving his division at the moment, when the siege seems really to be drawing to a close, will be very unfortunate, and she still much hopes that he may remain at Malta, whence he could return quickly to his post.""

The Duchess relented, and indeed it was chiefly fear of public opinion which had first led her to oppose her son's return. What influence she exerted on her niece is impossible to say, but on January 19, writing from Windsor, the Queen at last gave the Duke the encouragement he sought. "Pray set your mind entirely at ease about your return, and believe that neither we, or your own family or the Country, think otherwise, tho' we all *regret* the necessity, than that you are *entirely* justified from your broken health, and the decided medical advice you have received, in coming home on sick leave. Be assured my dearest George, that we *all* fully appreciate your devotion to your country and the service, and *fully* acknowledge your unflinching participation in all the danger, privations and anxieties of this very trying campaign. You have every right to be received as you will be, as one of *our* Heroes."[*] When the Queen saw H.R.H. at Windsor she thought him improving in health, but, as she told Lord Raglan, "he is much shaken and certainly would have been quite unfit for duty in the Crimea."[*] Louisa was also converted to the view that it would be acceptable for her husband to return. Just before leaving Malta on January 22, he wrote to tell her he was coming back, although he admitted, as far as his fever was concerned, he had nearly recovered. "But I say nothing of this, as it is better to give out that one is still far from well."

"The first quality of the soldier," said Napoleon, "is constancy in enduring fatigues and privations. Courage is only the second." In the heat of action, the Duke had displayed a gallant disregard of danger and sought the thick of the fight. But he did not possess the sustained fortitude which enables men to endure discomfort, fatigue, nights without sleep, cold, hunger, and the sight of suffering. Overwhelmed by responsibility and worn out by anxiety, he succumbed to fever and depression. Moreover, he longed to return to his wife and children, and he knew that a Crimean winter might kill him. Disillusioned and sickened by a war whose strategy he was powerless to influence, he accepted medical advice and returned home to recruit his strength.

The Duke was always overwhelmed by grief after a battle. On the evening of the Alma, he described in his diary the awful sights he saw. "When all was over I could not help crying like a child." After Inkerman, he was even more deeply affected. "We went over the field of battle to behold a field of blood and destruction and misery, which nothing in this world can possibly surpass. After dinner I had to ride to Lord Raglan to consult with him, and on my return I was so overpowered by all I had gone through, that I felt perfectly broken down." Writing to the Queen about the battle, he told her: "Our loss has been awful and I cannot deny that seeing all my good friends and fine fellows falling around me, has quite broken my heart."" Kinglake, in his book *The Invasion of the Crimea*, says of H.R.H. that he was brave enough himself, but too reluctant to risk his men, and too easily overcome by the horrors of war. "He was liable to be cruelly wrung by the weight of a command which charged him with the lives of other men. He was of an anxious temperament; and with him the danger was that, in moments when great stress might come to be put upon him, the very keenness of his desire to judge aright would become a cruel hindrance." He preferred to act on orders rather than be thrown back onto his own judgment. In view of the Duke's later conservatism, it is interesting that Kinglake describes him as having "no dread of innovations; and the beard that clothed his frank, handsome, manly face, was the symbol of his adhesion to a then new revolt against custom.""

Lord Wolseley, with whom H.R.H. was to have many notable encounters, the two men representing opposed schools of military opinion, was contemptuous of the Duke's courage. "I am heavily handicapped," wrote Wolseley to his wife in 1884, "in having to contend not only against ordinary prejudice and obstruction, but to overcome those difficulties presented to me in the form of a fat, clever, royalty.

. . . It is amusing to read the Duke of Cambridge on his own doings in Ireland. He fancies himself very much over what he did there, and being personally—as I have often told you—a man of the most *timid* nature he is *as* proud of having dispensed with police protection in Cork and Dublin as if he had led a storming party." Elsewhere he says that Lord Airey often told him that "H.R.H. is quite as great a coward morally as he is physically." In a letter written in 1884, in which he discussed sending Augustus FitzGeorge into the forefront of the battle, he says it would be interesting to see if the son could "stand being shot at" as "the father could not.""

Such accusations are strangely at variance with all other evidence. Colonel Gordon, writing to General Grey, Prince Albert's private secretary, said: "The Duke of Cambridge behaved very well indeed [at Inkerman] and I wonder how he escaped." Lord James Murray declared: "The Duke of Cambridge was everywhere [again at Inkerman] in the thickest of the fight, doing his best to direct and encourage his men, and you know how soldiers love and admire an officer who does so." Colonel Phipps told the Queen: "There is not a braver soldier in the Army, officer or man, than the Duke of Cambridge. I believe that there is not a man . . . but would lay down his life for him."" These tributes, written during the war by those close to H.R.H., have a better claim to credit than the secondhand recollections of a declared opponent of the Duke. Wolseley's correspondence with his wife was written in a vigorous, entertaining, and often highly exaggerated style. He did not need to weigh his judgments carefully, consider the feelings of others, or even bother overmuch about the truth of what he said. H.R.H. was the consecrated obstruction who prevented Wolseley, an impetuous and self-willed reformer, from having his own way, and therefore nothing that could be said about him was too uncharitable. But when all allowances are made, the conclusion can hardly be resisted that the Duke's return from the Crimea, if it was not disgraceful—for he was broken down in body and mind—was scarcely heroic.

H.R.H. left Malta on January 22, 1855. The ship was very crowded, and the noise made by the children aboard proved "a great annoyance." On the way home he again visited Napoleon III at Paris. He made little effort to conceal his gloom about the military prospects of wintering in the Crimea. Neither did he hesitate to attribute the responsibility for disaster to the French and English governments. *"Le Duc de Cambridge est arrivé à Paris exaspéré contre son gouvernement, découragé et décourageant a l'excès.'"* On January 30 he landed at Dover and took the first train to London. He had written to Louisa from Malta on December 21, telling her "not to meet him at the Railroad for fear he might break down in public." Instead, he arranged to go to Queen Street as soon as he possibly could. "Reached Town at six," he wrote in his diary, "and drove at once to St. James's, where I found my dearest mother and Mary, looking both very well. Then hurried up to Queen Street and was once again in the arms of my dearest Louisa and our beloved children. Never shall I forget the happiness of that meeting after all I had gone through. . . . Ramsthal [H.R.H.'s steward] was enchanted to see me, but so are all, wherever I go."

The day after his return he saw the Queen and was relieved to be well received. Her Majesty, "having come to London in consequence of the defeat of the Ministry and their resignation, sent for me and received me most kindly and graciously, together with the Prince. I was some time with her, and I lunched with her. Being still far from well and anxious to keep quiet, I did not go anywhere else excepting to see my own family." "George arrived and lunched with us," wrote the Queen in her diary. "He only reached Dover yesterday, and looks ill and much broken, bent, very thin, a haggard look, and wearing a huge beard. Poor fellow, it is sad to see him like that, and he was a good deal affected when he first saw us, but cheerful enough afterwards, though rather agitated."

Louisa was displeased that she saw so little of her husband on the first day of his return. She wrote him a letter on February 11, saying she could not bear partings, however brief. "Ah! how glad I shall be when Tuesday comes. I am so anxious to see you again. I cannot bear being separated from you for more than a few hours. I do so love you my dearest heart and have been separated from you for so long a period that I feel quite low and wretched. I hope you are enjoying yourself and that you like your visit, but I am quite certain you thought of me and will not be sorry to return to one who loves you with the greatest truth and sincerity. Fifteen years yesterday since we met and eight of those we have been married, what happy ones they have been (except for the last). I have been one of the happiest of wives and you say you have been the happiest of husbands and when you returned home you said you would not change for anyone in the world, for I was dearer to you than life itself. I was your all on earth. You know that must please me loving you as I do, and I therefore was much annoyed we could not spend that day together, it was most unfortunate, but generally happens that the Queen invites you upon days that I am anxious you should pass with me."

After a few months in England, the Duke completely recovered and wished to rejoin the Army in the Crimea. "On saying to George," wrote the Queen in her diary on June 6, "that I thought he ought to go out again, found that he was most anxious to do so, as he was not at all happy in inactivity." When the Duke heard the news of Lord Raglan's death, and again later of Simpson's resignation, he aspired to the chief command himself. Writing to Louisa on September 30, he says: "I want so much to command that

Army. That would be the height of my ambition, for if successful I should be a made man and no power on earth could shake me then. Ah Lu, what a glorious thing that would be would it not?"

Much of the summer of 1855 H.R.H. spent in trying to obtain a command. He had several interviews with the Queen, who did what she could to "pacify" him, for she regarded him as "agitated" and "excitable." "After luncheon," she wrote in her diary on October 31, "in spite of the rain, we took a walk with George, who talked very eagerly about himself . . . He aspires to be Commander-in-Chief, for which honour, he said, he must show his fitness. He wants to go back to the Crimea, but has not been chosen for a command. I am very sorry for poor George and feel for him, but much is his own fault (which he now sees) at not having gone back to the Crimea, as he ought to, six weeks after being home."

Early in 1856 the Duke wrote to Lord Hardinge, explaining the difficulties he had encountered in obtaining a command, and seeking the assistance of the Commander-in-Chief. "The kindness," he wrote on February 4, "I have ever received at your hands, prompts me again to address you on a subject, which we have before several times spoken about. It is now more than a year, that I have returned home and have been unemployed. Since that period I have made several efforts to be again placed in Command, and my anxiety was great to receive an important trust.'" His insistent efforts all proved vain, for although nobody was prepared to tell him so directly, the Government had decided early in 1855 not to give him another command. Lord Panmure, Newcastle's successor as Secretary of State for War in Palmerston's administration, wrote in March to Lord Raglan to tell him not to expect the Duke to return. "I may tell you in confidence that you will not see the Duke in the Crimea again, as I have advised him not to return. What effect this may have on you I know not, but I trust it may not disarrange any of your plans. I shall likewise endeavour to persuade Cardigan that his health is insufficiently reinstated, for his temperament is not such as to make him looked up to as a C.O. should be. All this, however, I communicate in the strictest confidence.'"

Lord Panmure himself bore the brunt of most of H.R.H.'s importunity. There were times when he received almost daily visits. On October 3, the Duke "went to the Horse Guards, where I saw all the authorities and heard a great deal of news of various sorts and kinds. Simpson has certainly resigned, but his successor is not yet known. I wish they would send me." Two days later he was back again at the War Office. "Saw Lord Panmure, with whom I had a long conversation about myself, and my anxiety to command the Army in the field. He seemed to fear there were great difficulties, but was very kind in all he said."

Lord Panmure, in considering a successor to General Simpson, wrote the Queen a review of all possible candidates for command. "Lord Panmure presents his humble duty to Your Majesty, and has the honour to forward to Your Majesty copies of despatches which have arrived by this mail. Lord Panmure cannot conceal from Your Majesty that in General Simpson's letter there are grounds for anxiety as to the present state of things with the Army. It is quite evident that General Simpson thinks himself unequal to the task of commanding the Army, and is anxious to be relieved from so weighty a responsibility. With this feeling so strongly expressed, Lord Panmure is of opinion that it would be unjust to the Army to leave it in trembling hands, and unfair to tax General Simpson's powers of mind and body beyond what he states himself able to endure. Under these circumstances Lord Panmure asked Lord Palmerston to hold a conference with Lord Hardinge at the War Department on this momentous crisis. They went over the list carefully and discussed the following selections as being possible.

1st. Lord Seaton. His age is seventy-six, and though his frame is robust for that period of life, he is unfit for exposure to such a climate as the Crimea.

2nd. Lord Hardinge. He stated that, if ordered by Your Majesty, he would obey, but he represented that he was physically unfit for the task.

3rd. The Duke of Cambridge. Your Majesty will, I trust, forgive me when I state that, admitting all His Royal Highness's hereditary courage, he might fail in self-control in situations where the safety of the Army might depend on coolness and self-possession.

To find the Duke an occupation, and to divert him from commanding in the field, Panmure offered him the governorship of Gibraltar. H.R.H. "anxiously considered the proposal," and "consulted two military friends in whose judgement I could confide, as also one or two members of my immediate family." In the end he came "to the conclusion that however honourable the post is that you have thought of for me, it is not exactly one that would suit my views and feelings. The fact is that the sphere of action is, if I may be permitted to express myself, rather too confined for a person of active habits like myself . . . Of course, I am perfectly prepared to take my share of active duty in the field, if it should be thought desirable that I should again join the army in the East, but otherwise I should wish for some employment at home, where I think I might perhaps be useful at the present moment in superintending the levies of various descriptions that are preparing for active service." When he heard the news of the fall of Sebastopol, the Duke again wrote to Panmure, begging to be sent out to the front. ". . . Poor Lord Raglan! how I wish he could have seen this great work accomplished under his own eyes! I am in despair, as you can imagine, at not having been present; this is a most painful feeling, really at times quite unbearable, and, indeed, I feel daily more and more ashamed at leading an idle life when the Army and my gallant and dear friends and comrades are all in the field. If this war lasts, I do beg and pray of you to employ me actively in the field."[n]

The active command for which he longed was denied him, but early in 1856 he was sent on an important mission. After the fall of Sebastopol, it was decided to hold a conference in Paris to discuss how best to prosecute the war against Russia. H.R.H. was appointed Senior Military Delegate representing England. Before the conference reached any decisions, however, the enemy came to terms, and one of the most futile and incompetently conducted wars ever fought was joyfully concluded.

As is customary after most campaigns, a good deal of acrimonious discussion took place in an effort to discover what went wrong. Kinglake's early volumes, published seven years after the peace, provoked bitter controversy, and the Duke became involved in the disputes. *The Invasion of the Crimea* is in all respects monumental, but its author, in attempting to make sense of conflicting accounts, sometimes depended upon unreliable evidence. "I have heard old officers of the Guards," wrote Fortescue, "who were present at Inkerman discuss with much amusement Kinglake's account of the Brigade in that action, knowing well the individual from whom he derived most of his information."[n] Sir George Lewis, Secretary for War at the time of Kinglake's publication, wrote to H.R.H. to say that he had just read the book, which he regarded as "a nasty pamphlet, or rather a collection of nasty and personal invectives, in the form of a history. I fear it is calculated to do the country much harm."[n] The veteran martinet Sir George Brown sent the Duke a detailed synopsis of the work, which he told him he read "with some *strain* on my patience . . . I have no hesitation in declaring it, so far as it has gone, one of the most injudicious and mischievous productions that has appeared in my time!" He described it as "quite unreliable," and he believed it "impossible that this work can ever be considered an authority on which any rational man could safely attach his belief." Brown thought that Kinglake's "vituperation and slander" would reflect on Lord Raglan, and he wondered who had advised Lady Raglan to put her husband's papers into such hands."

The passage in Kinglake's history which particularly incensed the Duke was one in which it was suggested that the First Division had been so dilatory that it had failed to give effective support to the Light Division. There was too much truth in the accusation for it to be anything other than objectionable. The Duke wrote round to other generals who had fought at the Alma, asking if they agreed with Kinglake's account, and, not surprisingly, none of them did. "In Mr. Kinglake's very detailed account of the battle of the Alma," he wrote to De Lacy Evans, "at the bottom of the three hundred and forty-first page, it is stated that you sent me a message, pointing out to me the danger of not advancing more rapidly in support of the Light Division with my Division the First. I certainly have no recollection whatever of ever having received such a message . . . I should therefore feel much obliged to you to let me know whether it was your impression that you sent me such a message, by whom it was sent, and to whom it was delivered. You can easily imagine if you have looked at the passage in question, that I am anxious to understand on what grounds Mr. Kinglake asserts that the First Division did not give effectual support to the Light Division, a view of the case I entirely deny the correctness of.""

De Lacy Evans sent back a most diplomatic answer, saying that he was in fact indirectly responsible for sending a message to H.R.H. suggesting that he should advance. However, being on higher ground than the Duke, he could see more of the battle, and gave his opinion that, with the necessarily restricted view of things which the First Division had, it was perfectly reasonable for it to have halted. "Strictly speaking I sent no communication in my own name to the First Division, but as will be seen, I caused a communication of importance to be made ostensibly from a higher source. . . . Colonel Steele, Military Secretary to the Commander of the Forces, a most active officer, came to me twice during the battle to ask how I was getting on with my attack . . . I asked him if he would undertake to go to the First Division and state that he was the bearer of orders from the Commander of the Forces, that that Division should forthwith pass the river and proceed as rapidly as possible to support the troops of Sir G. Brown." The second day after the battle, De Lacy Evans sat next to Raglan at dinner in his tent and Colonel Steele was opposite. He asked Steele if he had delivered the message. Steele said he had done so. "Lord Raglan then placing his hand on my shoulder said—'But I also sent the same order.' Your Royal Highness expresses anxiousness to understand on what grounds the effective support rendered by your Division could be questioned. I trust it has not been questioned. Because in my judgement no troops could have eventually more nobly performed their duty than those under your Royal Highness's command."'

The Duke also wrote to Sir Colin Campbell, created Lord Clyde in 1858, about this alleged delay of the First Division at Alma. The Field Marshal replied that "there can be no doubt that an interval, to some extent, did elapse," but he described it, with some reservations, as "justified and inevitable.'" Sir George Brown, the most outspoken of generals, who would never have hesitated to be offensive, had he believed the facts warranted it, and who, as commander of the Light Division, was in the best position to judge how effective the Duke's support had been, told H.R.H.: "I have always considered that the Guards came up *precisely* at the right time. Had they come earlier they would have been exposed to a heavy fire in passing through the vineyards and crossing the River . . . I did not look for nor see them until I wanted their assistance and then I found the Grenadier Guards formed and ready to come to my aid. H.R.H.

would in my judgement have done very wrong to have advanced earlier and thereby compromised their order by getting his troops prematurely involved in the attack." Brown could not speak savagely enough of Kinglake's book: part of the reason he had for believing Kinglake to be misinformed was that he had never once consulted the general commanding the Light Division. "He seems to have preferred placing faith and relying upon camp gossip, and on the idle reports and statements of irresponsible individuals to the more authentic information that he might have received from the General and superior officers of the Army." This "most atrocious book cannot fail to do endless mischief amongst ourselves and in the French Army and nation at large."[*]

The Duke finally saw the culprit himself. At twelve o'clock on February 17, "Mr. Kinglake came, and I had a long interview with him on the subject of his book. I discussed with him such parts as I thought unjust towards myself as commanding the First Division at the battle of the Alma. No one could behave better or in a more gentlemanlike way than he did, and I firmly believe it was not his intention to do me any injury. He seemed well disposed to set matters right as far as he could. He was with me an hour."

The confusions and blunders of the Crimean War necessarily led to a prolonged post-mortem. Some said it was the Duke of Wellington's fault, some accused Lord Raglan, others the Ministers. But the most persistent and unjustified efforts were made to blame Raglan's staff, in particular the Commissary General, Lord Airey. He was attacked by the press, and the Government attempted to blame him for its own shortcomings. The Duke of Newcastle even tried to drag Raglan into the conspiracy but was firmly rebuffed. "Am I," he asked the Secretary for War, "or are the writers of private letters in the best position to pronounce upon their [the staff's] merits?" General Simpson was sent out to investigate Raglan's staff and unobligingly reported: "The Staff here at headquarters have, I am convinced, been very much vilified. They are a very good set of fellows—civil and obliging to everyone who comes. I am speaking of the personal Staff, who have no responsibilities further than being generally useful. Nor have I any fault to find with Airey and Estcourt."[n]

The Duke of Newcastle next attempted to persuade Raglan to agree to Airey's being transferred to a command in the field, but was told for his pains that "if he be removed from the appointment of Quartermaster-General, a very great injury would be inflicted on the service and myself personally." Idle gossip was thought sufficient evidence to destroy Airey's reputation. Newcastle told Raglan: "This very day, an angry relative of an officer dying from sickness said to be brought on by avoidable causes, asked me how a Quartermaster-General was likely to attend to his important duties who found time to write long private letters to at least half a dozen fine ladies in London." Lord Raglan answered: "I can, of course, give no reply, to the charge of an officer dying from avoidable causes: but I can say this, that the Quartermaster-General can have nothing to do with these causes. He has not the charge of sick officers. General Airey pleads guilty to having written to Miss Hardinge who was in great anxiety about her brother, then confined by illness to this house, and to Lady Raglan to let her know how I was; and these are the only ladies he has written to except his wife. I really cannot understand any gentleman venturing to intrude upon you such an insinuation . . ."[n] Wolseley regarded Airey as one of the most capable soldiers he knew. The despicable attempt to blame him for almost half a century of parliamentary neglect was very much resented by H.R.H., who himself knew too well how ignorant chatter could be repeated as if it were Holy Writ.

Arguments over Kinglake, and the search for scapegoats, were the least profitable aspects of the vigorous re-thinking on military matters which followed the war. After 1856 a constructive period of reform ensued, and the Duke of Cambridge, who in that year succeeded Lord Hardinge as Officer Commanding-in-Chief, wholeheartedly gave his support to a number of important changes, many of which he is ignorantly supposed to have resisted bitterly.

Commanding-in-Chief

O N JULY 7, 1856, a great review of troops who had returned from the Crimea took place at Aldershot before the Queen. The Duke attended with his mother and Princess Mary Adelaide. As it rained the whole afternoon, H.R.H. "therefore showed Mama and Mary the Camp, and we went to all the old Regiments of my Division. All looked admirably well and received me with the very greatest cordiality and good feeling." It was so wet that the parade was cancelled and the Duchess returned to London. In the course of the afternoon, Lord Hardinge, while talking to the Queen and Prince Albert, was struck down by a stroke. The Queen at the time merely thought he had slipped, for his mind remained perfectly clear, and he apologized "for making such a disturbance." Two days later the Commander-in-Chief resigned, the whole of his right side being paralysed, and he died in September, killed, according to Queen Victoria, "by the Press."

The Prime Minister, Lord Palmerston, discussed the matter of Hardinge's successor with the Queen. She recorded in her diary on July 9: "Talked of Lord Hardinge's illness and our fear indeed knowledge, that he would resign, which places us in a great difficulty, for his loss will be immense. Lord Palmerston fully appreciates his great qualities and merits and the seriousness of his loss, for a man of his experience, cannot be replaced. Then we discussed his possible successor. Sir William Codrington we

agreed would be the best, but he is so much junior, that
unless he had gained a victory in the field, it would be
impossible to put him over the heads of others. Talked of
George, of his great regimental knowledge, his experience
of different armies, his devotion to the Army, and popularity, and all pointing to his being the *most* suitable.
Albert truly observed while for the Army it would be an
advantage to have a Prince of the Blood at their head, for
the Crown, it might not be a support, as any attacks
against him would reflect to a certain extent on the Crown,
and the Commander-in-Chief ought to be a support to the
Crown. We then went through the whole Army List, and
with the exception of Lord Seaton, who would be quite
the right man, were it not for his great age, we could find
no one worth considering." The next day the Queen received "poor Hardinge's resignation," and sent it to Lord
Palmerston, expressing her "opinion, that George was almost without a competitor." On July 12 she heard "that
the Cabinet, after due consideration, had concurred in
advising me to approach George, as successor to Lord
Hardinge. They say that the Army expects and wishes it."
"Viscount Palmerston presents his humble duty to your
Majesty," ran the letter recommending the Duke's appointment, "and begs to state that he has consulted with his
colleagues as to the advice to be tendered to your Majesty
in regard to the appointment of a successor to Lord Hardinge as General Commanding-in-Chief; and upon a full
consideration of the subject, the Cabinet are of opinion
that your Majesty's choice could not fall upon any General
Officer better suited to that important position than His
Royal Highness the Duke of Cambridge, and Lord Panmure
will have the honour of taking your Majesty's pleasure
upon the matter officially. It seems quite clear that there is
no General Officer senior to His Royal Highness the Duke
of Cambridge to whom it would in all respects be desirable
to entrust the duties of the command of the Army, and
there is no General Officer below him in seniority who has

claim sufficiently strong to justify his being preferred to His Royal Highness . . ."[n]

On Sunday, July 13, just as he was about to dress for an early dinner, the Duke received a note summoning him to the Palace. "The Queen saw me in the Garden, and in conjunction with Albert announced to me my appointment to the Commander-in-Chief of the Army. She was most gracious and most kind in her expressions of pleasure, as was the Prince. Thus I am placed in the proudest military position that any subject could be placed in: it is an onerous one, but I will do my best to do myself credit. I saw Lord Hardinge, who was aware of the appointment, and who I found rather better, but still very feeble." The Queen took the opportunity, as she recorded in her diary, to impress upon the new commander-in-chief the need for consulting her before taking any important decisions. "George came at seven, and I informed him of his appointment, and *embraced him.* He had just received Lord Palmerston's letter, announcing it, and is much pleased . . . We tried to give him good advice as to appointments and begged him always to consult us, before anything definite was done."

On the day of his appointment to supreme command of the Army, he wrote two notes to his mother. "Although nothing is yet known, I think I can tell you that it is decided and that I am Commander-in-Chief. I have received the following letter from Lord Panmure. 'I have much satisfaction in informing your Royal Highness that the Cabinet has cordially concurred in recommending you to the Queen as Lord Hardinge's successor. This is a step to which I rejoice in having been a party, and I have no doubt that it will be beneficial to the Queen, the Country and the Army to have your Royal Highness at the head of the latter.' " A few hours later on the same day, the Duke was able to write: "So it is all settled and I am Commander-in-Chief. I heard from Lord Palmerston, and the Queen sent for me to come to her this evening and announced it to me in the presence of Albert. She was very much moved, and I saw it touched her very nearly, but she was exceedingly gracious and friendly and kind to me, and we had a very nice conversation together, with which I was very well satisfied. It is a tremendous undertaking, but yet I am quite of good courage, for all are for me."

The Duke's aunt, the Duchess of Gloucester, who was especially fond of her nephew and deeply appreciated his kindness to her, indeed so much so that on her death she left him her house, wrote an excited letter to her sister-in-law, the Duchess of Cambridge. "You may judge, by your own feelings what mine are at our dear George's distinguished appointment . . . He is so looked up to and beloved by the troops, and the Queen is so fully sensible of all his merits, that the moment she could make him Commander-in-Chief she has done so. Dear sister, as you doubted when we parted that I should see you to-day, I write this note to wish you joy of this great and joyful event, which I know you have been so long looking forward to with so much anxiety, and it must make you feel very proud to be the mother of a son who has made himself so popular and beloved by all classes, and that the confidence of the Queen has so clearly shown itself as to have given him this responsible situation. From my heart I wish you joy, and dear Mary also. George wrote me a kind little note last night to inform me of this event and of the Queen's great kindness to him when she saw him on the subject. I could not fly to Kew at eleven o'clock last night, or I would have done so, and having no notice of when you might come to town to-day I put off writing, hoping you might call in passing Gloucester House . . . I wrote of course to the Queen the first thing this morning to express my joy and happiness, and I have had a letter from her full of affection and feeling for him. God bless you.'"

When, in September, Louisa heard of the death of her husband's predecessor, she wrote to the Duke: "So poor Lord Hardinge is dead. I am very sorry, for I think he was a man who was blamed for the fault of others. What an excitement you would have been in, had you not received the appointment some time ago, but that is now over and you have what you consider the greatest blessing in life."ⁿ This was not an overstatement. The post of General Commanding-in-Chief, the highest in the Army, which the Duke held for the next thirty-nine years, was one for which he had longed since the death of the Duke of Wellington.

Since the very earliest times an important part of the Crown's authority was its control of the Army. The office of Commander-in-Chief is the oldest in the military hierarchy; some writers have traced it back to 54 B.C. when Cassivellaunus put himself at the head of the English forces collected to repel Julius Caesar's second invasion of Britain. Oliver St. John, who defended Hampden in his resistance to ship money, was reluctantly forced to admit that Charles I had wide powers to defend the realm, and that "inherent in his Majesty as part of his crown and kingly dignity" was "his primitive prerogative of Generalissimo and Commander-in-Chief." At the Revolution of 1688 an attempt was made to subordinate the Army to Parliament, but it was far from successful. Officers still regarded themselves as serving the Crown, and as deriving their authority from commissions signed by the sovereign. The history of the office of Commander-in-Chief is largely the story of the struggle between the Crown and Parliament for control of the armed forces.

Various titles have been used to describe the Chief Officer of the Army: Captain-General, Field Marshal on the Staff, and General Commanding-in-Chief. Monk, Duke of Albemarle, was appointed Commander-in-Chief by Charles II. On his death, the King personally assumed control of the Army, and from 1670 to 1793, except temporarily in the emergency of war, the office remained dormant. In the eighteenth century the Secretary at War, a politician subject to the controlling authority of the Home Secretary, and unfortunately even more subject to the influence of those officers who possessed powerful friends in Parliament, assumed responsibility for Army discipline and the disposal of patronage. In 1793, on the outbreak of war with France, Lord Amherst was appointed Commander-in-Chief, and two years later was succeeded in the office by the Duke of York, who delivered the Army from political jobbery, restored its efficiency, and reformed its administration. The power exercised by the Secretary at War, or by the Commander-in-Chief, in the opinion of successive sovereigns, was a delegated authority belonging to the Crown; and for a time George IV contemplated assuming the office himself, until Lord Liverpool convinced him that the Duke of Wellington had a superior claim.

Although the Duke of Cambridge has been referred to as Commander-in-Chief, he did not officially assume that title until it was conferred upon him in 1887, the jubilee of his fiftieth year of military service. In 1856 he was gazetted as General Commanding-in-Chief, the distinction being that his name was not at the top of the Army List, and since he had been promoted over the heads of his seniors, he was the chief but not the first officer in the British Army.

Queen Victoria, "a soldier's daughter," was always intensely interested in Army matters. She frequently referred to "her Army," and the troops thought of themselves as "soldiers of the Queen." Writing to Lord Panmure on February 28, 1855, she alluded to "her noble, brave, and unequalled soldiers (whom she is so proud to call her own)." "You never saw anybody," wrote Lord Panmure to Raglan, "so entirely taken up with military affairs as she is."' Believing the Army to be her own possession, she was sensitively jealous of any threat to her prerogative. She insisted on signing every officer's commission, and would not contemplate suggestions for reducing the labour, because she was anxious to retain the "personal connection between the Sovereign and the Army." The Duke of Wellington had always told her that "it was of the utmost

importance to the stability of the Throne and the Constitution, that the command of the Army should remain
in the hands of the Sovereign, and not fall into those of
the House of Commons." For this reason he had urged the
Prince Consort to become Commander-in-Chief." At the
close of the century, Lord Roberts maintained that the
Sovereign "stands far above the exigencies or influence of
party," and hence was the proper person to dispense Army
patronage, and to inspire the devotion and loyalty of the
troops."

H.R.H. took over command of the Army in an age of
vigorous reform, and certainly there was ample scope for
improvement in the soldier's life. As Lord Wolseley said,
"to enlist was to be disgraced," and the low grade of recruits
was made an excuse for not improving their conditions.
Barracks were ill built, overcrowded, and insanitary. One
pump was considered enough for a battalion. Meals consisted of beef and potatoes. Abroad, conditions were worse
and the mortality rate was shocking. At Sierra Leone a
soldier's chance of surviving his term of service was four
to one against. Even in England, the death rate in the
Army was five times higher than in civilian life. Pay, after
various reductions, was about threepence a day, and discipline was maintained by branding and flogging. Parliament took better care of convicts "who were public enemies
than of soldiers who were a public safeguard."" The Duke,
by his constant efforts to improve the conditions of the
troops, became exceedingly popular with them, and earned
the epithet "The Soldier's Friend."

A year after H.R.H.'s appointment, Lord Clarendon, then
Foreign Secretary, told Greville how pleased he was with
the Duke of Cambridge, who had shown "a great deal of
sense and discretion, and a very accurate knowledge of
the details of his office." He had given "great satisfaction"
when summoned to Cabinet meetings, and was a better
Commander-in-Chief than Lord Hardinge had been. The

Queen, who was not always easy to please, was delighted
with her cousin's energy and zeal. On October 29, 1856, she
remarked in her diary: "Remained talking with George, after
breakfast, for some time, about military matters, and also
when we walked out with him later. I must say I think he is
much devoted to his office and very active and energetic, in
getting things into good and proper order." Again on October 23, 1857, she wrote: "The Army much talked about at
breakfast. George understands his business well, and he is
very keen about it. He spoke of the bad system of the
Government in not telling him *beforehand,* what is intended
to be done, merely taking sudden decisions, which he could
not always carry out." Certainly he was conscientious and
scarcely ever let pleasure interfere with business. "I was to
have gone today on a visit to Belvoir," he says in his diary
on January 2, 1868, "but thought it right to give it up, as I
did not like to be absent from my post while these Fenian
threats were going on."

A great deal of H.R.H.'s time was spent writing to
generals all over the world, with whom he liked to correspond personally as well as officially. He told Sir Hope
Grant, sent out to command the China expedition of 1859:
"I think that it is very desirable that privately and confidentially you should keep me well informed of all your
proceedings . . . I find this the best mode of dealing
with all the General Officers in Command in various parts
of the world . . ."

The Commander-in-Chief's letters, often several pages
long, and all written in his own hand, are a formidable
monument to his industry. If he had had no other occupation than keeping up this correspondence, he would have
been hard worked. It did not matter what distance lay between a commander in the field and the Duke at the Horse
Guards, his interest in the minutest details of organization
would be evinced by a constant flow of letters.

One of the first, if not the most considerable of the
Duke's reforms was to improve Army music. At a parade

to commemorate the end of the Crimean War, the massed bands struck up "God Save the Queen." The sound was so painful that H.R.H., who loved music and spent many of his evenings at the opera, was overcome by the noise. He immediately instituted a standard pitch, and founded a School of Army Music at Kneller Hall, once the home of Sir Godfrey Kneller, the artist and courtier who painted ten reigning sovereigns. The Royal Military School of Music set standards admitted throughout the world, and outside the school gates to this very day stands a public house: "The Duke of Cambridge." On August 13, 1857, H.R.H. went by train "to see the new Musical School I have formed. It seems admirably established and is working most satisfactorily . . . A charming locality and they play and sing wonderfully well." Nearly thirty years later, on May 28, 1886, he took Sir Arthur Sullivan to visit Kneller Hall. "Heard the band in the chapel first, and then a fine and powerful band on the Parade Ground. Was very much satisfied with the whole condition of things, as was Sullivan, who said he had no sort of suggestions to offer for improvements."

Many proposals suggested by the Commander-in-Chief were not so successfully accomplished. The trouble was nearly always the same. Successive governments, committed to retrenchment, did all in their power to reduce Army estimates, and little could be done without money. In January 1857 the Duke pressed upon the Government the need to train men for the Commissariat, but despite the lessons of the recent war, he was told that military expenditure had to be curtailed and that what he proposed would be too expensive. "The supplies of the Army," said Lord Panmure, "will have to be obtained in the most economical manner, in order to keep John Bull in a good humour." In one of the most prosperous decades in our history, and with the warnings of the Peninsular and Crimean Wars before them, Palmerston's Ministry wilfully allowed the Commissariat to become once more a token force. The crippling expenditure necessitated in war by perverse economies resorted to in peace suggests that parliamentary control of the Army has not always been exercised with undeviating wisdom; and the resentment felt by soldiers against ignorant and short-sighted political interference was based on heart-breaking experience. The Duke's career as Commander-in-Chief involved a ceaseless struggle against reductions in military expenditure, and he made many enemies in the fight, but his efforts saved the Army from much of the havoc wrought by ill-judged economies.

Both Tory and Liberal politicians regarded military matters primarily from a financial standpoint. Disraeli, as Chancellor of the Exchequer in Lord Derby's Ministry, thought Lord Hardinge "very prone to expenditure," and wishing to produce a popular budget, resented the expense of the "damned defences." The Liberals, the party of "peace" and "retrenchment," ever suspicious of the political threat of an Army, ceaselessly preached and practised every form of economy; but how peace could be promoted, "by denying to the Government the means for suppressing disorder," Cobden and his followers never explained. Both parties, moreover, were anxious to extend parliamentary control over the armed forces. "I fear," wrote the Queen to the Duke in 1857, "the Cabinet have been dabbling in military details again, for which they seem to have a singular predilection, and for which they are eminently unfit.'" H.R.H., writing on June 8, 1858, to Sir Colin Campbell, complained of constant attempts to extend civil control. "A restless spirit is abroad and a great desire for constant change . . . If we want any change it should be with a view of putting more military element into our organization, but I am afraid that is not the spirit of the age, which wants to introduce further civil control which must lead to harm, for an army never can be commanded or controlled by civilians. . . ."

The Queen supported her Commander-in-Chief in opposing reductions. "Only be stout and determined," she encouraged him, "and you may rely on our backing you up." Every year the Duke submitted his estimates to the Secretary for War, and every year he pleaded that ill-considered attempts to save revenue only cost more in the end. "What a deal of money," he told Sir Colin Campbell, "our economy fits have cost the country.'" In 1858 he protested "that in the present state our armed force is most deficient in number . . . I cannot answer for the consequences if something is not done at once to add to our military forces both at home and abroad." Again in 1860, he stressed the inadequacy of Britain's defences. "I am strongly impressed that in the present state of the world, England ought never to be in so deplorable a military position as she is at present for the want of troops, more particularly Infantry. I am well aware that it is a most difficult matter to find a remedy, as any additional force must require increased expenditure; but, on the other hand, the question we have to put to ourselves is, Are we justified in leaving matters in such a condition? I think we are not, and therefore I feel bound to bring the subject to serious notice." The following year he informed the Secretary for War that "I have no hesitation in saying frankly and unreservedly, that I consider this force [the Army, after it had been reduced by 14,000 men] *totally inadequate* for our present work and requirements.'" Sometimes his own generals, anxious to placate the Government, would suggest economies or agree that they were feasible. Lord Mansfield, Commander-in-Chief in India, whose political loyalties were suspect at the Horse Guards, was warned by the Duke that he would not acquiesce in reductions in the Indian Army. "The proposed reduction in rank and file in European Regiments of Cavalry and Infantry serving in India have not reached me officially, and though no doubt they will be accepted and approved by the Government, and consequently carried out, I shall feel it my duty to warn the authorities of the danger which in my opinion is incurred by making them. I am well aware that the financial difficulties are great, and that these have induced you to make these proposals, but looking at the vastness of our Indian Empire, at the extent of our frontier, at the distance of India from support, or at the suddenness with which difficulties have arisen before now, I cannot but think the economy is altogether a false one, and that the present European force serving in India ought not to be reduced by a single man for many years to come. In fact the financial difficulty ought to have been met in some other way than by the reduction of the army.'"

The support the Queen offered the Duke in resisting cuts in the Army was, in the estimate of some of her Ministers, given too generously. She very properly complained to Palmerston in 1857 that the Government did not appear to have learnt the lessons of the War against Russia. "The Queen is anxious to impress in the most earnest manner upon her Government the necessity of taking a comprehensive view of our military position at the present momentous crisis, instead of going on without a plan, living from hand to mouth, and taking small isolated measures without reference to each other." The Prime Minister, suffering from a surfeit of regal advice, neatly contrived to administer a rebuke to his Sovereign. "Viscount Palmerston . . . has had the honour to receive your Majesty's communication . . . stating what your Majesty would have said if your Majesty had been in the House of Commons. Viscount Palmerston may perhaps be permitted to take the liberty of saying that it is fortunate for those from whose opinions your Majesty differs that your Majesty is not in the House of Commons for they would have had to encounter a formidable antagonist in argument . . ."'"

The Queen and Prince Albert attributed the difficulties and sufferings of the Crimea to the "miserable reductions of the last thirty years." They protested that economies were being made even before peace had been signed, and the Queen told Palmerston that she "expected" retrenchments to be carried out "with great *moderation* and very gradually." In 1857 she referred to the position of the Army as "pitiable" and assured the Prime Minister that the measures taken to deal with the Indian Mutiny were "by no means adequate to the emergency." The Prince Consort, writing to Stockmar, told him that the disasters in the East showed what befell an Army "which rests upon civil government and the Press," and he complained that while politicians made "grandiose speeches" they let "our poor little army be wasted away." In 1869, hearing rumours of further economies, the Queen informed Lord Derby that if England were to be listened to in Europe she must be powerful and not regarded as "despicably weak in her military resources." She enthusiastically endorsed Palmerston's precept, which was more than in practice he did himself: "For a country great and rich to leave itself without the means of defence is not a method to preserve peace in the long run."

In 1859 two events occurred to awaken the public to the inadequacy of Britain's defences. The first was an invasion scare. Orsini, the year before, had thrown a bomb at Napoleon III, and many Frenchmen held England responsible for the outrage, partly because she had harboured the conspirator, and partly because she was reputed to desire the death of the Emperor. The Duke, anxious to appease, and believing that revolutionaries should be deported, suggested that Lord Panmure should persuade his colleagues to reconsider their attitude to immigrants. Panmure, however, remained defiant. "While quite prepared to make the most searching investigations for any breach of our laws on the part of those whom we harbour, or, more correctly speaking, who came to our shores, we must maintain the high position which we so proudly occupy of giving shelter to the unfortunate, of which shelter there is not a *party* who now attacks us who have not from time to time, availed themselves." The danger of a French invasion was, in reality, remote enough, but had Napoleon seri-

ously contemplated an attack, British military preparations
would have proved ridiculously insufficient. The second
event which increased awareness of danger was the publication in 1859 of Sir John Burgoyne's pamphlet "Observations on the possible results of a War with France under
our present system of Military Preparation." It had been
written as a confidential memorandum in 1846, but little
had occurred since to modify it. If the French invaded,
Burgoyne predicted, the English Army would be outnumbered ten to one. The English were so weak militarily that
they would have to surrender. The British Empire, in Palmerston's phrase, "existed only by sufferance," and unfounded optimism about perpetual peace obscured the
need for effective defence.

The Commander-in-Chief was sensitively aware of England's vulnerability. Parliament, in an emergency, was always inclined to place excessive reliance upon volunteer
forces, although the greater part of the Militia "served no
purpose except to inspire the negligent and ignorant with
a false feeling of security." British patriotism, it was
thought, was a sufficient substitute for training and organization. Fox in 1804 had advocated "an armed peasantry"
as "the great defence of a country" against invasion, but
Sir John Moore was not so confident in the effectiveness of
untrained forces. He once told Pitt, Lord Warden of the
Cinque Ports, that the place for volunteers would be on
the cliffs, where they would have a good view of the battle
being fought on the shore. In 1856 the coast was completely undefended, and Wellington's disclosure that, except immediately under the fire of Dover Castle, infantry
might easily be landed anywhere had inspired momentary
panic rather than appropriate action. H.R.H. took the matter up in 1861 and managed to persuade the Secretary for
War that money must be spent on defences. Sir George
Lewis, who in 1861 succeeded Sidney Herbert, accepted
the Duke's advice, with certain reservations. "I quite appreciate the advantage of fortifying our arsenals and naval

stations—but I cannot see the benefit of dotting little forts, like the old Martello towers, along our coasts. We have been building a little fort on the coast of Aberdeenshire of which I am unable to discover the use, unless it is to prevent the Norwegians from kidnapping the Queen from Balmoral, and it is now proposed to fortify the Scilly Isles —in order, I presume, to save Mr. Augustus Smith to the Nation."

H.R.H. agreed about the absurdity of some of the proposed fortifications but thought that the great dockyards and arsenals needed some protection. "At the same time there are parts of the coast which cannot be quite overlooked, and these must be attended to. For instance, Newhaven in Sussex, where a landing could easily be effected, and where there is a small port of disembarkation just opposite the French coast. I would certainly have a work there, and I hope you will allow it to be proceeded with. Then again I think the mouth of the Humber and of the Mersey are points which cannot be altogether overlooked, as they are the great emporiums of our trade. The Clyde again would be another point. As for Aberdeen, I say nothing in its favour, and I have still less to say for the Scilly Islands."" Resisting dangerous economies, and urging the Government to look to the defences of the country, occupied much of H.R.H.'s time and energy, even without wars and campaigns on his hands, and there was hardly a year of unbroken peace during the period of his Commanding-in-Chief.

The Duke of Cambridge as an old man was reputed to have a very low opinion of the Staff College and its products. Wolseley once suggested that a vacant appointment should be given to a Staff College Officer. "Staff College Officer," grunted the Duke, "what does he want a Staff College Officer for? I know those Staff College Officers. They are very ugly officers and very dirty officers."" This outburst, gleefully treasured by regimental officers who had suffered at the hands of objectionable students from Camberley, was not directed at all graduates, but against a minority who viewed the College solely as a means to promote their careers, and who took insufficient trouble to master their regimental duties. But toward the end of his time, the College "developed into a nursery of missionaries" who condemned H.R.H.'s convictions and set less store than he did on the importance of the Regiment. As a result, he still regarded "those Gentlemen who have been at the Staff College" with "the very best feeling" and considered that they had always "done remarkably well; but I prefer for the staff to have regimental officers."[n]

When he was in a playful mood he often pretended to abominate the Staff College. "One time when he was inspecting a district at home and when the gala feast in his honour at the general's house, which all the staff of the district are invited to, had arrived at the port and walnut stage, he was heard to lift up his voice and to remark to the general in loud-toned guttural accents which sounded all over the room, 'I'm glad to know, Sir ——, that you have no Staff College officers on your staff. [The staff were nearly all Staff College men, as he was perfectly well aware.] I don't like Staff College officers. My experience of Staff College officers is that they are conceited, and that they are dirty! Brrains! I don't believe in brrains. You haven't any, I know Sir, and as for my Military Secretary over on the other side of the table, and a damned good Military Secretary too, he's the very stoopidest man I ever came across.' "[n]

But as a young man, with the experience of the Crimean War vividly in his mind, H.R.H. was strongly in favour of maintaining a considerable staff and training it rigorously. "It is preposterous," he told Sidney Herbert, "to go back to the Staff we had before the War. Is it really wished . . . that we should again fall into this fatal error? I can be no party to such a plan, and I trust you share my views."[n] After the Duke had hardly been a month in office, he began to impress upon Panmure the need for a highly trained staff. "I am sure you will permit me to remark that it is really essential to the new formation that we should have a thoroughly efficient staff, for it was in this point we formerly failed so much, and it is necessary that Staff Officers should have opportunities for studying their professional duties, and how can they do so if a certain increased number to the old establishment be not appointed?" The Secretary for War in his reply made the usual excuses about cost, and H.R.H. begged him not to "give in too much to the cry against the Staff, for, believe me, if we have not a very efficient Staff during peace, we cannot have a really good one during war."

Ever since Le Marchant had opened his school at High Wycombe in 1799, some attempt had been made to train staff officers in their duties, but the reconstituted Staff College at Camberley—then named Cambridge Town—owed its existence very largely to the efforts and enthusiasms of the Commander-in-Chief. On December 14, 1859, the Duke laid the foundation stone of the present Staff College buildings. The Sandhurst Cadets formed a guard of honour. It was a sunny but piercingly cold day, and as they stood knee-deep in the heather, their toes felt like falling off from frostbite. H.R.H. laid the first block of masonry, instructed in the task by the architect. In a brief speech, the Commandant thanked him for the honour he had accorded the College, and said how fitting it was that the Duke should have undertaken the ceremony, since "the College has been your Royal Highness's actual creation."

H.R.H. was an advocate of every form of military education. Mr. Gleig, the Chaplain General, who was also Inspector General of Military Schools, was delighted with the interest shown in his department by the new Commander-in-Chief. In the old days, Gleig had been a close friend of the Duke of Wellington, but they had become estranged because of the Inspector General's introduction of school-masters to the Army. "By God!" exclaimed Wellington, "if there is a mutiny in the Army—and in all probability we shall have one—you'll see that these new-fangled school-masters will be at the bottom of it."

In 1862, not long after the opening of the new Staff College buildings, the Sandhurst Cadets mutinied. In the grounds of the Military College stood an old fort, originally constructed to give practical instruction in gunnery. After an enthusiastic start, the fort had fallen into disuse. Exasperated by irritating discipline, and provoked by the food offered them, the Cadets secretly provisioned this old redoubt, withdrew behind its solid defences, and refused to come out until their grievances were redressed. The authorities attempted to open negotiations but were warned to keep their distance. Eventually the Governor agreed to consider the Cadets' complaints, on condition they surrendered. He then proceeded to arrest the ringleaders before any redress was offered. Furious at this treachery, and refusing any talk of terms, the Cadets returned to the fort, which they held against all onslaughts. "Local fire was completely ineffective, and it was necessary to employ ordnance of the heaviest calibre: the Duke of Cambridge, whose weighty and lurid verbal metal reduced the fort. He saw that justice was done, restored the broken corporals to their rank, and left for London, the cadets' cheers ringing in his ears." The episode was characteristic of the paternal nature of the office of Commander-in-Chief.

At the end of every year the Duke appeared at the Staff College and inspected the Cadets. There were certain features of the visit which froze into ritual. After hearing the Director General of Military Education read a report on the attainments of candidates for the staff, H.R.H. was shepherded into one of the lecture halls, where "specimens of the work done during the year were submitted for his approval. 'Verr gude, verr gude,' the Duke used to grunt, as he passed some exercise along to the Adjutant General and the other big-wigs brought along in his train, who murmured their admiration. It was the practice in the second year for the seniors to carry out a survey of a considerable tract of country, each of them doing a different area representing perhaps a square mile or so. Colonel Richards then pieced these different sketches together and pasted them on to a vast board—no mean achievement, and one that called for much erasure, for a good deal of give and take, and for a liberal expenditure of pigments. Some officers would have coloured their woods the tint of cooked spinach, while others had preferred the hue of a young lettuce. Some would have depicted buildings in a delicate pink; others would show them like clots of blood. But in the Colonel's cunning hands these crudities disappeared, the work of his pupils became a harmonious whole, and when the vast board was hung up on the wall the result, at a distance at least, was pleasing to the eye.

"A regular programme was always followed. The Duke's attention was drawn to this work of art, and while he was gazing at it somebody, put up to it or knowing his cue, remarked in an undertone, 'But it surely must have taken an officer a long time to map out all that country all by himself.' 'Tut, tut,' interrupted H.R.H., 'you don't understand. It's the work of a whole lot of these officers each doing his separate bit. See here.' And he would peer and would point to some spot where the joinings of two bits of paper were particularly conspicuous. After that he went off to his lunch in high good humour, and all was well.'" On one occasion an irreverent cadet inserted on the margin of the combined map: "To the Grouse Moor." "Humph! Grouse Moor," grunted the Duke. "By Jove, you're lucky fellows having grouse shooting at your very doors. Didn't know you had grouse in these parts."

Luncheon provided the culmination of the ritual, although unfortunately, in an unimaginative desire to please, not wholly foreign to military catering, the main course was invariably the same. The Duke having once rashly expressed delight at being offered pork chops, word went round every mess in the Army that no dish was more appreciated by the Commander-in-Chief. Consequently, for forty years, he lived on a never-ending succession of pork chops, until he grew to dread the appearance of the once-relished delicacy. H.R.H.'s visits to the Staff College grew more frequent when his own sons were passing through the nearby Military Academy. On December 13, 1864, he "spoke to the Sandhurst Cadets on the impropriety of their conduct at Blackwater Fair . . . Dear Gussy [Augustus FitzGeorge] carried the colours and looked very well. He has passed a most excellent examination, eighteenth on the list without purchase out of the forty vacancies."

On the Parade Ground, the Duke of Cambridge was often "priceless." "His comments on his inspections were a joy to the select few who heard them. He once reviewed in Hyde Park the three battalions of Grenadiers who, after a long interval, happened to be in London together; and summed up as follows: 'In all my experience of reviews in England, Ireland or on the Continent of Europe, I have never witnessed such a damnable exhibition of incompetence as has been shown by the Grenadier Guards to-day. When the Cease Fire sounded, the First Battalion was firing at the Serpentine; the Second Battalion was firing at the Marble Arch; and God Almighty knows where the Third Battalion was firing. I don't.' " Once on parade he was storming against the habit of swearing in the Army and wound up his tirade by saying: "I was talking it over with the Queen last night, and her Majesty says she is damned if she will have it." H.R.H. was almost too expert in drill, and few deficiencies escaped his unyielding gaze. "Where are the pioneers?" he asked the colonel of a defaulting battalion. "I don't see them." "In front of the leading company, your Royal Highness." "Have they got their picks and shovels with them?" "Certainly, your Royal Highness.

Do you want them to do anything?" "Yes," said the Duke. "I want them to dig a very deep and very wide hole, and then bury this battalion in it."

The Duke did not confine his energies merely to inspecting. On field days he often personally took command, and it was a rare occasion if victory were conceded to his opponents. In 1861 H.R.H. was appointed Colonel-in-Chief of the Royal Artillery. On the morning after dining with them, a field day was held, the Commander-in-Chief taking over half the garrison with which to launch an attack, and Sir Richard Davies, the Commandant, who had commanded the artillery in the Crimean War, taking up a defensive position on high ground with the other half. "The Duke advanced his force straight at the enemy's position, no cover was utilized, and when the position was near, a magnificent battalion of marines, without taking the trouble to deploy, charged and captured it, having heroically disregarded the fire of three batteries, which slated them for some hundreds of yards across the open. Little attention was paid to tactical considerations and taking cover in those days. The decision arrived at by the Umpire . . . was that the Duke had been successful in his entirely direct attack, and that the honours of the day rested with him. We, on the opposing side, who had poured artillery and infantry fire for half an hour into the serried masses of His Royal Highness, were of an opposite opinion. Since those days I have been fortunate enough to acquire a large and varied experience as regards manoeuvres in other countries than my own, and I can recall no single instance in which a prince of the blood royal, who happened to be in command on one side, was not adjudged to have been successful."[11]

The Indian Mutiny was the first campaign with which H.R.H. was concerned as Commander-in-Chief. News of the outbreak reached England at the end of June 1857. In July, Sir Colin Campbell, who had served under the Duke in the Crimea, was appointed Commander-in-Chief of the Army in India, to succeed General Anson, who had died of cholera. "Colin Campbell came," wrote H.R.H. in his diary on July 12, "and I took him to the Queen to take leave of her, and she was most gracious to him. He then took leave of my mother and sister, and then I said goodbye to him, with really a very heavy heart, for I love that fine soldier and respect him more than any words can describe." Sir Colin, despite forbidding difficulties, managed to restore order in India, not without an abundance of advice from the Horse Guards. As always, H.R.H. was concerned for the welfare of the troops, and pressed Sir Colin in May 1858 to go into "summer quarters" and not risk exposing his men to the savage heat of the Indian sun. His anxiety did not end there, for he rebuked Sir Colin himself for moving about, as Wellington had done in Portugal, with an insufficient escort. Nobody, except the Duke of Cambridge, was in a position to criticize a commander in the field to his face. "I think that you exposed yourself a great deal. I cannot say anything against this, but I do hope that you will always bear in mind in this operation that the country looks to you to carry out the great work in hand, and that if anything were to happen to you I really do not know what we should do, as I know of *nobody* who could replace you efficiently . . . I have almost a mind to be *angry* with you. . . . Remember, my dear friend, you are not simple Colin Campbell, but Commander-in-Chief of Her Majesty's forces in India, and that the latter is a very different personage from what the former may wish to consider himself."⁷⁰

In the year of the Mutiny, the Duchess of Gloucester became ill. "No old nurse," she told Princess Mary Adelaide, "could have taken more care of me than George did."⁷¹ On April 30 at five o'clock in the morning, the Duke and his mother watched her die. "After sitting up during the whole night, at two o'clock the end of our dearest

Aunt was evidently approaching . . . Towards three all were in the room and Hawkins and Hills watching attentively said that it would not last many minutes. Still the struggle, without being apparently painful, was a long one, and at five fifteen after a deep sigh our beloved Aunt breathed her last without pain or suffering. It was an awful and most distressing moment. All behaved nobly . . . We had a short prayer before death and another after it. Nothing could surpass the solemnity of the moment . . . Dined alone at my home, and felt most wretched, for I have lost the best friend I possessed on earth."

The whole Cambridge family were deeply moved by her death. "We young people," wrote Princess Mary, "that is to say, George, Augusta, and I," loved her "as a second mother." She was an angelic being, and "I trust that one day I may follow her bright example, and resemble her in mind and heart as well as in name."[n]

The Duke had several meetings with the Queen and the Prince Consort to discuss the funeral arrangements. On May 8, the sad day arrived, although it "had the advantage at all events of fine weather. At eight fifteen I went to Gloucester House. Everything was ready, and at nine punctually the procession started for Paddington Station. It was a most dreadful moment to see the body of the beloved one carried lifelessly out of the house she had been mistress of and loved so well . . . Returned home to the Palace to breakfast, and at ten fifteen drove to the Queen's Private Station of the S.W.R. Thence by special train with the Prince of Wales to Windsor. Mama and my sisters joined us at Richmond. We were at Windsor at eleven thirty. Prince Albert had already arrived. At twelve the mournful procession began to arrive from Slough. All was admirably conducted. The funeral ceremony then commenced and was beautifully performed by the Dean reading and the Choir singing. Nothing could be more beautifully impressive, and not a dry eye was to be found in the Church. As to myself, no words can describe how I felt on the occasion. I was conducting to its last resting place that being whom I most respected and venerated on earth. May God have mercy on her soul, and may I have the happiness of joining that blessed soul in Eternity, however miserably unworthy I am!"

The following day, as one of the Duchess's executors, he went to hear the reading of the will. "It is a beautiful Will, not anybody forgotten, and her kindly feelings of charity expressed throughout all quite beautifully. There are things left to everybody: annuities to the servants, the plate to Mary and a good many jewels—and all that is not willed away to myself as her absolute heir. How beautifully she has ever behaved to me, really in a manner for which I can never feel or prove myself sufficiently grateful." Gloucester House, which the Duke occupied until his death in 1904, stood at the west corner of Park Lane. Although the house contained many fine apartments, he used three small rooms at the back, where the prospect was mainly roofs and chimneys. He also inherited from the Duchess many possessions which had belonged to her father, George III.

Another royal death, which took place in 1861, had a profound influence on H.R.H.'s career, for the Queen's protracted widowhood left him to perform many of her duties. In December the Prince Consort caught a feverish cold. Some attributed it to a hasty visit to Cambridge, undertaken after he had received the news of a romantic escapade in which the Prince of Wales had been involved earlier in the year. Others blamed the Eton College Volunteers, who held a review on the South Terrace at Windsor, which Prince Albert, dispite a chill, felt obliged to attend. It was a mild enough day, but although he was wearing a fur-lined overcoat, he felt as though cold water was being poured down his back.

The Duke was kept closely informed of the progress of Prince Albert's illness. Every day, sometimes even twice a day, he was sent a note by Sir Charles Phipps, the Prince's Private Secretary. "The Prince," he wrote on December 7, "I am sorry to say is not any better, indeed his disorder has again declared itself as a fever of the kind sometimes described as Gastric Fever. Symptoms are I am glad to say all favourable, but it is a very tedious disorder, and we must not expect improvement for a fortnight yet. Your Royal Highness knows the Queen well enough to be aware that Her Majesty cannot bear to be alarmed and therefore if Your Royal Highness writes to Her Majesty it should be in a cheering tone. I do not think that Her Majesty could at present see anyone, but she is perfectly calm and cheerful."

11 December: The Queen is quite well and keeps very cheerful, looking always at the bright side, but she is constantly, except when she takes a drive, attending the Prince, and if I am to speak sincerely to your Royal Highness would, I think, not be disposed to see anyone at present. The Prince is of course quite unequal to receiving anybody.

13 December: Although the Prince had not a good night last night the material symptoms have not, I am assured by the doctors, been prejudically affected by it, and His Royal Highness is not considered worse than he was yesterday.

13 December: Your Royal Highness will believe with what unspeakable grief I have to announce to you that the Prince Consort's illness has taken a very unfavourable appearance, and the doctors are in much and deep anxiety. They are not without fear for the night.

So alarmed was the Duke by the news, that he took the seven o'clock train to Windsor on the morning of December 14. "Found the Prince had got over the night and was a shade better, but I observed from the countenances of the medical men that they entertained but little hope of real amendment. Saw the Prince of Wales, who had arrived from Cambridge during the night. Did not see the Queen, but saw Alice who has behaved most beautifully

136

throughout." H.R.H. returned to London the same evening, only to be awoken that night with the news of the Prince's death, brought to him in a message from Sir Charles. "The most dreadful event that could, I believe, occur to this country has fallen upon it. My beloved master expired at ten minutes before eleven, so peacefully and tranquilly that it was hardly possible to say when his last breath was drawn. . . . The Queen, the Prince of Wales, and the Princesses, with the Prince and Princess of Leiningen, surrounded the bed and watched the last moments of the best man that I ever met with in my life. The Queen has shewn herself to be possessed of great strength of mind. Overwhelmed, beaten to the ground with grief, her self-control and good sense have been quite wonderful. If aid and support and assistance can be given her by those far below her —how many thousands there are who would give their lives up to such a task. But I am not fit to write to your Royal Highness for my heart is broken—though my feelings at such a time should not be mentioned.'"

On the fifteenth the Duke returned once more to Windsor, still too dazed to realize how fearful was the blow which had fallen. "Nobody can have any idea of how great the loss must be to the poor dear Queen and to the Country. I went to Windsor by eight o'clock train, arriving soon after nine. Found all at the castle in an awful state of consternation and despair, though as calm and resigned as it was possible, under the circumstances, to conceive. . . . I attended prayers in the Chapel at twelve, and after that saw the Queen for a moment. I found her fearfully affected, but still able to give vent to her feelings in a profusion of tears. She is behaving nobly in her heavy affliction."

The Duke was so agitated by the calamity that he took to his bed, and was forbidden to attend the funeral, although for a time he declared he would go, in defiance of the doctors' advice. His sister, Princess Mary, thought that "the worry and excitement had well nigh driven him into a fever."

Grieved as he was by the Prince's death, there had been moments when little love was lost between them. The Duchess of Cambridge "abhorred" the Prince Consort, possibly for supplanting her son in the Queen's affection; and Prince Albert was always suspicious of the Cambridges, and of their influence on the Prince of Wales. The Queen, writing to the King of the Belgians in 1863, recalled her husband's fear that "Bertie" would be led astray by his "Uncle" George. She refers to "a mad and very imprudent idea" that her son join the Cambridge family in Germany, "the very *worst* society for Bertie possible, which my Angel said he must be kept out of."[n]

The death of the Prince Consort left many offices vacant, and although the Queen felt unable to fill such posts immediately, she let the Duke know through Phipps that she proposed to appoint him to the Colonelcy of the Grenadier Guards. Writing from Osborne on January 6, 1862, Sir Charles said: "The Queen with a feeling which Your Royal Highness will well understand and appreciate feels an insuperable objection to an immediate filling up of the offices which have by so lamentable a misfortune become vacant. Such a course would be repulsive and intolerable to Her Majesty. But the Queen thinks it may be satisfactory to Your Royal Highness to learn that it is Her Majesty's intention, whenever the time for such an appointment shall come, to offer Your Royal Highness the Colonelcy of the Grenadier Guards. This is a subject upon which you may well imagine the Queen finds it impossible to write herself, as realizing the loss which makes all the rest of her life a blank to Her Majesty."[n]

Fortunately the life of the royal family was not all sorrow and mourning, and the wedding of the Prince of Wales in 1863 was, as the Duke described it, "a great day for Old England." The Cambridges were delighted with Princess Alexandra of Denmark and thought it "a charming marriage." The Queen also formed a high opinion of her daughter-in-law. "Dear Alix" was frequently employed to reform her husband. She was instructed, for example, to prevent his smoking cigars after dinner—in which, if she ever made the attempt, she was far from successful. "Beloved Albert so *highly* disapproved it, which ought to be enough to deter Bertie from it."[11]

For the Duke, an even more important wedding was that of his sister Mary. The Prince of Wales met Prince Teck at the court of the King of Hanover, and invited him to Sandringham. Further visits to England followed, and he became engaged to Princess Mary in March 1866, the proposal being made in the garden of Kew Cottage. The Duchess of Cambridge and the Duke were both delighted, for there had been anxious times when it seemed possible that no suitable offer would ever be made. Princess Mary was generous, impulsive, and entertaining, but she was a "mountain of a girl," and her massive proportions scarcely hinted at the attraction of her character. Prince Teck, however, was undaunted. "The young couple," wrote the Duke on April 6, "looked and seemed supremely happy. It is a great event in my family, and I must say I think it is a *very happy one*. He is a charming person and likely to make dear Mary an excellent husband. It is a real pleasure to see Mary so thoroughly satisfied at the resolution come to."

The wedding was arranged for June 12, but very nearly had to be postponed, because the date did not suit the Queen, who insisted that she must have "full three weeks rest" at Balmoral, and could not therefore return from Scotland until June 13. In the end she grudgingly changed her plans and attended the ceremony, which, though "very trying," was nevertheless "a satisfaction," and she trusted "the beginning of many years of happiness." In May 26, 1867, "dear Mary was confined at one minute before twelve o'clock," and gave birth to "a charming, healthy little girl with powerful lungs." This child, destined to become Queen Mary, was christened at Kensington Palace.

Her godfathers were her uncle the Duke of Cambridge (who was one day to become godfather to her eldest son, the present Duke of Windsor) and the Prince of Wales, later Edward VII.

The year of Mary's marriage saw the defeat of Austria in the Six Weeks' War, and it became evident that the Prussian Army, with its magnificent general staff under von Moltke, not only could win wars with lightning rapidity, but provided a lesson in organization and tactics which it would be dangerous to ignore. The Commander-in-Chief fully appreciated the importance of studying the methods of other armies. In 1864 he wrote to the Secretary for War, telling him that the Horse Guards were insufficiently informed about what was going on elsewhere, and suggesting that the expense—for he rightly anticipated objections on that ground—of military attachés was completely justified by their value. "In the present most disturbed state of Europe, when military operations and preparations are going on in so many states, I think it really would be of the greatest importance that we should have a Military Attaché at all our principal missions, such as Berlin, Vienna, Copenhagen, St. Petersburg and indeed I think it would be as well to extend this system even to America."[n]

One thing which made the Prussians' military system so effective was their vast trained reserves for use in emergency. The Duke in 1866 wrote a memorandum on the subject for the War Minister's consideration. He began by pointing out that in England there was "no sort of Reserve to fall back upon with the exception of our Militia." On the other hand, most continental powers were "in a position to expand their forces at the shortest possible notice through the powers of conscription." His suggested remedy was to allow regular soldiers after seven years' service to go on unlimited leave, on condition that they returned to the colours in time of war. Furthermore, he proposed that soldiers on enlisting should engage to serve

on the reserve if and when they left the Army." The plan
for forming a reserve by introducing a seven-year enlistment period was later taken up by Cardwell, who inaugu-
rated a scheme for short service.

In his old age the Duke acquired the reputation of ob-
structing changes and of suspecting anything which even
hinted at reform; and it cannot be denied that with increasing years he became more conservative and retrograde. "I am an old fashioned person," he wrote in 1883,
"and though fully prepared to go to a certain extent with
the spirit of the age, I am for letting well alone unless the
necessity for change is very clearly demonstrated." But in
his early years as a soldier he was wide awake to the faults
of the service and eager to make improvements. "Probably
there has been no short period more fruitful in Army reforms than the two years from 1859 to 1861, during which
Sidney Herbert, as Secretary of State for War, and the
Duke of Cambridge, as Commander-in-Chief, laboured
shoulder to shoulder for the good of the Service." The
period of military reorganization following the Crimean
War owed much to his inspiration. Officers were made
to realize that soldiering was "something more than filling
in the time between breakfast and lunch." Even the cavalry, that sacrosanct arm in which H.R.H. had received
his early training, came under his restless scrutiny. He
told the Queen, "I have long felt a great anxiety about
making some change in the Cavalry to simplify matters in
that branch of our Service in which at present there are a
good many anomalies." During the first twelve years,
from 1856 to 1868, in which the Duke was Commander-
in-Chief, he set up a department of Military Education, he
revolutionized the Staff College, he pressed for joint manoeuvres of all arms so that "officers and men should be
thoroughly trained and prepared for war," he called attention to the need for a trained Reserve, and he conducted
a continual struggle against reductions.

· · ·

The Duke's financial problems did not end with the Army estimates, for his own sons showed a capacity to spend money which would have been wholly admirable in a Secretary for War but which was disturbing in officer cadets. In 1858 H.R.H. had to send one of his A.D.C.s to Sandhurst to "pay George's bills and blow up the tradesmen for giving him so much credit." Five years later George was in money troubles at Malta, and in 1866 he had "lost at the Gibraltar races and is in great difficulties. It is too sad, for in every other respect he is a nice, intelligent and gentlemanlike lad."[n]

Adolphus, who was an officer in the Navy, frequently distressed his father by threatening to leave the service. "Adolphus expresses a wish to leave the Navy," wrote the Duke in his diary on March 31, 1863. "This I have refused, but have got him transferred to the Flag Ship of the Channel Fleet . . . which will give him a change from the dull station of the Cape." Later his ship took him to Australia, where his father warned him to be "prudent." "A young fellow is easily laid hold of by a nice and pretty girl, but it would be such a disadvantage to you to commit yourself in any way in this respect."[n]

Adolphus's wild oats were sown prodigally, and an angry correspondence ensued between father and son. The young man was accustomed to purchase extravagant presents. "You give no sort of reason," writes the Duke, "for buying those earrings worth £27 for some common woman, who would I should think have been well satisfied with the present of *one pound*, if not less . . . I regret the loss of that beautiful pin. Probably some other female friend of yours has walked off with it. It is most sad." In another letter, H.R.H. enclosed two extracts, "one from the *Morning Post*, the other from the *Army and Navy Gazette*, and I need hardly tell you how much I have been pained to find your name thus publicly noted in so discreditable a manner. Of course everybody talks of these things and instead of my sons' names being creditably brought to public notice, it comes before the world in the most unsatisfactory manner it is possible to conceive. This is now the second time that your name has come to public notice discreditably, and I confess to being both disgusted and very angry. I hear from every variety of quarters that you are most unprincipled in the non payment of your debts and in fact you owe money in every possible direction." He refers to a bill for £19 at a cigar shop, and mentions the earrings again. "Certainly they have not been bestowed on anybody at home. You have left heavy debts at Portsmouth. But even worse than all this you have borrowed money of Charles who in the kindness of his heart lent it to you, and who can ill spare it himself . . . Have you not actually had the meanness to owe ten shillings to a billiard marker who poor devil has not sufficient to live from day to day? Is this gentlemanlike, is this honourable, is this not enough to disgust and enrage the most indulgent Father . . . ? I will stand it no longer . . . I shall not again be found to listen to any of your excuses and subterfuges, which you may have thought have thrown dust in my eyes. Who is this person to whom these earrings have been given? You are ruining yourself by the bad company you keep. You think this very fine no doubt, let me tell you it is most dishonourable, very ungentlemanlike, and will not be tolerated by me, or indeed by Society at large. A man who behaves without honour to his neighbours in the payment of his just debts, must be ruined not only in purse, but in character." The Duke threatened to stop Adolphus's allowance if he did not mend his ways. "If you do what is right you know you will be well supported by me, if you do not, but continue in the sad course you now alas seem to have adopted, I shall decline to disgrace myself by having any share in your discreditable acts. Your very annoyed father, George.""

Despite his father's threats and entreaties, Adolphus continued to run up debts, and tradesmen, desperate for money, complained to the Duke. "It is utterly impossible to go on in this way," he told Adolphus. "I am more wretched about you and George than words can describe. If after this payment you do not keep out of debt . . . you must go to the wall and take the consequences of your folly. I am not going to ruin myself for you, of that you may rest assured." A letter arrived at Queen Street from a money lender. "Mama opened it by my advice and found it contained a threat that if you did not repay what you owed at once he would declare you an outlaw!" Distinctly declining to assist again, the Duke cleared £800 of debt as a twenty-first birthday present for Adolphus, telling him, what was only too apparent, that he had no idea of the value of money, and that "you boys will be the death of me if you go on in this way."" These troubles, however, were only a beginning. Before he had finished, H.R.H. was to pay over £100,000 to rescue his sons from financial disasters.

Apart from absences at shooting parties, and short visits abroad, Louisa and her husband lived happily together in Queen Street, with only an occasional cloud to overcast the radiance of their marriage. Louisa's jealousy sometimes erupted. "I have always thought," she wrote on December 8, 1856, "and still believe that there can be no love without jealousy." True to this maxim, she became suspicious of the length of a visit her husband paid to Sir George Wombwell at Newburgh Park, and provoked from him a protestation of innocence. "I swear to you my darling by everything most sacred, that I have ever kept the oath I swore to you that I am yours and yours only and ever have been so, and that I have *never* made love to any other woman or wished to do so."" To have written this must have left him feeling most uneasy.

Louisa, although society ignored her marriage, was nevertheless expected to behave as if she were Duchess of Cambridge, and H.R.H. was horrified to hear that she had even momentarily contemplated acting in private theatricals. "As regards the question you put to me about your taking a part in some private theatricals, I never thought darling that you put that question to me seriously, but now that I find you do, I must confess that I have *a very great objection* to it and hope you will *not* do so."[n] But generally she was free to live her own life, entertain her own friends, and give parties at which her husband was more a guest than the host. Queen Street was strictly her establishment and Gloucester House was his. "Went to Queen Street," wrote H.R.H. on December 20, 1865, "where Louisa had her annual little Christmas dinner, which went off very well. We had about thirty people, a very good sit down supper and kept it up till past three o'clock."

In 1867 Louisa became ill and was so crippled that she had to be carried from room to room. For the rest of her life she remained something of an invalid and bore her sufferings with unprotesting courage. "Louisa, though perhaps better on the whole, is in a very suffering state and really perfectly helpless. It is painfully sad to witness, and she bears her misfortunes with wonderful resignation."[n]

While Louisa was recovering at Buxton, the Duke was left to look after the house in Queen Street, and a crisis soon threatened. Writing to his wife from the Library of the House of Lords, he told her that there was servant trouble. "Ramsthal tells me that a very awkward thing has happened in Queen Street. The Cook told him this morning that Julia [a maid] had had a man in her room last night, and on her remonstrating with her, she refused to open her room door till she threatened to call a policeman." Then both the man and Julia were out all night. "When Ramsthal spoke to her this morning she said it was her *cousin*, which he explained to her made no difference, in his opinion, but Cook says it was a *Captain* somebody." H.R.H. asked Louisa what she would like done, warning her that if Julia were dismissed the cook might go too, for fear of being left alone in the house."[n] It was a domestic experience from which royal dukes are customarily sheltered.

Louisa, wishing to amuse herself in Buxton, asked her husband to send her the Queen's *Highland Journal,* which had recently come out. He replied that he had not been given a copy and had been unable to buy one, as it was already out of print. "It is a pity," he added, "that it was ever published." A day later, on August 11, he received a handsomely bound copy, "with a very pretty inscription in the fly leaf, 'To dear George in recollection of his dear friend and cousin, from his affectionate cousin.' Very nice I think, don't you?"

A Flood of Reform

IN THE AUTUMN of 1868 Disraeli decided upon a General Election. The Conservatives, despite having extended the franchise the year before, were heavily defeated, and Gladstone was returned to power with a majority of one hundred and twelve. The Duke watched the campaign with mounting anxiety. "The elections," he wrote on November 21, "are going most horribly against the government and I fear the next Parliament will be a most mischievous and radical one. God knows what they will not do!" The next day he heard rumours about the names of the new ministers. "Mr Lowe they say is to have the War Office. This would be *awful* for me." Writing to Adolphus Fitz-George on December 4, H.R.H. told him "it is generally understood that Mr. Gladstone is at this moment forming a new government. What this may lead to, Heaven only knows, but I presume it must end in considerable reductions in both Army and Navy . . . I regret all this deeply, though as you know, I take no share in politics. I confine myself to the duties of my office." On December 7, the new Ministry was announced. "Mr. Cardwell is the new Secretary for War, a most gentlemanlike man, with whom it will be pleasant to act. I confess, however, that I am under considerable apprehension that large reductions of establishment may be contemplated . . . although we have not a man or officer more than we really want or require."[11]

. . .

147

The new War Minister was educated at Winchester and Balliol, and derived from those institutions an invincible conviction that his high-minded liberalism involved a unique revelation of ultimate Truth. His Oxford career was impressive. He achieved a first in Maths and Classics, and was President of the Union. He was called to the bar in 1838, entered Parliament four years later, and at the age of thirty-two was appointed Secretary to the Treasury by Peel, who greatly admired his ability. Subsequently, he became President of the Board of Trade, Chief Secretary for Ireland, and Secretary of State for the Colonies. At the time of his appointment as Minister for War, he was fifty-five, six years older than the Commander-in-Chief.

During his political career he had formed an unfavourable opinion of the workings of the War Office. He was a man to whom economy and administrative competence were an end as much as a means, and whatever else might be said of his new department, it could not be claimed that it was either cheap or efficient. Cardwell believed that the Commander-in-Chief at the Horse Guards should be subordinated to the Secretary for War at the War Office. The Army, he argued, was a parliamentary army, and he, as the Minister responsible to Parliament, could not tolerate a divided authority. His party had been elected "to obtain the greatest amount of efficiency at the smallest cost," and this could only be successfully accomplished by means of "a complete reformation of a system now universally pronounced to be unsatisfactory." In a paper submitted to Gladstone," Cardwell outlined his plans for subordinating the military element to the civilian; for abolishing Purchase —the system of buying and selling commissions in the British army—and with it the aristocratic principle so offensive to the Liberal party; and for making the Board of Admiralty a model for the government of the Army. It was an attractive enough programme to radical minds, but, calculated to inspire the boundless indignation of the Queen, the hostility of the majority of the Army, and a stubborn rear-guard action on the part of its Commander-in-Chief.

Until he was appointed Viceroy of India in 1872, Cardwell's Under-Secretary of State was Lord Northbrook. He was a much more diplomatic person than his austere master, and skilfully sugared the bitter pill which H.R.H. was required to swallow. The moment the Liberals came to power, Northbrook was appointed chairman of a committee instructed to report on Army organization and to recommend improvements. It followed in the footsteps of an inquiry headed by sir James Graham, which in 1860 had reviewed the relationship of the Secretary of State to the Commander-in-Chief, and had investigated War Office organization. Graham told Cardwell: "I assure you the only word which will describe it properly is 'chaos.'" The War office had developed piecemeal over the centuries as a result of changes and compromises in which temporary exigencies had only too often obscured basic principles. It was haunted by the ghosts of extinct offices and Cardwell found himself curator of a constitutional museum. Northbrook advocated the ending of the "dual control" of the Army, the passage of legislation confirming the Secretary of State's complete responsibility for all military matters, and the transfer of the Commander-in-Chief and his staff from the Horse Guards to the War Office. These proposals, not surprisingly, were modelled on those which Cardwell had also outlined to Gladstone.

The Duke of Cambridge fought desperately to prevent his removal to the War Office, then situated in Pall Mall. It clouded the issue to pretend that this was merely an administrative simplification. The prestige of the Commander-in-Chief, even the prerogative of the Crown, was threatened by the move. For the Duke to be turned out of the Horse Guards "would be a degradation which would altogether alter his status in the estimation of the Army and public," and would, in his opinion, he told Cardwell in December 1869, "be most injurious to the interests of the Crown, the real head of the Army . . ." It was largely because what the Duke said was true that the plan appealed to the War Minister.

The Duke, in fact, never denied the Secretary of State's sole responsibility to Parliament, but what he claimed was that the Crown delegated to him the "active command of the Queen's forces," which could scarcely be undertaken by a civilian. In a letter to Cardwell he wrote: "It may be urged, and truly urged, that the Secretary of State for War is responsible to the country for all matters connected with the Army, and is also the adviser to Her Majesty on all military matters. I do not for one moment deny this; and you will do me the justice to say that I have ever held this to be the correct and constitutional view of the case. But the Secretary of State, being a high political functionary and a civilian, cannot, as such, take any active command of the Queen's forces, and these duties are consequently delegated to the Commander-in-Chief appointed by the Crown, and to whom the Crown, under the advice of her Ministers, delegates the supreme military authority."

Finding Cardwell stubborn, the Duke proposed a compromise. The Commander-in-Chief, he suggested, should have a room in the War Office and the Secretary for War should have a room at the Horse Guards. "There would be more give and take in the arrangement . . . We have now a telegraph between this office and yours. The most instantaneous communication can thus go on between us, and the touch of this magic instrument would bring me to you in less than five minutes . . ."⁗ It was an ingenious suggestion, but Cardwell was reluctant to be accommodating, although he was under bombardment from the Queen as well as from the Commander-in-Chief. One concession he could not avoid. While suitable quarters were being prepared for the Duke in Pall Mall, a building with fewer amenities than a workhouse, a section of the War Office had to be sent to the Horse Guards. Lord Haliburton was chosen for the unenviable task of heading the intruders, who were painfully aware of the frosty welcome in store. "To an absolute fearlessness Haliburton united that peculiar blend of tact and force which is only found in strong men. He was one of those fortunate people, who, without being thick-skinned in the vulgar sense, are impervious to hostile atmosphere. He marched his staff of clerks into their new surroundings as if they were merely moving from the west to the east wing of the old buildings in Pall Mall. It was not a case of smoothing over difficulties; they simply ceased to exist. On the morning upon which the transfer was effected the Duke came down in choleric mood, prepared to criticize the new department as if it were a regiment with a black mark against it paraded for annual inspection. He found everything working with the smoothness of a well-oiled machine. H.R.H. was an outspoken prince, and he ever gave frank expression to his feelings. 'Well, I'm damned,' was his only commentary."

The new War Office quarters were first used in 1871, the Commander-in-Chief, on the Queen's insistence, being provided with a special entrance. "Went to War Office," wrote the Duke on September 23, "where, alas! the dear old Horse Guards are now established. It is a sad change, and the state of discomfort from all being unfinished is something really quite dreadful, and makes me feel very unhappy." As an act of reverent, some called it childish, defiance, H.R.H. asserted his independence by heading his correspondence "Horse Guards," despite the move to Pall Mall. After preliminary protests, the Secretary for War let the matter rest. "I hear that Mr. Cardwell foresees difficulties about dating letters from Horse Guards when we are at the War Office, but I hope he will give way. It is all very well to break up old traditions but these are the very life and soul of an army . . ."

In order to complete the subordination of the Horse Guards to the War Office, Cardwell drafted an Order-in-Council defining the Duke's duties. The Queen, on June 28, 1870, signed it with much reluctance, for it removed the Commander-in-Chief from his sole and immediate depend-ence on the Crown. *Blackwood's Magazine* described the measure as "the severest blow that has been struck at the monarchical principle . . . since the times of the Long Parliament."

Cardwell, with his Treasury experience behind him, was expected by his colleagues to effect large economies in Army estimates, and this he achieved by making the colonies responsible for their own defence, and by reducing the size of the forces at home. Such reductions were effected despite vigorous protests from the Queen. She told Cardwell that she had serious misgivings about "the extent to which it is proposed to withdraw troops from the Colonies." She trusted the matter had been discussed and considered by the Cabinet. "The Queen could never forgive herself if she found that she had inadvertently given her assent to anything that could risk the safety of her colonial possessions." When this policy of denuding the Empire of regular troops involved the country in the Kaffir and Zulu wars in South Africa, the Queen wrote to Disraeli in 1879 underlining the lesson which "is again taught us," but which is so seldom heeded: "*Never* let the Army and Navy *down* so low as to be obliged to go to great expense in a hurry . . . We had but small forces at the Cape; hence the great amount having to be sent out in a hurry . . . All this causes great trouble and expense afterwards. If we are to maintain our position as a first-rate Power . . . we must, with our Indian Empire and large Colonies, be prepared for attack and wars somewhere or other *continually*. And the true economy will be to be always ready. Lord Beaconsfield can do his country the greatest service by repeating this again and again and by seeing it carried out. It will prevent war."" General Airey, writing to the Duke of Cambridge during the Franco-Prussian War, said that events in Europe led him to consider the condition of the British Army, and despite the Government's complacent assurances, he personally believed it lacked "everything that constitutes an army ready to take the field . . . The

consolation is that everything is remediable with money
—but money is wanted at the beginning—not in profusion
at the end which is our usual plan."⁗

The Commander-in-Chief implored Cardwell to reconsider the wisdom of these economies. In 1870, when the
defeat of France underlined the dangerous depletion of
military resources in England, he insisted on an interview
with Gladstone. "I felt the necessity," he told Cardwell, "of
telling him how strongly I feel the need for an increase in
men and horses." The Duke warned the Minister of War
of the perils of reducing the staff. "I hope the Staff may not
be cut down too much. When we went to the Crimea we
had no staff and felt the serious want of experienced officers for staff duties. If a thoroughly efficient staff be not
maintained in peace, you cannot have one when War
breaks out, and your army is thus rendered very helpless
and inefficient."⁗ But despite the Duke's entreaties, the
estimates, far from being increased, were reduced by over
a million pounds.

In a memorandum prepared for Cardwell on December
22, 1868, H.R.H. emphasized that emergencies were often
unheralded, and it was useless to reduce the Army in
times of apparent peace, thinking that, if the need arose, it
could at once be expanded. "There cannot be a doubt in
the present state of the world, and more especially of Europe, that, should troubles arise, they are likely to come
upon us suddenly and when we may least expect them. All
history leads us to this conclusion. Such was the case of the
breaking out of the Crimean War, which found us completely unprepared for so great a contest. Such was again
the case in the Italian Campaign of 1859, and more recently in the great German contest of 1866. Even our great
Indian Mutiny came upon us quite unexpectedly, so that
we have two instances affecting the very existence of our
Empire, the Crimean War and the Indian Mutiny, in which
the absolute necessity for instant vigilance and the power
of rapid increase of our forces have been clearly and palp-

ably demonstrated. It is to meet such sudden contingencies that the great Continental Powers have of late largely increased their already enormous means of military power . . . It would be impossible for us entirely to overlook what our neighbours are doing in this direction without taking warning ourselves in time . . . When it is considered that the whole of our Infantry of the Line at home amounts to only 49,291, of that in and on passage to and from our Colonial possessions to only 31,144, and of that in and on passage to and from India to 44,196, making a grand total of 124,631, and that at present we have nothing in the shape of a proper Reserve Force to fill up our battalions in an emergency, it can hardly be thought prudent or wise to diminish this force still further till some regular system has been devised and adopted to meet the very peculiar requirements of the present state of the world." How unavailing were these protests may be judged from the frequency with which they were repeated.

The Duke found it hard to become accustomed to the cataract of changes in which Cardwell plunged him. "I am endeavouring to reconcile my mind," he exclaimed, gasping for breath, "to the numerous changes which are proposed on so many subjects connected with Army matters, and I hope you will do me the justice to say that I have given every assistance in my power to carry out these changes. There are, however, two points to which I cannot reconcile my mind, the one is the large reduction in Establishment, the other the removal of such a large portion of the troops from the Colonies, and the actual military abandonment of some of these colonies by the entire removal of their garrisons. These two points are to me so serious that I feel bound once more to entreat of you to consider whether something could not be done to mitigate these two evils."⁷¹

History is so much orientated to the parliamentary point of view that, although events proved the Duke's predictions right, he has nevertheless been represented as a retrograde whose incessant obstruction prevented Ministers from reforming the Army. Military setbacks, instead of being blamed on the politicians who failed to anticipate them, were often ignorantly attributed to the Duke, although he unavailingly demonstrated to successive Secretaries for War that reductions would lead to disaster. He committed the unforgivable enormity of being right and he paid for it by being made a scapegoat.

Once a decision had been reached, the Duke loyally carried it out, although he felt it his duty to do all in his power to prevent mistakes being made while matters were still under discussion. To his own sons, for example, he was prepared to admit that he "fought" Cardwell in the hope that a Conservative Government would regain office. Writing to Adolphus FitzGeorge on March 18, 1870, he says: "We live in most anxious times, everything is being changed, everything is being cut down in a most frightful manner. In short nothing can be worse for both Army and Navy. I hold on and am determined to do so in the hope that better times may come." In another letter to Adolphus written on May 1, 1869, he observed: "Change is decidedly the order of the day, and our old institutions, which have made us the great nation as thank God we have hitherto been, seem to be a good deal threatened . . . The onslaught on the Army and Navy is very fierce, particularly on the former, but I am fighting a good fight and hope I shall get off victorious."

The Duke found the Queen a sympathetic audience when discussing Cardwell's shortcomings. As usual, she thought her cousin "agitated." "Saw George," she records in her diary on August 15, 1870, "and found him greatly excited. He told me of all his difficulties, of the obstinacy of Mr. Cardwell and want of knowledge of military matters in detail." Even Wolseley, who greatly admired Cardwell, admitted that the Secretary of State "was absolutely ignorant of our Army and War."⁴ This, however, he reckoned was not such a handicap as might appear, since the Minister availed himself so freely of Sir Garnet's advice.

The Duke of Cambridge, as Commander-in-Chief, worked with eighteen Secretaries for War. Their ignorance he soon took for granted, but the merit of civilian rule of the Army was lost on him. When regiments had to be sent out to Africa in 1879, they were so depleted that they had to be made up with volunteers. He discussed the matter one evening with his mother, and Lady Geraldine Somerset, who, as always, was present, and who recorded the conversation in her diary. "The Duke returned from Aldershot where he had this morning [February 18, 1879] inspected the troops under order for Africa; every day shows more the abomination of idiotic Cardwell's system!! Every regiment for service having to be brought up to its full numbers by 300 or 400 volunteers from other regiments, destroying all esprit de corps and solidity, starting on a campaign and then not knowing each other, not the officers their men, not one another's names!! The *idiocy* of the English constitution taking an ignorant *civilian*, a stupid *lawyer* full of theories, to organize the Army!!!"

The Duke and Cardwell each at times thought himself ill-treated by the other. Cardwell complained that the Duke sabotaged him, expressed his criticism of the Government too freely and too publicly, and was liable to say one thing to his face and something quite different behind his back." H.R.H. believed that the Secretary of State was too inclined to consult everyone but his official advisers, that he failed to obtain the Commander-in-Chief's sanction in circumstances where precedent required him to do so, and that he was always endeavouring to circumvent the Horse Guards. The Duke discussed his ill-treatment with the Queen. "I sat under the trees where George came and talked with some excitement of the state of affairs, considering that he had not been well treated, and I counselled moderation, calmness and great discretion." Previously she had spoken to H.R.H. on this vexed subject and agreed that the Government had behaved badly to him. "After luncheon saw George C. who talked very sensibly, but to whom they have not behaved very well."[n]

While Mr. Delane, editor of *The Times,* was dining at Marlborough House with the Prince of Wales on July 15, 1870, a note was slipped into his hands. The Duke, who was present, was as disturbed as his host to learn that France had declared war on Prussia. Hostilities could have been prevented, declared Sir Robert Morier, an expert on German affairs, "if for twenty-four hours the British public had been furnished with a backbone." This was too much for the Commander-in-Chief, who for over a decade had insisted that power politics presupposed the possession of power. "What the hell," he asked, "is the use of a backbone without an army, which we have not got?"[n] The next day H.R.H. received a telegram from Osborne. "Have telegraphed to Mr. Gladstone that steps ought to be taken for our safety and that Parliament ought not to separate without some measures being taken to increase our efficiency in Army and Navy, as no one can tell what we may not be forced into. The conduct of the French is too Iniquitous."

The outbreak of hostilities nearly produced a crisis at Mecklenburg-Strelitz. The British Ambassador at Berlin, Lord Adolphus Loftus, telegraphed to the Duke on July 21: "Persuade Grand Duke of Mecklenburg-Strelitz to return forthwith with his son. If his Royal Highness delays in joining Prussia and National movement he risks his throne . . . Young Prince should at once offer himself to King of Prussia for military service." Two days later the Ambassador enlarged on his telegram in a letter. He was relieved to hear that the Grand Duke and his family were returning at once to Germany. "I learnt," he told H.R.H., "that national feeling was becoming very strong in the Grand Duchy, that the prolonged absence of the Grand Duke was being ill viewed, and further that unless the Grand Duke came forward to give his adhesion to the popular movement, it was to be feared that some very stringent measures might be resorted to, and we have experience on such occasions Count Bismarck is a man of action. . . . I am happy to learn this morning that the Grand Duke has telegraphed to the King of Prussia, offering the services of the Hereditary Prince [Prince Adolphus] in the Army, and that the Grand Duke and his son are to return immediately." The Commander-in-Chief telegraphed to the Queen on July 24, asking her to find out through her daughter, the Crown Princess of Prussia, whether the King had received the Grand Duke's offer of help. "It would be most gracious of you if by some means through dear Vicky, or otherwise, you could ascertain if this offer of service has reached the King, who otherwise might assume that no such offer had ever been made." In the end it transpired that the Strelitz family were well received in Prussia, were invited to dinner by the King, and Prince Adolphus was attached to the staff of the Crown Prince. Loftus told Granville, the Foreign Secretary, that unfortunately the Grand Duchess had returned to Strelitz without seeing either the Queen of Prussia or the Crown Princess. "It would have been more politic for her Royal Highness to have done so." Princess Augusta could never forgive the Prussians for conquering Hanover in 1866, and her loyalty to the German Empire, established in 1871, of which the Grand Duchy became a part, was unenthusiastic. When she died in the winter of 1916, at the age of ninety-four, she sent George V a last message from the country with which he was at war. "Tell the King it is a stout old English heart that is ceasing to beat."

The Duke, soon after encouraging Prince Adolphus to join the Prussians, had an angry interview with a young English officer who had offered his services to the French and had fought with the army of the Loire. On returning to England, the offender was summoned to the Horse Guards and severely rated by the Commander-in-Chief.

He was informed that he had behaved abominably, broken countless Queen's regulations, disgraced the service, and was fortunate not to be court-martialled. After this fierce rebuke, the Duke paused and then muttered under his breath: "I am bound to say in your place I should have done the same." The young man's name was Kitchener."

The Duke followed the events of the Franco-Prussian War with a professional interest and kept a special diary of the campaign. His letters were full of the battles raging on the Continent, and when he heard of the proclamation of the Third Republic, he prophesied untold trouble for France and Europe. In a letter to Lord Napier of Magdala, September 8, 1870, he wrote: "The extraordinary events of the past week really surpass all belief and expectation. Marshal MacMahon's army, having got into a most unaccountable corner near Sedan, between the Belgian frontier and the Prussian Armies, has been defeated in three successive battles, and was driven into Sedan where the Emperor surrendered himself as a prisoner of war to the King of Prussia, and the whole French Army there assembled, about 80,000 men, have laid down their arms. There never was such a catastrophe befell a great country since the world began. The Republic has been proclaimed at Paris, and accepted apparently by France, which says it is determined still to hold out, and to stand a siege of Paris. The Germans are now marching on the French Capital, and according to all human calculations, I should say they would enter it within one week. What is next to happen, God only knows, but the events are certainly most grave and I fear it is the commencement of many wars and conflicts thoughout the world.'"

The success of the Prussians in 1870 was attributed to a bewildering variety of causes, but nobody disputed that conscription, and the large reserves thereby made available, played an important part in their military system. The Duke had already pointed out in 1868 that the English

Army lacked any adequate reserve. In 1870 Cardwell introduced an Army Enlistment Act, which provided that after a period of short service with the colours, initially six years, men could join the reserve: a nucleus of trained professional soldiers recallable at a moment's notice. As H.R.H. admitted at the Royal Academy Dinner of 1878, when Short Service "was first introduced by my noble friend Lord Cardwell, I had some doubts whether it would answer," but "I am happy to say that the success of the measure has been complete." Sometimes setbacks encouraged the Duke to revert to his former suspicions of Cardwell's plan, and certainly he did not always speak of it so enthusiastically, but as he had himself emphasized the urgent need for a trained reserve, his criticism was confined to deploring the loss of the old, veteran soldiers, and doubting the value of new, untried recruits.

The Queen was even more doubtful than her Commander-in-Chief about the merits of Short Service. When in 1882 she telegraphed to Wolseley after his victory at Tel-el-Kebir, she "squeezed a drop of lemon juice over her honeyed congratulations." "The Queen," ran part of her message, "is glad to hear that Sir Garnet entertains such a high regard of her Household Cavalry; she would remind him they are the only Long Service Corps in the Army.'" Lord Roberts, a more knowledgeable, if less vociferous critic than his Sovereign, who was one day to be Commander-in-Chief, made a speech, after his Kabul campaign in 1880, opposing Short Service. "Young soldiers," he said, "of eighteen or twenty, may be, and probably are, individually as brave as their comrades of maturer age, and as well able to fight when everything is *couleur de rose;* but I will never admit that young soldiers, or those new to each other, are as reliable, in times of difficulty, as old and tried soldiers. What is it that has enabled a comparatively small number of British troops, over and over again, to face tremendous odds, and win battles against vastly superior numbers? The glorious annals of our regiments give the answer—discipline, *esprit de corps*, and powers of endurance—the three essentials which are absolutely wanting in the young soldier . . . The origin of the short service system was, I understand, the necessity of having a reserve of trained soldiers in England. I fully admit this necessity, but, even after the experiences of 1878, I take leave to doubt whether we can always depend on securing the services of the reserve we are slowly forming, and of this I am quite certain that we are sacrificing our army to obtain a reserve, which, except in the case of a great national danger, it is evidently not intended to make use of."[n]

On February 21, 1871, the Commander-in-Chief was denounced in the House of Commons. "Mr. Trevelyan brought forward his motion to-day in the shape of an attack upon myself, and my administration. Nothing could be more satisfactory than the debate, which was entirely in my favour, and in which many friends spoke out well, nobody more so than Bernal Osborne. The Division gave a majority of one hundred and eighteen against Mr. Trevelyan, the numbers being two hundred and two against eighty-three, so I hope this disagreeable question is now disposed of." Trevelyan's motion was that: "In the opinion of this House no scheme for military organization can be regarded as complete which does not alter the tenure of the Commander-in-Chief in such a manner as to enable the Secretary of State for War to avail himself of the best administrative talent and the most recent military experience from time to time in the British Army." Trevelyan, the biographer of his uncle Lord Macaulay, was one of Gladstone's more radical subordinates, and despite courteous references to the Duke's good intentions, his insistence that the Commander-in-Chief should not be a permanent official was something of an indiscretion. The motion provoked speaker after speaker to rise in H.R.H.'s defence. Lord Eustace Cecil claimed that if the officers of the Army were asked if they wished the Duke to continue in his command, an immense majority would say that there was no better man to be found. Cardwell declared that "if there is one thing which would be more mischievous than another, it would be to have the smallest suspicion of politics" introduced into the office of Commander-in-Chief. Mr. Osborne, whose speech H.R.H. particularly appreciated, suggested that Trevelyan had merely regaled the House with a dissertation he had many times starred in the provinces. "I believe," he said of the Duke, "a more honest and conscientious man and a man better fitted for the post, never presided at the Horse Guards." Turning with scorn to Mr. Trevelyan, he continued: "He endeavours to raise a cloud around the Horse Guards; he talks of purchase, Army agents, flogging, marking with the letter "D," and contagious diseases." He puts all these together, and he endeavours to blame them on the Duke of Cambridge."

The Secretary for War was informed that his Sovereign trusted the Commander-in-Chief without question. "The Queen," she told him on an earlier occasion, "cannot shut her eyes to the fact that a disposition exists in some quarters (she fears even among some of the subordinate members of the Government, as, for instance, Mr. Trevelyan), to run down the Commander-in-Chief, and generally to disparage the military authorities as obstacles to all improvement in our Army administration. So far from this being the case, the Duke of Cambridge has always acted most cordially, as the Queen is sure Mr. Cardwell will already have found, with successive Secretaries of State, in promoting and giving effect to all well-considered measures of improvement, and ever since he has been at the head of the Army H.R.H. has deserved the Queen's entire confidence, and is entitled to her best support." Cardwell himself was not so fortunate. When Queen Victoria heard that the Speaker of the House was about to resign, she at once suggested Cardwell as his successor, because he was "disliked by the Army," "knew nothing of military matters," and was unfit for his post."

Of all the military measures of Gladstone's Government, the one which provoked the fiercest storm was the abolition of Purchase. Purchase had arisen in the seventeenth century as an attempt by colonels charged with raising regiments to recover, in part, the expense of so doing, by requiring the officers they appointed to buy their commissions. These, in their turn, sold their commissions to their successors. Although William III attempted to abolish the practice, it was energetically supported by vested interests, and Parliament, ever eager to maintain an army cheaply, did not feel inclined to terminate a system which saved the taxpayer money. "The system," as Fortescue observed, "being utterly illogical, iniquitous and indefensible, commended itself heartily to the British public."

There were a number of powerful arguments in favour of abolishing Purchase. It was inevitably an aristocratic system, and soldiers without money, whatever their ability, became "bent and bald under that cruel game of golden leap-frog of which they are the eternal victims.'" Many officers hardly troubled to learn the rudiments of their profession, not caring a farthing what their superiors thought of them. Promotion was by bank balance. Guards officers would take hansom cabs to join their battalions in Hyde Park, and considered themselves overworked if their day did not end with luncheon. A cavalry officer was reputed to have remarked: "Soldiering would be all right if it only consisted of the band and the Mess; no damned men or horses." Yet it was such people who in times of need performed feats of staggering heroism, and subalterns, should fate so decree, crushed rebellions and ruled empires. When Purchase was abolished, *Punch* published a notice to "gallant but stupid" young gentlemen. "You may buy your commissions in the Army up to the thirty-first day of October next. After that you will be driven to the cruel necessity of deserving them.""

The fact that so many officers were gentlemen sufficed to condemn the system of Purchase in the eyes of radicals. The author of "A Letter on Army Reform," published in 1855, analysed the various reasons why schoolboys joined the Colours. "The reasons," he discovered, "which procure commissions for boys desirous of entering the army are various. One obtains his commission because he has a friend at court, another because he is a neighbour of the Commander-in-Chief, a third because his mother is a very agreeable woman, a fourth because his grandfather lost a leg at Barossa. But in no case are the personal merits of the applicant considered for one single moment. Whether he is robust or puny, intelligent or dull, well educated or ignorant, is never inquired; if he has 'interest,' he gets his commission; if he has not 'interest,' he does not get it . . . It is also a *sine qua non* at the Horse Guards that all applicants for commissions shall be 'gentlemen,'—i.e. that their parents shall never have been actually engaged in any retail trade, or in any mechanical or agricultural calling, by which they have earned their bread. No previous military education or training, no long and good service as a non-commissioned officer, gives an applicant for a commission in the British army without 'interest,' a preference over the idlest and dullest schoolboy with 'interest,' who ever sought refuge from the Greek grammar in a red coat; on the contrary, the latter is certain to succeed in obtaining it—the former to fail." Gentlemen might well be "gallant fellows, ready and anxious to fight but averse to face vicissitudes of those climates which kill many, many more British soldiers, than the bullet or the sword, and too much accustomed to the luxuries and amusements of home society either to bear their fair share in the tedium and peril of colonial service, or to look upon military life otherwise than as a dashing and casual pastime, rather than a serious and permanent profession. And these are the men who claim to have given a high tone to the British army, and who invariably carry off its prizes; they aver that it is to the leading of 'gentlemen' like them that our military renown is due, thereby implying that without them that renown would never have been achieved. To show the utter absurdity of such a claim we need look no further afield than to the records of two of the most distinguished brigades in the British service—the Guards and the Marines—the one the most, the other the least, aristocratic corps in her Majesty's pay. Is there a pin to choose between them; and, if there be, in whose favour is it?"

In 1856 a Royal Commission had inquired into "The Sale and Purchase of Commissions in the Army." It found there was "little inducement for officers to acquire proficiency in the science of War," knowing, as they did, that they might "look forward with confidence to the attainment of high military rank" so long as they had "a sum of money available to purchase promotion." The subaltern without the means to buy himself advancement might serve "during all the best years of his life in distant stations and in deadly climates," and yet, however enthusiastically he performed his regimental duties, however industrious, experienced, or gifted he might be, it availed him nothing, unless he was "able to buy the rank to which his qualifications entitled him." The system was prejudicial to discipline: old officers could hardly be expected to show deference to young men promoted over their heads because they were rich enough to buy seniority. The report concluded by describing the system as "vicious in principle, repugnant to the public sentiments of the present day, equally inconsistent with the honour of the military profession and the policy of the .British Empire, and irreconcilable with justice." Despite this striking condemnation, nothing whatever was done.

Even before Cardwell became Secretary for War, he had censured the system of Purchase. Indeed, he said that to mention it was to condemn it. "It is not known in any other country; it would not be tolerated in any other service; and it is not admitted in the Artillery, the Engineers, the Marines, or the Navy." Abolishing the system would do exactly what his opponents said it would: give England a professional officer class, which was what the country needed. "My impression is that if we pass this bill . . . its effect would be to attract to the Army the aristocracy of merit and professional talent, which is after all the true aristocracy." Those who argued that Purchase was the very life-blood of the regimental system were answered by a series of pointed questions. "Is there no regimental system, no *esprit de corps* in the non-purchase regiments? Is there no *esprit de corps* . . . in the regiments of Prussia? Is there none in the Navy?" Cardwell admitted the heroism and gallantry which had always been displayed by British officers. "But if there is one lesson which we have learned from the history of the late campaign it is this—that the secret of Prussian success has been more owing to the professional education of the officers than to any other cause to which it can be ascribed. Neither gallantry nor heroism will avail much without professional training, in these days when arms of precision shoot down soldiers at immense distances."

The Commander-in-Chief held very different views on Purchase from those of the Secretary for War. "I should, of course," he told Cardwell, "deeply regret any change in the system of Purchase, for, however theoretically objectionable, I think it has worked favourably in the interests of the service. It has enabled us to officer our army with gentlemen, and it has kept our officers comparatively young in years compared to the other armies of Europe." In advocating Purchase, although admitting it to be "theoretically objectionable," most Army officers regarded the Duke as defending their interests, and some of the arguments they advanced were not without substance. Promotion by selection, they feared, might cause "ill-feeling in the Army and encourage officers to hate each other." A professional army would make England like Prussia, "neither more nor less than a military despotism." Moreover, this "out of date Army" had secured an Empire on four continents, had humbled the pride of Napoleon, and had forced the Tsar of All the Russias to sue for peace. Was it wise to tamper with a system which had proved so triumphantly successful? The Treasury, if Purchase were abolished, would have to find huge sums in compensation, retire officers on pensions, and might even be compelled to consider paying them adequately—the existing rates being much the same as they had been in the reign of William and Mary. A subaltern's expenses were reckoned at £157 annually and his pay at £95, leaving a deficit of £61. The net pay of a lieutenant colonel, after deducting income tax and interest on the price he had paid for his commission, amounted to the magnificent sum of £170 a year. Besides, if promotion were to be by merit, alleged or actual, the Commander-in-Chief would be exposed to intolerable pressures. Yet if it were arranged by seniority, the stagnation which existed in the non-Purchase corps would pervade the entire army. What would happen to the cavalry, in which youth and daring were imperative, if it were commanded by elderly officers? Finally, it was asserted that men of property, men with a stake in the country, were a perpetual guarantee against army dictatorship and military adventures.

The purchase of commissions was defended by many eminent people. Wellington had argued that it brought into the service "men who have some connection with the interests and fortunes of the country besides the commissions which they hold from His Majesty. It is this circumstance which exempts the British Army from the character of being a 'mercenary army,' and has rendered its employment for nearly a century and a half not only not inconsistent with the constitutional privileges of the country, but safe and beneficial."" Palmerston believed that it was "only where the Army was unconnected with those whose property gave them an interest in the welfare of the country . . . that it could ever become formidable to the liberties of the nation."" When Sidney Herbert had considered the possibility of modifying the system, he encountered strong opposition from the Queen, the Prince Consort, the Commander-in-Chief, and Lord Panmure, who in 1871 resisted Cardwell's bill when it was debated in the House of Lords. "In so doing, he was actuated by a sense of the political security which is afforded to a State by having its army officered by men belonging to the higher classes, or, at least, having a stake in the country, and in this connection he recalled the dictum of De Narbonne, War Minister in France during the Revolutionary Period, who declared that the effect of giving promotion solely for merit would not in reality be favourable to political liberty, because a Staff composed of soldiers of fortune would be much more likely to support a Dictator than would a body of officers who were already bound to the ancient institutions of their country."" Lord Salisbury predicted that the principle of "seniority tempered by selection" would soon resolve itself into one of "stagnation tempered by jobbery."

The Duke of Cambridge, in resisting the abolition of Purchase, opposed it so energetically that he came into serious collision with the Government. Gladstone was anxious to force H.R.H. to support abolition in the Lords, partly because he knew what harm was done to the cause by the fact that its opponents suspected that the Commander-in-Chief shared their views. "There is a general feeling," Cardwell told the Duke, "that the measure of H.M.'s Government, if not actually deprecated, is certainly not cordially supported by Your Royal Highness." This impression is "strengthened by your not having taken an opportunity of saying anything publicly in its favour." The Secretary for War reminded H.R.H. that he had spoken in the House at the time of Trevelyan's motion, of the Duke's "cordial assistance." "Is it right," he asked, "that I should defend you in the House of Commons on the ground that you have given us your cordial assistance . . . and then find that we are impeded in carrying out measures by an impression that they are not cordially supported by you?"

To require the Duke to deny publicly what the Ministers privately knew he believed was to precipitate a crisis. The Government purposely placed him in a dilemma; as they saw it, he must be compelled to co-operate or to resign. He, however, maintained that provided he loyally endeavoured to carry out the Government's policies once they had become law, he was under no obligation to support measures in the Lords which he believed ill judged. On the contrary, his office required him to maintain a strict political neutrality, which was hardly compatible with delivering partisan speeches at the crack of the Government whip. He maintained that it was unusual for princes to vote, and that not only was the Commander-in-Chief not a politician, but there was no necessary reason why he should be a member of either the Lords or the Commons.

On June 3, 1871, he wrote to Cardwell defending his refusal to speak or vote on Purchase, and argued that this refusal was consistent with loyal support of the Government. ". . . It has ever been understood by myself, and certainly been admitted by all previous Governments, that the officer holding the position of Commander-in-Chief could have and ought to have no politics, and I have consequently most scrupulously abstained from ever taking part in any political discussions. . . . Whatever measures Her Majesty's Government may decide to adopt in conjunction with Parliament, it will be my duty and my desire cordially and loyally to carry them out, and so long as this line of conduct is adhered to by me, I do not see how it can be assumed that I am not, to the fullest extent, carrying out my duty by the Sovereign, by the Government, by the Country, and by the Army." Cardwell replied, through Airey, that whatever may have happened before, the view of his colleagues now was that "after fairly discussing and combating all measures with opinions and advice" it would be regarded as the Commander-in-Chief's duty to "acquiesce." If he failed to do so, "the Government are *more* than prepared at once to remove him." The gloves were off. The Duke must surrender, resign, or be dismissed."

In this emergency H.R.H. turned to the Queen for support. "I understand," he wrote to her, "that you are likely on Saturday to see Mr. Gladstone, and I would venture to suggest to you that it would be a great assistance to me in maintaining the neutral position I have always tried to keep as Commander-in-Chief of Your Army . . . if You would strongly impress upon Mr. Gladstone the absolute necessity of not pressing me on the matter of support in the House of Lords when the Army Regulation Bill comes up for discussion . . . If ever the Commander-in-Chief is required to depart from his strictly neutral position, his tenure of office would inevitably have to depend on every change of Government, and by this means the office would become a political one, and with such a change the interests of the Army would be handed over to political interest."

A few days later he wrote to say that he had seen Gladstone and Cardwell, but that they had remained adamant that he must vote and speak for the bill. "Mr. Gladstone added that he considered the responsibility of the acceptance or rejection of the measure by the House of Lords would now be in a great measure on my shoulders, and if the Bill were rejected in the House without my having voted or spoken in its favour, the result would have very grave consequences to myself and to the Army, for as he expressed himself the ground would be cut away from under his feet, for he could not defend me against the attacks of his more advanced followers, and that not only would he be compelled to abandon me, but also he feared the office of Commander-in-Chief would go with me . . . The interests of the Crown are deeply involved. They must not suffer from any false step on my part." The Duke added that

Lord Russell, Lord Dalhousie, and, he believed to some extent, Lord Grey, although Liberals, "take a view adverse to the Government plan."[n] The Prime Minister in fact threatened that if the Commander-in-Chief failed to support the Government in Parliament, either he would be dismissed or his office would be modified. Some of the Duke's friends thought that Gladstone, by this high-minded blackmail, had put himself so thoroughly in the wrong that H.R.H. would be justified in threatening to disclose the whole proceedings unless the demand was withdrawn.

The Queen, as requested by her cousin, wrote to Gladstone, expressing the hope that the Commander-in-Chief should be allowed to remain outside politics. She told him that she thought it would be wrong for the Duke to be forced to support the Government in the Lords. "The Queen thinks that few more serious evils could arise, both to her as sovereign, to the Army, and to the country, than the fact of the position of the Commander-in-Chief, and indeed of other officers holding high military commands, being looked upon in any way as political . . . That the Duke will honourably and cordially assist the Government in carrying out any regulations which may be enacted, the Queen cannot for an instant doubt, but she strongly deprecates any course of conduct being expected of him, which will place him in open antagonism to the opposition and thus render his position nearly untenable in case a change of Government takes place."[n] Galdstone, however, replied that there were several precedents for the Commander-in-Chief voting in the manner suggested, and he predicted that if the bill were rejected without H.R.H. supporting it, there would be "an immediate movement in the House of Commons against his Royal Highness; nor can your Majesty's advisers undertake to answer for the consequences . . . It is, in the mind of the Government, clear that the influence of officers connected with the Horse Guards has been used adversely to the measure: and that public opinion even ascribes a similar use of influence, by the expression of unfavourable sentiments, to his Royal Highness. Doubtless this opinion is erroneous; but it is much to be desired that the effects produced by it should be removed.'" On July 9 the Queen had an interview with Gladstone "and talked of George C. and what Mr. Gladstone had written to me. I begged him to see George, which he said he was most willing to do, protesting most vehemently against any intention of making George depart from his neutral position; but it was not wished he should in the slightest degree give his opinion now, or in favour of the Bill, only advise its adoption. On my urging he should not be pressed to vote, Mr. Gladstone said . . . for George's own sake, it will be better that he should vote."

The episode ended in anticlimax. The Duke made the required speech, which Granville in a telegram described as "skilful as to his own position, and fair towards the Government." The Queen wrote in her diary on July 15: "Read George's speech, which is extremely good. While maintaining the neutral position of the Commander-in-Chief, he gives the Government that support which it is wise he should. I have written to compliment him and tell him so." As the Prime Minister had suggested, H.R.H. contrived to advocate the passing of the bill by his fellow peers, without supporting the measure itself. It was a piece of Sophistry which came naturally enough to its proposer but which did not so readily recommend itself to the Duke. And then, after all this flood of controversy, the Lords destroyed the bill by amendments, and the sale of commissions was finally abolished by Royal Warrant, not by Act of Parliament. All the excitement, high words, even menaces, turned out to be merely much ado about nothing.

Had the Duke not spoken in favour of the bill for abolishing Purchase, the Liberals, by their own admission, would have blamed him for its defeat. But the very Government which was prepared to hold him responsible for reverses was happy enough to take upon itself credit which was rightly his. Cardwell's biographer, Sir Robert Biddulph, an admirer and subordinate of the great reformer, speaks of the Secretary for War determining to "introduce" manoeuvres into the British Army—as if the plan was the product of his own, unaided genius. In fact, of course, the Commander-in-Chief had been stressing the need for large-scale exercises since 1852, and the manoeuvres held at Aldershot in 1871 owed more to the Duke's inspiration than to all the Members of the Cabinet put together.

The Aldershot manoeuvres were the first to be held since 1853, and they were repeated the next year, but, owing to the expense, no further exercises on such a scale were contemplated again until 1898. Manoeuvres were so exceptional an undertaking in the British Army that a special Act of Parliament had to be passed each time they were held. The military operations of 1871 were planned for September, and lasted about a fortnight. The Duke resided at the Queen's Pavilion at Aldershot and considerable numbers of military observers from abroad attended. They expressed themselves delighted by the civility and hospitality with which they were received, but most refrained from commenting on the technical aspects of the proceedings, except that "many foreign officers unhesitatingly declared that the Duke of Cambridge thoroughly understood his business as a General in the field."" Three divisions were involved. The Prince of Wales commanded a cavalry brigade "with an interest and vigour," according to the Duke, "which it is truly gratifying to observe." But both officers and men displayed bewildering ignorance of the rudiments of fieldcraft. It was with the greatest difficulty that they pitched their tents. The horses of the First Life Guards stampeded before operations ever began, frightened by a flock of geese. Carts broke down, rations were mislaid, and harnesses fell to pieces. The *Quarterly Review* described the manoeuvres as "a shameful performance," proof of administrative deficiency, and "a spectacle of open humiliation." Nevertheless, it was far better to discover such shortcomings during peaceful exercises than in time of war. The following summer manoeuvres were held on Salisbury Plain and Cardwell managed to persuade Gladstone to attend. He hoped that if the Prime Minister were seen taking an interest in the Army it might help to dispel military hostility to the Government. The success of this device was not conspicuous. It needed more than a brief glimpse of the great statesman to persuade most soldiers that the Liberal party was not their enemy.

Toward the end of 1871 the Prince of Wales caught typhoid at Sandringham and his life hung in the balance. The illness followed the same course as had his father's, and the Queen dreaded her son would die on December 14, the day of the Prince Consort's death. Sir William Jenner warned the royal family that the Prince might succumb at any moment, and the final crisis took place on December 13, the eve of the dreaded anniversary. The Queen hardly left her son's bedside for a moment. Hour after hour she sat holding his hand in an agony of anticipation, listening to his heavy, uncertain breathing. Suddenly he turned toward her, stared at her wildly, and asked: "Who are you?" The Queen's self-possession was on the verge of dissolution when the Prince whispered gently: "It's Mama. It is so kind of you to come."

The Duke of Cambridge, after anxiously following the first stages of the illness from Gloucester House, joined the family gathering at Sandringham on December 9. The account of the fever he gave in his diary would have provided a worthy contribution to *The Lancet*. He first heard of the Prince's illness on November 23. "Of course," he wrote, "this makes one feel very anxious." Four days later: "The accounts from Sandringham are very alarming. Sir W. Jenner and Dr. Gull are in constant attendance; the fever is excessive, the delirium severe. 28 November. Matters very grave at Sandringham. The Prince was very ill indeed yesterday and great anxiety felt. He is very delirious and in a high state of fever. 29 November. Accounts from Sandringham very anxious. I asked leave to go, but was requested not to come at present. The Queen, I rejoice to say, goes there to-day . . . 2 December. The accounts from Sandringham this morning prove that the crisis on Thursday night was a most grave one, and that great danger existed for a time, but that it is happily gone over for the moment. 4 December. Matters seem gradually to improve, but the fever, alas, continues. 8 December. The accounts this morning from Sandringham are most alarming. Last night a serious crisis seems to have set in. The fever has greatly increased, with decided congestion of one lung. Alfred [the Duke of Edinburgh] came to see me in great distress, poor boy! He is going at once to Sandringham. The Queen is also going again . . . Worse telegrams kept reaching me all day, and this afternoon one from Alice was so bad, that the end seemed at hand. I telegraphed for leave to go down myself, for I felt most miserable. I decided upon going down in the morning at all hazards. 9 December. Got a telegram from Alfred during the night, saying I might come. Sent off for a special train. Got rather better account this morning. The night was quiet and the spasm seemed to have passed away. 11 December. The awfulness of this morning, I shall never, never forget as long as I live. Between six and seven the General [Sir W. Knollys] knocked at my door to say we were sent for to the house. I rushed out of bed, dressed hurriedly, and ran to the house in intense agony. The morning was desperately cold, and the damp rose from the snow on the ground. On arrival found all assembled near the dear patient's room: a severe paroxysm of difficulty of breathing having come on after frequent attacks of a similar character during the whole of a most restless night. All looked bewildered and overcome with grief, but the doctors behaved nobly, no flinching, no loss of courage, only intense anxiety. I went into the outer lobby, where the medicines were being prepared, and nourishment mixed, and could hear the heavy breathing of the dear Prince, but was struck by the power of his dear voice, for he continually talked wanderingly, whenever the breath was sufficient to do so. After some time of intense anxiety, the paroxysm subsided and we began again to hope, but our hopes were faint indeed! However towards ten, matters seemed rather to mend, at all events to quiet down. Later, however, matters looked very bad again, as at four, violent delirium again set in. Had a long interview with Jenner and Gull, who said the case was not hopeless yet: but the anxiety was great. 13 December. Grateful again this morning that we were allowed to pass through the night without having been called, but the night was bad, and the delirium with incessant talking continues uninterruptedly. The anxiety and grief at the house are intense, all looking forward to tomorrow with intense alarm, that being a most ominous day, the anniversary of the death of the Prince Consort. Everybody writes, everybody telegraphs, all being intent for news. The alarm and consternation and excitement in London are terrific, the loyalty displayed by the entire nation is sublime. 14 December. The ominous day has arrived and yet, praised be God, he lives, and he has slept at times during the night, with a less amount of delirium, so that again we hope. 15 December. The Prince has passed a quiet night with a great deal of sleep, all the symptoms are improved, and we begin to look with hope to the future . . . God has, in His mercy, heard all our prayers, and we have indeed cause to be grateful to Him. Am going to bed comparatively happy, after these fearful days of suspense."

During her son's illness, the Queen took entire charge of the large family gathering at Sandringham, and prevented his being smothered by solicitude. Arrivals and departures depended upon her instructions, and she guarded the Prince's door like a sentry. Ponsonby, her private secretary, described how he went toward the garden

1A Augusta, Duchess of Cambridge

From a portrait by Sir William Beechey

From a portrait by Von Angeli

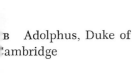

B Adolphus, Duke of Cambridge

From a portrait at Windsor Castle

2   H.R.H. Prince George of Cambridge

From a portrait by Winterhalter

3   Mrs. FitzGeorge

4   Visit of the Sultan to The Duke of Cambridge, at Constantinople

5   The British Troops on the Heights of Alma

From a portrait by John Lucas

6   Major General H.R.H. Prince George of Cambridge, K.G., in 1847

7A H.R.H. Mary Adelaide, Duchess of Teck

From a photograph by Ellis and Walery

*m a photograph by Ellis
l Walery*

H.R.H. Augusta,
and Duchess of
cklenburg-Strelitz

8   Field Marshal H.R.H. The Duke of Cambridge, K.G., in 1900

by a side door, when he was "suddenly nearly carried away by a stampede of royalties," headed by the Duke and brought up by Prince Leopold, "going as fast as they could. We thought it was a mad bull. But they cried out: 'The Queen, the Queen!' and we all dashed into the house again and waited behind the door till the road was clear."

The Duke became obsessed with the idea that something was wrong with the drains. He conducted a tour of inspection, proclaimed Princess Louise's room uninhabitable, which in view of the congestion in the house was somewhat trying, and finally discovered a sinister smell in the library. An expert was sent for and declared he could detect nothing. The Duke grasped the man by the shoulder and led him round the room. "My dear fellow come here—don't you smell it? Well come here, till the man at last said he did, to save himself from being pulled about the room. On this admission Jenner spoke to him seriously and the Duke violently. The man however had nothing to do with drain pipes but was only the gas man, and tried to say so once or twice, but no one would listen and he was finally dragged upstairs where the stink, they say, was suffocating. Luckily however the gas man was the right man, for it turned out after much rummaging that the smell was an escape of gas and on his doing something to his pipes the smell has entirely ceased."

The Duke's anxiety was felt from the heart, for he was extremely fond of the Prince of Wales. "I have always said their dear R.H.'s are the most *charming* couple, and the most delightful hosts it is possible to conceive, and all who know them *must* love and like them." The Prince returned the affection, and having known the Duke "alike in boyhood and manhood as 'Uncle George,' their mutual relations remained for life those of an affectionate uncle and nephew. The Prince owed to his 'uncle,' whose profession was the army, his youthful enthusiasm for that service, and after 'Uncle George' succeeded his father in the Dukedom and became Commander-in-Chief of the Army, there was much confidential intercourse between him and his 'nephew' on controverted questions of military organization in regard to which the Duke was stubbornly loyal to anti-quated standards . . . The genial heartiness of the Cambridge household pleasurably contrasted in the Prince's boyish eyes with the serious demeanour of the rest of Queen Victoria's English kinsfolk."[n] This "genial heartiness" was much frowned upon by the Prince's mother, who regarded it with intense suspicion. Writing to the Duke of Connaught in 1875, the Queen deplored her children's fondness for races, no sport, in her view, for royalty. "To my great grief," she wrote, "I hear that dear Bertie *loses* money at races! For *him* to do this is dreadful. . . . Now tho' you are the younger brother I know that he respects and looks up to you—as well he may—which alas! none of you can do, as I wish you could, to Uncle George. . . . Nothing is worse for a country than when the higher classes indulge in frivolity and vice." She begged the Duke of Connaught to reform his brother and to "say you know the terrible anxiety and grief it is to me."[n] Prince Albert had once accused the Cambridges of leading his eldest son astray, and the accusation was therefore not abandoned lightly.

A great Thanksgiving Service was held at St. Paul's on February 27, 1872, to celebrate the Prince's recovery. The Queen had serious misgivings. She dreaded the fatigue "which I think will be too much for Bertie," and although "willing and very anxious to show my warm acknowledgement of the loyalty and sympathy shown on this occasion, I do not—I must say—like religion to be made a vehicle for a great show. The simple Thanksgiving, more than a month ago, was the right religious act."

The Duke was greatly moved by "the loyalty and good feeling of the people" and thought the ceremony "the most heart-stirring thing I ever witnessed." For some time Queen Victoria's retirement had encouraged criticism and even republicanism, but the country, united in rejoicing over the Prince's recovery, again showed "itself a great and powerful monarchical nation." "The morning looked fine," wrote the Duke in his diary, describing the Thanksgiving ceremonies, "and the day turned out beautiful for the occasion, though the wind was cold. At eleven thirty drove to Buckingham Palace with my two State Carriages and three Equerries with an escort. There joined the Queen's procession, which started exactly at twelve, the Speaker leading, then the Lord Chancellor, then myself, and then the Queen's procession following. It was a most glorious sight, the crowds enormous, their enthusiasms and loyalty overpowering and unbounded, the troops lining the Streets the entire way there and back. We went by Stable Yard, Pall Mall, the Strand, Temple Bar, Fleet Street and Ludgate Hill. The ceremony in the interior of the Cathedral was simple but very impressive. About 14,000 people were accommodated. The Archbishop of Canterbury preached. We returned by the Holborn Viaduct and Holborn, Oxford Street, the Marble Arch, Hyde Park, and Constitution Hill, and were home by three thirty. The whole thing was magnificent, and a great national success. The Queen was delighted, and the Prince got through it well, though he was fatigued at last. Lord Lucan commanded the troops, Prince Edward the Infantry, and Sir Thomas MacMahon the Cavalry. The order and regularity were splendid." For some time the Duke had been eager for the Queen to emerge from seclusion. "I only wish," he wrote on June 20, 1867, "the Queen would oftener consent to appear in public, as it is so much desired by everybody and is so necessary and essential in these times."

While the Duke was staying at Goodwood in the Easter of 1873, he received news of the death of his steward Ramsthal, who had been in his service since he was nine years old. "The blow has quite stunned me. Nobody can ever replace the dear faithful old man, who has for forty-five years shared my fortunes in life, and has never once

left me . . . May God have mercy on his dear soul."
H.R.H. left Goodwood to attend the funeral, "a respect due
to the memory of one who had served me so well and for
whom I entertain so strong an affection, regard and esteem." The Queen, who after the Prince Consort's death
formed deeper friendships with her servants than with
most of her subjects, wrote an understanding letter of
sympathy. "Let me now tell you how grieved I am at the
great loss you have sustained in the death of your faithful
and excellent steward and I may add *friend*. No one perhaps can more truly appreciate your feelings than I do,
who know what it is to have an attached, devoted and
faithful confidential servant. Indeed such a loss is often
more than those of one's nearest and dearest, for a faithful
servant is so identified with *all* your feelings, wants, wishes,
and habits as really to be *part* of your *existence* and *cannot*
be replaced . . ."[n]

The visit of the Shah of Persia in June 1873 involved
the Duke in a plague of ceremonies. The reports which
proceeded His Majesty from Berlin, the first capital of his
European tour, thoroughly alarmed the Queen and she
consequently decided to lodge her guest in Buckingham
Palace while remaining herself at Windsor. The Shah, unaccustomed to the society of European ladies, behaved in
so uninhibited a manner as to give grave offence. The
Persians made purchases in carriage loads, but the delight
of the Berlin shopkeepers soon dwindled to dismay when it
was discovered that paying played no part in the practice
of the Imperial court. The apartments occupied by the
Persians in the royal palace were left like a slum struck by
a cyclone. Nobody, not even the Grand Vizier, ventured to
tell the Shah that he must try to be punctual, that before
being seated himself he should wait for the Empress to sit
down, or that loud, Oriental shouts at dinner were inclined
to startle the company. The Shah preferred to eat most of
his meals alone, sitting on a carpet, and this was perhaps

fortunate, since his behaviour at public banquets was unpredictable. He liked putting his arm round his neighbour's chair, and it was his habit to chew his food for a moment and then examine it. If for any reason it displeased him he threw the remains under the table. The Shah, on reaching England, seems to have accommodated himself better to Western ways, for the Duke makes no mention of any such barbarities. "18 June. In uniform to the Station at four forty-five to meet the Shah of Persia on his arrival, together with the Prince of Wales, Christian, Teck and my whole staff. Alfred and Arthur went to Dover to fetch him. The impression he produced on me was favourable. We all drove in procession to Buckingham Palace, where he lives. On leaving the Station, rain commenced and became very heavy before we arrived at the Palace. The road was lined with Troops, and crowds received him most enthusiastically. 19 June. The Shah came to pay me a visit, soon after one o'clock. His manner is dignified and good, and he understands French fairly, but without speaking it well, though he does so a little. He stayed about a quarter of an hour . . . Dined at Marlborough House, a large Full Dress Dinner for the Shah and all the Persian Princes and leading Attendants. No one could have behaved better or been more dignified than he whilst at dinner. We were only men. 24 June. Went to Datchet by Special Train with the whole of my staff at one thirty from Waterloo, arriving at two thirty. Went direct to Frogmore, where had luncheon, and rode up to the Castle at three to attend the Queen and Shah to the great Review in Windsor Park. The Shah was late in arriving, his train having been delayed . . . The Shah rode with us, the Queen and Court followed in carriages . . . The crowd on the ground was enormous and most enthusiastic . . . At the conclusion of the Review the Shah presented me with one of his own diamond swords, a magnificent gift by which I was greatly gratified and pleased."

. . .

In November of 1873, while visiting her daughter in Mecklenburg-Strelitz, the Duchess of Cambridge had a stroke which left her an invalid for the remaining sixteen years of her life. She was brought back to England in the following May, but at the end of the year had another attack. The Duke, with his eye for clinical detail, wrote in his diary on December 19: "While dining out a message came summoning me to Kew to bring Sir William Gull. Fortunately we were both at hand and started at ten forty-five and were at Kew by eleven thirty. Found dear Mama better and recovering from an attack probably of the heart from indigestion, which seized her about nine, and for the moment took away all consciousness and rendered her rigid. Gull found the pulse and heart extremely feeble, but the momentary danger seemed past. Still it is a painfully critical state of things and the anxiety at her advanced age is distressingly great."

The Duke's life in these years was punctuated by a sad and weary round of illness. His own gout was growing worse and at times he was so crippled he was forced to bed. The twinges of agonizing pain to which he was liable sometimes kindled a temper which at its sunniest was scarcely sanguine. And, added to all his other worries, Louisa's health, although gradually improving, still gave grounds for concern. In 1868 he bought her a little house at Horley, then in the wilds of the country, which she named Cambridge Lodge. It was hoped that rural life would hasten her recovery. "At eight o'clock went down to Horley by train to see Louisa's little cottage," wrote the Duke on June 15, 1868. "It was a lovely day but intensely hot. Walked to the house about a mile. It is a very nice quiet little place and will in time be very pretty. Found Louisa all the better for her stay there and much pleased to see me there. George was there also."

Louisa now spent less time in Queen Street than in younger days, for she was often advised for her health's sake to leave London. Whenever he could, her husband would visit her. "Please dearest," he wrote to her on August 13, 1869, when she was staying at Buxton, "keep my coming dark. Warn your servants not to say who I am. At these watering places people are a horrid bore and Mayors and inhabitants immediately want to get up addresses. I found this to be the case the first time I went to Scarborough and I had no peace during the whole time I was there." Despite such excursions, Louisa still spent much of the year in Queen Street, and she generally arranged to leave London when the Duke was paying visits in England, or travelling abroad. Occasionally she met her husband's colleagues. She was present, for example, at an informal dinner given for Cardwell at Gloucester House on December 18, 1870. But she was not particularly excited by politics, and showed little desire to meet the great men of her husband's world. Her interests were centred round her family, her friends, and her pets. She particularly loved dogs. When the Duke visited Queen Street in 1869, on the anniversary of Inkerman, he found "poor Louisa in a dreadful state of affliction at the death of her dear little dog Nelly, which I regret greatly myself. She thinks the dog was not properly treated medically after pupping." The grief she felt at the death of this animal betrayed her compassionate heart, for she dearly loved all who surrounded her. Neither age nor pain nor separation diminished for an instant her passionate devotion to her husband, whom she still loved with the same burning fervour of the early days of their marriage.

Damming the Deluge

GLADSTONE'S great reforming Ministry came to an end in 1874. Its policy, according to Disraeli, had been one of "blundering and plundering," which harassed every trade, worried every profession and menaced every class, institution and property in the country." The Liberals, in part, attributed their defeat to the Licensing Act of 1872. "We have been borne down," said their leader, "in a torrent of Gin and Beer." The ensuing Conservative Government, which lasted six years, allowed the Army a period of consolidation after the avalanche of change which had swept over it. Disraeli first appointed Gathorne-Hardy as Secretary for War; and when in 1878 he was raised to the peerage as Earl of Cranbrook and became Secretary of State for India, Colonel Stanley, Lord Derby's heir, succeeded him.

Gathorne-Hardy found the Duke loyal and conciliatory, although no enthusiast for new ways. "H.R.H. is frank and friendly, and evidently expects and respects difference of opinion; he argues without any peremptoriness, and accepts without any ill-feeling an adverse decision." The hundreds of letters the Commander-in-Chief addressed to Hardy displayed, in his opinion, "an extraordinary knowledge of all the minutest details of the work of his office." The Radical press echoed the sentiments of the Secretary for War about the Duke's conservatism, but without qualification or restraint. An article in *The World*—a disreputable but vigorous journal—on August 19, 1874, demanded the resignation of the Commander-in-Chief, on the ground that he obstructed progress. "During the last twenty years," declared the article, "war has developed from a mere trade into an abstruse science, and it is progressing with daily accelerated strides. The task of commanding the British Army has therefore enormously increased, and the Duke may well feel that it is now beyond his powers. He alone has stood still, while the whole military world was advancing. He has clung obstinately to the past, has resisted every measure of reform till it became an accomplished fact, and then has done his best secretly and insidiously to render it inoperative . . .

"We can hardly say that the Duke of Cambridge has even put himself at the head of the retrograde clique, for he is not the man to head any party; rather have the retrogradists got in front of him and pushed him backwards. . . . If minute attention to buttons and straps, and careful supervision of marching past and parade movements, are the qualifications of a great commander, not even Moltke can hold a candle to his Royal Highness . . . He seems to consider drill the be-all and end-all of a soldier's training, instead of a means by which an object is to be attained. We are by no means sure that he does not share the opinion of some fossil colonels, and looks on manoeuvres as calculated to ruin regiments. These conservative tendencies of the Duke by no means proceed from want of talent. His natural abilities are good, but he is utterly without mental culture, and knows nothing whatever of the scientific part of war. As a rule, the royal family are not given to reading, and in addition the Duke has always been surrounded by a little clique, the members of which, finding themselves very comfortable in the positions which with little merit of their own they have secured, wish to retain those positions, and consequently have ever sought to keep down men of energy and originality. Nothing is so obnoxious to office-holders as innovations. . . . Besides the tendency of all recent progress, all the new regulations, has been to give merit a chance of rising; but if merit rises, what is to become of patronage?

". . . An officer of some standing and given to speak his mind very plainly observed not very long ago, 'The country may have a royal duke, or it may have an army; it cannot have both.' . . . Officers who write are his aversion, and contributors to the press are invariably kept in the background till their reputation with the public becomes so great that they cannot be suppressed any longer.

". . . If, therefore, War is to be cultivated as a science, if our military system is to be improved, if our organization and tactics are to be based on sound principles, and to be brought into harmony with modern conditions, the sooner his Royal Highness resigns his command the better. We admit, however, that his resignation would be received by the profession with varied and mixed feelings. He has certainly made himself popular with the men. The fact that he, a prince, should have devoted himself to soldiering as if he had to earn his bread by it, and that he has in two bloody actions displayed the hereditary courage of his race, has had something to do with his popularity. He is also in appearance and manner a soldierlike man. The lower orders like the bluff bearing and vehement outspoken language which were the characteristics of the Tudors . . . He always goes much into detail—men with his description of mind always do; and he is therefore credited with having always been engaged in studying to promote the soldier's welfare. . . . As to the officers, there are many who would regret his retirement. His hearty manner, his undoubted good nature, his wonderful memory, in which are treasured up, not only the name and face, but also the career, of nearly every officer in the service, make the unreflecting majority blind to his defects. Those defects are, however, serious. He is extremely vituperative on very slight provocation, and not seldom publicly addresses officers of rank and standing in the most humiliating language . . . The last person who speaks to him is the one by whom he is influenced . . . Finally, his chief vice—a blind Conservatism—is attractive to the majority, for in the army all old things are generally looked upon as good; and a Conservative body of officers naturally sympathize with a Conservative Commander-in-Chief.

"A large and thoughtful minority, however, appreciate the Duke's character more justly. They perceive that his energy is chiefly spent on trifles, that his activity is mainly displayed in rushing wildly about the country holding routine inspections."

The views expressed by *The World* were, as it admitted, only those of a minority, but the minority counted Wolseley among its numbers. The Duke was inclined to suspect that some of the newspaper attacks upon him were directly inspired by Sir Garnet, who detested the traditional field day because he believed it detracted from the ultimate purpose of military training: preparation for actual war. "I have just returned from one of those most tiresome field days," he once wrote, "in which the Duke of Cambridge delights, but which to me are hateful in the extreme. I am not good as a dissembler, and I keep my temper with difficulty when I see and hear so much that tends to rub up the wrong way every military instinct I possess." On another occasion, he told his wife: "I hear the Duke was most annoying at Aldershot. The Field Day was abominably bad. He assembled all the junior officers when it was over and said: 'Very fine horses, very well turned out; looking very well; splendid men and well drilled; but damned bad officers.' "

The Commander-in-Chief's outspokenness could only have been salutary. His constant round of tours and inspections would have achieved little if he had dispensed nothing but insincere flattery. But he was no more inclined to dissemble than was Wolseley, and it was just because he was quick to criticize that his compliments were gratifying. There were times, however, when his brusqueness provoked resentment. "They have been comparing this inspection with the last," wrote Colonel Henderson, a lecturer at Sandhurst in 1894, "when the old hero of many banquets grunted ferociously at the pile of schemes, maps, etc. and then darted off to revel in pork chops and other delicacies, giving us to understand that we were very dull dogs."

Traditional field days and parades may have disgusted military reformers, but they provided a magnificent spectacle which greatly assisted the work of the recruiting sergeant. Chatham was a military station the Duke frequently visited, and the splendour of his reviews so impressed itself on the mind of a child who watched them that he vividly recalled the excitement of the occasion over half a century later. "For me, it was the army that occupied the fore-ground of the picture,

> 'The army that fights for the Queen,
> The very best army that ever was seen!'

and certainly it was an incomparably more picturesque and colourful army than anything you imagine today. It was, moreover, conspicuously under royal patronage: for no circus, nor even the Salvation Army, then in its youthful prime, that put down a glorious drumfire barrage once a week under my nursery window, could vie for entertainment with what seem to me to have been the fairly frequent occasions on which His Royal Highness, the Duke of Cambridge, came down in his capacity of Commander-in-Chief, to review the Chatham Brigade. As our house was right above the station, we could see his whole cavalcade mounting and getting under way—the expression 'glittering staff' was certainly no misnomer, with the whole street in spate with cocked hats and scarlet and decorations; and when the grand old warrior led it under the railway bridge, it almost seemed as if his whiskers would have brushed the brickwork on either side.

"As one who had been habituated to play soldiers, to think soldiers, and to daydream himself a soldier, I kept an almost photographic impression of that spectacle, and it explained much since to me that would have otherwise been obscure. The battlefield was a magnificent open space called the Lines, with the ground from the South edge falling abruptly down to the valley in which lie Rochester and the Medway . . . It was along that edge that the enemy had taken up his position, having presumably climbed up out of the valley, and lain down for a breather. I say 'his'—but as a matter of fact there were at least ten of him, each man being supposed to represent a hundred. I did not suppose any such thing. It was only fitting that the Queen's forces should exceed these Frenchmen, as I visualized them, in quantity no less than in quality. It was on this devoted ten, lying conspicuously on their stomachs—for there seemed to be no question of entrenching—that the whole Chatham garrison staged a long, leisurely attack over ground suggestive of a billiard table. Undeterred by the massacre of the Prussian Guard at St. Privat under rather similar circumstances eighteen years previously, they advanced in three closely packed and accurately dressed scarlet lines, lying down at frequent intervals, as much, I imagine, for the purpose of correcting their alignment as of popping off blank. In the second or third line a score or so of men would ever and anon spring simultaneously to their feet to discharge an equally simultaneous volley. I should think that under these circumstances even ten men, counting one as one, with a sufficient number of cartridges, could have accounted with their Martinis for a greater part of the assailants; unless they had been conspicuously bad shots, which, under His Highness's system of training, they most likely were, since a straight shot was accounted as nothing in his eye compared with a straight line. However, at long last, the spoil-sport bugles went, just as the final charge was being prepared and the invaders were about to be bayoneted and pitchforked, before my delighted eyes, over the crest. Then the victors formed up intact, and with bands thundering out the regimental tunes, marched triumphantly past the Duke, who I think must have enjoyed this part of it most of all. For peace-time soldiering it was the most impressive spectacle that anyone could conceive. But when something of the sort had been tried against a rabble of unsoldierly Boers, not so long before, there had been a rather different tale to tell! But that would be no bar to its being tried again, in due course, against the selfsame enemy.

"Of course it will be said that a small child was perfectly incapable of appreciating the deep motives behind all this martial pageantry. And that would have been true; for I had no idea at the time of the mastering anxiety that possessed the staff and the commanders, which was that on no account whatever should proceedings be prolonged for a single second beyond the hour fixed for H.R.H.'s lunch, which always consisted of chop and tomato sauce. Any failure in this respect would be notified to all concerned in royally unpublished terms, for the Duke had inherited from his uncles, of the Regency generation, a command of varied and picturesque imagery far beyond the resources of Billingsgate.'"

In January 1879 the Government declared war on King Cetywayo, the Zulu leader, who threatened Britain's supremacy in South Africa. The campaign began disastrously. Cardwell had so weakened colonial defences that Natal had only a battalion with which to resist a ferocious and numerous enemy. Lord Chelmsford, who commanded the troops in South Africa, told the Commander-in-Chief that the Zulus appeared to have no fear whatever of death, and "although mowed down by hundreds at a time never faltered in their attack. Englishmen liked the foe to come on bravely but rather injudiciously, and to be 'mown down' by guns that never jammed. They liked him to be easily surprised and bamboozled, and then they paid the highest compliments to his 'unavailing heroism'; Mr. Kipling probably compensated him with a poem in Cockney dialect." But if he declined "to be surprised and bamboozled, the public journals were apt to describe the ensuing disaster as a 'treacherous massacre.' "" At Isandhlwana, Cetywayo captured an important base camp, full of essential stores, equipment, and ammunition, and in the process destroyed most of the troops defending it. "It will be a melancholy satisfaction to your Royal Highness to know," wrote Chelmsford, "that the imperial troops fought in the most gallant manner, and that their courage and determination is the theme of wonder and amazement amongst the natives who saw them fight and who escaped to tell the tale."[n]

The Duke pressed the Government to authorize an increase in the size of the Army. Early in the very month in which war was declared, and despite the campaign being fought at the same time in Afghanistan, reductions had been contemplated. The Conservatives were as shortsighted as the Liberals when it came to military expenditure. In view of the reverses in Africa, reinforcements had to be dispatched, and H.R.H. was authorized to promise Chelmsford two regiments of cavalry, two field batteries, a company of engineers, and six battalions of infantry. Within a fortnight, the troops were collected, embarked, and had sailed: the Commander-in-Chief inspected them before their departure.

"To Aldershot," wrote H.R.H. in his diary on February 18, 1879, "to inspect the several corps for service at the Cape . . . The troops looked well, but there are a very large number of volunteers and young men, which is certainly a great disadvantage. The spirit among them, however, is excellent, so I hope they will do well. 19 February. Went by train from Fenchurch Street to Tilbury Fort to inspect the Third Batt. 60th Rifles before embarking for South Africa. They looked a strong, healthy set of young men and most orderly and regular. Passed over to Gravesend in a tug, and then saw the Draft of two hundred and fifty men from Winchester from the First Batt. and the Depot, an equally fine body of men and in excellent order.

"22 February. Went with the Duke of Connaught and my staff to Hounslow by train, and thence drove in my wagonette to the Cavalry Barracks, the snow preventing my seeing the 17th Lancers on the heath before embarkation for S. Africa. Saw Regiment on foot parade in Barrack Yard, a splendid body of men in the finest possible order and made up with excellent Drafts from 5th and 16th Lancers. 26 February. Went from Waterloo with my staff to Portsmouth, and there saw 58th Foot embark in the *Russia* . . . The Regiment looked very efficient and fit for work, and the vessel was a good one. Then on board the *Palmyra* in which the Royal Engineers embark tomorrow, also a good vessel. From thence by special train to Southampton Docks . . . There saw 94th and drafts for 57th on board the *China,* a fine vessel, but very crowded with troops. Then went on board the *England* in which Head Quarters, 17th Lancers, and General Marshall were all admirably put up and ready to sail, and then over the *Spain,* which was ready to take on board next day the left wing of King's Dragoon Guards with Generals Clifford and Newdigate. Saw the *China* and *England* sail and then returned to London."

According to custom, the Government decided to blame the commander in the field for failures which might with more justice have been attributed to policies dictated from Whitehall. On May 28 they appointed Wolseley as Commander-in-Chief in South Africa, although by the time he reached Natal, Chelmsford had defeated Cetywayo at Ulundi. The Duke wrote to congratulate the superseded general on his victory, and generously supported him against an ungrateful Government. "Above all, and before all, let me congratulate you and the gallant troops under your command for the glorious news which reached me by telegraph yesterday of your entire and signal success at Ulundi, ending in the complete defeat of the Zulu Army under the direct command of Cetywayo . . . Nothing, as far as can be judged by the necessary shortness of the message received, could have been better done, and happily with comparatively small loss on our side, and the moral effect thus produced will, I sincerely trust and confidently believe, put an end to the war . . . The general demonstration of joy and satisfaction felt by the public at large is all that could be wished, and it would give you intense pleasure to see it as I have been enabled to do the last two days. There is universal rejoicing from Her Majesty downward, and the feeling is as sincere as it is general . . . Let all the troops know how greatly I am gratified." Chelmsford, in acknowledging H.R.H.'s congratulations, thanked him warmly for all his support. "Whatever the result may be, and whatever verdict may be passed upon me as a General, I shall never forget Y.R.H.'s kindness or the generous support given to me at a moment when it was most needed.""

The Duke, hearing rumours that Wolseley was to be sent out to the Cape, was greatly disturbed. On May 24, he discussed the prospect at St. James's with his mother, and he told the Duchess and Lady Geraldine that "he plainly saw that they are determined to send Garnet Wolseley out to the Cape!! We had a long discussion about him and the *danger* of him! and *his* being at the bottom of the whole Cardwell system!!" If Chlemsford needed to be superseded at all, H.R.H. would have preferred Lord Napier as his successor. "Monday 26 May 1879. I forgot to mention that yesterday I saw Lord Beaconsfield on the question of Sir Garnet Wolseley being sent out as Chief Commissioner and Commander-in-Chief in South Africa, and this morning I called on Lord Salisbury and saw him on the same subject. The Cabinet decided today to send Wolseley. I should have infinitely preferred Lord Napier, but he was thought too old, which I cannot at all admit, as he is as hard a man for work as I know anywhere." Writing to his son Adolphus on June 4, he says: "Wolseley's appointment was not pleasant to me though I think it was necessary to do something at once as matters at the Cape were going on badly. I admit Wolseley's intelligence but I cannot see why he should be the *only* man in the Army we have left for duties requiring energy." It was undoubtedly hard on many officers that Parliament and the public had come to think of Wolseley as England's "only General." As usual, Sir Garnet took out to South Africa a carefully collected staff, chosen from the not very large circle of his supporters and admirers in the Army. Their appointments infuriated the Duke, who detested the "Garnet Ring." "Went to the office," he wrote on May 29, "where found to my great annoyance, that Stanley had sanctioned all Wolseley's friends, a long list of whom he had handed in, to accompany him out to the Cape. This puts me out very much . . ."

Once Wolseley arrived in South Africa he continued to offend the Duke. Lady Geraldine's diary is full of conversations in which Sir Garnet is abused. On August 3 the Duke "read us the telegram he had just received today from Sir Garnet Wolseley, in which he too *impertinently* says: 'Lord Chelmsford wishes to return home and *I* have given him permission to do so'!!!! For want of taste, of tact, of good feeling! so stamps the fellow for what he is a prig and a pretentious snob! No gentleman." On August 8 H.R.H. received another "offensive telegram," full of "claptrap as to all *his* reductions of expenditure! Full of attacks upon Chelmsford! In short full of self-sufficiency, arrogance, impertinence! A *cad* indeed!!" Two days later the talk at St. James's again returned to "that brute Garnet Wolseley. His insufferable pretensions! The offensiveness of his despatches, full only of himself!"

The new Commander in South Africa arrived to find the war virtually over, but after some months it flared up once more. In 1880, the Liberals were returned to power, and as at the General Election Gladstone had attacked the whole philosophy behind Disraeli's imperialism, the Boers in South Africa consequently expected the withdrawal of British forces. In December, finding this hope disappointed, they rose in revolt and won the victory of Majuba Hill. Rather than continue a war which threatened to involve all South Africa, Gladstone granted the Transvaal virtual independence. Having conceded to force what had been denied to discussion, the Government left their enemies victorious, distrustful, and resolved, if need arose, to resort again to arms.

The Duke was utterly dismayed when he heard that the

Prime Minister was negotiating terms. In a letter to Adolphus written on April 14, 1881, he refers to "this terrible peace in South Africa," which he considered "too awfully humiliating." "The country is lowered in every sense of the word and our influence at home and abroad dreadfully damaged. My own idea is that we shall ere long have to fight again at the Transvaal and indeed in South Africa generally." On December 15, 1881, the Duke presented the Minister for War with his annual review of the Army. The report concluded with a pointed rebuke for the Government. "In submitting my usual annual report upon the state of the Army, I have this year to allude only to one war in which our troops have been engaged—that with the Boers; but this has been a most unfortunate one. During the short period of one month we suffered three defeats . . . After, on 27 February, obtaining, by a difficult night march, possession of the Majuba Hill—a decisive tactical point—we were driven headlong from it in a rout so complete and disastrous that it is almost unparalleled in the long annals of our Army. When this last victory of the Boers was won, a force had been collected in Natal from this country and from India sufficient to have crushed with certainty the insurrection and restored the tarnished prestige of our arms; but for reasons other than military an armistice, followed by a peace, was concluded with the Boers upon terms which were certainly depressing to our troops, and upon which I abstain from making any observations."

The reverses which the British Army suffered in South Africa revived the controversy about the merits of Cardwell's system of Short Service. The Duke constantly complained that the reinforcements consisted of "mere boys." Even Wolseley admitted that many of the recruits needed a year or eighteen months of service before they became efficient soldiers and had "done growing." Lord Napier, the veteran of Magdala, who had probably seen more fighting than any general in the service, was badly shaken by the news from the Cape. "One thing appears clear," he wrote in 1881, "that the stubbornness of the British soldier, which used to cover all the blunders of the Commanders can no longer be counted on, and those who are playing tricks with the Army, are still in power and unconvinced . . ."⁸ The first significant test of the new system in action proved that the fears of its opponents were not as groundless as its advocates had alleged them to be.

Among those who volunteered for service in South Africa was the Prince Imperial, the great-nephew of the first Napoleon and the remaining hope of the Bonapartists. He had been a cadet at the Royal Military Academy at Woolwich, where the Duke had watched his progress with pleasure. "Saw the Cadets," he wrote in his diary on February 15, 1875, "who drilled and looked well. The Prince Imperial drilled them remarkably well when called upon. The Empress Eugénie was present throughout the day. She went with me to see the drawings, then into the Gymnasium, where the Reports were read and the Prizes given. The Prince Imperial took the seventh place in the List, a most excellent position for a Cadet eleven months younger than the greater portion of his class, and who had to do his study in a foreign language . . . Saw the rides, which were excellent. The Prince Imperial took the first place, also first in fencing." The Queen also watched the young Prince's career with affectionate interest. She telegraphed to the Empress congratulating her "at the success of the dear young Prince Imperial," and she told the Duke that she felt sure the Academy would always be proud that the young Prince had distinguished himself in their school, "and above all, *behaved* so well!"

The Prince's first request to go out to South Africa was rejected by the Government, but he persisted so vigorously that at length they yielded. The Queen was touched by his desire "to go out with and serve with my brave troops." She saw him before he set sail for the Cape, feeling "glad I am not his mother at the moment." She particularly told the

Duke that "we know he is *very* venturesome," and that he should on no account be allowed near the enemy. H.R.H. accordingly wrote to the High Commissioner of South Africa, Sir Bartle Frere, telling him that the Prince Imperial was coming out merely as a "spectator."

On the evening of June 19, 1879, Princess Augusta and Lady Geraldine went to the French Play, the piece being entitled *Les Deux Mondes*. They were joined by Captain George FitzGeorge. "In the middle of the third act the Duke came, from his Scots Guards dinner in a very short entracte. We tried to tell him the story! very badly! The *fourth* act had just begun when a man came in looking for the Duke, went up to him and whispered something on which the Duke threw a tremendous start! Aghast! A sound of distress! Passed a bundle of telegrams the man brought him, and went with him into the little anteroom behind our box, where he stood reading them. My heart sank with envy, presently he came into the box again, whispered to P.A., who exclaimed with *horror,* 'Good God!' I asked him what it was? And he whispered to me!!! 'The Prince Imperial is killed!!' Good God! The horror! The pain! and dismay, poor, poor, poor, Eugénie!!!!! I read the telegram: 'Killed in a reconnaissance in which he dismounted from his horse, was surrounded by Zulus, and shot!' Good God! It is too dreadful. The Duke went off *at once* to Lord Sydney about breaking it to *unhappy* Eugénie! Of course P.A. should also have left the theatre *at once!* But strange as she is! and always for keeping a thing *secret* and a mystery, we sat *through* the play!! It was too terrible to do and of which I, of course, did not hear a word more and only sat in *pain.*"

The Duke regarded the news as "overpowering in its terribleness." The next day he wrote in his diary: "The news of the Prince's death is really overwhelming and no words can describe the dismay it has caused. How it could have happened that the Prince should have been allowed to get into so exposed a position is quite inexplicable."

On June 21, H.R.H. visited the Empress. "I settled to go to

Chislehurst this morning and proceeded there at twelve o'clock. . . . I was at once received by the poor Empress, who behaved too beautifully and heroically in her awful sorrow and grief. She conversed with me for nearly an hour upon this sad, sad business, and not an unkind or ungenerous word ever passed her lips. Her fate is fearful to contemplate; all hope in life gone for ever with this dear gallant boy. I myself feel quite broken-hearted."

The Queen was haunted by the Prince Imperial's death. "How horrible. How dreadful," she telegraphed to H.R.H. from Balmoral. "I am quite overwhelmed by the stunning news, and in such sorrow for the poor dear Empress who has lost all. We leave at one today." A letter followed the telegram, in which grief was mingled with imperious rage. The Queen's letters, as Lady Geraldine once observed, were inclined to be "peremptory, despotic as no Eastern potentate." Surely, she asked, it was arranged that the Prince was never to leave Lord Chelmsford's staff? How could he have been allowed in so exposed a place? "No doubt, he, poor dear brave young man pressed to go, but he ought *not* to have been allowed." Just in case the Duke was not suffering agonies of self-recrimination, she emphasized the extent of his responsibility for the tragedy. "I can't tell you how it haunts me, and has upset me, and for *you* who arranged all for his going it is most painful." Two days later the Queen visited Chislehurst. "I went this afternoon and sat with the dear Empress, and it is quite heartbreaking to see her—so gentle, uncomplaining and resigned, yet so broken-hearted. *And* one can say *nothing* to *comfort* her! I never felt anything more, and am quite miserable and overwhelmed by it! Poor dear! She asked me, did I think it *possible* it might not be true, and that it might be someone else? But I said I thought *that* was *impossible*, for his dear remains were at once recognized!"

On the same day that the Queen paid her visit to the Empress, the Duke defended the Government and the Horse Guards in the House of Lords. He read the letters of introduction which the Prince had been given for Frere and Chelmsford. "All I can say is . . . after having read these letters, that I think, so far as the authorities at home are concerned, everybody must feel that nothing has been done by them to place the Prince in the position which, unfortunately, resulted in his death. We all deplore, deeply deplore —I am sure that everyone in this House, every man, woman, and child in this country, everyone, from the Queen on her Throne down to her humblest servant, must feel and deeply deplore—what had occurred; but certainly, as far as the authorities are concerned here, I feel that nothing has been done to produce such a catastrophe as that which we all so much lament. I have already said how deeply I sympathize with the bereaved mother, and I am sure your Lordships fully share that feeling."

The most distressing feature of the Prince's death, as far as the Army was concerned, was not so much that he had found his way into a position of danger, although that by itself was regrettably careless of the authorities, but that some of those with him fled at the appearance of the enemy and left him to his fate. The Commander-in-Chief wrote to Chelmsford, asking for a detailed investigation. "That he should have gone to the front with so small an escort, and with a junior officer, Lieutenant Carey, alone in his company, requires explanation of the fullest kind; as also does the fact of his having been killed, poor lad, with two of his escort gallantly fighting for their lives, whilst Lieutenant Carey and the four other men who were with him returned to camp, apparently much frightened, though otherwise quite unharmed . . . At present the feeling of horror, distress, and I may say dismay, is intense, and it will require the most clear account and the most searching investigation to satisfy the world, both at home and abroad, that he was not abandoned to his fate by the officer and men who were with him . . . The condition of the poor Empress is of course lamentable in the extreme, for with this lad all her hopes are buried in the grave for ever. Had the poor dear gallant young fellow been killed in a general action, or by your side, or by the side of one of the superior officers, it would have been the will of God it should be so, and nothing further could have been said; but that he should have met the fate he did, in the manner in which thus far the telegrams describe it to us, is the point which causes so much painful comment, and which seems to all, including myself, to be so inexplicable.'"

The Empress behaved nobly. She begged that no one should suffer, and requested an end to all investigations. She declared that her only consolation on earth was that her son had died a soldier's death, and she wanted no recriminations. *"Mois qui ne peux plus rien désirer sur terre, je demande cela comme une dernière prière."* She derived a sad satisfaction from the company of her son's charger, which was sent back from South Africa and was stabled at Balmoral, with a magnificent horse which had belonged to the Emperor. "The poor Empress," wrote the Queen, "who is staying here with me, can't separate from them."

Just before the Empress left for Scotland, one of her ladies-in-waiting wrote to the Duke, describing a dreadful episode which had taken place at Chislehurst. "Her Majesty is much the same, *very, very* sad, and she looks so pale and ill! She was busy last week, some boxes having arrived from South Africa. She insisted upon seeing them unpacked, and in one of these trunks was the poor little Prince's shirt, all covered with blood. The sight of it, of course, renewed her grief.'" The Duke did everything in his power to help the Empress. He had known her ever since his visit to Paris on his way to join his division in the Crimea, and now in her grief he paid her constant visits and wrote her many letters. The Commander-in-Chief was still no more hardened to death than he had been at Inkerman and at the Alma, and was always desolated by casualties. The numerous letters of consolation he wrote in his lifetime were no mere token tributes: they came straight from the heart.

. . .

The war in South Africa raised an issue on which Wolseley and the Duke found themselves utterly opposed. As a young man, H.R.H. had held ruthless opinions, but he modified them as he increased in experience. Writing in 1857 to Sir Colin Campbell, who commanded in India, he had told him: "Let me know from time to time who are your best officers, in order that we may push them on, and also who are useless that they may be got rid of." "It is essential," he declared in another letter, "to weed the Army of non-effectives, especially in the higher grades."ⁿ Soon, however, he discovered that such methods of selection were too unsettling for the Army, and he became increasingly inclined to advocate promotion by seniority. He admitted that in wartime there might be arguments for departing from this principle, but he maintained in the ordinary course of events any other method of selection would give general dissatisfaction in the Army, would involve "serious injustice to individuals passed over," and since the Army was "scattered all over the world performing a great variety of special duties," it would be next to impossible to compare the merits of officers who had served in different quarters of the globe. The heart-searching and jealousies which selection might engender would greatly outweigh any alleged advantages. The proposal that promotion should be decided by merit naturally appealed most to those Army officers who believed themselves possessed of outstanding qualifications. The vast majority, who had no pretensions to superior ability and were inclined to suspect the intellectual soldier, were perfectly content with a system which regarded length of service as more telling than any other military accomplishment. The Duke's advocacy of "seniority" was therefore popular in the Army, and it cannot be doubted that this means of promotion maintained harmony in the higher ranks of the service. If junior officers, on account of their supposed ability, were to be promoted colonels over the heads of elderly majors, serious ill-feeling might ensue. Moreover, what constituted ability and who possessed it were matters of definition and opinion. Favouritism might easily vitiate selection. Officers inclined to a particular school of military thinking, without any conscious desire to favour those who held similar opinions, might nevertheless be tempted to imagine that those who thought as they did deserved advancement. If there was always a danger that promotion by seniority might deprive an outstanding junior officer of scope for his talents, and could even perhaps place in important commands those unqualified to hold them, there was equally the risk, if promotion was confined to merit, that the efficiency and goodwill of the Army might be corrupted and that ability would be misjudged.

Wolseley had always agitated for merit as the sole passport for preferment. The real test of an officer was not length of service but his record of achievement. "He urged in season and out of season that merit should have precedence over seniority. He begged the Duke when there was a question of promoting an officer of doubtful value in the field: 'Give him orders and ribbons, but don't give him the men's lives to lose.' Capacity to command troops in war, he protested, should be the one test of fitness for promotion in an army . . . The counter-argument ran that peace training often provided a very inadequate proof of capacity to lead in the field, and that a process of selection might open the door to favouritism and jobbery."[m] Lord Roberts, who disagreed with Wolseley on most military matters, shared his views on promotion. "I cannot forget," he wrote in 1890, "the lessons taught me in 1857, when, with scarcely an exception, every officer in a high position had failed." He could not accept what the Duke told him in a letter on the subject of promotion by seniority: "I found it always answered better than simply to select what might be a better man if by so doing I hurt the feelings and prospects of a deserving officer."[n]

On arriving in Natal to take over command from Lord Chelmsford, Wolseley wrote to the Commander-in-Chief on June 30, 1879, on the subject of his successor, should he be killed in action. "I cannot say too much for the zeal of General Clifford. I do beg and urge upon the Government in the most earnest manner that he should be given a commission as second in command to succeed me in the event of my being shot; that is always supposing H.M.'s Government is not disposed to promote Colonel Colley to that position. He is the ablest man I know, and in the interests of the public service, if they alone are to be regarded, it would entirely be advisable that he should succeed to the command here in case of my death." The Duke in his reply repudiated the idea that Colley could momentarily be contemplated as second in command. "As regards the officer who would take your place in the event of anything occurring to disable you, of course this duty will devolve on Major-General Clifford, a very hard-working and able officer, in whom every confidence could be placed. I cannot at all agree in the advisability of preferring a very junior officer like Colonel Colley, however able he may be. No Army could stand these sort of preferences without entirely damping the energies of senior officers, and the balance of the advantage is very decidedly, in my opinion, in favour of the senior officer unless otherwise disqualified."

Wolseley had all the Irishman's persistence in argument, and was not prepared to give ground, even to the Commander-in-Chief. Writing from Pretoria on September 28, he re-stated his position. "When I wrote regarding a man to succeed me in the event of my being disposed of, I naturally assumed it would be the object of the Government that the ablest and most fitting man should succeed me. When the interests of the State are, in my opinion, concerned, I always feel it to be my duty to speak very plainly, even although I may not, when doing so, be able to do all I would, under other circumstances, do for a man like General Clifford, whom I have long known as a friend and admired as a soldier. In my humble opinion, all private interests or liking should be ignored, and all questions of professional seniority entirely put on one side when the great interests of Her

Majesty's Empire are at stake. It was under the influence of these feelings that I recommended General Colley to succeed me in preference to any other officers who were senior to him in South Africa. He is *immeasurably* the ablest man here: this is a point upon which I know there are no two opinions on the part of men who know the officer I refer to, and Your Royal Highness is aware of the high opinion I entertain of General Clifford. It is but due to Her Majesty and to the State that the country should have the services of the best man to command Her Majesty's troops in the field entirely irrespective of what his present rank may be." The Duke, however, was not convinced. "I can assure you I take no exception to your giving me your opinions freely in your private letters, only I cannot see that the public service is benefited by our going out of our way to put some officers prominently forward on all occasions, however valuable they may be, when there are others available quite equal to perform good service also if chance be only given to them. I quite admit that the public service is the *first consideration,* and I *invariably* look to this myself. But I consider the public service is much *depressed* if certain officers are constantly brought to the front. . . . I am the first to admit that Brigadier Colley is a very able man and superior officer, and it is quite right to place every confidence in him; but there are plenty of opportunities for making his abilities of use to Her Majesty and the State, without, by so doing, injuring the feelings of others . . . No man has the public interest and service more at heart than I have, and I have nobody specially whom I wish to serve, but the *whole Army* and body of its officers in general."

When, in 1882, Wolseley was given command of the Egyptian expedition, he took advantage of his right as Commander-in-Chief in the field to correspond direct with the Secretary for War, Lord Hartington. "There are now serving under my command," he told him, "some regimental Lieut.-Colonels who are entirely unfit for their positions—men who, although entrusted by regulations with the command of over eight hundred soldiers of all ranks, could not, with due regard for the lives of those soldiers and the honour and interest of the State, be allowed any independent command before an enemy . . . I hold that it is criminal to hand over in action the care of the lives of gallant soldiers to men who are deplorably ignorant of the elements of their profession. A system must be entirely and radically wrong under which officers of this stamp can obtain the position of Lieut.-Colonels in H.M.'s Army. . . . In a system of promotion by seniority neither care nor judgement need be exercised, and the fitness of an officer for his position is, in the main, left to chance. . . . An officer thus arrives at the highest position in a regiment, not in consequence of his qualifications, but simply in consequence of his place in the regimental list, frequently in the face of known disqualifications for such a position. . . . In the Navy—the sister service of the Army—the officers to command ships are selected with the greatest care. Should not equal care be taken in choosing an officer to command a regiment or battalion?"

The Duke recognized Wolseley's great ability, but regarded him as "a desperate reformer" who failed to look "to the consequences in military affairs, which is a great mistake and misfortune . . . You cannot change without serious risk the military arrangements and organization which have made our power so great . . ." When Wolseley went out to the Cape in 1879, taking as his staff the usual group of friends, H.R.H. was not properly consulted, and consequently felt himself to be the victim of duplicity. He complained to Stanley that "Sir Garnet Wolseley has made my position very uncomfortable and I can assure you I feel it most deeply. The selection of a large number of special friends is a serious blow to my position as Commander-in-Chief . . . Men have gone out *against my judgement* and this is well known to themselves and friends. Consequently they look to their patron Wolseley and no longer to me." The Duke pointed out that Wolseley must have warned these officers to be ready to go before consulting anyone. "This is a degree of double dealing I am not accustomed to by a General Officer in high position and which shakes my confidence in his future and my power to be of any use to him, for where there is not confidence, there is not that cordiality which is so necessary in these matters . . . I am deeply *mortified* that after twenty-three years service in the past such a state of things should have arisen."[n]

Early in 1880 there was talk of Wolseley being sent to India to succeed Sir Frederick Haines as Commander-in-Chief. The Duke resisted the suggestion, and Haines was persuaded to remain a little longer in the East. Lady Geraldine described how on February 8 H.R.H. had seen the Queen, who had written "an admirable letter to Stanley! Quite perfect! All that he wished her to say! Told us of the presumptuous letter of Garnet Wolseley that caused it, in which he quite over-reached himself and overshot his mark! Thinking to 'catch' her by speaking of the gallant *Highland* Regiment rushing to the attack with their bagpipes in the front, without naming the other Regiments at all! who had behaved quite as gallantly! and also that he wished he were in England *to help* her to carry through the views of the *Prince Consort!* In both of which he quite missed his aim! as she *only* saw his object and is extremely disgusted!! But she is anxious if he can be kept in hand, that he should be employed at the Horse Guards here where they think he can do less mischief than elsewhere! She is particularly indignant at the allusion to the Prince Consort which she says is *totally* false as he never at all had such views!!"

Wolseley soon got to hear of the opposition to his appointment and on March 20 wrote his wife about "the formidable Royal party which is against me, with that silly good-meaning man the Duke of Cambridge at its head . . . It will crush me if it can, and as I am not a Party man I fear it may do so . . . I have just had a letter from that silly man Ponsonby, the Queen's Private Secretary, telling me Her Majesty is offended because I said in a letter I wrote to

him, that we have never had any substantial reform in the
Army since the Prince Consort died, and that were he living
now, Army reform would be in a very different position from
that it now occupies. This is certain, for Prince Albert was
a very sensible man and not one that was likely to have
taken all he was told by the Duke of Cambridge as gospel.
However the Queen is a woman and can know nothing of
war or of modern warfare, so she naturally leans upon her
cousin of Cambridge who knows as much of modern warfare
—or indeed of any warfare, as my top-boot does. She
naturally adopts H.R.H.'s views, and because he hates
the modern views I hold on military subjects, she thinks
that I am the radical he paints me to be. I detest radicals
. . . . Mr. Gladstone's views are abhorrent to every instinct
within me." The Liberals "are church wardens and parish
vestry men more than Englishmen—I am a jingo of the
jingoes of the highest acceptation of that title, and yet I am
represented by people like the Royal George as radical!!!"
Wolseley was nearly always contemptuous of those who did
not agree with him, but one cannot blame him too severely
for resenting being lectured on war by the Prince of Wales.
"Let him stick to his tailoring, that is his province," was Sir
Garnet's aside to his wife, "and keep his breath for his own
porridge."

At the General Election of 1880 Gladstone had emerged
from retirement, attacked Disraeli's imperial aspirations,
with which H.R.H. fully sympathized, and followed a policy
in South Africa which led to untold expenditure in men and
money. Childers, who in Gladstone's previous Ministry had
been First Lord of the Admiralty, was chosen as Secretary
for War. The Duke watched the progress of the election
with increasing despair. Lady Geraldine noted on April 8:
"A little after six came the Duke very low and depressed at
the dark prospects! *His* position is dreadful! And he is more
to be pitied than anyone! Which brute will he get?? And
have to stand by and see his Army *destroyed!* And when

the sneaking dirty policy of the Brutes has drifted us into a war, then get the blame and discredit because there are neither men or materials for use! *Ungrateful* task for an ungrateful country! No wonder he is depressed." On April 11 Lady Geraldine wrote: "The Duke read us his letter from the Queen in which she tells him she will send for Hartington, he being the *leader* of the Opposition, and one of her *first* duties will be to see to the selection of a *safe??* man for the War Office! She expresses her astonishment at the so entirely unexpected revolution of public opinion! But attributes it to no dislike of present policy, but to mere love of change and the notion that hard times and oppression may be helped by that!" The only spark of comfort was that H.R.H. would not have Cardwell again at the War Office. "One good thing he heard, that Cardwell is going, is quite weak! So, thank God! *he* at least is unfit and incapable. . . ." Cardwell's illness had begun in 1879. By 1883 he was out of his mind, and he died at Torquay in 1886. Even Wolseley, whom many accused of obsequiousness to the Liberal party, was opposed to their being returned, for although he applauded their responsiveness to military changes, he resented their indifference to imperial needs. "If we have a change of Government," he wrote to his wife, "we shall have no more fighting for some time to come anywhere, for Gladstone and party would not I believe fight for the Isle of Wight if it were taken possession of by an enemy: they would find fifty reasons for concurring in the policy of masterly inactivity and some would I have no doubt go as far as to express great astonishment at it having been left so long in our possession.""

Childers and the new Government soon began contemplating changes and reductions. Opening a new year in his diary, the Duke wrote sadly in 1881: "The year commences under deep anxiety for the future of this country and for us all who love and respect our old institutions. Under God's blessing these clouds may be dispelled, but at present nothing can be more gloomy . . . At twelve at-

tended meeting at the War Office. It has been decided to
make great changes in the Army in spite of my earnest re-
monstrances, but I have not succeeded in them, which I
deeply deplore." Childers, it seemed, was always "full of
new projects," many of them "most prejudicial to the Army
and extremely distasteful to myself." "We talked," wrote
Lady Geraldine on December 29, 1881, "of the Duke's busy
day, long War Office meeting, of Childers *busybody!* interfering in everything, wanting to change *everything!* wanting now to do away or regulate by authority the Officer's
Mess!! Of Garnet Wolseley supporting the Duke on the
point! Of how utterly false Childers is, how he lies!" Lady
Geraldine even went so far as to attribute the "blackguard
articles in the radical papers" to the pen of the Secretary
for War. The Duke told the Prince of Wales that Childers,
far more than Wolseley, was his great enemy. Writing to the
Queen in 1886, H.R.H. told her that "Mr. Childers was not
'persona grata' at the Horse Guards, as you well know, and
I think was more imbued with his own interests and vanity,
than the good of the Army. I doubt not he meant well, but he
was not a success."[n]

The Duke, who still continued to date his correspondence from the Horse Guards, was greatly disturbed to receive a letter from the Secretary for War suggesting the
time had come to cease doing so. The Commander-in-Chief
wrote in great agitation from Kissingen, where he was
drinking the waters to alleviate gout. He declared that
great issues were at stake. "We have had so many changes
of late, and the old landmarks have been so largely swept
away, that it is most undesirable to make any more, and
believe me that old traditions in army matters are of the
greatest value to the Service generally, and consequently
to the State."[n]

Childers maintained, even more vigorously than Cardwell
had done, that the Commander-in-Chief was the servant,
not master of the Secretary of State for War. Talking to
Dilke, he "broke out against the Duke of Cambridge who

'went chattering about the place, refused to behave as a subordinate, and wrote direct to the Queen.' "" This implied a very exalted definition of the Minister's prerogatives, and certainly if the Duke was sometimes known to err on the side of extravagant claims, Childers was not to be outbid. It required an almost insane confidence in his own importance to suggest that the Duke might only address his cousin on military matters after having first sought the Minister's permission. In a speech delivered at Pontefract on January 19, 1882, the Secretary for War harangued his audience on the need for subordinating the services entirely to Parliament. He attacked those who imagined that the Army was the Queen's. Soldiers were not "soldiers of the Queen"; they were members of an Army of the House of Commons. The Queen could do no wrong only because her acts were those of her responsible Ministers. "No act of discipline can be exercised, no appointment or promotion can be made, no troops can be moved, no payments can be made, without the approval, expressed or implied, of the Secretary of State.""

During the two years in which Childers was at the War Office the Duke had constant occasion to write to the Queen—without permission. The Queen, so the Duke told Lady Geraldine on March 16, 1881, "was *very* kind and gracious, very nice to him, declared staunchly she would '*never*' allow the office of Commander-in-Chief to be done away with, 'she would *never stand that!*' Alas! the Queen's 'nevers' and 'not standing' seldom last a day!!!"

In July 1881 the Commander-in-Chief was provoked to such desperation that he sent in his resignation. It had been an exceedingly hot summer, and some men had died of sunstroke at a field day at Aldershot. Childers wrote H.R.H. a letter which the Duke regarded as a censure upon himself. Consequently on July 16 he sent a message to the Queen to say he intended resigning. "I was greatly astonished," wrote the Queen in her diary, "and said censure of George had never been implied, but only a record to be kept, that field days, should in future not be held in the middle of the day. The letter had been couched in most civil terms." To the family circle at St.James's Palace, the story assumed a different significance. "Then the Duke," wrote Lady Geraldine on July 17, "gave H.R.H. [his mother] detailed accounts of his 'passage of arms' with the Queen! who has been behaving very *badly* to him about those deaths from sunstroke at the Aldershot Field Day. Childers decided to write the Duke a most *offensive* letter, as he *alleged* by desire of the Queen! imputing the *blame* to him. The Duke did not really believe he had her sanction! Certainly could not accept such a letter and absolutely refused to admit that *anyone* was to blame! and sent Ellice and Whitmore to Windsor to Ponsonby, to enquire whether the letter had the Queen's sanction, and to say, if so as the Duke could not accept such a letter, he had but one course to pursue: to send in his resignation! It appears that the Queen *had* seen the letter! . . . but 'did not read it, at all as the Duke did, as imputing blame to him'! Some shifty doubtful excuses, but the fact remained, the Queen *had* sanctioned a letter being written to him. On their return with this information, the Duke sat down and wrote to the Queen, sending her his resignation! 'No longer enjoying her confidence and support he could no longer hold the command he for many years had had' etc.!! This he sent her. Shortly after, before she could have received this, crossing with it, he got by messenger, a most amiable letter from her!! full of apologetic excuses! that she had never understood this so, never meant it, etc., etc.!!! and begging he would think no more of it! He had to write again, thanking her, accepting the apologies, which therefore rendered his other letter and resignation nugatory, but saying that as this letter of Childers to him of course remains on record, he thought at least the Queen ought to have it nullified."

The appointment in 1881 of Wolseley as Adjutant General led the Duke to threaten resignation for the second time in the year. The Adjutant General's office was one which necessitated constant co-operation with the Commander-in-

Chief and, moreover, provided its holder with dangerous opportunities for introducing changes. The Liberal Government wished to appoint Wolseley so that he would be in an effective position to resist the Duke's rear-guard action against reforms. It was in vain that H.R.H. protested that the new Adjutant General would disrupt the harmony of the Horse Guards: that was precisely the Prime Minister's intention.

In the very year in which Wolseley's appointment was being angrily contested between the Duke and Childers, Sir Garnet aggravated the hostility of the Horse Guards by his complicity in various critical articles published in 1881 which condemned traditional Army arrangements and advocated the very changes which Wolseley and his friends were known to desire.

The Duke of Cambridge had suffered too much from newspapers to regard them with favour, and as Sir Charles Phipps once told the Prince Consort, "fear of the press" was "inherent" in him." The Duke of Wellington had always suspected officers who wrote for the papers, a practice he described as "croaking," and indeed he forbade officers to write for publication. Not only did he regard the habit as subversive of discipline, but he attributed to it much of the ignorant but dangerous criticism which the Army constantly encountered. "As soon as an accident happens," Wellington declared, "every man who can write, and who has a friend who can read, sits down to write his account of what he does not know, and his comments on what he does not understand, and these are diligently circulated and exaggerated by the idle and malicious, of whom there are plenty in all armies. The consequence is that officers and whole regiments lose their reputation and a spirit of party, which is the bane of all armies, is engendered and fomented."

Wolseley's opponents were inclined to blame him for attacks in the press which, although expressing his views, did not actually proceed from his pen. But he was guilty of writing many provocative articles and of delivering speeches peppered with rash indiscretions. The newspapers, for which Sir Garnet provided an unending supply of copy, were always eager to publish his articles or those of his friends. Wolseley's set, the Garnet Ring, in 1879 was given a new nickname. "The Duke," wrote Lady Geraldine on October 13, "told us of a capital new name they have got now—besides the old original 'mutual admiration society'! which is so good! They call them now: 'the press gang'! That is excellent." At the first night of *The Pirates of Penzance,* it did not need George Grossmith's admirable make-up to enable the audience to discover who was "the very model of a modern Major General." Indeed, the phrase "All Sir Garnet" was the Victorian way of saying "all correct."

The Duke was naturally wounded by some of the things said about him in the newspapers, and mischief-makers were quick to allege that Wolseley was their author or inspirer. Major George FitzGeorge suggested to Wolseley that it might be advisable for him to clear up growing misunderstandings, and taking the hint, Sir Garnet sought an interview with the Commander-in-Chief. "Had a long interview with Wolseley," wrote the Duke on November 26, "who gave explanations and assurances that recent attacks were neither directly nor indirectly inspired by himself, nor did they come from him. Certainly these assurances were remarkably decided, and appeared frank."

The Duke told the Queen that he had seen Wolseley. "Saw George C.," she wrote on December 4, "who was quite quiet and thanked me for my assistance, regretting all the trouble I had had. He hoped things would go on better now, and with right, blamed Mr. Childers very much, spoke of the shameful atrocious articles in *The Times,* which no one knows who they were written by. George is convinced that they were inspired by the War Office. Sir G. Wolseley he now exonerates, after having talked with him, and he hopes he will behave well . . . Mr. Childers has written to me, to the effect, that Sir G. Wolseley will abstain from writing and speaking on military matters whilst he is in his present position." Lady Geraldine was not quite as prepared as the Duke to accept Wolseley's assurances. On November 29 she wrote: "The Duke told us how well satisfied he is, he has had his explanation from Wolseley and how great the mistake was Wolseley did not speak openly to him before! With his *marvellous* power of forgiveness and real utter forgetfulness of injury, that fine and rare quality of his, ready to *forget* all injury done to him at the first word of apology! And from his own truth and loyalty his ready belief in that of others, he is now 'perfectly satisfied' that Wolseley had nothing to do with those articles! and convinced now they have honestly spoken together, he and Wolseley will get on capitally! Altogether he is much happier, quite happy now! and altogether another man from that he was last week!!" A few years later, Lady Geraldine came to the conclusion that Childers rather than Wolseley instigated the press attacks. The Queen, she wrote on December 14, 1884, has "fully found out how Childers *lies!* which the poor Duke had such sore reason to discover while he was at the War Office, where he always affected to be *so put out* at the abominable newspaper articles which without doubt, emanated from himself!"

Wolseley gave Colonel FitzGeorge an account of his interview with H.R.H. "I had a satisfactory interview with His Royal Highness, and was very glad I acted upon your advice. I tried to impress upon him how impossible it would have been for me in the position which I occupied to have seen him earlier on the subject of the newspaper articles that had given him pain. In the first instance it was some time before I knew that I had been put down as the author or inspirer of the articles, and when I was told it by Mr. Childers I said to him frankly that I felt it insulting to me to imagine I had anything to do with them. I think it is rather hard that I should be set down as the author or inspirer of everything that appears in the Press against the administration of the Army. But let that pass; I urged as strongly as I could that in my opinion it would have been most indelicate of me to have seen the Duke about articles discussing me as Adjutant General: it would have looked as if I wished to ask for the berth, or to force myself upon His Royal Highness. I had never asked any one for it: if I had asked any one for it I should have gone straight to the Duke, although I should have felt, of course, that he would not have given it to me."ⁿ

Lord Napier was disposed to blame Childers for this epidemic of press criticism. "Mr. Childers," he wrote from Gibraltar, "behaves shamefully in permitting such breaches of official confidence, but the same action has characterized the proceedings of the leaders of that party." Some of the articles had been so well informed that it was presumed that they were written with knowledge derived from official sources. "I hope," Napier continued, "the Duke will not pay attention to these malignant and base attacks, but will hold his own, and if Wolseley is forced upon him, will keep him in order." "I was very glad," he wrote a few months later, "to see the *St. James' Gazette* and the *Army and Navy* reply to *The Times.* Mr. Childers must see the false ground he was getting on and that these shameful and false attacks on the Duke make H.R.H.'s position much stronger. I cannot believe that the Country will allow a clique to worry out a Commander-in-Chief who possesses the confidence of the army in his justice and knowledge of the Service."ⁿ

The efforts of the radical press to force the Duke to resign encouraged many generals, and even a former War Minister, to express their confidence in H.R.H., and their hope that he would not yield to such pressure. "Though I have felt much sympathy," wrote Lord Cranbrook, "with your Royal Highness under the mean and malignant attack to which you have been subjected I have hesitated to write in case I might seem to be meddling in matters which no longer concern me. I cannot however recall the frank and cordial relations with you which made my tenure of the War Office so pleasant to myself without expressing my sense of the injustice which is done to you by an anonymous press, under which personal enmity conceals itself. The fact that Your Royal Highness' position precludes you from replying makes the false insinuations the more cruel. I have reason to know the want of truth in the suggestion made that you have impeded the progress of changes which the Secretary of State had decided upon. Your opinion, as was your duty, you freely gave but never failed to act upon decisions even though averse to them. I cannot say that I am surprised, though shocked, at the subtle attempts to disparage you."

General Steele, in command at Dublin, wrote assuring the Duke of the confidence of the army. "I cannot resist," he declared, "writing a line to Your Royal Highness on the subject of those vile articles in *The Times,* evidently the production of Brackenbury dictated by Wolseley. I look with perfect dismay on the future; but I trust Your Royal Highness will not give way and entertain for one minute the idea of resigning the position of Commander-in-Chief. You may take my word that not only the older officers, but the young ones also look with dread at the prospect of the army passing into the hands of that self glorifying clique. The subject is freely discussed over here and I hear but one opinion. The intention of forcing you to resign is so obvious that I am sure Your Royal Highness will forgive me for writing so plainly and assuring you of the confidence that the large majority of the army feel towards you.""

Wolseley, even after his appointment as Adjutant General, and despite the fact that he held an official position, continued to write and speak as if independent. It would be difficult to deduce from his recorded utterances that he was himself one of the foremost figures in the military hierarchy. In 1887, the year of the Queen's Jubilee, Wolseley made a number of speeches in which he arrogantly claimed that he had reorganized the Army and rid it of inefficiency. The Duke was furious. Lady Geraldine on April 24 recounted a conversation in which "we talked of the *impertinence* of

Wolseley not attending the banquet last night! because he preferred to go to a *press* dinner, to fawn upon and be fawned upon by the press!! He had much better have let it alone, for as usual and invariably he made a most egotistic speech, glorifying himself and offending everyone else! taking great merit to himself for having at last succeeded in getting rid of the *theatrical* side of the British Army!!!!! and in reducing our curiously constituted Army to a real fighting organization!!!! Such insolence! *Always* that insolent tone as though the Army had never done anything, never been heard of, never existed until under, by, and through *him!* Such arrogance! How marvellous a thing it is, he *never can* make a speech without offending someone! He is no gentleman, it is all summed up in the fact that he is a regular thorough *Irishman,* that most detestable and intolerable of all God's creations."

The next day Lady Geraldine asked the Duke "whether he had brought Wolseley to book! as to the meaning of his impertinence about his 'having got rid of the theatrical side of the British Army'? He had, and the fellow explained he meant as to uniforms! Was there ever anything so ridiculous as a cocked hat? Fancy a cocked hat in a campaign!! to be buttoned and hooked up to the chin!!! The Duke answered he had worn a cocked hat all through the Crimea and had thought it a very comfortable headdress! And as for being buttoned up, he supposed he preferred to see the dirty shirts of the men!! remarking also that nothing can be more buttoned up and stiffer than the Prussian Army, supposed to be *the* great military model! to which Wolseley answered 'Oh! the Prussians? Theirs is *the most* theatrical Army in Europe!' The Duke then asked him *what* Army then he deigned to approve? The fellow then said, in every way the most admirable and praiseworthy and sensibly dressed Army *he* had ever seen was the *American!!!!* After *that,* there was no more to say! A filthy Republican rabble! Wolseley went to the room of one of the others and affected great inno-

cence, asking 'What did I say? I really don't know! Give
me a paper that I may see! I am such a fool I always say
something that is taken ill'!! A regular odious Irishman."

On May 4, less than a fortnight later, Wolseley again
"rejoiced us with one of his delectable speeches! at some
function in the City; he told General Harman à propos of
his Press Association speech, that he was so *annoyed* he
had most particularly begged there might be no reporters
present! on which the Duke very pertinently remarked *he*
was not in the habit of begging his speeches not to be reported as himself he had no intention of saying anything he
saw reason to be ashamed of!!" Later in the year Wolseley
referred contemptuously to barrack-square drill as the end-
all and be-all of military training. The Duke protested that
the Adjutant General had no right to make such criticisms
in public speeches. Sir Garnet, evading the question of his
right to denounce the policy of the Commander-in-Chief, replied: "I have been always in touch with the officers who
advocate progress and who attach the greatest importance
to military training, that is, to the highest form of drill. These
men think our military training is too much sacrificed to
show parade movements, and that the soldier can be better
disciplined both in body and mind by being taught the duties
and evolutions he *must* practise before an enemy, than by
parade movements only possible in peace."

The Duke was not to be diverted from the issue of Wolseley's indiscretion by discussing the rights and wrongs of
what he had said. "With reference to the letter I have just
received from you, and in which you say that you, in the
main, agree with me, though you adhere to your views, I
really don't think there can be much, if any, difference at
all between us, as the more that drill is adapted daily to the
details of intended movements, the more I shall be pleased
. . . I am at all times most willing to attend to any suggestions or recommendations . . . to make training or equipment in any way more adapted to modern requirements.
What I really do object to is that in public addresses made

from time to time, very disparaging expressions occur of our old system as compared with what you would wish to have done . . . I am sure that you will feel with me, that the Adjutant General of the Army when writing in public periodicals on military subjects, carries great weight in his utterances, and that it is not desirable that in that capacity he should express himself on controversial matters, which are sure to elicit comment of various kinds . . . It is undesirable for officers of the Army on full pay to express their opinions in any other way than by the legitimate channels of communication to the Commander-in-Chief."[a]

The Duke opposed Wolseley's appointment to the post of Adjutant General on two grounds. First, he believed Wolseley's military views to be too revolutionary; and second, he maintained that Wolseley was incapable of discretion and would prove an intolerable colleague. It was for these reasons that H.R.H. refused to recommend Wolseley to the Queen. He explained his position in a letter to Lord Hartington, for a time the Liberal most trusted by the Royal family. "Writing to Mr. Childers, with whom I have always been on the best and most cordial terms, I happened to tell him that I could not think of Sir G. W. as the future A.G. because whilst being on perfectly friendly terms with Wolseley, he belonged to the new school which I did not. At this expression Childers seems to have taken alarm and to have supposed that I meant to imply that I wished the new A.G. to work under me, in a direction entirely opposed to the present system. Such an idea did not cross my mind but what I intended to convey was that whilst Wolseley and I are on perfectly good terms as between man and man, his views and mine on almost every subject are so divergent, that in that special position in which he virtually is my 'alter ego,' I could never feel that confidence in him, which it is *essential* in the interests of the Public Service as well as to my own comfort and even usefulness as a public officer, should exist between the C. in C. and his right hand man the A.G. But in saying this I did not intend to convey the idea that I wanted to create opposition to the present order of things. I have, much against my personal feelings, accepted them and having done so I should fail in my duty were I not to try to carry them out, but I must be allowed to do so through men in whom the Army and myself more particularly have real confidence, and not through the man who has never failed to take every opportunity of insulting the Army, and speaking and writing in a sense which he must have known must be distasteful to the present head of his profession, whom I consider he is bound loyally to serve and not to oppose." The Duke continued that it would not help, as suggested by the Queen, to make Roberts Quartermaster General, "because the Q.M.G. is entirely subordinate to the A.G. I cannot start with an A.G. *against* whom I am *guarding* myself in all directions. I must trust him for *himself.*"[n]

In his official letters the Duke exercised some restraint in his criticism of Wolseley, but in his conversations with his mother he spoke of him as a "firebrand," as "underhand, untrue, false, disloyal, overbearing and bumptious to a degree! Self-opinionated and riding all rough shod." He complained of "the serious harm and hurt he does the Army with his theories and innovations and favouritism."[n] Wolseley, who was only five foot seven inches, had some of the urge to assert himself that Napoleon had: a comparison he would not have considered far fetched. Beside the Duke, an impressive mass of a man, he certainly looked, and possibly felt, very small. Unconsciously he cast himself in the role of David defying Goliath.

Childers told the Duke bluntly that the new system in the Army could only be made to work successfully if administered by those who looked upon it favourably, and although the Commander-in-Chief always loyally endeavoured to implement decisions to which he was opposed, it was essential to have some senior officers who looked upon reforms with enthusiasm. "Your Royal Highness referring to Sir Garnet Wolseley, says that while personally you and he are perfect good friends, professionally you are as far as possible divergent; You, Sir, having been consistent in your Military opinions, whereas he belongs to a new school; and it is on this latter ground, and not because of any personal objection, that you would not wish to see him appointed Adjutant General. . . . Since 1869–70, new principles in military administration have been introduced and are now fully established. They have no connection with party politics, for they have been accepted as fully by the Conservative party during their six years of office from 1874 to 1880, as by Mr. Cardwell who introduced them, and by myself who have completed them. . . . Now, Sir, I must remind you that to all these changes Your Royal Highness is and has been (to use the word in your letter to me) consistently opposed . . . And, Sir, you will forgive my saying that your opinions are well known to the Army, and that officers cannot but hope to find favour with you by advocating as many do, disapproval of the policy of 1869 to 1881. That Your Royal Highness, as head of the Military Department is perfectly loyal, and that you give a cordial support to the Secretary of State I should be the first to proclaim. But now that the policy which you, Sir, have consistently opposed has become the established policy of the country, I think the time has come when the Secretary of State is entitled and bound to take care that among those who have to give effect to it, the principal officers under Your Royal Highness should be identified with it in sentiment; and especially that the Adjutant General should be an officer known to the Army to be of the new, and not of the old, school. . . . It is impossible that any policy can be worked heartily and 'with a will,' unless a fair proportion of those who administer it look upon it favourably and even cordially."[n]

At a meeting at the War Office on October 10 to which H.R.H. had been summoned from a tour of inspection at Plymouth, the Secretary for War attempted in vain to persuade the Duke to recommend Wolseley's appointment. "I firmly refused to consent to such an arrangement, much to his vexation I could observe." That deadlock had been reached soon became known. The *Court Journal* of November 19 announced: "The most straitened relationship exists between Mr. Childers and the Duke of Cambridge. The former knows absolutely less than nothing about Military administration and organization; while as every soldier will testify, the Commander-in-Chief knows not only every move but almost every individual officer . . . It is now a combat between ignorance, as represented by Mr. Childers, and knowledge, as represented by the Duke."

An appeal to the Queen was the next inevitable move in the struggle, and the Duke decided, in his dealings both with his cousin and with the Secretary for War, to throw the threat of resignation into the scale. The Queen originally took the line that the appointment was out of the question. "Saw Sir H. Ponsonby," she wrote in her diary on September 16, "about a letter George had had, from Mr. Childers, about the Adjutant General, which annoys him very much. Mr. Childers wants Sir G. Wolseley, which is impossible, and which would cause George to resign." However, when it became evident that the Government was determined to appoint Wolseley, and was not to be browbeaten by missives from Balmoral, the Queen began to advocate compromise. As Lady Geraldine complained: "Alas! the Queen's 'nevers' seldom last a day!"

On October 17 the Duke sent the Queen a copy of a letter he had received the day before from Childers. "I cannot tell you how it has distressed me, for it places me in a most difficult position, for either I shall be compelled to accept as Adj. General an officer in whom I never can feel the slightest real confidence and sympathy, or it obliges me to ask you to consider whether the time has not come when as an honourable man, I cannot any longer continue to hold the office I have endeavoured to fill to the best of my ability in the interests of the Sovereign and of the Army . . . You know that I frequently of late have accepted changes which I have not and could not approve of. I have done so in the interests of the Crown and of the army, as I thought my retirement might lead to complications and difficulties of a very grave character. But there is a limit beyond which I could go not, and that limit as it appears to me, has by the present action been attained . . ."[n]

Lady Geraldine described in her diary the Duke's reception of the letter from Childers which provoked this threat of resignation. "The Duke told us!! he has a letter from that *brute* Childers!! . . . coolly telling him: Garnet Wolseley is to be Adjutant General! and he has submitted the appointment to the Queen!!! It is *the most outrageous insolence ever perpetrated!!!* And in every way *too abominable!* Nasty brute of a fellow. And what a humbugging lying brute! A *'radical'* through and through, with all that is disgusting, hateful, contemptible, despicable, dishonourable, in those of that party."

Sir William Harcourt was staying at Balmoral when the Duke's threat of resignation arrived, and he wrote to Gladstone describing the consternation it caused. The Queen apparently had approached Harcourt hoping to obtain his advice, but he was forced to tell her that "it was impossible for one Secretary of State to invade or intermeddle with the affairs of a department of a colleague." Harcourt attributed the Duke's hostility to "strong personal antipathy . . . The question as I understand it is really one of 'incompatibility,' which between husband and wife is often regarded as a good ground of amiable separation. It seems almost idle to hope that the Duke and Sir Garnet can live conjugally together." Harcourt went on to say: "I have not ventured myself to offer any suggestion, but I have endeavoured to lay before you the situation as it is. It is very like the dramatic position in *The Critic* when all the parties are at a deadlock each with his dagger at the other's throat, and how it is to be terminated is not obvious. I fear not by the formula, 'In the Queen's name I bid you all drop your swords and daggers.' The only thing I feel strongly is that the resignation of the Duke should if possible be averted. The

Queen evidently looks to you to help her out of the scrape, of the gravity of which I think she is entirely aware . . ."[n]

The Queen, recognizing that the Government would never retract, and anxious to avoid the Duke's resignation, tried personally to persuade him to accept Wolseley as Adjutant General, arguing that H.R.H. would be in a better position to control him if he were made an official subordinate. "The Queen has so much to do this morning," wrote Ponsonby on her behalf, "that Her Majesty has scarcely time to write fully to Your Royal Highness and has commanded me to do so. The Queen fears that Mr. Childers thinks the success of his Army Reforms depends on the Assistance of Sir Garnet Wolseley. She believes that he fully appreciates the loyal support he has received from Your Royal Highness but that he considers Sir Garnet's aid at present almost a part of the new scheme which Your Royal Highness has undertaken to support. Her Majesty quite agrees with Your Royal Highness but thinks it would be impolitic to raise a serious controversy on this question and having given her approval to the *trial* of the new Army plan the Queen feels obliged and bound to give it every chance of success. Sir Garnet Wolseley seems just now to be a sort of half irresponsible adviser to the Secretary of State. Would it not be better that he should hold the really responsible position under Your Royal Highness? The Queen understands that this is the opinion of many distinguished officers, who while disliking the new reforms and heartily supporting Your Royal Highness' position, point out that to object to Mr. Childers' wish to have Sir Garnet as Adjutant General would expose Your Royal Highness to all the attacks of those who declare that the shortcomings of the new plan are due to the attitude taken by the Commander-in-Chief. The Queen asks if Your Royal Highness would not think it preferable to send for Sir Garnet Wolseley, to tell him frankly the reasons which have made Your Royal Highness object to his appointment and then to come to an understanding with him for the harmonious conduct of the business of the office, insisting on pledges being given that no communication with the Press or Parliament should ever take place. The Queen merely mentioned this in case Your Royal Highness should find no other solution possible."

The Commander-in-Chief received this letter while staying with the Prince of Wales at Sandringham. The Prince was strongly in favour of his "Uncle George" resisting the Queen's attempted compromise, and doubtless the letter the Duke sent to Balmoral was influenced by his host's views. "My dear Cousin," he wrote, "I received here yesterday morning a letter from Sir Henry Ponsonby, written by your direction, which has given me much pain and distress, in as much as it seems to me to modify very considerably the views you so graciously expressed to me in your last letter. From that I was under the impression that you would continue to back up my strong conviction, on public grounds, against the appointment of Sir Garnet Wolseley as Adjutant General. Sir H. Ponsonby's letter on the other hand makes me fear that I am in error in this respect and that you think it undesirable that any further opposition to the appointment should now be made. If I were in doubt as regards the importance of the step about to be taken by the Government as regards this matter, any misapprehension has been entirely cleared up by an article in this day's *Times*, which virtually, and no doubt by inspiration from high quarters, actually announces the decision come to by the Government, and that moreover in terms *most offensive* to the high office with which you have entrusted me, and which I have now filled for so many years. The Adjutant General in this article is pointed out to be the officer who is expected to give advice and carry out the orders and directions of the Secretary of State; and the Commander-in-Chief's functions are entirely ignored or set on one side. Indeed all the attributes now belonging to my office are specified and layed down in detail as belonging to the position of the Adjutant General, and it is further asserted that the Adjutant General is the Queen's Adjutant General, and that the Commander-in-Chief's position is one of much more recent date. This may be the case, but certainly not in the spirit and sense in which the relative positions of those two officers have stood towards one another as long as the present generation can remember. Such being the view now put forward in so clear and decided a manner, I hope you will permit me to put before you how *impossible* my position must become if I accept such conditions. I could not serve you, or do my duty by the Army or the Country if I am not a *free agent* in the first place, and if I am not to retain in *fact* as well as in name the powers hitherto entrusted to me. If it can be pointed out in any way that I have failed in my duty, I hope no hesitation would prevent such a statement being put forward. But suddenly to be placed in an inferior and degraded position would be unbearable to myself, and would I feel sure be unacceptable to you. I shall probably be told by the Government, represented by the Secretary of State, that he is not responsible for the article in *The Times*. This technically is most likely the case, but nobody will ever persuade me that what is stated in that *Times* article is not inspired by somebody in authority, whoever that somebody may be."

Ponsonby had said that H.R.H. had not made any "positive charge" against Wolseley. "I only declined," explained the Duke, "to do so in writing. I considered, as I still do, that the appointment rests between the Secretary of State and myself before submission to you, and *not* with Her Majesty's Government, such being a purely *Military* and *not* political appointment. To you I am only too happy to state my objections. I consider in the first place that Sir Garnet is *not* the officer I deem at present best qualified for the Post, or as having the strongest claims to it . . . In the next place I think the Army wants *rest*. Such great changes have been introduced, that time should be given to allow matters to settle down. Sir Garnet Wolseley's great object seems to be to go further and further, and to upset the little that is left of the old spirit of the officer by indiscriminate selection, by carrying education to the extremist limit, by letting men go to the Reserve after three years service, and in a variety of ways intensifying the sweeping changes that have already been effected. Thirdly I think the mode of his introduction into the office of Adjutant General would be a direct slur and imputation upon me, and on the manner in which I have performed my departmental duty as military adviser of the Secretary of State and as such a serious insult would be offered to me in my official position. Lastly Sir Garnet's close connection with the Press, and his strong expressions on Military matters in speeches and writings . . . would prove most detrimental to the interests of the Army, and would certainly turn military matters into subjects for political discussions, which in my opinion, should on all accounts be avoided when military questions are involved . . . I fear there is now no alternative left to me but to withdraw from a position which has become unbearable, certainly not by my seeking, but by the extraordinary manner in which a particular officer has been forced upon me for the post of all others which requires mutual confidence and sympathy.""

Sir Francis Knollys, the Prince of Wales's Secretary, told the Duke: "If your Royal Highness wishes to ensure real assistance from Balmoral, I venture to express an opinion that you must continue to show them a firm front and an earnest determination to resign." When it became known that Wolseley's appointment was inevitable, the Prince himself recommended to the Duke that he withdraw from his command. "Now," the Prince wrote, "that it seems inevitable that Wolseley is to be Adjutant General you will have to decide as to whether after all you have said—it is compatible with your dignity to retain the position as Commander-in-Chief. Deeply as I would regret your resignation for the sake of the Queen, for all of us her children, for the Army and for the Country, it would be far better for you to do that than become a cypher and the mere tool and subordinate of Messrs Childers and Wolseley—besides what would your position be with the Army? When officers come to your levees, to your office and write to you to ask you to do this and that, what answer can you give them? Simply that you must refer the matter to Mr. Childers. By your remaining you play into the hands of those who have made your position virtually untenable—by resigning you will always be a thorn in their side—but what is far more important—you will be able to benefit the Army to which you are so devoted and for whom you have worked for upwards of twenty-seven years as their Commander-in-Chief, far more—when your hands are unfettered—in your place in the House of Lords and on many other public occasions you will be able to speak your mind out—and point out the utter fallacy of this new army organization—and prove to them why you could not hold your present post any longer . . . After long and mature consideration the conclusion that I have come to is to offer this advice, in which all those who esteem and love you will I am sure concur—and if I have spoken plainly you will I am sure forgive your very affectionate nephew and cousin, Albert Edward.'"

When it became evident at Balmoral that somebody was urging the Commander-in-Chief to resign, the Queen was horrified to discover it was her own son. Ponsonby, writing to the Duke on December 2, mentioned that "the Queen asked me who could possibly advise your Royal Highness to resign as it would be such a serious mistake to do so, and she went on to say she was sure the Prince of Wales had strongly urged you to maintain your position. Her Majesty stopped and asked me if this was not so. Of course I had to tell the Queen that I believed His Royal Highness took the very opposite view of the question. But I said nothing more as to where I derived this information."

In the end, Wolseley became Adjutant General and the Duke was prevailed upon to give up all thought of resigning. To save his face, he was not required to recommend Sir Garnet to the Queen, but merely offered no objection to the appointment. The announcement, on H.R.H.'s insistence, was so worded as to emphasize the subordinate position of Wolseley to the Commander-in-Chief. Although in the years ahead there were to be many disputes between the Duke and his Adjutant General, H.R.H soon came to appreciate Sir Garnet's ability as an administrator, and both men at least shared a common distrust of political interference in the Army.

"The Duke told us," wrote Lady Geraldine on July 16, 1882, "that it has turned out fortunate at this moment that he has Sir Garnet Wolseley as Adjutant General instead of Sir Charles Ellice! First he is much more hard working than him, or Horsford, and being on his mettle to make his famous *system* answer, he is determined it *shall* answer if he can make it, and works tooth and nail for that object; and above all! that he being here, no one can pretend it is not effectually worked and fails for want of being properly and fairly carried out. The Duke says of him he is decidedly clear headed and an able administrator; and that what is very amusing is that these fellows have themselves given themselves their *master* in him!!! He *wanted* the Duke to refuse all conference with the Cabinet Ministers and organize alone!! Which *unfortunately* is impossible."

The Duke and Wolseley

O F ALL Liberal measures to reform the Army, Childers was responsible for the most unpopular: the Territorial System. The idea was first proposed in 1877 by a committee under Stanley which recommended, among other proposals, establishing territorial regiments that would combine regular soldiers with the Militia. The proposal was rejected by Disraeli, and the mere suggestion of it alarmed the Queen, who feared it would threaten regimental *esprit de corps*. The Duke told her: "I have no hesitation in saying, that anything more distasteful to me than the recommendations of the recent Committee with reference to the Territorial Regiments I cannot conceive. The whole of my evidence before that Committee was against that one particular change." In a speech delivered in 1878 he declared that "the Army of England could not be localized. I have ventured to point out the variety of service for which our Army is called upon. We may look upon ourselves as an Army in a mobilized state, and if it is mobilized, you cannot make it a local Army. The Militia and Volunteers are essential for local service, whereas the Army of England can never be local beyond its depots, for I think it a pity to attempt to imitate foreign armies because our conditions of service abroad are necessarily different from those of any other country."[n]

Childers, however, was determined to pursue the matter, and set up a committee in 1880 to examine how best to implement Stanley's proposals. A plan was suggested, but the Committee's chairman, Sir Charles Ellice, warned the Secretary for War that "they could not conceal from themselves that the fusing together of so many Regiments hitherto separate, and the consequent alteration of titles and abolition of numbers surrounded with associations, will inflict a shock on the feelings of officers and men of those battalions which will thus lose their cherished designations." Undeterred by this warning, Childers decided upon making the change.

The Duke, unable to persuade the Secretary for War that the plan was disastrous, wrote first to Ponsonby and then to the Queen. "My province," he told Ponsonby, "will be to carry out this plan to the best of my ability. But anything more distasteful or detrimental to the *esprit de corps,* and therefore the best interests of the service, I cannot imagine. . . . That the Army should be thoroughly disgusted by such a condition of affairs, which is now to be perpetuated by the proposed order of things, is not to be wondered at. I, alas! can only *warn,* and I do so, I fear, even at the risk of appearing obstructive, but *I am not so,* and I am only doing my duty as entrusted by the Queen with the chief command of the Army." Hearing that Childers was going to Osborne two days after Christmas, he wrote to the Queen, hoping she might "have an opportunity of preventing the mischief that must result from Territorial Regiments, with the entire destruction of *esprit de corps.* These are no days to play tricks with the Army . . . I hope, therefore you will see Your way to making some stand upon the old Regimental system of our glorious Army. It has stood many shocks, and has done its duty nobly by the Crown and by the Country. It is worth saving. However, You are so well-informed upon all these matters, that I need not remind You of them. All I can say is, that nothing can be worse than the present prospect, and the new proposals are to my mind, as regards Territorial Regiments, graver than anything that has yet been done or suggested . . . and will be most unpalatable to the Army as a whole.'" This plea represented

H.R.H.'s second attempt to enlist the Queen's support. Earlier in the month, on December 7, he had asked for an interview. "Saw George C.," wrote the Queen in her diary, "who was in a great and frantic state, about the proposals for the Army and the linking of battalions . . . I tried to reassure and quiet him."

Neither the Queen nor the Duke could prevent the introduction of the Territorial System, but, as Ellice had prophesied, it was bitterly resented by the Army. Napier wrote to H.R.H. saying that he fully appreciated "the trial that Your Royal Highness has under the present administration. The evil advice of interested soldiers misleads men at the head of affairs, whose object is to please the people with a show of economy."[n]

In 1882 the Liberal Government found itself committed to war in Egypt, to avenge the massacre of Christians in Alexandria and to protect the Suez Canal. When the Cabinet finally decided upon intervention, it reached two characteristic decisions: to appoint Wolseley to command the expedition, and to authorize a wholly inadequate force with which to conduct the campaign. The Duke and the Adjutant General both agreed on the need to send more troops than was first envisaged, and H.R.H. persuaded Childers, for once successfully, that unless 15,000 men were dispatched, it would be "most hazardous," and "quite unjustifiable by all the rules of war." He discussed, on August 19 at St. James's, "the utter folly and madness of this absurd carrying on War on a Peace establishment!" He talked of "Childers always declaring his famous organization failed because the last Government did not carry it out fully and now *he* does exactly the same, only under infinitely *worse* conditions! as they were at peace whereas now they have a great war actually on their hands of which *no one* can foretell the dimensions it will assume! Idiocy!! and all this penny wise and pound foolish only to ask a vote of credit one *half* of that they ought to have asked and to say to the Duke of Cambridge see how economical we are! At what risk? at what cost?? Of how the *next* measure of these *vile* fellows will be to do away with the red uniform!! then the last vestige of the old army is gone!! that army that conquered the world in red! the *poor* Duke! it is heart breaking work, struggling with these brutes inch by inch! fighting bravely against their destruction of *everything!*"

On September 13, Wolseley won the battle of Tel-el-Kebir, and as a result Egypt came under British control. "The Duke," wrote Lady Geraldine the day after the battle, "is not only immensely pleased with the whole thing, but with Wolseley's management of it all, his disposition, and use of his troops." Colonel George FitzGeorge, on his return from the campaign, visited the Duchess on October 5. "He gave *high* praise to Wolseley! The confidence he inspires, his cheeriness and good humour, thought for others." The Duke was delighted with Wolseley's present to him of three rifles found in Arabi's bedroom, and for a short time the Adjutant General was almost forgiven his faults and shortcomings. Moreover, not only had he sent Colonel George home with the dispatches announcing the victory of Tel-el-Kebir, but he had telegraphed for Augustus FitzGeorge to join him in Egypt. H.R.H. was not to know with what reluctance Sir Garnet had acted. "In his last letter the Duke of Cambridge said that his son Augustus was now quite well and anxious to come out; what could I do but telegraph for him? This is very unfair upon me . . . Perhaps old mother FitzGeorge would like to come also?"[n]

A great parade was held to celebrate the triumphant return of the troops from Egypt. The Duke told his mother and Lady Geraldine about the ill-feeling caused by the Queen's arrangements for the review. "Spoke of the Review on Saturday, and the successful efforts of the Queen to make it as unpleasant and inconvenient for everybody as possible! and to prevent anyone but herself seeing anything! long discussion as to how on earth to manage that the family should be enabled in some degree to see! the Duke and the

Prince alone to be allowed to be on horseback by her carriage. Of the Princess Royal coming all the way from Berlin for it, and seeing nothing!" The quarrels which began some time before the parade broke out again on the day itself. Childers was "much affronted at not having had a place in the cortège!! the pretension!!! Probably he thinks he ought to have been on horseback at the door of the Queen's carriage instead of the Duke!!! He takes it very ill."" The Princess Royal cried throughout the proceedings and the Duke of Albany was exceedingly dissatisfied with the way in which things had been organized. He thought it a mistake that the Duke of Connaught rode in the Queen's carriage, and the festivities of the day were overshadowed by disagreeable dissensions.

The campaign in Egypt led to a proposal to introduce khaki uniform: a practical enough proposal, but calculated to inspire apoplectic opposition. At St. James's the idea was deplored. There was talk of the "scarlet that conquered the world in the happy days before they [the Liberal reformers] were born and the House of Commons reigned!!! And now our troops are to wear dust colour because red is *too dangerous* in war!!! Disgusting!"" At the age of fourteen the Duke had deplored changes in uniform. He had written to his father in 1833: "You cannot conceive how sorry I am that the handsome dresses of the Hussars are to be changed."" Now that he was over sixty he regarded alterations with increased distaste.

Wolseley's views on uniform were defiantly unorthodox. As a young soldier, he had been forced to fight in the jungle "in a scarlet cloth jacket buttoned up to the chin, and in white buckskin gloves." He nearly melted in the tropical heat and never forgot the experience. As soon as he was in a position to flout regulations, he discarded his official uniform whenever he possibly could, in favour of a "sloppy, badly fitting khaki Norfolk jacket, a dreadful garment that looked as if it had been cut out with a knife and fork. Look at any photograph of the conqueror, taken on his return. He is in this horrid little jacket: a wide expanse of neck and throat is bared by the amazingly wide collar (surely of his own design too), around which hangs his G.C.M.G. in so slovenly a fashion as to defy every regulation governing the wearing of such a dignified decoration. His K.C.B., stars, medals, and other decorations are spattered higgledy-piggledy and all awry over the garment, from high up on the shoulder to a crumple under the lapel near the top button-hole, through which runs a watch-chain, festooned right and left across the breast, each end running to earth in one of the patch pockets on either side . . . The hair is just a flagrant flouting of the Queen's Regulations. How could the Duke (despite his umbrella, which he always carried with an air), the epitome of full-dress majesty, or in civilian dress the most imposing frock-coated, silk-hatted dignity—how could he with sincerity bring himself to appreciate this perky sloven who seemed to exercise devilish ingenuity in discovering means of jarring his nerves?"[n]

Eccentricities of dress might be expected in Wolseley, but it grieved the Duke when a member of the royal family defended khaki and described it as an "inestimable boon." Writing from Cairo soon after the victory at Tel-el-Kebir, the Duke of Connaught recommended the "dust colour" uniform. "The clothing supplied to the men—viz. red serge and blue serge trousers—was thoroughly inappropriate to this climate and the men suffered terribly from the want of a cooler and more comfortable dress. Khaki is the only sensible fighting dress for our men, and had they been dressed in it like the troops from India, it would have been an inestimable boon to all. At the present moment the clothes of the troops from England are in such a state that you would be horrified to see them, whereas the troops from India look just as clean to-day as when they disembarked. I hope you will forgive the private and unbiassed opinion of one who only has the efficiency and well-being of the Army at heart. My opinions may not be worth much, but still I know that you like hearing things, and have always allowed me to tell you what I think."[n]

On April 2, 1883, the Commander-in-Chief made a speech at the Mansion House on the abomination of doing away with the red uniform. Lady Geraldine next day described it as "an admirable speech," and she referred to Lord Wolseley, who inspired so much of this restless desire for change, as "unreliable and untrustworthy . . . a man who will do or be anything and everything that will only push his fortunes. Perfectly courteous and outwardly civil but not to be trusted across the road!" Louisa read her husband's speech and warmly congratulated him on it. "I was so glad love," he wrote back on April 4, "you looked at my speech. I was very anxious to say what I did about the *red* uniform, about the last vestige of the old English army, Wolseley, Childers and Co. want to get rid of, but I hope they will find this more difficult than they anticipated." Toward the end of the month, H.R.H. wrote to Sir Evelyn Wood, a protégé of Wolseley's, then in command of the Egyptian contingent. Wood, like Sir Garnet, preferred whenever possible to dress as a civilian; this habit drew a kindly rebuke from the Duke. "Will you forgive me," he wrote, "if I venture to give you a little hint about appearing always in uniform. Foreigners look to this far more than you may imagine. In England these things are not much noticed, but abroad they are, therefore as present Head of the Egyptian Contingent, I would suggest your appearing always in strict uniform and enforcing this also upon all your Europeans . . . Pardon this little suggestion."[n]

In the summer of 1884 the Liberal Government once more found itself reluctantly involved in a campaign in Africa, this time in the Sudan. The operation was designed to rescue Gordon from Khartoum, where he was surrounded by the forces of the Mahdi. Wolseley, of course, was chosen to command the expedition. Gladstone, for as long as he dared, tried to ignore Gordon, who, far from arranging the withdrawal he was instructed to undertake, in fact committed the Government to further fighting in the Sudan. Eventually, public opinion compelled the Prime Minister to send troops to relieve the beleaguered town, but the decision was taken too late and preparations were inadequate.

In May 1884, the Duke complained of statesmen "who prefer to be blind than to see what is particularly disagreeable to themselves and against their constantly repeated theories." In the following month he wrote to Sir Donald Stewart, Commander-in-Chief in India: "Nothing has as yet been settled as to future action in Egypt and this delay is I fear fatal to early success. This being Whitsuntide the Government have *all* been out of town . . . Valuable time is lost and as usual I fear we may again be too late." Obviously suspecting that the Army would be blamed for the delays and indecision of the Ministry, he concluded: "I name this to you confidentially, that you may not suppose that it is the Military Authorities who are to blame." The next month he wrote again in despair: ". . . As usual we shall be *too* late and when action is to be taken we shall be entirely unprepared for carrying it out. I have preached and prayed on the subject till I can do so no more, and the result must be on the shoulders of the politicians."

Several months after the decision had been taken to attempt Gordon's rescue, Hartington, who, toward the end of 1882, succeeded Childers at the War Office, still apathetically resisted demands for more men. "Even now," wrote Lady Geraldine on February 10, 1885, "the vile Government grudgingly *forced* to action, are doing it in the most miserably half-hearted way! Fighting and struggling against every single man to be sent out! Hartington declaring at every suggestion, that his delectable 'colleagues' 'will jump down his throat'! The Duke's labour immense to get the proper force sent out! Always met with: 'Why so many?' 'Is it necessary?' and of course not attended to, the matter referred to Wolseley, who answers, all for the greater number, and telegraphs: 'The more the better, we must run

no risks!' Curious alteration from his previous views!! Of
Hartington's intolerable apathy and unutterable indifference! And his ignorance! resisting the Duke's *very strong*
arguing to call out the Reserve 'Not now'! of course! Delectable policy of 'Too late' !! What's the use? What are we
to do with these fellows with nothing to do for a month?
Imagining they could be called out today and fit and ready
tomorrow! What a man for a Minister for War!!"

Wolseley, writing from Nubia in October 1884, told the
Duke: "The more I study the question on the spot, the more
certain I become that this Nile route is the only one that
could ensure Khartoum being reached by a British force."
A river attack required boats. As the local craft "leak horribly and founder at the least provocation," Wolseley asked
for vessels to be sent from England. "What sums of money
might have been saved if the Government had purchased
some of those stern-paddle steamers I recommended to their
notice months ago. It is always, and under our present form
of Government, must, I suppose always be the same. No
Ministry will expend a thousand pounds to-day to save the
expenditure of £5000 which people can see will be inevitable in six or eight months' time.'"

The Adjutant General and the Duke were in entire agree-
ment over the deficiencies of the Government, but they seriously differed, as usual, on the question of selection of staff.
"Wolseley," wrote H.R.H. in his diary on August 30, 1884,
"takes his usual entourage of Staff Officers. It is a pity he
will always take the same men, but he clings to that particular idea and mode of conducting military operations. I
think it is a very unfortunate thing for the *esprit de corps*
of an army, which must damage it." It was one of the Duke's
favourite sayings that the British Army was too small an
army to be divided into parties. "We don't want to have any
cliques or divisions in it. We cannot afford it. We want one
Army, the King's Army." The exclusiveness of Wolseley's
disciples, known as the Garnet or Ashanti Ring, engendered the very rivalry and jealousy which the Commander-

in-Chief believed to be dangerous to the good feeling of the Army as a whole.

When it became clear that Wolseley proposed to gather his old favourites about him for the expedition to the Sudan, the Duke wrote, warning him that his partiality was becoming notorious. "As to the quality of the superior or Staff Officers for purposes of war: you say very few men have the absolute requirements for active service in the field in the superior grade, so that you could tell the number off your fingers. I confess to having a better opinion of our officers in general than the view you take . . . The more fresh blood is tested on these occasions the better, and I think it a most unfortunate system to confine yourself to only a very limited number of men. You have an excellent Staff about you, I have not the least doubt; that you should like to have a certain number of these men whom you know intimately, and are therefore up to what you want, is most natural, and indeed essential. But if you never go beyond this particular batch of men, you work these and bring *nothing on*; and this I think another serious misfortune to the interests of an Army called upon, like ours, to serve in every part of the globe."" In further letters the Duke returned to his contention that it was best for the Army to "give every man a chance, and not merely pick out the plums of the military cake."

Wolseley for once selected his staff with rather more caution and chose a number of officers from outside the Garnet Ring, but he continued to insist on the inefficiency of the majority of high-ranking soldiers. "No one can at all times be more anxious than I am to bring out young untried men, for I know how inefficient and ignorant of war are most of our Major Generals. I often look over the list in that grade and shudder as I contemplate the possibility of nine out of every ten of them ever falling by any public misfortune into any command. Why therefore keep them on? Your Royal Highness is so soft hearted and good natured, that many an old gentleman is kept on in the army whom it would be better to let 'die in peace' and replace him by a young man . . . As I grow old myself, I feel this more strongly every day. There is a dash and daring and bright energy about youth that is worth all the caution and experience of old age. It is those youthful qualities which tell in war, especially in these desperate savage wars which so frequently devolve upon the British Army."[n]

During his voyage to Egypt in September 1884, Wolseley wrote to the Duke, requesting the formation of a Camel Corps, to consist of forty men chosen from each of a number of picked regiments. The Egyptian Army he dismissed as virtually useless. "I am convinced they should never stand in the open if charged by anyone, even by a herd of old apple-women from England." The majority of British troops were too young and would "not be able to stand the hard work." For this reason Wolseley was anxious to form his Camel Corps from the élite of the Guards, Household Cavalry, and Rifle Brigade. That he could not depend upon the regular battalions under his command was a damaging testimonial to the merits of Short Service, of which he had been so enthusiastic an advocate. The Duke, on first reading of the proposal to form a Camel Corps from some of the best regiments in the Army, told Wolseley: "It almost took my breath away." The principle he believed "unsound" and he only temporarily accepted it because there was no other way to form the sort of unit which Wolseley required. But he objected to any scheme which destroyed regimental spirit. "After all, that is the life and soul of this Army, and every other Army."

Wolseley, realizing that the Commander-in-Chief was troubled about the wisdom of his Camel Corps, sent him a letter designed to convert him to the project—which, incidentally, constituted yet another devastating indictment of the quality of soldier produced by Cardwell and Childers. "It would be simple folly to take the ordinary soldier . . . and pit him against an Arab warrior. Only fancy what chance a street boy from Whitechapel or a Clodhopper from Staffordshire, perspiring from every pore and mad from thirst, would have against the Arab, who has been bred up to fighting and whom fanaticism now gives a recklessness of death that makes him a serious enemy to the very best soldiers in the world. I should not feel myself justified in taking ordinary soldiers into action against him as long as I can get better men for the purpose . . . I may throw away my own life if I like, but I am bound by conscience, by honour to the men who trust in me and follow me, that I endeavour to save life as much as possible, even although I may run counter to the Queen's regulations and to the old peace customs of our Army in my endeavours to do so. I beg your Royal Highness to view what I do in this light.'"

The expedition to save Gordon failed. Time had been recklessly thrown away by Gladstone, and Wolseley reached Khartoum too late. The Government then determined to withdraw troops from the Upper Nile, contrary to the advice and wishes of the Khedive, Baring, Wolseley, Kitchener, and Sir Redvers Buller. As Wolseley wrote to H.R.H. in May: "To fly in the face of the advice given to them by everyone on the spot is a strong measure, and bespeaks great confidence in their own judgement. I am afraid, however, their action is solely influenced by party politics. The party exigencies of the moment have more weight than the interests of our Empire. This is plain speaking; but I think the time has come for all men who love their country to speak out, no matter on which side of the House they may sit, or with which they may sympathize.'" As a result of this withdrawal, the Mahdi overran the whole area, the native allies of the British were barbarously massacred, the country was laid waste, and eventually a large army under Kitchener had to be dispatched to recover the Sudan. The policy pursued by the Government from beginning to end was foolish to the point of madness, and the disasters which ensued were exactly those which had been predicted by the Commander-in-Chief.

Lord Hartington, as Secretary for War, very soon lost

the esteem of the royal family. He enraged the Queen by suggesting that she had behaved unconstitutionally in telegraphing her congratulations to Wolseley on his success at the battle of Abu Klea in 1885. Hartington wrote from the War Office, asking Ponsonby if it was Her Majesty's "desire to adopt the same course on other, similar occasions." He said that he could not help thinking that "it would on the whole be most convenient that any message from the Queen should be sent through the Secretary of State." The Queen justly described this proposal as "very officious and impertinent." She complained to her Secretary: "The Queen has the right to telegraph congratulations and enquiries to anyone, and won't stand dictation. She won't be a machine. But the Liberals always wish to make her feel *that*, and she won't accept it."

Wolseley, writing to his wife on his way back to England from the Sudan, prophesied: "Old George Cambridge must now be shaking in his shoes as he thinks of the returning firebrand that will soon be on his back." Wolseley was always a fighter and in England the Duke was the "first enemy." In moments of depression he admitted defeat. "I am tired and sick of my present position . . . The resistance of an irremovable Royal Commander-in-Chief has beaten me." Party changes, involving a succession of Secretaries for War, "who neither knew Joseph nor understood his schemes, nor had the least notion about military affairs," added to his difficulties." "I am tired," he told his wife, "having been worried by that old obstacle to all progress I mean H.R.H. until I could have murdered him with pleasure—it is too bad that England should have to pay so much by loss of military efficiency for the very doubtful honour of having this clever cunning old retrograde as Commander-in-Chief.""

Wolseley's letters display again and again this sense of frustration. Before setting out to the Sudan, he described himself as "too much worried and worked and thwarted by that mountain of royalty H.R.H. of Cambridge . . . The Duke has to be coaxed and flattered and terrified as one would act in dealing with some naughty little girl or some foolish old woman. I know nothing more wearing, because it is trying to the temper. Oh defend me from having to deal with royalties anywhere, and yet when I say this I cannot but feel how justly one's own servants might say the same thing about each and all of us." Soon after his return, he regretted that the Commander-in-Chief never seemed to leave London. "What a misfortune it is that 'George' has no country house—if he had he would take holidays like all the rest of the world instead of spending his Xmas and Easter in the society of that rope dancer." When one of the Adjutant General's favourite schemes was opposed by the Duke, he burst out: "If the future of the Army is to be decided according to the views of bow-and-arrow generals, I despair of it."

At times the Duke forgot all his troubles with Wolseley. On August 10, 1882, the Queen wrote in her diary: "After luncheon George C. came to see me. He is staying with Bertie on board the *Osborne*. He praised Sir Garnet Wolseley very much, saying he had behaved uncommonly well to him." Wolseley was opposed to Gladstone's imperial policy, he was impatient of political interference in the Army, although admittedly only when it failed to accord with his own ideas, and he had sent George FitzGeorge home with the Egyptian dispatches. These points in his favour contributed to friendlier feelings. Later, when Louisa was dying, his sympathy touched the Duke. "You have taken so kindly an interest," he wrote to Wolseley, "in my beloved one's illness that I must tell you myself that dearest Mrs. FitzGeorge passed away very peacefully this morning in my presence, and surrounded by her children. I know I shall have your sympathy in this to me most severe affliction." "The Duke read us," wrote Lady Geraldine on September 19, 1882, "a very nice good letter to him, from Wolseley, he gives great praise to Major George, whom he says he finds very useful indeed, always ready for work and 'doing it right well' when he has it to do, and that he will make a very efficient staff officer . . . The Duke read us also a very nice letter he had from Lady Wolseley, in answer to his congratulating her on her husband's success, she says how much Wolseley values the Duke's opinion, and how much he owes him."

Lord and Lady Wolseley exceeded the requirements of courtesy and overstepped the boundaries of truth in such flattery of the Commander-in-Chief. Lady Wolseley knew perfectly well that her husband—somewhat arrogantly, it must be admitted—regarded the Duke's opinions as worthless. "I cannot describe to you," he once told her, "the rubbishly nature of the Duke of Cambridge's letters to me. They are simply childish. I think it is high time he retired." Moreover, far from believing himself indebted to H.R.H., Wolseley rightly considered that his advancement had more than once been obstructed by the Duke's influence. "It is a curious fact," he told his wife in a letter dated August 5, 1892, "that I have not to thank that great German Bumble Bee for anything I have." Wolseley's kindness to Major Fitz-George was unashamedly calculating. "I am sending that fellow FitzGeorge home with my despatches which ought to endear me to the Duke for ever." His entertainingly scurrilous confidential letters provide a distasteful contrast with the flattering insincerities he employed in his attempts to humour the Commander-in-Chief. Unfortunately for Wolseley, H.R.H. was too shrewd to be deceived for long, and he saw plainly enough that he had to deal with a man "who will do or be anything that will only push his fortunes" and who was "unreliable and untrustworthy."[1]

The Queen, partly forming her opinion of Wolseley from conversations with her cousin, regarded him as a self-seeking adventurer. Disraeli, who recognized the Adjutant General's ability and was anxious to improve his relations at court, told the Queen in a letter dated August 24, 1878, that it was quite true "that Wolseley is an egoist and a braggart. So was Nelson." In a letter to Lady Bradford, Disraeli remarked: "Nothing can give you an idea of the jealousy, hatred, and all uncharitableness of the Horse

Guards against our only soldier. The Horse Guards will ruin this country unless there is a Prime Minister who will have his way, and that cannot be counted on. You cannot get a Secretary of War to resist the Cousin of the Sovereign with whom he is placed in daily and hourly communication. I tremble when I think what may be the fate of this country if, as is not unlikely, a great struggle occurs with the Duke of Cambridge's Generals!'"

In 1885 Gladstone's budget was defeated, owing to the fact that the Irish Members in the House voted with the Conservatives. The Liberals resigned and for some months Lord Salisbury was Prime Minister. At the end of the year he held a General Election, as a result of which his political opponents won a majority of eighty-six. Campbell-Bannerman became the new Secretary for War, and the Duke was so pleased to get him instead of Childers that he wrote enthusiastically to the Queen to thank her for her part in the appointment. "I hope you will allow me to assure you how grateful I feel to you, not only on my own account but specially as regards the interests of the Army, that you insisted on Mr. Campbell-Bannerman coming here as Secretary of State, in preference to Mr. Childers. The former is a very nice, calm and pleasant man, well known by all here and who knows the War Office work and with whom I have no doubt I shall be able to get on very smoothly and well.'" Gladstone's victory was short-lived, for he split his own party by his advocacy of Home Rule for Ireland. When in the early summer of 1886 the measure was rejected— Hartington, Chamberlain, and Bright all opposing it—he was forced to fight yet another election.

The excitement over the Home Rule election was immense, and the conversation at St. James's centered on Gladstone's iniquity. "Six thirty came the Duke!" wrote Lady Geraldine on June 25. "We spoke of the prospects of the elections." Some people were sanguine, but the Duke was less hopeful. "Truly his satanic Majesty helps Gladstone and he, alas! is very difficult to fight against! Of the utterly incomprehensible and marvellous aberration of the Sydneys in their *insane* love of Gladstone!! Lady Sydney having said her eyes were so inflamed and sore, but it was in a good cause; reading Gladstone's speeches!!! Of her brother, Lord Clarence, being nearly as insane: of somebody having said to him, but how is it *possible* that you, whom I believe to be an upright honest man, *can* swallow all the lies Gladstone tells? And he answered: Ah! that is because you do not understand him! He has such a wonderful mind that he can see *all* sides of a question, all around it! Now if you asked an ordinary person, is that screen in front of us gold, or silver? They would answer at once: gold! But Gladstone would never answer so! He would say: 'Well! To us now it appears to be gold, but in certain lights, at certain angles, it may etc. etc. . . .' and this a sober-minded honest man considers *admirable!!* The first preliminary to being a Gladstonian is, to get rid of every *shred and particle* of commonsense and common honesty." By July 6 Lady Geraldine and the Duchess appear to have persuaded themselves that Gladstone was "quite mad and always had a keeper in attendance." They discussed "the scandal of his iniquitous family knowing this, to keep it dark, and let him thus ruin the country. . . . We could, of course, talk nothing but the election." Eventually, to the delight of the inhabitants of St. James's Palace, Lord Salisbury was returned with a secure majority, Home Rule was rejected, and the Army, at least for a few years, could expect to be left alone.

Lord Salisbury appointed W. H. Smith as Secretary for War. He had already occupied the office during the brief period of Conservative Government the year before, and of all War Ministers he was best liked by the Duke. Smith, as a young man, had enormously expanded his father's news agency in the Strand by securing a monopoly of Railway bookstalls and by developing a circulating library. He entered politics in 1868 and was appointed First Lord of the Admiralty in Disraeli's Government in 1877. The Duke described him as "a very sensible, prudent and able man and an excellent administrator."" Moreover, he was entirely unassuming. On July 16, 1885, Lady Geraldine wrote: "The Duke told us Wolseley has been to Osborne to see the Queen and at his return told him she is so rejoiced and *happy* to be rid of Gladstone and his filthy lot!! She is like a school girl set free from school! Of the tact and taste Mr. Smith showed this morning at the reception of the Camel Corps, remaining tranquilly among all the rest of the crowd, till the *Duke* called him up to him! as per contra to abominable Cardwell who used to *try* to take the salute!!!"

Smith was the only Secretary for War to stand up to a Chancellor of the Exchequer on the issue of reductions. Despite all the pressure that Randolph Churchill could bring to bear, he stood fast, and the Chancellor, insisting upon a cut in Army estimates, sent in his resignation. Smith, on Christmas Day 1886, wrote an account of the contest for the Commander-in-Chief. "I am not at all surprised that Y.R.H. was startled with the news which *The Times* gave on Thursday morning. I was quite prepared for it, as the Chancellor of the Exchequer had been urging me to cut down my estimates heavily for some time, and when I had arrived at an approximation to the amount I should have to ask for, he came to me on Monday to go through the figures, and for nearly two hours he used every argument in his power to persuade me to reduce them. I could not see that it would be consistent with my duty to do so, and he left me saying he should resign his post, which intention he carried out the next morning.""

Randolph Churchill's resignation was a bluff that failed. Thinking himself indispensable—a common, if dangerous delusion—he imagined Lord Salisbury would insist upon the required reductions. In fact, his resignation was accepted and his career ruined. The country was surprised and bewildered, and nowhere was the news more excitedly discussed than in the Cambridge family circle. On December 23 the Duke paid his daily visit to his mother. "Our first word, of course!! was of the tremendous bombshell, the thunderclap that burst upon us this morning; Lord Randolph Churchill's resignation!!! Lord Salisbury himself they say knew it only yesterday morning, and half the Cabinet heard it only by the papers this morning!!! He resigns because he persists in refusing the estimates demanded by the War Office and Admiralty as *necessary* for the defence of the country and agreed to as such by Lord Salisbury, this being to catch a clap trap popularity by a marvellously 'economical' budget!! On the one hand so self-opinionated, overbearing, masterful, so erratic, uncertain and *dangerous* as he is, he is really a good riddance! But on the other hand certainly as Leader of the House of Commons is irreplaceable, disastrous loss!! God alone knows how dangerous and hurtful he may be to us, out of office! It is perfectly infamous of him to have resigned at so critical a moment, and reveals in a most unfavourable light his self-seeking egotistic nature and total want of patriotism! It *ought* greatly to injure him with the nation! But will it? Yet! as the Duke observed, going out thus upon the question of defences, stamps and commits him for ever to the clap trap doctrine of 'reduction' and peace at any price! And when eventually he resumes office, as he will, woe betide us! He will outbid Bradlaugh and Labouchère in 'cutting down'!! He is a nasty fellow! without a shred of principle but that of the advancement of Lord Randolph Churchill!"

As a result of the Chancellor's resignation and the death of the Foreign Secretary, Lord Iddesleigh, a Cabinet reshuffle took place in January 1887. Lord Salisbury took over Foreign Affairs, Smith succeeded the Prime Minister as First Lord of the Treasury, one of the rare occasions when the two offices were separated, and replaced Churchill as leader of the House of Commons. Goschen became the new Chancellor and Stanhope became Secretary for War.

"We talked," wrote Lady Geraldine on January 4, "of the excessive *bore* it is for the Duke losing Mr. W. H. Smith, *just* as he has got his hand in and is au fait with it all! He is himself *exceedingly* sorry to go and says he just feels now he has thoroughly mastered the whole thing and is at home, then he goes! In this *idiotic* constitution, the moment a man is *well* in the saddle and thus thoroughly understands his business, comes this stupid shuffling of the cards and immediately he is removed to another place he knows nothing about and a fresh man substituted to begin again with the ABC and learn what he has to do. A rotten system all through."

In his long experience with War Ministers, there was no other occasion on which a Secretary of State stood his ground against his colleagues. Excuses, apologies, sometimes self-justification, was what the Duke had learned to expect. Gathorne-Hardy in 1878, at a time when the Russians were at the gates of Constantinople and war in Europe threatened, unwillingly accepted reductions he knew to be dangerous. "With a reluctant hand," he agreed to cuts, despite his conviction that the Army was already too small. "Such a scraping and paring," he told H.R.H., "as I have been going through has made me miserable but there are limits which I cannot overpass." Two years later Stanley was excusing his surrender to the Chancellor with the argument that the economy was too depressed to justify even essential expenditure. And he advanced this theory at a time when Britain was the richest nation in the world. "I assure your Royal Highness that nothing but the state of the country would lead me to assent to, and still more to propose, such reductions as are intended—but with thirty thousand people living on charity in Glasgow, and even more, I believe in Sheffield, we *cannot* ask for more taxation."[n]

In presenting his estimates to Stanhope, the Duke told him in 1888 that he wished "to place on record, that hitherto he had been more guided in his annual demands for men by what he thought he had some chance of getting, than by what he knew to be the total military requirements of the country." H.R.H. and Wolseley wholeheartedly agreed that party politics vitiated the problem of military expenditure. Writing in 1883, Wolseley declared: "The interests of the Army have been subservient to the parliamentary or, more properly speaking, I should say to the party necessity of keeping its total cost down . . . The world is not in a condition that warrants us to continue in a state of complete unpreparedness for war." The Duke told the Goldsmiths' Company in 1881: "Army organization, and *all* army matters should *never* be a question of Party, it is a pure question of *patriotism,* how it gets dragged into Party Politics is as a question of money!" The parties rivalled each other in their zeal for reductions. "He wished he could persuade them when they had to vote on army matters not to think of their constituents but of this great Empire and her need of defence!"*

1887 was a great year of public ceremonies for the Commander-in-Chief, for it was the Golden Jubilee of the Queen's accession, and also the fiftieth anniversary of his joining the Army. As usual, long before the day of the ceremony itself, acrimonious discussions took place, and the Duchess of Cambridge, to whom gossip was a chief solace in affliction, heard from the Sub-Dean of the Chapels Royal, "who had it from the Queen's head coachman: that the 20th June unluckily falling upon a Monday, her 'most gracious' *cannot possibly* (!!!) spend a Sunday in poor London! So she comes up from Windsor to Paddington, starts *thence!!!!!* in procession, to drive to Westminster Abbey, with a *bonnet on,* as Mr. Payne the coachman, deplores!! for the thanksgiving service, and then back to *Paddington* to get out at Slough to be received by the Eton boys. Thus not staying in London one night!!! . . . When she ought to come up the 19th and remain till the 29th: only ten days after all!!!"* In the end, the Queen was prevailed upon to change her plans. As the Duke wrote in his diary on the day itself, the great Jubilee was "an immense success. London was in the Streets quite early in the morning, indeed during the whole previous night, and the weather was magnificent, bright sunshine with a cool breeze. I left my house, riding 'Guardsman,' a quarter before ten, and rode with my staff to Buckingham Palace. The several processions started thence in succession, the Queen being the last to leave; I riding by the side of her carriage. The streets were lined with troops the entire distance. The crowds were quite enormous and the enthusiasm throughout the entire route unbounded. Nothing could have been finer or more heartstirring. The Abbey was reached at twelve thirty where the scene was touchingly magnificent. The return route was equally fine and the enthusiasm overwhelming. We got back to Buckingham Palace without any accident or mishap by two thirty, where there was a great State Luncheon of Royalties in one room and suite in another . . . Dined again at the Palace—another State Banquet. The greatness of the Empire has been brought before the World in a most marked and satisfactory manner."

Lady Geraldine's account of the Jubilee was less restrained. "Greatest and most *perfect* success ever known! The most splendid and most thrilling pageant ever seen! The most touching and magnificent display of loyalty and attachment possible to conceive. The whole thing beggars description and I cannot attempt it, but leave it to the newspapers . . . I gave H.R.H. an account of the marvellous sight, the wondrous success it had been! The masses and *millions* of people, *thronging* the streets like an anthill, and *every* window within sight, and every roof of every house, men hanging on to the chimneys! there was never anything seen like it! And their enthusiasm! . . . The Duke who rode on Lifeguardsman, by the door of the Queen's carriage (and looked so well!! all say, and I alas!! preceding them in the procession could see nothing of him!!) told us he had never seen anything like the enthusiasm anywhere!! It was one continuous roar of cheering from the moment she came out of the door of her palace till the instant she got back to it! Deafening."

251

Four days after the ceremony in London, a Naval review was held at Portsmouth, which the Duke attended in his Trinity House uniform. He returned to London the following evening and gave his mother a description of all that happened. "The Queen in the *Victoria and Albert* followed by all the official boats, a long line! steamed through the whole line, each ironclad manning the yards! such *few* of them as still have such things! and cheering and firing a salute as she passed them! A quite magnificent sight!! And such a splendid day for it!! So hot, not a ripple, yet a most beautiful air. The illuminations at night were quite lovely! Altogether the Duke was immensely pleased! Quite delighted, a marvellous display of the power and greatness of the Nation! . . . The Duke lamenting and regretting naturally that Prince Adolphus had not taken the trouble or thought it worthwhile to go down for it, saying it was such a fine thing and rare occurrence, it was a *great* pity he should not have seen it, produced a little ruffle!!! For the Grand Duchess took it up hotly and Toko to Prince Adolphus for being so inert and wanting in interest! saying he had better remain at home altogether; certainly not undeserved, and in fact wholesome for him to listen to, but painful for all of us sitting around! and distressing for the Duke. Of the Prince of Wales having been perfectly happy in a new uniform!!! having just got himself made *Admiral of the Fleet!!!!* The Queen had the Empress Eugénie on board."

With such a crowd of royalty collected in London, there was a great deal of wrangling over precedence, a subject which appeared of epoch-making consequence to those whose feelings were ruffled. H.R.H. was more amused than concerned by the outraged excitement of some of his thwarted relations. "The Duke," observed Lady Geraldine on June 27, "who is so *rarely* grand seigneur and above all this miserable pettiness, knowing he is always Duke of Cambridge and can never be less whether he sits at the top at the bottom or in the middle!! said so sensibly, if they all come, prepared to take everything amiss and be offended at all and everything, they had better have made up their minds to stay away!"

The Jubilee celebrations concluded with a huge garden party, which the Duke attended. On June 30, he regaled his mother with an account of Gladstone's behaviour on the occasion. "The Duke gave us a full account, how very pretty it was, and well done and well managed; the Queen doing her part admirably again; she spoke to great numbers, going about a great deal, right and left. That brute Gladstone stood in the forefront of the circle before her tent while she had her tea, bang opposite her, hat in hand; she said to the Duke: 'Do you see Gladstone? There he has been standing hat in hand, straight opposite me this Half-hour, determined to force me to speak to him! But I am as determined *not* to speak with him!' So he continued to stand the *whole* time! But when she came out of the tent, instead of coming out in the centre, upon him, she went out at the end, and went along the line to the right, then made a circuit and took the other line to the left and most skilfully avoided him so that she neither spoke to him nor gave him her hand. But alas! the Duke heard afterwards, which is too *exasperating,* when she had so successfully and markedly avoided him, the brute contrived to get round to *inside* the house and placed himself so, that when she passed through the house to go away, at the last moment she came all suddenly *upon* him, round the corner, and was forced to give him her hand!!! Too provoking. *I* would *not* have done it even then."

Before the celebrations of his own Military Jubilee, the Duke paid a short visit to Germany. Nearly every summer he drank the waters at Baden and Kissingen, supposedly to alleviate his gout, although the cure, if anything, appeared to aggravate his symptoms. On August 16, while staying at Kissingen, the Duke had dinner with Bismarck. Adolphus FitzGeorge, who accompanied his father, wrote a long account of the evening's entertainment. "Today [August 15]

Prince Bismarck the Chancellor of the Empire called on my father, he was accompanied by Baron Rottenberg, who Stevens [the Duke's A.D.C.] and I entertained in my bedroom while the Prince was with my father. They had a half hour's conversation . . . The Prince had a great reception from the people on leaving and he had already remarked to my father that at one time here the people spat in the street as he passed, by way of insult; whereas now they overwhelm him with civility. The Prince looks very much thinner and better than when I saw him at Berlin last year . . . The Prince asked us to dine tomorrow evening at six o'clock."

On August 16 the Duke's party drove to Bismarck's lodgings. "He occupies a fine room nicely furnished . . . We sat at a round table at one end of the room. Bismarck had two fine beasts a dog and a bitch in the room, they are his companions and constantly in the room with him. They are, as he explained, a cross made many years ago between a Danish boar hound and a grey hound and the breed was established by a Duke of Wurtemberg who found that the boar hound was too heavy to run down the deer and that the grey hound was not heavy enough to pull the deer down, hence the reason for crossing. The breed has established itself as a distinct breed and is as he says the only bastard breed in animals that has established itself permanently. The breed is called Bastard in the German equivalent. Dinner was very fair. Bismarck apologized for it saying he had to leave his cook at Berlin on the way from Varzin down with a fever. The wines were numerous including sherry and port, hock, moselle, Burgundy and beer. Bismarck drank champagne and beer. He took peas, they were very badly cooked and hard as bullets. The Doctor objected and consequently he took a second helping. In the middle of dinner he said it was the anniversary of the battle of Mars-le-Tour in which his two sons took part in the celebrated dragoon guards charge, now an historical event . . . At dinner he spoke principally to my father in German but

told the above story to us in very good English. After dinner
we adjourned to the far end of the room my father sitting
on the sofa, Bismarck at the end of the table and we others
round it. He had three large German china pipes packed
full of tobacco at his side and commenced puffing away
vigorously and so continued to do during the rest of the
visit. He at once went into a constant flow of conversation
in English entirely, explained to us the different way land
property was dealt with in different parts of the Empire,
criminal laws, savings banks etc. and the charming part of
it was that he did not address his conversation to my father
particularly but to all of us generally . . . I remarked on
the facility with which he talked our language and he explained that he had learnt it as a child, but that he had not
talked it except to our Ambassador at Berlin since the year
1862, but that he kept it up by reading the political articles
and telegrams in *The Times,* 'tho' he knew all about it
beforehand, and never found anything in them new to
him,' and further, that he read English books occasionally.
On my asking him what sort, he said 'short and light or I
should never get through them.' My father made some remarks as to Prince William the Crown Prince's son being a
little rash in his sayings and Bismarck said that he talked a
great deal too much. Mr. Gladstone was then pretty hotly
abused all round. He [Bismarck] said he was very sick of
being at work being nearly worn out like a gambler constantly playing for very high stakes. I expressed a doubt
as to his being satisfied with nothing to do and he said that
he delighted in being in the country watching the growth of
young trees pushing their way upwards: this struck us all
as being a very remarkable characteristic of the difference
between his character and Gladstone's. Gladstone likes to
cut down trees, destruction being his strong point, Bismarck
likes to watch the growth of the trees, the growth of the
Empire being his strong point, and so the conversation went
on. About eight o'clock beer was handed round, we had
only just had coffee and brandy, and I refused upon which

he said 'You must not refuse beer in Bavaria' and I consequently partook as did we all, and so the cure was temporarily thrown to the winds. At eight fifteen about, we took our leave shaking hands with the old man and I can assuredly say I never spent a pleasanter and more interesting evening; it is not everybody who has the chance of an hour's chat with the great German Chancellor and I feel pretty honoured and shall remember it so long as I live as an event in my life. I was much struck with his eyes. They are very piercing. He is tall and upright, his clothes fitted him very badly (plain clothes) hanging about his body. He probably had them made before he lost so much flesh."

The Duke's military anniversary fell on November 3. "I have been overwhelmed," he wrote in his diary, "with telegrams and letters of congratulation both from abroad and from home." The Kaiser and the Emperor of Austria were among the many hundreds to send him messages. The Queen wrote a kind letter from Balmoral. "Let me congratulate you again," she said, "and let me express my warm thanks for the very valuable services you have rendered to me and to our Country, of which I am deeply sensible. That you may long be spared to command my brave and gallant troops is the earnest wish of your very affectionate cousin, Victoria R.I." The Queen created the Duke Commander-in-Chief by Letters Patent, "which office has been in abeyance since the death of the Duke of Wellington, as I have hitherto held the office of 'Commanding-in-Chief' . . . This is an honour of which I may be justly proud, and I cannot deny that I am so."

A great banquet was held on November 4 in the Duke's honour. "At eight thirty attended the great dinner of two hundred at the Hotel Metropole, given in my honour by the Senior United Service Club, Lord Napier of Magdala being in the Chair and the Prince of Wales on my right. All the Field-Marshals were present and a very large representative body of Officers. My health was most warmly and cordially welcomed and the whole thing passed off admirably, my speech in reply being very well received. . . . I was presented, by the united body of Officers who attended, with a very handsome gold Cigar Case, as a Memento of the event of the banquet given by them in commemoration of the occasion."

The dinner was a spontaneous tribute of the Army, and such was the enthusiasm for it that a great number of officers had to be turned away. The Prince of Wales, Lord Napier of Magdala, Lord Wolseley, Lord Lucan, Sir Redvers Buller, and many other distinguished soldiers attended. The incident of the evening which touched the Duke most deeply was a telegram he received shortly after the banquet began. "To Field Marshal the Duke of Cambridge," it ran. "My thoughts and heart are with you. I rejoice over the recognition of your service. I send my blessing to the best son that ever lived. Your loving mother, Duchess of Cambridge." Those who watched him receive the message feared he had received bad news, for tears ran down his cheeks as he read it.

"The speeches excellent," wrote Lady Geraldine next day, having studied all the newspapers and having heard that evening the Duke's account of the dinner. "The Prince first rate, and as for the Duke he excelled himself! the enthusiasm immense!!!! and all from the heart. The gold cigar case was presented and the Queen and the Prince together gave him a very pretty present, a pencil about four inches long in the form of a marshal's baton, very pretty indeed, so well modelled. . . . Sir Edward Whitmore came, and gave us a most satisfactory full detailed account of the whole evening! Told us he never saw such unanimity of enthusiasm! He thought they would break down the tables and smash all the bottles and glasses, with 'applause'! Declared he had not felt so happy for years, and thought the Duke was really happy, it was all so spontaneous and affectionate. At six thirty Lord Napier of Magdala came; from whom we had further accounts of the evening! After he had come in but a few minutes came the Duke! He thanked Lord Napier again for having presided so well, and come all the way over from France for the purpose; thanked H.R.H. for her *charming* telegram which had greatly touched him; as it did all those round about him to whom he showed it."

Unfortunately, there were two small clouds in an otherwise radiant sky. His sister, the Duchess of Teck, completely ignored the Jubilee. Lady Geraldine, who never liked Princess Mary, was exultant with indignation. "He has received I rejoice to say! tokens of regard, esteem, affection and interest! except!! solely, only, and alone *one* not!!! H.R.H. Princess Mary Adelaide!!! Not a sign or sound from the White Lodge!!! nor from anyone of the family!! It is too inconceivable!! and too *bad*." Three days later, on November 6, she commented on Princess Mary's improbable excuse for overlooking the great anniversary. "She *swore*, that none, not one single member of the blessed family ever heard one single syllable upon the subject or had a dream the Duke had or could have completed fifty years service, far less anything as to any celebration of it!!! A *remarkable* 'fact' when for two whole months past it has been *constantly* referred to in the papers, which it is to be supposed *some* member of the household sometimes reads!! And when here we have never ceased to talk of it!!!"

Lady Geraldine was not strictly accurate when she said that Princess Mary was the only person who forgot the Jubilee. The Duke of Clarence, the Prince of Wales's eldest son, made the same regrettable mistake. On the day of the Senior United Service Club dinner, Lady Geraldine wrote: "Prince Eddie *here*, at Marlborough House, his own near relation, known him intimately from his birth, an officer under his command, neither comes to him, nor writes to him, nor takes the slightest notice!!!! His own uncle and Commander-in-Chief!!!! Too bad; it is no want of proper feeling, but sheer stupidity!! Alas! that fatal apathy and inertness, sleepy apathetic laziness and total want of initiative. But the White Lodge people are far more curious and incomprehensible! Unpardonable omission! Not one single one of the whole family has taken the very smallest notice!! It is too outrageous." For Lady Geraldine, no occasion was complete unless it offered an opportunity for ill-natured grumbling. Possibly the surfeit of affection she bestowed upon H.R.H., who inspired in her agonies of undeclared love, deprived her of charity toward the rest of mankind, for she rarely erred on the side of being over-indulgent, except when discussing her beloved Duke.

Family Affairs

GREATLY as the Duke loved his wife, she was not alone in his affections. In her last years Louisa was an invalid, and when she was out of London her husband craved for company. The Duke told Wolseley, in the summer of 1890, "that he missed the society of some lady to whom he could be attached and in whom he could confide, and that he hated his big house at this season . . . Poor old fellow, he must have society. How I pity those who require it.'"

Strangely enough, the lady to whom he was devoted was, like his wife, called Louisa. She was the third daughter of Sir George Wombwell of Newburgh Park, Yorkshire. In 1840 she had married Henry Beauclerk, a descendant of Nell Gwynn's son, the Duke of St. Albans. They had no children and appear to have separated. Mrs. Beauclerk lived at Number 13, Chesham Street, Belgrave Square. They first met at a ball at Almacks in 1837, when Prince George was just eighteen; he was introduced to her by Adolphus FitzClarence. They began to see much of each other in 1847, the year in which H.R.H. married.

The first mention of Mrs. Beauclerk in the Duke's diary is made thirty-four years after they met. Presumably she was omitted for so long a time for fear the entries might be read. On November 20, 1881, he wrote: "I heard that L.B. was very seriously ill, which is of course a great distress to me." Five days later, he became more hopeful: "After some very bad reports and much anxiety heard that my dear friend was better." Mrs. Beauclerk was known to the Prince of Wales, and the Duke kept him informed of her illness. "I was sure you would take a kindly interest about Mrs. Beauclerk. My anxiety on her account during the last few days has been *very great*, but I hope since the measles have come out, that her illness is fully accounted for and thank God she is to-day I hope really doing well." He had been very anxious, "but that to me is nothing if God's mercy only gets her well through her serious illness." Three days later he wrote again with more cheerful news. "Thank God I can give a very good account of our dear friend. She is progressing very favourably and I trust that tho' great prudence and care will be required, she is now on the road to con-valescence. The relief this is to my mind I cannot describe to you. It is like awaking from a horrible dream which has been haunting me for the last five days.'" So agitated was the Duke by Mrs. Beauclerk's illness that he himself became un-well. The Duchess of Edinburgh told Wolseley that H.R.H. had given her a full account of "Mrs. B's internal arrange-ments, or perhaps I should say disarrangements. She tells me the Duke is very nervous about the fat red-faced old lady to whom she says he is very much attached.'" It was characteristic of Wolseley that he should have described the poor lady in terms so unflattering. Lady Geraldine said: "Her figure, her whole appearance was quite marvellous! No one could have judged her more than fifty-six to fifty-eight." But then in all probability this was the Duke's opin-ion, and his attachment to Mrs. B. was such as to discourage dispassionate assessment.

Mrs. Beauclerk recovered from measles, but toward the end of 1882 she was again ill, although nobody thought her troubles serious. Two days after Christmas, the Duke at five o'clock in the evening paid his "usual visit to Chesham Street, where I hoped things were better, and where I said goodbye to my dearest and most beloved Louisa, the friend and joy of my heart and life, for the last time, little dreaming

that I should never see her again alive." Early in the morning of December 28 Louisa Beauclerk died of a clot of blood
—an illness which afterwards the Duke could never hear
"mentioned without a shudder, knowing how it brought
him the destruction of all his happiness on earth."[n] "This
dreadful day," he wrote in his diary, "which has brought on
me mourning and grief was commenced by the terrible, the
crushing news, that my dearest and most beloved Louisa had
suddenly grown worse in the night and had died without
much suffering about six fifteen this morning. To me the
loss is irreparable and my grief is overwhelming. The idol of
my heart and of my existence is gone from me for ever. I can
now only hope and pray that we may meet again in Heaven.
God will be good and merciful to us and will forgive us our
sins . . . I did not leave the house all the morning, but at
five thirty went to see Miss Emily Wombwell [Mrs. Beauclerk's sister]. The meeting was dreadfully awful, but she
was all goodness, and kindness and affection, and I bless
her for it. I had some dinner at home and then went to St.
James'. Told my dear Mother what had befallen me and she
was good and kind and affectionate and sympathetic. I had
in the morning asked my son George to tell Louisa what had
happened. He too was good and kind, and Louisa behaved
nobly, only requesting the subject might not be mentioned.
The pain and grief of all this is too awful and overwhelming
and I am entirely *crushed* by it. God help me."

"Most sad, sad day!" wrote Lady Geraldine after hearing
the Duke break the news to his mother. "What sadder or
bitterer than to see a poor human heart crushed with grief!
all life, worth calling life at an end for it! a sorrow immeasurable and inconsolable. . . . In the evening came the
Duke! H.R.H. instantly saw how upset! how stricken! and
asking him what it was? he told her! his dearly loved friend
Mrs. Beauclerk died this morning at six o'clock!! The blow
is fearful! 'as a sledge hammer' splintering his poor heart to
fragments. . . . Loving and tenderly, and most touchingly
he spoke of her . . . showing the marvellous depth and un-

bounded tenderness of his unequalled love for her through an unswerving friendship of over thirty-five years! a life time. How rare, good God! how rare to find a man capable of such deep all-absorbing enduring tender love! . . . H.R.H. deeply moved by his *profound* grief!"

The Queen, when she heard the news, was less sympathetic. The Duke of Connaught mentioned in a letter: "I saw Uncle George who I found terribly broken by Mrs. B's death, he was quite miserable and cried dreadfully, I felt quite sorry for him." "I should pity your Uncle George," came the remorseless reply, *"very* much if it were *not such a discreditable* attachment; a married woman in *society*—and the mother [Mrs. FitzGeorge] of his sons alive. I believe Mrs. B. had a bad influence over him and from her home many things got repeated which did Uncle George great harm." The first the Queen heard of Mrs. B. was when the Duchess of Teck in 1878 explained that her brother was unable to assist her financially, because "he had his own family to support and a *still more* powerful influence, Mrs. Beauclerk, absorbed *all* he could give.""

Most people seem to have regarded Mrs. B. as a delightful person. General Clifton told the Duchess of Cambridge: "What a *good* influence she had upon him and how clever a woman she was." Lord William Paulet lamented her death greatly, "saying what a grievous loss she is to the Duke!"" On the day after her death, H.R.H. wrote: "Sympathy comes to me from all sides and respect and affection is shown to her dear memory. The pain, the sorrow, the reality of the affliction, increased upon me. My poor darling Angel died of a clot of blood in the vein of the left leg suddenly flying to the heart and death came upon her rapidly and without a struggle. God have mercy upon her dear soul."

On December 30 George FitzGeorge breakfasted with his father and was "full of kind and warm sympathy, but no real consolation, for *she* is gone and my loss can never be repaired." Louisa, on hearing about Mrs. Beauclerk, was "most generous" and took the announcement "in *sorrow* and not in anger, and therefore the subject is not referred to by me, but the position is a most painful one."

On New Year's Day the Duke wrote to his wife. It was not an easy letter and he made it short.

My own Louly, My dearest Wife,

According to good old custom my *first* letter in the New Year shall be addressed to you.

God bless you dearest and let me add from my innermost heart, forgive me.

Ever your very own

Most affectionate and devoted husband,

George

On January 7, the day before the thirty-sixth anniversary of his wedding, the Duke dined at Queen Street; "probably it was the best thing to do, however painful." He described it as "a very unpleasant dinner to me," but he was "advised" to go, and "all were kind and good and it passed over." Louisa was wonderfully forgiving. "Your kind and affectionate letter," he wrote to her on January 17, "reached me this morning, and I thank you from my heart for the generous feelings it evinces, and which I only too gladly reciprocate. I know my darling, that you have a great, great deal to forgive, and you have done so with a noble spirit, which touches me more than words can express and I can only say God bless you for it; and I will do my very utmost to soften the sorrow I have caused. It is so painful a subject dearest that I do not like to touch upon it, but I feel that your anxiety is to do everything that is affectionate and good by me, however blameable I am."

How much, if anything, Louisa knew about Mrs. Beauclerk before George FitzGeorge's announcement is impossible to say. As early as 1855, she was at least aware of Mrs. B.'s existence. Writing from Frankfurt in September of that year, she told her husband: "As I was sitting at table d'hôte today a Gentleman bowed. I looked and who should

it be but Mr. Beauclerk . . . I think he is much altered
. . . He said he had not seen you since you wrote to Mrs.
Beauclerk and asked them to dine with you at Brussels,
two or three years ago. I was astonished to hear it." Two
years later, when the Duke was staying with the Wombwells at Newburgh Park, Louisa was evidently suspicious,
for he wrote to her on October 8: "You asked me why I remained so long at G. Wombwell's. There is no reason further than that I had shooting every day, that I don't like
travelling on Sunday, and waited till Monday."

Lady Geraldine, who did not care for Mrs. FitzGeorge,
was enraptured by Mrs. Beauclerk, and although a savagely jealous person, never appears to have resented Mrs.
B.'s singular position. On the contrary, she became lyrical
when describing the "romance." "Too touching," she wrote
on December 30, 1882, "the proof of the *unbounded* tenderness of his immeasurable love and devotion for her
. . . Certainly there never was affection so *perfect,*
never such love, on the part of a *man!* Never! It is really
marvellous that at his age, and at her age! his love has not
only all the *adoring* devotion, but all the bright freshness,
blindness, glamour, *romance* of early youth!"

The Duke's diary was ordinarily little more than a list of
engagements, but in 1883 he used it to unburden his grief.
His fearful sense of loss, the memories that revived the
bitterness, the shock, the agony of separation are all recorded. "My heart is broken," he wrote on New Year's Day
1883, "it can never again be what it was, for I shall never
in this world see again the dear departed one, and no
other human being can ever give my poor heart that happiness and that bliss, which I was permitted to enjoy for so
many years in her blessed society . . . I saw Arthur
Wombwell, who was kind and good to me, as all her family
are thank God. I also today went to Church in Dover
Street and felt so strong an impulse to take the Sacrament
whilst her dear body was still on earth, that I stayed for the
Communion, which certainly comforted me. I feel ashamed

to confess that I had not taken it for many years, not I think since the death of my dear Father, when I took it at Cambridge House with my family. I hope God will forgive me for this and accept my sorrow at this neglect, which I now offer to Him in the spirit of devotion and love towards the spirit of the dear departed one. Later I went to the Office and at six I went with my faithful Dickins to her house, and stood by her dear coffin for the last time on Earth. It was in the Dining room and looked so solemn and still it was awful . . . I prayed . . . to the Almighty for forgiveness for that blessed spirit and for myself, in the hope that pardon would be granted to us both, and that we might be permitted, however unworthy I feel I am, to meet again in Heaven. May God hear my prayer in mercy and grace."

January 2 was the day of the funeral. The Wombwells begged him not to attend the service. "To which," wrote Lady Geraldine, "as he believes it to be for her sake, he acquiesces, but in fact they did it really for his sake! dreading how he *must* inevitably break down at it, which would be so painful! Prince Teck goes to it, which gives the Duke *great* gratification." In his own diary the Duke wrote: "This was the dreadful day of the funeral at Kensal Green. She expressed a wish herself, in letters she left, to be buried there and the family strictly carried out her instructions. I rejoice to think it was a bright sunny morning, the only day of sunshine we have had for a long time, and it felt to me as if Heaven by this grace had welcomed her dear soul into the region of the blessed . . . I wanted to attend the funeral, but it was thought that her memory would be more respected by my absence, and finding that the family particularly wished this, I did not go myself . . . At one forty-five I drove with Tyrwhitt to Kensal Green, and by her just closed grave stood and prayed, a brokenhearted man. The place was selected by Miss Emily and Arthur, and is beyond the Chapel in a nice quiet spot. I looked about me where I should purchase at once a vault for myself, for I will ensure then that I may be buried near her, which I had determined to be for years, and had indeed left a paper attached to my will to this effect, which was my intention ever since 1849." The Duke's desire to be interred at Kensal Green was observed by his sons, and there he lies buried in a vault beside his wife, a short distance from Louisa Beauclerk.

Evening after evening he discussed his loss with his mother, and Mrs. Beauclerk for a time was the chief topic of conversation, apart from an occasional criticism of Wolseley's latest outrage. The Duke described "her loveliness, her charm, her beautiful eyes!!" He talked "of her kindness, her generosity, never having heard her say an ill-natured word of anyone." He told his mother: "I positively believe, if it were humanly possible to love her more than I did then, I really loved her all these late years even more than formerly."

The Duke in his visits to St. James's made pathetic attempts to appear cheerful. Three days after Mrs. Beauclerk's death, Lady Geraldine deplored "the pain of seeing him, hitherto the joy and sunshine of this house, whose dear, bright visit was the enlivenment of H.R.H.'s day— thus bowed to the earth with grief! his very *existence* at an end." After he had partly recovered from the first overwhelming shock, he made "valiant, noble efforts to throw off his crushing sorrow while he is with his mother," trying "to be with her as usual and talk, and amuse her—while one knows how utterly broken-hearted he is."

Sad associations and anniversaries constantly revived his grief. On March 20, 1883, he visited Chesham Street for the last time before the furniture was put in store. "At twelve o'clock went to the poor dear little house to take a last look at it, as *her* things are to be packed up and the carpets and curtains put away. The grief and sorrow I feel at seeing all *her* things, but she my *beloved one* gone for ever, was terribly painful, and yet I am glad I went once more. God have mercy on *her* dear soul." Later in the summer, when Lady Geraldine was dining at Gloucester House, the Duke went into his writing room "and showed me the armchair and cushion in it in which she was when he last took leave of her the evening of the 27 December!!! It has been brought to him from Chesham Street and another armchair of the same kind and 'the little table on which we used always to have our tea'!!!"" For his sixty-fourth birthday Prince Edward of Saxe-Weimar sent H.R.H. "a little present and some lovely roses and flowers and these quite upset me, for they reminded me so of the dear offerings and flowers that were sent to me on this day by my *beloved* and *departed* friend. Her dear face is ever before me today and I can think of nothing else." Two days before Christmas the Duke discussed with his mother how Emily Wombwell had "now got all Mrs. Beauclerk's things arranged in her house!! Of how he knows them all! Of her giving him yesterday an album she had found amongst Mrs. Beauclerk's things, filled with all his speeches and everything concerning him." As Lady Geraldine had for many years devotedly kept just such a scrapbook, she remarked: "Curious *resemblance!*"

The Duke clung for consolation to relics of Mrs. B. He derived a sad pleasure from a starling which she had kept for fifteen years, and every morning took it out of its cage and fed it on worms. The very day she died, his letters to her were returned, and these he read with a melancholy fascination. On February 4 he told the Duchess that he was "reading over letters to Mrs. B." Some went back to 1849. "It strikes him so how without fail thro' *all* and *every* of them there runs the same never changing strain of *entire devotion* to her! when away wishing only to be back with her! If absent for only two or three days shooting, always 'the party is pleasant enough but would that he were back with her! how he longs for Saturday, or whichever the day, that he is to return! how he will not fail to come to *her* on arriving.'" The resemblance between such letters and those which he wrote his wife is striking, and the suspicion of insincerity arises. In order to keep Mrs. FitzGeorge ignorant of her rival, duplicity was unavoidable. But, although the Duke failed to conduct his "romance" without deceit, there was no pretence about his devotion to his wife. It was evidently not a situation to which either lady could be reconciled; nor did circumstances make it easy for the Duke to be honest without hurting feelings. The dilemma was intricate but not unprecedented, for other husbands have made room for two in their hearts, although few have remained so faithful—if the term may be used in such a context—to the lady of their second choice.

The first "sad anniversary" of the loss of his "beloved and adored friend" found the Duke longing for reunion in death. "God knows," he wrote, "what I have since suffered in sorrow and anguish of mind. Real happiness in this world has quite left me and the distance of time in no sense mitigates this feeling. I miss *her* and feel *her* loss every hour, I may say, moment of the day, and *nothing* can ever replace her to me . . . Standing by *her* dear grave, I longed to be *with* her even in death!! Would that it could have been so." Lady Dorothy Nevill, in her *Memoirs*, printed a letter she received from the Duke. At a casual glance it would seem to refer to the death of Mrs. FitzGeorge, but since she died on January 12, the mention of "Friday next, 28th" establishes that H.R.H. was, in fact, speaking of Mrs. Beauclerk. "My Dear Lady Dorothy,—May every blessing attend you even at this *terrible period* as you call it . . . To me the time is a *most painful* one, for my thoughts are entirely absorbed by the *events* of this time last year, which you can well imagine cause very sad reflections and give me so much sorrow and grief. Friday next, 28th, was the sad day which *ended* my *happiness* in this world. I shall not fail to come and see you with pleasure after these sad days are over, and when I can make myself a little more agreeable, I hope, than I possibly could at present."[n]

The Duke paid constant visits to Kensal Green, and continued so doing until the last year of his life. "At one fifteen drove to Kensal Green," he wrote on January 15, 1883, "and once more visited the grave of my beloved one, a painful, but to me essential duty, and asked again in prayer for her forgiveness for my many shortcomings towards her and God's merciful pardon for the sins of that dear soul and for my own, which are so much, much greater." On the second anniversary of Mrs. Beauclerk's death, he declared: "The sorrow of my heart has in no respect been mitigated by time, as some said it would. After attending a service at Dover Street I went to Kensal Green and there deposited a wreath on *her dear grave*. Several others I found already there, a proof that *she* is not forgotten by others as well as myself." In 1887, in the midst of his military jubilee, he did "not forget *her* dear memory, in the congratulation and honours that have been accorded to me," and visited her tomb on November 5. At the end of the year, on December 28, a day "ever to be remembered with deep sorrow and grief," he wrote in his diary: "It is now five years since my *beloved friend* was taken from amongst us. I went at ten to the Cemetery with Dickins to depose a beautiful wreath on *her* tomb. It looked so peaceful . . . but oh! how sad! Never shall I forget that dreadful day and a loss which is irreparable." In 1897, when the Duke was seventy-eight, fifteen years after Mrs. B.'s death, he paid his annual visit to Emily Wombwell and to Kensal Green on the "sad Anniversary." His grief was neither counterfeit nor consolable, and its intensity provides a measure of the vehemence of his love.

Despite the distractions of Chesham Street, the Duke's own family made large demands on his affection, and indeed there were moments when his devotion to his children was almost overwhelmed by aggravation at their improvidence. Louisa, so he assured her, he continued to adore "as I did the first day we met." "My feelings," he wrote on September 6, 1878, "are unchanged. If my letters have been feeble in their expressions in this respect, believe me my darling, this can only be caused by *age* creeping over me, which may make the pen less free in its expression, though the heart is as warm as in the earlier days of our devotion."

The Duke's diaries contain hundreds of references to dinners in Queen Street. Generally they seem to have been family gatherings, consisting of Georgina, Mrs. FitzGeorge's sister, Charles Fairbrother, Louisa's daughter, who married Captain Hamilton in 1859, and the three FitzGeorge sons. The Grand Duke and Duchess of Strelitz occasionally dined. Louisa spent part of her year either at the cottage at Horley or at various health resorts. Whenever the Duke travelled abroad, or visited some country house for a shooting party, he wrote almost daily to Louisa, but his letters throw little light on the everyday life of Queen Street. He is at his most communicative in times of disaster. Thus on June 29, 1882, he writes: "When I got to Queen Street found Louisa in the greatest distress her dear little dog Prince having been run over and killed by the wheel of a carriage near Bayswater Gate. It is most sad, for he was a most dear and affectionate little fellow and Louisa's constant companion, and I was myself, as was everybody, most fond of him."

In 1886 Louisa suffered a greater affliction when her sister Georgina died. In his diary on April 15 the Duke described his own part in this sad event. "Rode early, then busy at home, later walked to the office. I had only just reached it, when I got a note from Louisa to say that dearest Georgina had just passed away in an attack, which had suddenly come over her. I at once went up to Queen Street, and found dearest Louisa and everybody there in great distress and I myself entered most fully into their feelings of sorrow and grief. Georgina had during the last few days been much less well, for we had been in hopes that she was gradually mending . . . She had been downstairs for some time, had even walked out into the street one day that it was mild, just in front of the house, and had sev-

271

eral days dined with us quietly when I came there. The last day she came downstairs was on Tuesday, and I saw her downstairs for the last time on Monday, when she appeared better. On Tuesday however she felt so unwell with spasms in her chest, from which she had been suffering of late, the result no doubt of the want of power of digestion, that she went up to bed before I came to dinner. Wednesday she remained upstairs all day very unwell, had a very bad night with great pain and much vomiting, and when Louisa went up to see her today, she found her very feeble and suffering but quite herself and entering still into conversation with her, though but little. She had her beef tea and brandy for lunch, when Louisa left her, scarcely had she gone, when the nurse who had been again sent for that morning, and had only been there a couple of hours, was suddenly called to by dearest Georgina to come . . . She had hardly got her arms around her when she gave a vacant stare and poor dear she was *dead,* the doctors were immediately sent for, but all was over and no more could be done, as she was gone from us for ever. It is *too too* sad, and the suddenness of the event quite overwhelming. I stayed some time in the house and saw poor dear Georgina after she had been laid out, when her countenance was calm and placid. I then went home, later to St. James's, and unfortunately had a dinner which I could not get out of, much to my distress."

Except for Augustus, the Duke's sons caused him much anxiety. As he had himself made an original marriage, his children listened to his advice on the subject with a certain scepticism. The orthodox, even old-fashioned views he was disposed to express, were so inconsistent with his own practice that they failed to impress his sons.

Although the Queen had been distant with George FitzGeorge, the Prince of Wales was more affable. In 1877 he invited George and Augustus to Sandringham, "where," the Duke told Adolphus, "they are getting on swimmingly, though both have had a tumble out hunting." The Duchess of Cambridge never set eyes on her grandsons until 1878, when "she expressed a wish to become acquainted" with them. The meeting was a wild success; the FitzGeorges became constant visitors at St. James's, thus opening new horizons of discussion. "In the Afternoon," wrote the Duke in his diary on January 4, "took George to St. James's to be introduced to my dearest mother she having affectionately expressed a wish to see all the boys. It went off very well and she expressed herself as most pleased with George." Two days later Augustus was taken to see the Duchess, "who was much pleased with him. It is so nice of her to have done me this out of affectionate kindness."

In January 1883, while the Duke was still overwhelmed by the shock of Mrs. Beauclerk's death, Colonel George decided to retire from the Army. He had frequently threatened to do so before, much against his father's will, but now, having decided to write for the newspapers and to speculate in the city, was obdurate. "Says he cares nothing for soldiering, does not wish to be a General, knows he can never be C. in C., but 'Secretary for War I *can* be and that I *intend* to be.'" "Too bad of him," was Lady Geraldine's comment, "to annoy his father at this moment." "George is going to have something to do with a newspaper [*The Sunday Times*]," wrote H.R.H. to Louisa on May 15, 1883. I am convinced people do not like associating with anybody regularly connected with the Press." The Duke attempted to enrol Adolphus's support against his brother. "I hope," H.R.H. wrote to him on January 10, when the scheme was first made known, "you will help me in persuading your brother George from doing the most foolish and imprudent thing that was ever contemplated by a sensible and really intelligent man. He has sent in his resignation of his commission and is thus going to throw away the excellent position he has made for himself in the Army, with the object of being a writer in the Press!!!! the most horrible occupation a man can possibly take to . . . I am in utter despair." Some years later he told his wife: "I must try to prevent further mischief with this *dreadful* Newspaper and the speculative companies, which are not occupations for a high cast Gentleman who wishes to belong to good society to be involved in. I hope and think that in this you agree with me." George FitzGeorge was fascinated by enterprising business deals, but either the dice were loaded against him or he had no head for figures. Neither newspapers, nor a brewery, nor the Empire threatre, all of which lost heavily under his ownership, ever made him the fortune he expected. On the contrary, the Duke rescued him from a series of financial disasters. Writing to Adolphus FitzGeorge in December 1893, H.R.H. tells him he has seen Farrer, the family solicitor, and after talking matters over very fully, "it breaks my heart to say it, I really believe the best thing for George himself, and specially for his poor dear little children is to let him go bankrupt. It is *horrible* to me but I am afraid it is the only decision which is justified by the sad position of affairs."

George's marriage to Rosa Baring, which took place on November 28, 1885, did not altogether please his father, principally because Rosa's first marriage had ended in divorce. "Poor fellow," he wrote to Adolphus fifteen days before the wedding, "I don't think he is doing a wise thing for himself." H.R.H. was first introduced to his son's wife on April 10, 1886. Somewhat grudgingly he described her in his diary as "a handsome woman certainly, with agreeable manners." "The Duke does not dislike her," wrote Lady Geraldine, "and says she is a good looking woman." No doubt inspired from St. James's, he soon managed to find ground for criticism. His daughter-in-law was "made up, and very extravagant in her dress." Her constant visits to Paris to buy clothes were watched with disapproval. Mrs. George's Christmas present from the Duke in 1894 was a looking-glass and a handbag, and they were presented to her with accompanying jests.

Although Adolphus FitzGeorge abandoned his early extravagance, his father was dismayed by his views on marriage. While his ship was in Australia, he became engaged to a girl from Sydney. "The most foolish and thoughtless of all possible proposals," was how H.R.H. described the idea in a letter to his son written on May 18, 1869. "The idea," he continued, "of your committing yourself to a promise of marriage to a girl who has not a sixpence and whose family are anything but nice, according to your own showing, is so preposterous that I should have thought your own good sense would have at once prevented you from so senseless a proceeding." The Duke pulled strings at the Admiralty, Adolphus was transferred to the English Channel, and the marriage was abandoned.

In 1874 Adolphus again decided upon matrimony, and once more the Duke was opposed to the idea. He believed his son was not rich enough to marry and that a wife would prejudice his Naval career. "I adhere to my opinion," wrote the Duke on October 5, "that matrimony ought not to be thought of by you for some time to come . . . I write this of myself and from nothing that was said at Horley!" The next day he wrote again to Adolphus, arguing that it would be "most foolish and imprudent" to marry. "It is only fair by all parties that they should clearly understand that I have not given my consent to your proposal and that I considered that it was not to your interest to marry at present and that I considered the prospect of living on £1,200 a year a very miserable one indeed . . . You cannot say that this is a very deep or long standing affection. The young lady has moreover been brought up in much comfort and luxury." The Duke maintained that Adolphus should go back to sea, not act rashly, and try to forget the girl, whose name was Sofia.

In two further letters, written on October 11 and 17, H.R.H. produced additional reasons for his opposition. "The more I think of your proposed marriage the less I like it . . . I tell you candidly I do not like the connection. It really would be extremely distasteful to me . . . I am so fond of you boys that I want you to belong to my society and not a lower sphere which this would certainly be." A marriage such as Adolphus was contemplating would prevent his getting on in the service, in society, and in the world at large. "Professional society such as that in which you have been living more or less all your life is very different from a civil connection of a kind that would take you entirely away from me." H.R.H. assured his son that his advice was very sensible and should be seriously considered. "You are now in love and don't look beyond the present time."

"Had a long interview," wrote the Duke in his diary on November 22, "with George and Adolphus in Queen Street connected with the wish of the latter to marry, to which in his interest, I am much opposed, but upon which he is unfortunately very determined. I have now got him to promise, that he will at all events wait for two years or thereabouts." By September of 1875 Adolphus was still anxious to marry, and Mr. Holden, Sofia's father, having at first hesitated, now gave way. The Duke refused to give his consent but left the final decision to his son. "Whenever Miss Holden becomes your wife, you may depend upon it that she will receive every consideration and good feeling as such from me." The Duke made it clear that he would not attend the wedding. "I am not in England" at the time arranged, "but even if I were I don't think with my views on the subject it would be honest on my part to attend. That every blessing may attend you is my ardent hope and prayer because I have a real and sincere affection for you and your brothers, not because I think you are doing a wise or judicious thing, which to this moment I think you are not." "I take it for granted your brothers will support you at the wedding, but you could hardly expect your dear Mama to go all the way to Hull and back when you know that moving about is not easy for her.'"

Adolphus was naturally distressed that his parents refused to attend his wedding and wrote to his mother: "I cannot express to you the bitter disappointment it is to me that George, dear old boy, is to be the only one of my family present at the wedding tomorrow, however in this world we must be thankful for small mercies and thank God I shall not be submitted to the degradation of having to stand unsupported. He at least will see me safe through my wedding . . . Dear Gussy has failed to come at my earnest request by telegraph, pleading that it was too late, it may have been the case. I trust it was." Adolphus attributed Louisa's refusal to the influence of his father. He tells her that all his friends have "pocketed their pride" and consented to come. "I don't blame you, I believe you would have liked to have come. I believe it is all Papa's fault. God only knows why he should have been so cruel."

The Duke wisely determined to make the best of things, once the marriage was an accomplished fact. "One thing is certain," he told Louisa in a letter written from Paris on September 13, "the marriage having taken place it is better not to be on bad terms. There is no necessity for any great *intimacy* with the family at all events. You were quite *right* to decline the invitation to go to Hull for the wedding, it is just what you say, it would have given a certain amount of sanction and countenance, which it is best to avoid." On September 21, Adolphus's wedding day, the Duke wrote in his diary: "Dined with Louisa at home. She afterwards went to meet Dolly, who was alas! married today at Hull to Miss Holden, the daughter of a Solicitor there. When appointed to the *Rapid* [a ship of which he was given command] Dolly telegraphed me to give my consent to an immediate marriage before his departure. I left it to him to decide and he has consequently taken the step. May it turn out to his advantage. I regret it for his and mine . . . but must now make the best of it!" On the following day he met Sofia. "Dolly came with his young wife to introduce her to me. She seems cheerful and lively, but I did not think her very pretty. She is short and inclined to be stout. All passed off well, as it is best now to be on friendly terms. I took leave of them, as they leave today for Southampton to embark tomorrow for the Mediterranean, where the *Rapid* is."

The Duke's opposition to Adolphus's marriage was rather singular. Mr. Holden was a rich and successful solicitor, and by Victorian standards his daughter was a thousand times more acceptable as a bride than was an actress, however remarkable she might be. As soon as the Duke got to know Sofia, he relented. He told Adolphus on September 19, 1876, that he would be delighted if Sofia wrote to him from time to time. "I have every regard and good feeling for her on your account my dear Dolly as well as her own, and therefore you need be under no sort of anxiety on that account." He even instructed his son in the proper manner for his wife to address him. "She should commence her letter 'My Dear Duke' which is the right thing."

In quite a short time the Duke came to regard Sofia as an ally, whose influence on his wayward son might be exerted for good. When Adolphus in 1876 wanted to give up command of the *Rapid* because he suffered so badly from seasickness, his father thought resignation might be mistaken for cowardice at a time when war with Russia threatened, and he discussed the matter with Sofia, who entirely agreed with him. "Really my dear fellow," he wrote to Adolphus on July 25, "to read your letters one would suppose I was your bitterest enemy, whereas I am your *best* friend and there is not a wish of my heart that is not for your benefit and advancement in life. And in this sentiment I further assure you that I include Sofia, who is I know just as much interested in all that is good for you as I can be." Sofia and the Duke between them eventually succeeded in persuading Adolphus to retain his command. H.R.H. in a letter to his daughter-in-law, on August 18 tells her: "A young fellow without occupation must lead a miserable life in the long run, even though for the moment he may fancy the prospect . . . A life of idleness is a life of misery." The letter concluded: "I remain my dear Sofia yours very affectionately, George." It was a tribute to her charm and to the Duke's generous nature that, within a year of a marriage he had earnestly opposed, she had become "My dear Sofia" and he was her "affectionate" George.

Adolphus, as a married man, almost ceased to cause his father annoyance. It is true he continued to think of leaving the Navy. "You have known," he wrote in 1889, "how I always loathed and hated my profession." The Duke told him: "You think the Navy is made for you and not you for the Navy," and when in 1877 Adolphus contemplated becoming Secretary of the Hull Dock Company, H.R.H. wrote him a letter on June 13, complaining that nothing any longer surprised him, "for I have found out, alas, that you are never disposed to take my advice . . . but I was astonished nevertheless when you tell me that you were inclined to take the Secretaryship of the Hull Dock Company. To me this seems a most outrageous idea . . . But I suppose as usual I shall be told, that you know better than I do, and if you are determined to sever yourself from all connection with the service the more fool you that is all I say. But it disgusts me beyond measure."

Interference in the upbringing of children is a grandparent's prerogative, and, urged on by his mother, the Duke freely availed himself of his rights. In 1884 Sofia organized a charity bazaar, which the Prince and Princess of Wales consented to patronize. It was thought at St. James's that Adolphus's daughter, Olga FitzGeorge, might be present. Accordingly, on July 15, H.R.H. wrote to his son: "I don't know if you intend Olga to be there. She is so young that for her I should say it would be better not, but of course you must do what is best. I hope if she goes you will take care that she is very quietly dressed. You know I think at times she is dressed too conspicuously, which I don't think is at all good for a child, for it turns their head. My mother has spoken to me about this once or twice, so I am anxious you should take care about this for tomorrow particularly. This is of course for *yourself only*." When there was some idea of Olga acting in a play, her grandfather wrote: "appearing on the stage is not desirable for this nice little girl."

Adolphus, although more sensible about money than he had been in his early days as a young Naval officer, was still disposed toward extravagant ways, and occasional rumbles of displeasure erupted from Gloucester House. In 1892 he and Sofia moved into Number 12, Eaton Square. It was, in Lady Geraldine's phrase, "a charming house—a palazzo!! The *poor* Duke's pocket!!" The Adolphus Fitz-Georges usually spent part of the winter in Monte Carlo, which the Duke, after a visit in 1893, described as "a Hell upon Earth as regards Society . . . How you and Sofia can go and stay there year after year in those stuffy and stinking Gambling Rooms I cannot conceive and I confess to you honestly it *annoys* me more than I can express, and I think it very *lowering* to a Gentleman and Lady to be sitting at the tables day after day with such *degrading company*."[n]

Besides his visits to Chesham Street and Queen Street, hardly a day passed when the Duke was in London without his seeing his mother at St. James's. His appearances were eagerly awaited by the old, stricken Duchess and her infatuated lady-in-waiting. Lady Geraldine resented other visitors when the Duke was there, wishing to devour every moment without distraction. "At nine thirty the Duke came," she wrote, describing "a cosy pleasant evening," "H.R.H. with her work frame! He with his little table making 'Patiences'! I with my knitting. And pleasant talk." Another evening "was bright and lively and full of fun! Wound a ball of wool and was very gay!"[n] Once, when the Duchess of Teck left one of her sons at St. James's, the Duke played with him, "going on all fours pretending to be a big dog!"

The Duke was an excellent mimic and kept his mother in fits of laughter with his imitations. "At eight fifteen the Duke came! and dined with Princess Frederica [of Hanover] and me. Nine fifteen up to H.R.H. He was in the highest spirits! and too amusing and funny. Gave us the most amusing representation of General Bruce in command at Edinburgh, and his *boots!*" Another time, "he took off for H.R.H.'s amusement the way the present curate reads! Too *amusingly!* and was too funny and droll! imitating him so exactly!!" Even his near relations were not spared. "He took off the Duke of Cumberland's voice and manner in arguing a point, so *inimitably* cleverly! so to the life! It gave the Duchess a *fit* of laughter! *too* good!"" This gift of mimicry proceeded from a sharp eye for detail and a capaciously retentive memory.

The Cambridge family, while rejecting most of the vices of the Regency period, retained something of its gaiety. It was for this reason that the Queen and Prince Albert regarded their circle with suspicion, and it also explains why the Prince of Wales, detesting his mother's sombre court, was attracted to "Uncle George." One night the Duchess "dreamt she refused two kings, and the Duke said he was sure he could persuade Lord William Paulet to marry her!! which he did! and the marriage was arranged! Thereupon much reciprocal chaff!!" It was very "unlike the home life of the poor dear Queen." But conversations were not always frivolous. "We had a very *earnest* religious talk! upon the prevalent unbelief in the World! and upon the Lord's Prayer! on which the Duke spoke so touchingly with fine and simple trust!""

Often there was music in the evening. Lord Ormathwaite, in his recollections of life at court, described how the old Duchess of Cambridge, although "paralysed and a great sufferer . . . would sit in her sitting-room at St. James's Palace cheerfully receiving her friends whenever well enough. She was devoted to music, and at the suggestion of the Prince and Princess of Wales, Tosti, the composer of many lovely songs, used to visit her often in the evening about six o'clock and play to her. Knowing my fondness for music, she kindly allowed me to come on these occasions and sit in the room. It was most pleasant. The Prince and

Princess of Wales and many of the Royal Family used to drop in, but the Duchess was most particular that there should be no interruption of the music, and being the doyenne of the Royal Family she was allowed to have her own way. Apropos of the old Duchess being the doyenne. When she died, Queen Victoria said: 'Ah me! There is the last one gone who had the right to call me Victoria.' The Duke of Cambridge used also to drop in sometimes at these little parties. The Duchess, however, discouraged her son's visits at this hour as he invariably fell asleep on his chair and interrupted the most pathetic parts of the singing with loud snores!'" Although the Duke was rather prone to fall asleep in the evening, he was extremely fond of music, and often went to the opera three times a week. He did, however, draw the line at Wagner. *Götterdämmerung* he called a "wild and improbable opera which I think horrible but dear Stephens [an A.D.C.] thinks divine."

The Duchess always gave a family party on Christmas Eve. In 1886 the three FitzGeorges were invited to St. James's. "It was like the prettiest of bazaars! H.R.H. bore it all most beautifully!! I was quite astounded! She was far beyond my expectations! and so enjoyed the pleasure she was giving, that we could really not induce her to break up, and go to bed! though we repeatedly tried to do so, till at length the dear Duke, always kind and thoughtful, took the law into his own dear hands, and insisted on saying good-night and *drove* all away! standing sentry till he got them out! God be praised for his dear mercy in letting us all once again spend this evening in joy together!!!" The Duke was unfailingly attentive and considerate. The Duchess described her son "as like a sheep-dog with a flock of sheep," driving her guests away when he thought it was time for her to go to bed. "As fast as he hunted some away on one side they came back again on the other."

The Duchess lovingly appreciated her son's affection, and when he was out of London her conversation often turned to discussion of his thoughtfulness. On leaving for Germany in 1878, he paid his mother a farewell visit. "After supper the Duchess talked much of him and his exquisite goodness to her, and how readily he would have even now given up his journey for her sake if she had allowed it." On her eighty-ninth birthday, Lady Geraldine "went into her and had the pleasure of reading to her a *dear dear* note from the Duke which touched her to the heart! So kind! She spoke most lovingly of him and how *angel* good he is! Of his golden heart and *charming* nature . . . his boundless attention and goodness to her!"[n]

Both the Duchess and Lady Geraldine agreed that the Duke's readiness to forgive an injury was characteristic of his generous nature, and they contrasted the vendettas of the Prince of Wales with H.R.H.'s willingness for reconciliation. The Duchess "spoke of how strongly marked and beautiful a trait this in his character, and always has been! His tutors and governors always remarked it, saying however severely they punished him, he always the next time they met, bounded up to them with the same friendship and affection! And so he has been through life, I never met *anyone* who can so thoroughly and really forgive and *forget!* If annoyed and displeased he can be angry at the moment, but once having forgiven, he utterly and absolutely banishes it from his mind! So that if, some time after you by chance allude to it, you find he has *literally* forgotten it and you would really have to *recall* it to his mind. A very beautiful trait indeed! which arises from his golden heart and most charming nature."[n]

The Duchess loved to discuss her grandchildren, and their visits were always welcome. "Colonel George came in," wrote Lady Geraldine on August 28, 1883, "and paid a nice visit till eleven ten. He told us he was travelling South to Carlisle and made friends with a man in the carriage with him, getting into much conversation with him, after dining together at Carlisle they exchanged cards, on reading George's name, the man said, 'Ah well you have the best father in England!'!! Nice, and *wise* man!! He was a Mr.

North of Cumberland." But sometimes George FitzGeorge fell out of favour. He was inclined to be argumentative and, even worse, radical. "Again a long argument upon the new and old military systems, upholding alas! considerable Cardwellian principles. At last the Duke broke off and spoke with H.R.H. of other things." Lady Geraldine became "more and more convinced Captain George is very argumentative and opinionated and terribly *modern* in ideas of 'reform'!! so called! and for discarding all *former* views! and I cannot bear his *tone* with the Duke!" Despite these shortcomings, when Lord Charles Beresford in 1882 told the Duchess that George was "a capital campaigner! always full of fun, and really an admirable caterer!" he gave her a great deal of pleasure, particularly as he concluded his eulogy by saying he thought George "very clever, and to sum up, he has a head on his shoulders.""

The Duke was fond of discussing his family problems at St. James's, and the collapse of George FitzGeorge's business ventures was a sadly familiar theme of conversation. "The Duke told us," Lady Geraldine wrote on May 19, 1884, "he has settled the affair of making Colonel George his A.D.C. A great worry, annoyance, and trouble it has been to him, alas! And finally of course can only be settled by the Duke having *as usual!* to pay an enormous sum for him!! He will listen to no one, least of all to the Duke! So far wiser than himself and with such true instinct for what is right and well to do and to leave undone! which Mr. George has not at all!! All the trouble he causes the Duke with these silly companies he not only gets into but *heads!!!* without capital! He is too tiresome. But the poor Duke having again largely and generously *paid* for him and advanced a *large* sum has freed him from the brewery." When in the following year Colonel George left the Army for the *Sunday Times*, Lady Geraldine described him as a "donkey" who, had he remained where he was, "might now command the Regiment!! If he had not been so obstinate and self-willed about quitting! but! he would not care to command it! Cares for nothing but idiotic newspaper scribbling!!" And then, having always been jealous of Mrs. FitzGeorge, she adds: "How preponderating must the *wretched* blood on the *other* side be!!!""

Much of the conversation at St. James's revolved round the Queen, and there were moments when the talk was neither amiable nor loyal. The Duke sometimes complained he was ignored by Her Majesty. "He read us the Duke of Connaught's telegram to say the Queen would 'not *have time* to see him before she goes abroad'!!! Discussion concerning this rude ungraciousness." When he visited Windsor after Christmas in 1877, he was kept "quite as an 'outsider' they told him—the Commander-in-Chief!!—*nothing*! Neither the Queen, nor Dizzy who was there.""

At St. James's it was believed that the Queen was too friendly with Lord Wolseley. On January 14, 1884, they discussed "the *strangeness* of the Queen showing such unmeasured favour to Wolseley." "To my mind," Lady Geraldine observed, "so *unloyal* of her!!" Among other signs of this excessive partiality was the invitation to Osborne of Wolseley's thirteen-year-old daughter. Wolseley himself was utterly unaware that he was a chosen favourite; on the contrary, like the Commander-in-Chief, he believed himself to be scorned and rejected. "I am sick of Royalties," he wrote to his wife, "and never wish to see one of our Royal family again: I think I used to be the greatest loyalist in England, but the cruel treatment I have received from the Queen, I can never either forgive or forget." In September 1882, he enclosed a letter to Lady Wolseley which he had just received from the Queen, "the only one she has ever honoured me with. I think you will agree with me that it is as cold-blooded an effusion as you have ever read: her only sympathies and solicitude are for her own selfish self and her family . . . I should esteem it a favour if the Queen would not write to me unless she can write to me in more gracious terms than in this stilted, freezing epistle. However let us forget this subject: I have done well for my country and if my country's sovereign does not appreciate my services I cannot help although I can pity her."

The Cambridges attributed some of the Queen's eccentricities to her living too much in the society of servants and of listening to foolish advice. "They discussed the peculiarities of the Queen," wrote Lady Geraldine on July 17, 1886, "how she sent a note to H.R.H. saying that if the Grand Duke of Mecklenburg-Strelitz who had just arrived from Germany, should wish to see her, 'Will you tell him that I cannot see him because I am just off to Osborne!!!!' Too odd. Moreover! the fact of her just going to Osborne on Tuesday!! at the very *instant* in all human probability of a change of ministry!! H.R.H. spoke of how strange it is of the Queen to send him such a message! Of her being so ill surrounded!" The Prince of Wales, when his mother's *Journal* came out, told the Duchess that he was indignant and disgusted at the Queen's publishing it. But then, he said, there was "no one to prevent her committing such acts." The Duke, who did not himself read it until some time after its publication, was informed at St. James's that it was an "atrocious" work. "We told him, how besides its *offensiveness* it is so badly written! Such bad vulgar English! So miserably futile and trivial! So dull and uninteresting."

The Prince of Wales's hostility to the Queen's *Journal* was nothing to his indignation that his son Prince George was never invited to shoot at Windsor until he was twenty-one. "You would hardly believe it," he told the Duke, "that, I being heir to the throne, this is the first time that my son has *ever* shot in Windsor Park!" As Prince George was among the best shots in England, and had been one of a "family party" at Sandringham which shot six thousand head in three days, the omission was remarkable.

The conversation at St. James's very often drifted back to recollections of former times. "We talked," wrote Lady Geraldine on January 29, 1887, "of the extraordinary and inexplicable hallucination of George IV that he commanded the Xth Hussars at Waterloo!!! Speaking one day of it before the Duke of Wellington and referring to him for corroboration, the Duke of Wellington bowed, and said: "Your Royal Highness's memory is better than mine!'" But, despite her age, the Duchess lived very much in the present and was quite as happy as gossip about Wolseley as the Prince Regent. "We spoke of the Dinner last night [May 21, 1887] to Sir Frederick Stephenson at which the Duke was, having been very successful! Colonel George said the Duke made a capital speech which was highly appreciated! Speaking of General Stephenson's modesty he said, 'We all know there are *some* generals, and it is not necessary to mention any names, but there are *some* who are very fond of always blowing their own trumpets! Now General Stephenson *never* blows his own trumpet! and as he does not you will perhaps forgive me if I blow it for him and somewhat loudly!'" When Wolseley went up in a balloon at Chatham, Lady Geraldine, after regretting that "the cord was not cut!" commented: "It's so like him, that having been most *violently* and abusively opposed to the use of balloons, since he went up in it, he returned in a violent state of enthusiasm about it."

The Duchess was always interested in foreign affairs and the doings of her numerous German relations. The death from cancer of the Kaiser Frederick III caused consternation at St. James's. The Duke, on June 16, 1888, "showed us a *charming* telegram he had received from the *poor* unhappy little Empress!!! in answer to his. 'Many thanks! He was so fond of you, loved England so much, you will not forget him, I know!'" Five days later, H.R.H. "told us of a really admirable letter he wrote today to the young Emperor William, giving him as his uncle, good sound advice! alluding to his differences with his mother, which he was able to do as Prince William had frankly spoken with him about them! and offering 'as he is very fond of her,' if at any time he could be of service between them, to do all in his powers to smooth matters, which it would give him great happiness to effect."

Apart from the family, Wolseley, Cardwell, and Childers, Gladstone was the public figure most discussed at St. James's. Lady Geraldine loathed him with extravagant frenzy. The Duchess was more temperate but was certainly no admirer of the Liberal statesman. The Duke, while opposing his policies, sometimes expressed a reluctant respect for his character and attainments. On April 2, 1883, Lady Geraldine was told by the Duke of his "visit at Sandringham which he liked very much, amongst old friends. Told us of Gladstone cutting down a tree! The absurdity!! Previously divesting himself of hat, coat, waistcoat, rolling up his shirt sleeves and unbuttoning his shirt front!!! The curious sight of the Prime Minister of England at seventy-four in this garb at this work watched by the heir apparent, the Primate, and the Commander-in-Chief!!! Of how admirably Gladstone read the lessons at both the morning and evening services yesterday! worth going a distance to hear." During the following evening, the Duke returned to the subject of the Prime Minister and spoke "of his wonderful energy and earnestness, and the extraordinary charm and fascination there certainly is about him personally, but loathing his politics as one does and all the harm and mischief he has done and does, yet one cannot help being charmed with him while you came in personal contact with him! The precise reverse of Beaconsfield. Of what a goose Mrs. Gladstone is! And how strange those four clever men, Peel, Derby, Disraeli and Gladstone should have married four such silly women!"

Miss Taylor, a lady-in-waiting called in by the Duchess to assist the indefatigable Lady Geraldine, was of Liberal sympathies. Once she became so indignant at hearing constant abuse of Gladstone that she stormed out of the drawing room of St. James's in an angry sulk. The Duke described Miss Taylor's behaviour as "outrageous." Lady Geraldine considered "she ought to be well whipped! a

thorough good thrashing is what she ought to have."
Princess Mary was disposed to be more generous and said
she considered "everyone has a right to their own opinion."
Once, when Miss Taylor's father was visiting St. James's,
the Duke happened to come in and the Duchess, to put
him in the conversation, said: " 'Mr. Taylor is just telling
me how conservative the city is.' 'I know,' said the Duke,
with meaning, leaning across to Mr. Taylor, 'I know! Excellent Conservatives. *I wish everybody else* were so too.'
The Duke then proceeded—on purpose!—'Oh! all the mischief is that *scoundrel* Gladstone!' so that Mr. Taylor could
not doubt of *His* Royal Highness's opinion of Miss Ella
Taylor's outburst.'"

The Duke, on April 20, 1887, sent Lady Geraldine "a
most cleverly drawn envelope!! the stamp placed so as to
form the head of the Queen as she kneels with it laid upon
the block, Gladstone with the most wicked expression of
exultant hate and fury, with his axe raised about to chop
it off! So cleverly done." The St. James's circle were very
angry with the Prince of Wales "for heading the list of
congratulations on Gladstone's birthday with a fulsome
telegram to the brute. To *my* mind it is too disgusting and
sickening! and *despicable!* He assured the Duke he had
telegraphed in *his* name as well as his own—thank *God*
it was only a joke."

When the Prince of Wales failed to come up from Sandringham to the funeral of Lord Iddesleigh, Lady Geraldine
was angered by "the knowledge that had heaven in mercy
delivered us from the curse of Gladstone's existence, the
Prince of Wales would have run, with ten special trains and
twenty extra engines, and enveloped in yards and folds of
crepe, to do honour to his funeral! and curry favour with
the plebs." Gladstone's invitation to Sandringham made
Lady Geraldine's "blood boil. And I asked the Duke if he
would not invite Mr. Parnell and Mr. Dillon to dinner
tonight to meet the Prince as his most fitting companions
and the most suited to his taste? It is really too disgusting.

The Duke defended him, it being the exigencies of his position, but there is a way and a mode of doing things."'"

Toward the end of 1888, the Duchess became more seriously ill, and on April 6, 1889, she died, at the age of ninety-two. The Duke, at the time, was inspecting the troops in Ireland. "Poor dear Mama!" wrote the Duke in his diary. "So kind, so good, so devoted to me and oh! how much I shall miss her dear presence, but for her, dear precious darling, a happy release from prolonged sufferings." He immediately left Dublin for London, where he arrived on the morning of April 7. At St. James's he "found poor Lady Geraldine very calm and composed though painfully sorrowing. I at once went to my dear Mother's bedroom, and saw her dear face lying peacefully and composedly on her bed of death, a happy expression on her beloved countenance. It was a terrible moment, though for her, dearest soul, a happy release."

The Duchess's end had come so suddenly that none of her children were with her. Apart from the nurses and Lady Geraldine, there was only one member of the royal family present. The Princess of Wales was at Marlborough House, and hearing that the Duchess was dying, she hastened across to St. James's. "Aunt dear, you know Alix," she said, as she approached the bedside. But there was no response.

The funeral took place at Kew Church on April 13, "exactly in the same manner as that of my beloved Father, at her express will and to our complete satisfaction." The hearse was escorted to Kew by the Life Guards, and the coffin was "surrounded by a profusion of the most lovely flowers I ever saw collected." The Queen was at the service and sat between Princess Mary and Princess Augusta. It was the only funeral she ever attended, except for her son Prince Leopold's. "The mournful ceremony was conducted in the most beautiful and solemn manner, a large number of my dear Mother's old friends being present." After the

Queen had returned to Windsor, she wrote to the Duke: "It was a melancholy satisfaction, I assure you, for me to have been with you all three at that very impressive and touching ceremony. . . . It is a sad and solemn feeling that there is no one above us any longer, and that *we* are now *the only old ones left.*"[n]

While the Duke was still mourning his mother's loss, Louisa became seriously ill. "I was much alarmed," wrote the Duke on July 30, "by the accounts about dearest Louisa this morning." The doctors were "evidently very anxious about her." "I therefore gave up going down to Goodwood for the race meeting and party, as I had intended . . . Sir Alfred Garrod went to see Louisa at five and both he and Dr. Sims found her very much less suffering than they had expected and thought she was progressing slowly but decidedly, they were therefore hopeful. I sat with her later on and read to her and she seemed to like it and was much less suffering."

From the end of the summer of 1888, Louisa lay under sentence of death and, despite great pain, managed to disguise her suffering from her husband. Occasionally, however, she surrendered to outbursts of anguish which doused her gaiety and charm. The Duke one day insisted that Sheppard, the Sub-Dean of the Chapels Royal, should come back to Queen Street with him and be introduced to his wife. "Sheppard made as if he would stay in the hall till the lady had been prepared for his visit. 'What the devil are you stopping there for?' said the Duke. 'Come up with me.' They proceeded upstairs and were ushered into a room opening into the bedroom where the patient lay. The Duke passed through the door and told Mrs. FitzGeorge that he had brought the Sub-Dean to see her, of whose kindness to his mother he had so often spoken, upon which, to Sheppard's consternation, he heard her say with emphasis, 'Indeed he is the last person I wish to see!' and, on his being introduced, she turned her head away and refused to speak. After a long pause of much embarrassment to all, Sheppard made a courteous effort to take leave, upon which the lady relented and said, 'Mr. Sheppard, you have shown me more courtesy than I have you, and I hope you will come again,' which he did seeing her constantly for the few months which preceded her death.'"

By the beginning of 1890, Louisa was so seriously ill that the Duke began to fear the worst. "No improvement," he wrote on January 7, "in the condition of my dearest love . . . She says herself she feels very ill and there cannot be a doubt of the fact. It makes me feel very, very anxious though I still *hope* for the best but I *fear* for the worst. I went to Queen Street and then to the office. Went back to Queen Street, dined there, and sat with Louisa, about whom I am *very uneasy*." On the following day he wrote: "Our Wedding day which we have always kept together. . . . Louisa seemed just a shade better to-day, so I proposed to her to take the Holy Communion with me tomorrow to which she *gladly assented*." On January 9 the Duke "after being busy at home in the morning went at once to Queen Street to meet Mr. Sheppard. Dearest Louisa appeared stronger and better and was able to keep her dear eyes open which she could not do the last few days. She *rejoiced* at taking the Holy Communion with myself, Loulings [Mrs. Hamilton] and dear good faithful Rowley [the nurse], was quite herself and most keenly attentive during the celebration and seemed none the worse for it. To me this service has been an immense satisfaction, and I thank God, for his great mercy in enabling her to take it before passing away from amongst us." On the tenth Louisa became unconscious. "Sims came in the early morning to tell me, he had been sent for to Queen Street, as dearest Louisa was in a very serious state. I at once went there with Gussie. Her eyes were in a peculiar condition and she had difficulty in recognizing those about her, and spoke and took nourishment with the greatest difficulty. I think she recognized my voice and said in a very low tone, 'God bless you dear papa' but it was very indistinct. It was evident that the end was approaching. I went home for breakfast and returned to Queen Street. Mr. Sheppard came at one, and we had prayers by her bedside, but she was too far gone to hear them or to be able to attend to them, the brain had evidently begun to give way. I again returned home to write some letters and then went back to Queen Street, she was lying in a peacefully unconscious state though still able to hear occasionally and I think she again made a great effort to say 'Bless you dearest' but that was all. From that time she did not speak again. We passed a most miserable day and after being together and having a second prayer just before dinner, remained there all night expecting the end. She lay there quite calm and placid, breathing quiet, pulse good, extremities still warm but peacefully unconscious. Sims came several times, but there was no change."

Louisa was unconscious throughout the eleventh and died early the next morning. "My beloved wife breathed her last calmly, peacefully, softly at about four o'clock this morning. We had been expecting this painful event all through the night, but lungs and heart were so sound, that they continued to perform their functions till their strength gave way under the weakness caused by absence of all nourishment, which could no longer be taken in the unconscious state she was in. All her children as well as myself, the little nurse, dear Rowley, and the female servants were surrounding the death bed . . . May the Almighty have mercy on her dear soul and give us strength to brave up against the overwhelming loss we have sustained. After coming home, I at once wrote to Ponsonby and the Prince of Wales asking the former to announce it to the Queen, which he kindly did and I later on received a most affectionate message from Her Majesty, which I highly appreciate and which would have been such a joy to my beloved one, had she known the fact. The Prince of Wales called on me to express his sympathy and sorrow at my heavy affliction. I had some hours' rest and then went to Queen Street where dear Mr. Sheppard gave us a short touching service at the death bed side. My beloved one lay lovely in death still amongst us. Her countenance was beautiful, quite young to look at, though seventy-four in actual age. The sorrow of my heart has this consolation that my beloved wife is now in peace and rest after her terrible and very prolonged sufferings, and God will be merciful to her Soul. She was so good and kind and affectionate and true and generous-hearted, and my little home of fifty years with my beloved Louisa is now come to an end."

The day after Louisa died, the Duke wrote to the Queen.

My dear Cousin,

Your most dear and gracious letter, and warm sympathy, have deeply touched me, and gives me *great consolation* in my heavy affliction. With all the greatness and importance of your position, nobody knows more about real affection than you do, my dearest cousin, who have had such painful trials to go through alas! on so many occasions. Your sympathy is a blessing to me for which I thank you from my very heart, and beg to remain,

Your most dutiful and devoted cousin,

George"

On January 14 the Duke "returned home, breakfasted with the boys, went to Queen Street and had a last look at my beloved wife, now beautifully laid out in the shell of the coffin, so calm and placid and quite young in the face, nothing painful about it, my bracelet on her dear arm, which she always wore, and which she will take with her to the grave."

The day of the funeral, January 16, was warm and sunny. At eleven thirty an open hearse, smothered in a mass of magnificent wreaths and followed by five carriages, set out from Queen Street. The Duke and his three sons were in the first carriage. In the second were Louisa Hamilton, Colonel Charles Fairbrother, Rose, and Sofia. Lord Wolseley and Colonel Du Plat, equerry to the Queen, formed part of the procession. At half past twelve the mourners reached the cemetery, where they were joined by the Duke of Teck, his wife being detained by "influenza," and a large number of friends. The crowd surrounding Kensal Green was so vast that barriers had to be erected and the entrance gates closed. After the coffin was lowered into the grave, it was hidden by flowers. The Duke's wreath was designed with a cross of violets in the centre, and the words "To my Dearest Louisa" picked out in white. The vault was lined with ivy and laurels, and was covered by a great marquee. "The last sad day has come," wrote the Duke, "and is painful in the extreme. Went at eleven to Queen Street and at eleven thirty the mournful procession moved from the dear little house. I followed the hearse with my three sons . . . All along the route the sympathy and good feeling evinced was very marked. Arrived at Kensal Green Chapel exactly at twelve thirty. Dear Mr. Sheppard read the burial service quite beautifully. All our friends attended in large number, and there was a great crowd outside all very respectful and sympathetic. She is buried behind the chapel in a piece of ground I bought for myself some years ago where I purpose to be laid myself by her dear side. Nothing could be more solemn and appropriate."

After the service, the family drove back to Queen Street. There the will was read; it was "most just and generous to all her children. Horley goes to Charles, the Queen Street home is settled on Augustus with all the furniture in it on the payment of £800, her jewels are divided amongst her children . . . I am executor with Bateson."

The Duke remained in England until the end of the month; then he left for Cannes. The day after the funeral he spent a painful afternoon looking over his wife's possessions in Queen Street, "my sons all most affectionate and good to me." On January 19, he went with Augustus FitzGeorge to the grave, "looking so nice and peaceful, but oh! how sad. Also went to the grave of my dearest friend."

Finally, a week after the funeral, he went "to Queen Street to take affectionate leave of the dear old house, including the poor dear room in which she died, where I have spent so many happy years of my life with my beloved wife. It overwhelmed me with grief and sorrow." At Cannes, away from all associations connected with Louisa, he nevertheless longed for her "indescribably" and especially missed "hearing from or writing to her daily, as has always been our habit since we first met." The very first thing he did on his return to England was to visit Kensal Green. "Very busy all morning," he wrote on March 19, "many people looking in upon me. I had before gone to the cemetery to visit my beloved wife's tomb. It was a sad, sad, visit and yet I was relieved in making it. George went with me. The wreaths were still being crowded on the grave, a painful spectacle, then also looked at the other poor grave nearby, which looked peaceful and well looked after." He had only returned from Cannes reluctantly, hating "the idea of going home where I shall feel my isolation more than ever, for I really have lost with dear Mama the *Home* and the daily life connected with it absolutely and entirely and there is nothing to me that can replace it on my return."

The Duke, who never forgot anniversaries, lived over again in January 1891 the miseries of Louisa's death. "My thoughts," he wrote, "were entirely absorbed with the sad recollections of last year, for this was the night that my beloved Wife Louisa passed away from amongst us. Oh! how I deplore her loss, to me so great and irreparable. No words can express the intense sorrow that oppresses and depresses my heart." Writing to Adolphus on January 13, he tells him: "I daily, hourly I may say, miss her dear presence from amongst us. She was so good and true to me, such a real friend, always giving the best and soundest advice, and so thoroughly unselfish, and having only mine and all of your good at heart. In short my dear Dolly I feel thoroughly miserable and can only hope and pray *she* is now in a better world, where ere very long, I may be per-

mitted to join her again." In 1892, on October 31, Louisa's
birthday, he wrote in his diary: "How many happy days I
have spent with her this anniversary in former days!! Now
how all is changed and how isolated one feels. It is very sad
and I felt all day greatly depressed."

From everything that the Duke did, said, and wrote, it is
evident that he was devoted to Louisa, and it appears that
his passion for Mrs. Beauclerk in no way diminished his
affection for his wife. Mrs. FitzGeorge's position—as the
Daily Telegraph obituary expressed it—"was one scarcely
without difficulty or disadvantage. But so considerable was
her natural grace and dignity, so marked her tact and intelligence, her experience and judgement, that she easily surmounted any of the inconveniences that may have lain in
her path." The fact that Louisa could not inhabit the Duke's
official world enabled him to live two lives and to escape
from the official flunkery of Gloucester House, literally by
the back door, into the cosy family establishment in Queen
Street.

Lady Geraldine, no doubt expressing the view of the
Duchess and, certainly in this instance, of the Queen, deplored the marriage and detested Louisa. Her opinions, of
course, were poisoned by almost hysterical jealousy and
her views on marriage were narrowly aristocratic. Moreover, her references to Louisa amount to little more than
sinister hints, mysterious allusions, and criticism of her
manners, which neither the evidence of Mrs. FitzGeorge's
letters nor of her husband's correspondence and diaries in
any way supports. On December 2, 1906, Lady Geraldine
noted that she was reading Sheppard's *Life* of the Duke.
"The Chapter on my Duchess's death is deeply touching
and beautiful! but the following Chapter!!! turned all to
gall." It was devoted to Mrs. FitzGeorge.

In 1884, the conversation at St. James's turned to the
circumstances of the marriage of the Grand Duke of Hesse.
"The Duke spoke strongly on 'when a man, through some

unfortunate accident, makes a great mistake he must abide by it!' Yes! upon that alas! *He* has honourably acted all his life, and cruelly suffered for it, poor true and good heart." Two years later Lady Geraldine recorded a remark Lord William Paulet made to the Duchess. "We spoke much of the Duke! which is always pleasant to do! for he has such a just appreciation of his work! Such a properly high opinion of him, such a deep feeling and regret for the never sufficiently to be lamented sacrifice of his existence."''

Sofia seems to have shared Lady Geraldine's opinions of her mother-in-law. On March 9, 1904, shortly before the Duke's death, Lady Geraldine visited Kew Cottage, where "Mrs. Dolly" was staying. They had a long discussion about the Duke's health and then the conversation turned to the old days. "So much, so much she told me! and so much which corroborated all that I have thought and believed . . . One very curious thing she told me, that all of the three sons were christened at the Chapel Royal Savoy!!! too strange! One detestable thing she told me of '47!!! [the year of the Duke's marriage] Oh! but the pain of it all! It would even poison the paper destroying it utterly! leaving nothing! Nothing! Nothing!!! And, O God! the price paid!!!" Soon after the Duke's funeral, Lady Geraldine deplored his being buried in that "hateful mausoleum." On March 30, 1904, she wrote: "Oh! how I detest his being at Kensal Green! and what *pain* the whole thing is." Sofia again told "me many things about *her* that entirely corroborated much I have seen and heard from others, and my own intimate convictions . . . This made me more than ever miserable and still yet more embitters the bitter thought of where he lies!" Later, Mrs. Dolly, talking of her brother-in-law Augustus's "disastrously offensive manner," said: "He is so *exactly* like his mother. *Exactly* her voice, manner, tone, and character!"

Lady Geraldine's views were more often than not expressed with extravagant vigour, but they were recorded after all in a private journal, with no thought of publication. She was neither obliged nor accustomed to weigh her words, and her likes were as passionate as her dislikes were vehement. Her hopeless infatuation for the Duke, her unthinking acceptance of social conventions, and her distracted jealousy, all encouraged her to blackguard Mrs. FitzGeorge. Her ill-defined accusations contain, at worst, therefore, only a grain of truth. That the Duke's married life was happy is proved by his utter dejection when Louisa died. And while she lived he never expressed even one fleeting moment of regret. In taking her for his wife, he had wittingly defied convention. It had been no hasty decision: indeed, strictly speaking, it had been reached too late. Lady Geraldine's attempt to represent it as a rash and precipitate indiscretion, while plausible enough as a theory, is without substance in fact, and her malicious prattle in no way detracts from one of the great romances of the nineteenth century.

Commander-in-Chief

WHEN the Duke heard that W. H. Smith was to leave the War Office, he was very despondent. "Thinks all and everything is going to the dogs! Most depressing and despairing reports this evening [January 7, 1887]. Edward Stanhope is to go to the War Office, the Duke knows nothing at all of him for or against, hopes he may do! But we spoke of the unutterable harm to the Service of the State, of the inane and idiotic practice of this *eternal* shuffling of the cards and the moment a man gets to know and thoroughly understand and be capable of his work, whisk! he is moved off to something fresh of which he knows nothing! Now not only no Government lasts twelve months but the self-same Government never can have its Ministers at their same posts for six or four months!! They have had *four* Secretarys of State at the War Office within a year!!!!"

Although Stanhope was a Tory, the Duke quickly grew to distrust him, and thought him in some ways worse than Cardwell or Childers. Smith was deeply regretted. "We spoke," wrote Lady Geraldine on April 15, 1888, "of how admirably well Mr. W. H. Smith had led the Commons for the year past! Of the *very* high regard and esteem, the very *high* opinion of him, the Duke has! 'He is such a *gentleman!* such a man of his word! you can so entirely trust him.' He has such solidity and stirling worth."

After working for a few months with the new Secretary for War, the Duke decided that he was "an odious prig" and "far away the worst War Minister he has yet had to endure, knows *nothing on earth* of the subject, yet believes himself so mightily clever he will not ask or take advice from *anyone*, and acts entirely off his own bat, then when shown what a mistake he has made 'Ah well! *it is done!*' "

Stanhope did not improve on further acquaintance. He was so "impertinent" that the Duke was once more driven to threats of resignation. Describing an interview he had with the War Minister on January 16, 1889, H.R.H. told Lady Geraldine "he had had a most unpleasant meeting at the War Office today! That little *beast* Stanhope more nasty than ever! No War Minister he has yet had *ever* assumed the insolence of tone towards him personally of this *beastly* little whippersnapper who might be his son. Nasty filthy little prig! Childers and even Cardwell were always, at least outwardly, civil courteous and deferential to him personally! To schoolmaster him as a chidden schoolboy was reserved for the Conservative Government to do!! He told him plainly today if it goes on it is quite impossible for him to stay."

Mrs. Mitford, another of the Duchess's occasional ladies-in-waiting, was lectured by the Commander-in-Chief on the shortcomings of the Secretary of State. Lady Geraldine thought it "imprudent" to talk so freely before such a "dangerous gossip." Indeed, H.R.H. was liable to let his indignation outrun his discretion and was not always careful in his choice of an audience. Mischief-makers were only too ready to repeat what he said—such reports being sometimes invented, often distorted, and invariably embellished. On this occasion he "spoke with Mrs. Mitford of that shining light Edward Stanhope, to show her how wretched a creature he, alas! is; as he proved to her by too many instances, what a regular little pettifogging lawyer he is, and so overbearing and opinionated, worse than that so unreliable and not truthful! telling one man the Duke has agreed to so and so, or even that the Duke *wishes* so and so, when the Duke has unmistakably and repeatedly urged on him the exact reverse! and while pretending to hold the military authorities responsible, representing them to the public as being so, he *does* all off his own ultra-civilian bat, without consulting them at all; tomorrow he is to bring in, in the House of Commons a bill concerning the national defences, and he has never consulted the Duke upon a word of it!!! Or even shown it to him!! nor to the Adjutant General! and then, he quibbles so *beside* the truth! Before the Estimates were made out, he said to the Duke and the rest of the military authorities, 'You must not ask for more men, because the Chancellor of the Exchequer *will not give them.*' In the face of this of course the military authorities did not ask for them; thereupon, without mentioning a word of these preliminaries, or any details of how or why, in the House of Commons he shields himself from attack by the all-round assertion: 'They were never asked for'!! So disingenuous! It is indeed a miserable task to have to work with such a Minister!'"

Wolseley's assessment of Stanhope was much the same as the Commander-in-Chief's. He described Stanhope as "nothing more than a little party politician dressed up as a Statesman . . . I have striven hard to help him to make up for his absolute ignorance upon every point large and small of his work, but to no purpose. He is a prig pure and simple . . . I long for a rest or power; at present I have neither and have to serve a ridiculous Commander-in-Chief who knows nothing of War and a real first class prig (i.e. Stanhope) who only cares for party politics." The Adjutant General opposed Stanhope so vigorously that the War Minister sent him as Commander-in-Chief to Ireland to get him out of the way. "Little Stanhope nearly ruined me," wrote Wolseley, in retrospect, "and I often think I ought to have stood up and fought the little cunning, jealous and suspicious sparrow, without any mercy. I think I could have killed him but I had pity on him for I despised him. You ought never to lose a chance to kill an enemy or a man as hostile as he was to me whenever you can. He was an underhand little reptile that I scotched only when I should have killed him." In a letter to Sir Henry Ponsonby, Wolseley described Stanhope as "this smallest of minded men whom it has ever been my fortune in life to meet and to do business with."[n]

Lord Wolseley, on April 23, 1888, made one of his famous speeches. It was widely reported by the press, and the Duke, although he thought that the Adjutant General had no business to be so outspoken, could not but sympathize with the sentiments expressed. "We spoke of Wolseley having made a very trenchant speech last night, a *tremendous* onslaught on *all* governments, of whom he says they sacrifice everything to Party! Everything done or left undone, to suit Party needs and interest. Most *strictly* and accurately true! but the Duke considers he has no business to be so outspoken, being an official, and therefore bound to greater reticence. Though *I* still cannot but feel it is well the truth should sometimes be spoken!! The fact is Wolseley is very angry at a great deal that is doing at present, very sore, and utterly disgusted with Mr. Stanhope whom he thinks (and small blame to him for it!) a conceited ass!"

In May 1888 the *Daily Telegraph* published a sensational article headed "England in danger—no guns, no men." It referred to the "deplorable neglect of Parliament and the mischievous system adopted by successive ministries in deliberately hiding the truth from the people." It maintained that the Army was too small, its equipment obsolete, and its barrack accommodation inadequate. The paper claimed that these charges proceeded from the "highest military authority." The Duke when he read the article "was much put out . . . I requested Harman to go to try to find Mr. Lawson and ask him what it meant, as I knew nothing of such a statement or announcement . . . Harman returned saying that the 'highest military authority' referred to was not myself." That evening H.R.H. answered a question put to him in the House of Lords about his responsibility for what had been said. He told their Lordships that nobody could have been more astonished than he was himself when he noticed "this extraordinary sensational article . . . I can only say that I have reason to believe that 'the highest military authority' which I admit that, up to this moment, I believed I was, is intended for somebody else."

Sir Henry Ponsonby, in explaining the episode to the Queen, attributed the confusion which had arisen to the fact that the *Daily Telegraph* had based its article on a speech made by the Commander-in-Chief. A short time before, the Under-Secretary for War, addressing the citizens of Guildford, had told them that the responsibility for providing an efficient army rested with the military authorities. This was too much for the Duke, whose demands for recruits had been rejected, and who was indignantly fighting to prevent excessive reductions. Both H.R.H. and Wolseley replied by publicly declaring that the Army was too small, and that it was iniquitous to hold them responsible, when try as they would, the Secretary of State refused them money and men. As Ponsonby declared with surprised satisfaction: "His Royal Highness and Lord Wolseley are entirely agreed on the subject." Although the Government was angry, "Lord Wolseley's friends are strong in his favour, and maintain that the Duke of Cambridge and he have done a real service in creating an excitement about the Army.'"

If the Commander-in-Chief retained any illusions about Stanhope or Conservative Governments, they were dispelled by the appointment in June 1888 of a Royal Commission to report on War Office organization under the chairmanship of Lord Hartington, who had recently left the Liberal party over the issue of Home Rule. It reported in 1890 that the complete responsibility of the Secretary of State to Parliament and the country for all Army matters must be accepted as definitely established. Among its recommendations, "almost buried by diplomatic tribute and complimentary verbiage," was the proposal to abolish the post of Commander-in-Chief and to remodel the War Office on the lines of the Board of Admiralty. A chief of staff, corresponding to the First Naval Lord, was to be the senior military official. The Duke regarded the whole report as "deplorable." Before he had time to do more than thumb through its contents, he was in a flurry of indignation and excitement. Stanhope was subjected to a heavy fusillade from the Horse Guards, and the Queen, at Windsor, was overwhelmed with letters, telegrams, and visits. She did, however, reassure her agitated cousin by insisting that she was fully determined to retain the post of Commander-in-Chief unimpaired. When Ponsonby submitted one of the Duke's letters to her, expressing alarm at the Hartington Report, she endorsed the memorandum: "This cannot be allowed for one moment, and Sir Henry should take steps to prevent this being even discussed. V.R.I."

During the next few days Ponsonby received a bewildering array of additional instructions. He was directed to tell Smith—who had been a member of the Commission—and Stanhope how shocked the Queen was "at the nature of the Army Commission report so far as the Horse Guards are concerned: and would you tell them both she entirely disapproves of the idea of a Board such as that at the Admiralty, and cannot listen to it for a moment." Next he was told that the Queen proposed to write to the Prime Minister, Lord Salisbury, and inform him that she had "talked fully over the subject of this truly abominable report," that she quite agreed with the Duke that its recommendations were "reckless" and "incredibly thoughtless," and moreover that she was "beyond measure shocked" that they "should have emanated from a Conservative Government." Writing to her private secretary, she told him: "The Queen wishes a satisfactory arrangement, but the C.-in-C.'s position must not be lessened or weakened. One of the greatest prerogatives of the Sovereign is the *direct communication,* with an immovable and non-political officer of high rank, *about the Army.*"

The Commander-in-Chief underestimated the Queen's vigilance, for she was ever sensitive to the remotest threat to prerogative and did not require his prompting to appreciate the damage which would be done to the monarchy if the Hartington Report were accepted. But whether she needed the Duke's advice or not, it was none the less proffered unsparingly. To emphasize the gravity of the situation, H.R.H. again talked of resignation, a threat so frequently employed that its effectiveness was diminishing. He warned Ponsonby that as "Mr. Stanhope leans to the side of the Commission," its recommendations would be accepted "unless the Queen is *very, very firm* and *decided.*" Ponsonby reassured the Duke: "I think Her Majesty will consent to no great change which is opposed by Your Royal Highness, and Lord Salisbury apparently does not approve of any alteration in the position of the Commander-in-Chief.'"

The Duke never discovered that, at the time of the publication of the Hartington Report, there was an even more sinister threat to his position than the proposal to abolish his office. Ponsonby wrote at the Queen's command a letter to the Prince of Wales, understandably described as "strictly confidential," since "it would obviously lead to serious difficulties if the Duke of Cambridge were to hear of it.'" The plan, which was to be kept from the Commander-in-Chief, was proposed by Lord Wolseley. In a number of letters to Ponsonby, he discussed the Commission's suggestions. To abolish the office of Commander-in-Chief he regarded as a "step backwards." "We sorely want a doctor I admit, but Brackenbury and Co. have sent us an executioner.'" His solution was to persuade the Duke of Cambridge to resign and to replace him with Prince Arthur, Duke of Connaught. The Queen thought the plan decidedly attractive, although she foresaw difficulties.

The Cabinet considered the proposal but finally rejected it. What induced them to do so, Wolseley could never discover. Stanhope merely informed him the reasons were "political." "What I conceive to be at the bottom of the matter," Wolseley told Ponsonby, "is that they have made up their minds to do away with the office of Commander-in-Chief

. . . It is hard that a man should be held to be disqualified for high military command because he is the Queen's son. Behind all this matter is the Duke of Cambridge. Harting-ton, and all the Secretaries of State here in my time, have suffered so much at his hands, have had all needful reforms in the Army so blocked by him that one and all were deter-mined never to have another Prince here who might prove equally immovable and irremovable. I am so fond of the Duke of Cambridge that I hate even thinking of this, but I am sure it is true, and I think everyone who has been long here knows this as well as I do." Ponsonby replied by point-ing out possible objections to the appointment of the Duke of Connaught and stressing the difficulty of overcoming opposition. "Before I for ever relinquish the subject," came the answer, "I wish to fire one more shot in what I believe to be the interests of the Duke of Connaught and of the Army. If what I say is high treason I hope I may be forgiven. I may as well be hanged as high as Haman as on an ordinary gallows. In writing this note I wish above all things in the interest of the Army and therefore of the State to adopt some line of conduct that will secure us in the future as in the past a Commander-in-Chief.

"To secure to any future Commander-in-Chief the powers which the Duke of Cambridge inherited from the Duke of Wellington, I am well aware the Duke of Cambridge has himself rendered impossible.

"No Government of any shade of politics would ever or could ever again allow anyone to be able to prevent nearly all reform in our military organization as the Duke of Cam-bridge has done for years past; as you know that his action has more than once produced between the Queen and her Cabinet a strained condition of things that was to be depre-cated on every ground.

"In our endeavours to retain the post of Commander-in-Chief in the Army, this fact must be recognized, for I am sure it was in the minds of many who sat upon Lord Hartington's Commission. If we succeed in retaining the post at all, we must be prepared to see it shorn of much of its present importance. I know privately that it is Mr. Stanhope's wish to retain the Duke of Cambridge as Commander-in-Chief for another two years longer. He will then be seventy-three years of age. The idea is then to get rid of him and have no successor to his office, but instead to have a Chief of the Staff to the Secretary of State for War. In other words, some political creature of his own.

"The Duke of Cambridge says many times every week that he will at once resign and consults me and Harman as to the propriety of doing so. Between ourselves, I don't think he has the least intention of ever doing this until he receives a hint from the Queen that he should do so.

"Now I come to my proposition: Why should not Lord Salisbury allow the Duke of Connaught to succeed him at once? If necessary make the tenure of that office seven, or even five years. . . . My own selfish object in bringing this forward is, that under the Duke of Connaught the Army would be brought up to date in all matters of military instruction, organization, and tactical efficiency. Personally, I like the Duke of Cambridge so much that I hate saying this, but it is well known to all the rising officers in the Army that, as long as he continues to be Commander-in-Chief, this much wished for condition of things is impossible, is not to be thought of. It is not the Duke of Cambridge's fault: he was educated in a bad military school and cannot forget the lessons it taught him, nor can he take in and learn those which modern war has taught all foreign nations.

"I hope it may not be thought that it is from any ill-feeling towards the Duke of Cambridge I write this. In my heart I entertain strong feelings of personal attachment to him. No one can know him, and see him daily as I have done for years, and not admire his amiable qualities. But in the interests of the Army I would like to see him replaced by the Duke of Connaught *at once*. . . . As a punishment for my treason don't send me an ultimatum of 'resignation or of compulsory removal.' I give my views for what they are worth. They may be foolish, they are certainly honest."

Not only did the Cabinet reject Wolseley's plan, but the Queen in the end decided that it was impracticable and that she could not "seem to advance the interests of her own son." On August 7 she wrote in her diary: "Saw Sir H. Ponsonby later, about a remarkable letter from Lord Wolseley, strongly urging that George C. should be got to resign, Arthur to be appointed his successor. This I consider an impossibility, though it might in some ways be a good thing. Arthur is of the same opinion." But she entirely agreed with Wolseley that her son was handicapped by being royal. "It is too shameful keeping him out of all important places on account of his birth." Moreover, she suspected that "the Government think most foolishly Arthur would be as retrograde and old-fashioned as the dear Duke of Cambridge, whereas he is the very reverse." In the end the proposals of the Hartington Committee were set aside, the claims of the Duke of Connaught were rejected, and the Commander-in-Chief remained in unchallenged possession at the Horse Guards.

One criticism which was levelled against H.R.H. during the discussions on the Commission's report was that he could hardly be performing his duties satisfactorily when his health apparently required him to spend long periods abroad. The Queen was well aware of what was said and did little to encourage these trips overseas. "Tho' I granted you the desired leave," she wrote on December 29, 1891, "I must impress you with the necessity of it not exceeding on any account four weeks, as I am sure that your frequent and lengthened absences are not good and enable those who are inimical to the office of Commander-in-Chief to argue that if he is so often away it shows that we can do without him." Admittedly, H.R.H. was an indefatigable correspondent, but there were times when his presence at the Horse Guards was much to be desired. The Tranby Croft scandal was such an occasion.

In September 1891 the Prince of Wales stayed at Tranby Croft for the Doncaster races. His host, Arthur Wilson, was a rich shipowner from Hull. Among the guests was Sir William Gordon-Cumming, Colonel of the Scots Guards. Sir William was accused of cheating at baccarat and was induced to sign a paper promising never to touch cards again. He maintained his innocence throughout, but agreed to the arrangement to avoid a scandal involving the heir to the throne. His fellow guests, for their part, undertook "to preserve silence" about the accusation which had been made, and there the matter should have ended. Subsequently the story leaked out and Sir William brought a slander action against Mrs. Wilson and other members of the house party. The case, which lasted seven days, came before Lord Chief Justice Coleridge on June 1, 1891, and the Prince of Wales reluctantly appeared as a witness for the defence. The press, suffering from one of its more acute fits of morality, attacked him unmercifully for indulging in such wickedness, and published to the world the horrifying news that the counters which had been employed were stamped with the Prince's monogram. The Queen's eldest son, it seemed, was so depraved a gambler that night after night he risked losing money to his friends, if not his immortal soul to the devil. A verdict for the defendants was returned, but the public behaved as if the Prince had been on trial.

The Queen contemplated the proceedings with profound distaste. She instructed the Duke of Cambridge, on his return from his visit to Egypt, to lecture her son on the evils of gambling—a task one might have thought the national press had rendered superfluous. The Duke, on arrival at Sandringham, lost his nerve—if, as Wolseley once unkindly observed, one can lose what one has never possessed." He tried to persuade Sir Francis Knollys to deliver the Queen's message, and on Sir Francis declining to do so, it failed to reach its destination." H.R.H. told his son Adolphus: the "scandal is painfully disgusting and anything more unfortunately managed from beginning to end I cannot imagine."

When the charges made against Sir William became public, Lord Coventry, one of the guests at Tranby Croft, brought the case to the attention of Sir Redvers Buller, who in 1890 had succeeded Lord Wolseley as Adjutant General. He wrote to Buller rather than to the Commander-in-Chief because the latter was in Egypt. "We feel it incumbent upon us," he declared, "to place the facts officially before you that a full enquiry may forthwith be instituted into so grave and serious an accusation against a gentleman holding Her Majesty's Commission."" Sir Redvers thereupon investigated the affair and reported his findings to the Queen and the Duke.

In a letter written to Ponsonby on February 13, the Adjutant General gave a lucid summary of all that had occurred. He argued that if Sir William were required to resign from his regiment, or if a court martial were immediately held, such proceedings would prejudice the civil trial then pending. Buller, after consulting the Judge Advocate General, decided it would be unjust to institute a military inquiry before the action for slander had been decided in court. In writing to the Duke, he mentioned two features of the affair which he regarded as unsatisfactory. He maintained that no hostess should ever have permitted one of her guests to be watched, almost trapped, as Sir William had been. Hearing of the suspicions that had arisen, she should have contrived to avoid any further games of baccarat. A conjurer could be procured, or some wretched guest conscripted to sing, recite, or play the piano. Perhaps if all other contrivances failed, they might, as a last desperate resort, even fall back on conversation. The second irregularity, as Buller saw it, was that, all having sworn to preserve secrecy, the story should later have come out."

The Commander-in-Chief was opposed to the idea of delaying military proceedings until the civil trial was over. "Impress upon the Secretary of State," he telegraphed to

Buller, "I consider honour of Army requires immediate action on military part. How can an officer accused of cheating be allowed to wear Queen's uniform?" The Prince of Wales, who, in truth, had had much to endure, was in no mood for temperate measures. He felt even more strongly than his Uncle George that an immediate court martial should be held. A court martial, if it found Sir William guilty, would dispose of the civil action, and would moreover avoid publicity for the Prince.

Lord Wolseley, writing to his wife on February 12, said he was "very much amused" by a letter he had received telling him that the Prince of Wales was "furious with the way in which Buller had disposed of the Cummings scandal —postponing all military action until the civil trials come off in November next." The Prince was indeed angry and agitated for a court martial. Writing to H.R.H., he declared: "It is enough to make the great Duke of Wellington rise from his tomb and point his finger of scorn at the Horse Guards— over which he presided so long and with such honour! Not only the officers but even the men are affected by the Adjutant General's decision. The conduct of the A.G. is inexplicable but he cannot have the interests of the Army at heart, acting in the way he has. I always knew he was a born soldier—and equally imagined he was a gentleman, but from henceforth I can never look upon him in the latter category!"* If the Prince was to be credited, Buller's sense of fair play, a quality which many have considered to be among the foremost attributes of a gentleman, deprived him of the right to be so regarded. With a fine disdain for the traditions of English justice, the heir to the throne took Sir William's guilt for granted, and the idea of a trial, or of weighing evidence, seemed to him a waste of time. Cumming's version of the affair, so he told the Duke, "was false from beginning to end." He had "not a leg to stand on, and his protestations of innocence are useless. His conduct throughout has been simply scandalous."*

Sir Francis Knollys, writing on his master's behalf, pro-

312

tested against the Adjutant General's postponement of military action, which sanctioned "a man of whose guilt no impartial person can for one moment entertain the slightest doubt, to remain from February to November in Her Majesty's service because his Solicitor, in order to gain time, says the case will be prejudiced by the authorities allowing a court of enquiry to be held . . . and after nine or ten months all the details of this lamentable affair will be again brought forward and discussed to the great edification of the Republicans and Socialists." However, Knollys continued, the Prince is glad "to hear that the Guards Club are going to take the matter up." "Everybody wished Your Royal Highness had been here, in which case an immediate enquiry would have been held." As it is, the slander trial "when it comes off will be a great calamity to the Royal Family, to Society and the Army."[n]

The Prince of Wales was not alone in begging the Commander-in-Chief to use "his influence to insist upon this fellow being tried by the military authorities as would be done in every civilized country in the world." The Duke of Fife wrote protesting against "this most unfortunate and extraordinary decision." He declared that "the action of the Adjutant General had filled everybody with amazement" and that, to preserve the honour of the Army, measures must, at once, be taken." But Buller had already committed the Duke, who supported the decision, although disapproving of it. The affair not only was unfortunate for the Prince and the Army, but had inadvertently given undue prominence to H.R.H.'s absence abroad. Knollys, writing to Ponsonby, observed: "The Duke of Cambridge is playing the part of Antony, with Cleopatra up the Nile, in Egypt,"[n] and he vigorously complained about the Commander-in-Chief's being absent from his post for nearly three months.

The lady whom Knollys dubbed Cleopatra was Mrs. Vyner. Bob Vyner was a rich Yorkshire squire, who in 1865 married Eleanor, daughter of the Reverend Slingsby Duncomb Shafto. She became an intimate friend of the Prince of Wales, cultivated the Tecks, and numbered the Duke of Cambridge among her most ardent admirers. "After talking to your mother," Frank Harris once told Lady Alwynne Compton, "one feels a sort of intimate sympathy with her, almost as though it were love." "The curious part of it is," replied Lady Alwynne, "that she is in love with you for the time being, she's extraordinarily sympathetic."[n]

After the Duke fell a hopeless victim to Mrs. Vyner's charm, Lady Geraldine regarded her with venomous malice. "Great God in heaven!" she wrote on December 11, 1891. "What *can* he see in her? What can he? What *can* attract him? Of all the *absolutely uninteresting unattractive* women I have ever seen she is far away the most entirely so, she has not an *attraction* of any kind, she is really very *plain*, singularly undistinguished, not the *ghost* of a figure, fat, podgy, shapeless yet at the same time arms like a knitting needle! A *most* silly way of going into fits of giggles into her pocket handkerchief about nothing at all, a provoking way of talking, not an attraction in the world. And O God, O God, most clearly and decidedly to me, has not a spark of real feeling for him!! I am as sure of it as anything on earth!" Lady Geraldine, contrasting her own devotion to the Duke with Mrs. Vyner's flighty affection, described it as bearing the same relation "as a farthing rushlight to the great sun." It was Lady Geraldine's conviction that the Duke's association with Mrs. Vyner had ruined his character, and she deplored the influence of the "*hateful* Vyner lot." "Have been reading the old, old journals," wrote Lady Geraldine on November 13, 1893, "it is all like a strange trance and dream to me, for he is now a totally, entirely, absolutely, *utterly different man*, in *all* and every way and *everything!!!* from what he was then! When I read of and remember him *then*, as he was! and see and hear him now, it is positively as though it were two altogether different persons! Inconceivable!!"

The Duke first became acquainted with the Vyners at Homburg in August 1888. "That fatal time!! that *ended* all life for me," was how Lady Geraldine described it in 1894 as she was reading through her diaries. "Reached another volume," she noted on June 2, "of the dear past!! which volume I see goes as far as July 1888! just before the end of my life!! As in a month from then it was *destroyed* by the vile hateful *Diablesse*." In February of 1889 the Duke stayed a fortnight at Cannes and enjoyed himself so much that he spent part of the winter there for the rest of his life. He always put up at the Hôtel Prince de Galles, where he occupied the same "charming apartments." It was conveniently close to the Château St. Anne, the Vyners' "quite beautiful" villa, with its "delightful and beautifully kept garden, quite perfection." Bob Vyner rented the shooting on the island of St. Marguerite, and many "charming excursions" took place across the bay. The Vyners entertained nearly all distinguished English visitors to Cannes. The Prince of Wales paid many visits to the Château, and even Mr. and Mrs. Gladstone were invited. "He made himself most agreeable," wrote H.R.H. on February 17, "and is looking very well." That Mrs. Vyner fraternized with the arch-traitor did not help endear the *Diablesse* to some of the Duke's friends. When the visit ended, on February 28, H.R.H. wrote in his diary: "Alas! My stay here is come to an end to my great sorrow for I have *delighted* in it, and only long and hope to be able to come again in future years."

After Louisa's death in 1890, the Duke saw even more of the Vyners and their circle. Writing in his diary on December 30, he commented: "The last day of rather an eventful year, of much sorrow, though latterly also of much comfort." In 1891 he went to Egypt to join the Vyners there. On his way out, Mrs. Elizabeth Butler entertained him. "We had the Duke of Cambridge to luncheon. He arrived yesterday on board the *Surprise* from Malta, and Will, of course, received him officially, but not royally, as he is travelling incog., and he came here to tea. To-day we had a large party to meet him, and a very genial luncheon it was, not to say rollicking. The day was exquisite, and out of the open windows the sea sparkled, blue and calm. H.R.H. seemed to me rather feeble, but in the best of humours; a wonderful old man to come to Egypt for the first time at seventy-two, braving this burning sun and with such a high colour to begin with! One felt as though one was talking to George III to hear that 'What, what, what? Who, who, who? Why, why, why?' Col. Lane, one of his suite, said he had never seen him in better spirits. I was gratified at his praise of our cook—very loud praise, literally, as he is not only rather deaf himself, but speaks to people as though they also were a 'little hard of hearing.' 'Very good cook, my dear' (to me). 'Very good cook, Butler' (across the table to Will). 'Very good cook, eh, Sykes?' (very loud to Christopher Sykes, further off). 'You are a *gourmet,* you know better about these things than I do, eh?' C.S.: 'I ought to have learned something about it at Gloucester House, sir!' H.R.H. (to me): 'Your health, my dear.' 'Butler, your very good health!' Aside to me: 'What's the Consul's name?' I: 'Sir Charles Cookson.' 'Sir Charles, your health!' When I hand the salt to H.R.H. he stops my hand: 'I wouldn't quarrel with her for the world, Butler.' And so the feast goes on, our august guest plying me with questions about the relationship and antecedents of everyone at the table; about the manners and customs of the populace of Alexandria; the state of commerce; the climate. I answer to the best of my ability with the most unsatisfactory information. He started at four for Cairo, leaving a most kindly impression on my memory. The last of the old Georgian type! 'Your mutton was good, my dear; not at all *goaty,*' were his valedictory words.'"

Mrs. Vyner, although sometimes callous about the pathetic attentions of her elderly admirer, did provide him with that companionship for which he ever hungered, and which, in younger days, had been supplied by Mrs. Beauclerk, by the Duchess of Cambridge, and by Mrs. Fitz-George. When he left Cannes for England on March 1, 1894, he did so "with a very heavy heart, as regards those of the dear 'Château.' " Whether Bob Vyner was equally sorry to see him depart remains a matter for conjecture.

Lady Geraldine, after leaving St. James's, took a small house in Upper Brook Street. Whenever the Duke was in London, he visited her constantly, and she was often invited to Gloucester House. Mrs. Hamilton, on December 15, 1893, even invited her to Queen Street, to meet H.R.H. "At eight o'clock in a hansom to Queen Street!!! to meet the Duke!! What turmoil of strange thoughts and feelings at going in for the first time into *that* house! Curious that I should have lived to know and frequent *both* houses." The conversation at Brook Street was often of life in the old days, and whenever it turned to the present, Lady Geraldine's obsession with Mrs. Vyner somehow nearly always won the upper hand. "We talked of the new play which came out last night at the Haymarket, *A Woman of No Importance* by Oscar Wilde! Of what an *animal* he is! The Duke saw him last year at Homburg where he bored him to death, because the *beastly Diablesse* chose to think it smart to be by way of being 'amused' by him!!'"

On Christmas Eve 1893, when the Duke called at Upper Brook Street with his present, a quarrel arose which made H.R.H. purple with rage and left Lady Geraldine sobbing and broken-hearted. "Sore wounded at every point, all round, everywhere, and deeply grieving in my soul for the way he is now entirely giving up ever being at the Horse Guards, neglecting his duty! *he!!!!* who *lived* for duty, and before this pernicious foul *vile influence* was the most conscientious man that breathed and the hardest worker! Grieving for this sad inconceivable change and all it entails and how it plays into the hands of those who *want to get rid of him* and invites the attacks of such curs as Labouchère . . . I foolishly asked what was to become of the Horse Guards for the three months absence?" The discussion became angry, and Lady Geraldine accused H.R.H. of sacrificing everything for Mrs. Vyner. Her repressed passion and jealousy erupted and a tearful scene ensued. Lord Roberts, himself to become Commander-in-Chief in succession to Wolseley, said that "for some time before the old Duke was retired, he practically did nothing—the ordinary routine of the office was carried by Gipps."¹ So the accusations Lady Geraldine blurted out in the heat of argument were more than half-truths, and that, of course, was what made them unacceptable, that was why her front door banged so violently, and that accounted for a scowling old gentleman seen storming down Upper Brook Street in the season of goodwill.

Among Lady Geraldine's menagerie of aversions, the Duchess of Teck held a prominent place. Her "beslobbering and beslavering the vile Diablesse" was "absolutely sickening," particularly as she had been "infamous" and "past all language abominable to and about poor unfortunate Mrs. Beauclerk!!! and relentlessly persecuted her!" The Duke occasionally joined Lady Geraldine in her censures. He was vexed when Princess Mary in discussions with the Queen misrepresented the financial help he had given her. Everything about his sister was vast and generous: the way she looked, the way she ran into debt, the way she forgave and forgot animosities. When Wolseley succeeded H.R.H. as Commander-in-Chief, she saw no reason to make that the grounds for a vendetta, although to ask her brother to invite Wolseley to dinner was perhaps imposing something of a strain on his geniality. "He has observed for himself, I rejoice to say, what *riles* my whole being, the sickening way Princess Mary is kowtowing all she can to odious Wolseley and making all the fuss imaginable of him and is *profoundly* disgusted with her!! as well he may be! He told me of her rascally bad taste, when he was consulting her as to whom he should invite to meet her last night, suggesting he should invite the Wolseleys! But he frankly told her his opinion of it and of her suggesting it!! Tonight he has a big dinner of twenty for all the Horse Guards staff and to which he has had to ask Wolseley—not pleasant! but of course in his present position at the Horse Guards not to be avoided, that is quite one thing, to ask him with his wife for last night, a footing he has never yet been on, is a very different thing!!"

As Wolseley grew older, he grew very little more tolerant or modest. He was convinced that most soldiers were bigoted traditionalists, and that he, and a select few officers, alone appreciated the revolution taking place in warfare. "I have just been to an Alma Day parade," he wrote on September 20, 1887. "It is a fine thing to keep alive the memory of those old battles, if we really remember how and why they were won. They are damnably mischievous if we think because they were won we must always win again. Half the Army is still living, not on the memory of the Crimea, for which God be praised, but of the Peninsula." The Duke, in his eyes, was the embodiment of the old school. "When that Royal personage is present," he said of a field day at Aldershot, "the whole thing is merely skittles he believes is like War. It is sad to think that the English people who pay so much for this little army, can only have a plaything kept up to amuse Royal princes who know as much of war as I do of Theology."

Wolseley, who saw H.R.H. at close quarters, was aware of how old he was becoming. "Poor man," he said in 1894, "he looks bundled up like an old clothes bundle." But pity him as he might, the Duke's infirmities led Wolseley to the irresistible conclusion that he was unfit for office and should, if necessary, be ignored, circumvented, or removed. Wolseley's practice of ignoring his chief naturally led to resentment. "Quite between ourselves," the Prince of Wales told Ponsonby in 1888, "there is no doubt that Wolseley gets hold of Stanhope behind the Duke's back to work his own schemes. . . . W. is doubtless a very able man and if we were engaged in another war would command our army in the field, but he is false to the backbone, and can never be trusted. He is I know thoroughly disloyal to the Duke and much more so than he has any idea of. However there he is, in a position of great power and there he intends to remain."

In his last year of office the Duke was seventy-six, and there were times when life became almost too much for him. On returning to Gloucester House from Cannes the year Louisa died, he wrote in his diary on March 23: "I got back all right and am well enough but oh! so *sad* and so worried. I dislike my life and all the worries connected with it and shall be glad when I am out of all these troubles, which seem to grow worse and worse every day I live." Such moments of depression and despair were exceptional; but he had reached an age when most of his friends were gone, and hardly a day passed without him deploring the deaths of those that remained. "I came home," he wrote on New Year's Day 1894, "to begin the year in my room alone, thinking of the past and of many dear kind friends and relations many of whom have passed away for ever, but are dear to my memory." All around him the old order was changing. At "dear old Rumpenheim," the summer residence near Frankfurt where he and his German relations congregated every year, the installation of central heating appeared to him desecration. That it was superfluous, Lady Geraldine knew to her dismay. In the tropical heat of August, she once complained, the arrangements are "as though we were living in the North Pole in December!"

The Cambridges were so long-lived a family that Queen Mary used to refer proudly to the "Cambridge constitution." The Duke, despite his gout, his failing hearing, and the partial loss of the sight of one eye, was remarkably vigorous for his years. "My seventy-fifth birthday," he recorded in his diary, "a good old age, but happily I can still do a great deal, as proved today, when I was over seven hours in the saddle." Lady Geraldine, on July 13, 1894, was told by the Duke "of the intolerable number of dinner engagements he has! night after night! how much too much it is. Of *alas!!* how seedy he has been!! Poor dear heart! Actually stayed in bed all Tuesday—what that tells to one who *knows* him! He whom nothing on earth can induce to stay in bed *half* a day when most imperatively necessary with some serious bronchitis or most severe gout!! But was so utterly *done,* he simply felt he could not get up! said he would stay in bed the morning and then stayed on and on and finally did not get up till dinner time, shows how he had been over-taxing himself and how *much* too much he has been doing. It is fabulous! Literally no man of *forty* does any one day what he does the whole of every day, day after day, week after week, month after month! It *is* too much. I am so thankful he did at last for once take a bed day!"

The Duke was a very large man, and his visits to Baden and Kissingen entailed dieting as well as drinking the waters, and seeing Mrs. Vyner. "I am delighted, and feel as light as a *feather!*" was his comment on discovering he had reduced his weight to a little under sixteen stone. Lady Paget, who met him at Kissingen, described him as "very stout heavy and gouty. How he can stand the bumping about on fiery horses over bad roads in this torrid heat I do not know. Every night a rayless copper sun sets in a sky of brass and the leaves hang scorched and motionless on the dusty trees. The Duke is like Princess Mary, very English, he has a great deal of common sense, but lacks energy to enforce it. He swears, but he is kind. He generally hangs or leans upon the person nearest him. I found his weight prodigious in some of our morning rambles. After dinner, and even at dinner, he gets very sleepy, and his head drops on the shoulder of the lady nearest him.""

The Duke continued shooting until a year or two before his death. At the age of seventy-four he killed over two hundred head himself one December day at Sandringham. The total bag was 3,564, shot by ten guns. Owing to the failing sight of his right eye, he shot with a gun that had a crooked stock. H.R.H., as Ranger of the Royal Parks, would often shoot the ducks on the Serpentine early in the morning, but Labouchère objected to the exercise of such rights, particularly in Richmond Park, and suggested that some arrangement should be made "with that eminent warrior the Duke of Cambridge, so that H.R.H. may disport himself elsewhere than in a park intended for the recreation of the public."ⁿ

While shooting at Sandringham he saw a certain amount of the Prince of Wales's sons: the Duke of Clarence, Prince Eddie, and Prince George, the Duke of York. H.R.H. was fond of them both, and did what he could to assist the Duke of Clarence's military career. But although he thought Prince Eddie "charming," and "as nice a youth as could be," his "unaffected" simplicity, and "lamentable ignorance" were serious drawbacks to getting on in the world. The Duke was inclined to blame Dalton, the Prince's tutor, for having taught him nothing. "He [Prince Eddie] sat one night next the Duke when the talk turned on the Crimean War: *he knew nothing about it!!!!* Knew *nothing* of the Battle of the Alma!!! It is past all conceiving! One other sad failing he has from the Prince, he is an inveterate and incurable dawdler, never ready, never there!"

After returning from a visit to Aldershot during his mother's lifetime, the Duke told her of his successful inspection, and spoke of Prince Eddie's incurable apathy. "He cannot learn his drill, so that he is not *yet* in the ranks! The Duke wanted to try him in some most elementary movement, the Colonel begged him not to attempt it as the Prince had not an *idea* how to do it! The Duke of course not wishing to expose him, let it alone!" After two more years at Aldershot, the Prince had made better progress than expected, but he had still a distressing amount to learn. "We talked of how right alas! our judgement of stupid Dalton was, who taught Prince Eddie *absolutely nothing!!* Major Miles the instructor he has been under at Aldershot is quite *astounded* at his utter ignorance. . . . It is clearly Dalton's fault, for it is not that he is unteachable, as Major Miles, having found him thus ignorant, is equally astonished how much he has got on with him and thinks, under the circumstances his papers are infinitely better than he dared to expect. He has his father's dislike for a book and never looks into one, but learns all orally, and retains what he thus learns."″

When, toward the end of 1891, the Duke received the news that his niece, Princess May, was engaged to the Duke of Clarence, his pleasure at the excellence of the match was not unqualified. Then, early in the New Year, while H.R.H. was at Cannes, he received a telegram on January 11, from his sister Mary, announcing that "Dear Eddy had been attacked at Sandringham by influenza in a very serious form." Two days later the Prince contracted pneumonia. "We are all dreadfully staggered by the suddenness of this serious account, which we so little anticipated." The following morning, when he returned from a stroll, "several telegrams awaited me. I guessed the worst: poor dear Eddy had passed away. He died this morning at nine fifteen. It is a fearful catastrophe, so sudden, so unexpected and in the very prime of life and in apparent health when I last saw him this day week. It is really overwhelming. One can hardly realize the painfully sad event which has so suddenly come upon us and the results which may arise out of it."

The Duke was very fond of Princess May. He praised her "immensely! as 'charming'! and a very sensible woman." He was therefore delighted when she afterwards became engaged to Prince George, of whom he had an equally high opinion, although he was opposed to the wedding being arranged so soon after Prince Eddie's death. During one of his visits to Upper Brook Street he told Lady Geraldine about a function at Richmond, "where the Duke of York opened the new foot-bridge and automatic lock, and described to me the curious and interesting construction of the latter; of how well the Duke of York does, his *remarkably* good manner, and speaks well with a very good clear distinct voice and enunciation; but how much he, the Duke, regrets the Duke of York told him the other day he 'can't bear London, and *going out* and *hates* society,' which he thinks a very great pity, and misfortune in his position." And again, in another conversation, "the Duke said he had seen the Duke of York in the morning just returned from Aberdeen; praised him immensely, has a very great liking for and excellent opinion of him, declares he has a 'charming nature'! If so, certainly he gets it from his angel mother! The Duke is extremely fond of him and rates him very high."[n]

The wedding took place on July 6, 1893. "The streets were crowded last night and London almost impassable. My house was full of my friends and others having been asked by me to come to my house and see the Procession pass. Left for Buckingham Palace in State with Augusta and thence we all proceeded in four distinct processions. Volunteers lined Constitution Hill, the troops the streets. The crowds were enormous. The ceremony was well conducted and everything passed off admirably, we returned from St. James's in a similar procession to Buckingham Palace, where there was a State luncheon given by the Queen. Stayed to see the Duke and Duchess of York leave for Sandringham. The streets were lined with troops all the way to Liverpool St. Station, and their reception admirable. Dined in the evening at Marlborough House, a party of forty-eight, all Royalties. We all went to a stand looking over the wall in Pall Mall to see the crowds pass for the illuminations which were general and the crush in the streets marvellous. Weather lovely." There was one disagreeable episode at the celebration at Buckingham Palace. The Queen, on seeing Mr. Gladstone, who for the last time was again her Prime Minister, avoided shaking hands with him and gave him "only a very stiff bow." Undeterred by this frosty reception, he passed behind her and sat down in her tent unasked. "The Queen indignant said to P.A. [Princess Augusta] 'Does he perhaps think this is a public tent!!' "[n]

Gladstone's victory in the 1892 election brought Campbell-Bannerman back once more to the War Office. Before his appointment was announced, the Duke was terrified that some extreme radical would be wished upon him.

When the news became known that Dilke had won a seat, it was feared that the Prime Minister, "lying canting hypocrite that he is," might even "give him the *War Office!!!!* Of how his first act will be to get rid of the Duke and abolish the 'Commander-in-Chief'!!!! *brutes!*—He wishes, if one can possibly speak of wishing, in such a choice!—he might get Campbell-Bannerman back again, who at least is personally decent to deal with." "Mr Campbell-Bannerman," the Duke had told the Queen in 1886, "is a very nice, calm and pleasant man, well known to all here [Horse Guards], and who knows the War Office work, and with whom I have no doubt I shall be able to get on very smoothly."[n]

The fear that the new Liberal Government would attack the Commander-in-Chief soon proved to be justified. Gladstone, who retired in 1894, left it to his successor, Rosebery, to strike the fatal blow. Finally the Duke was forced to resign, but not without an immense struggle. In April 1895, H.R.H. made a speech emphatically declaring that he had not the slightest intention of retiring. When the Prince of Wales hinted to his uncle that resignation might become necessary, and that the Queen could not indefinitely resist her Ministers' advice, the Commander-in-Chief told the Prince that he wished at least to remain at his post until 1896, when he would have completed forty years in office. He was fortified in this resolution by the support of Colonel Augustus FitzGeorge, who now lived with him at Gloucester House and helped manage his affairs. Bigge, Ponsonby's assistant and, in June 1895, successor, wrote to Knollys: "The Prince of Wales has heard on the very best authority that *Augustus* FitzGeorge is at the bottom of the Duke's line of conduct. The Duke does exactly what this son tells him, and if they want the matter to be settled they must 'square' him."[n]

On May 7 the Queen had a long interview with the Duke in which he told her that his anxiety was to do what was in the best interests of the Crown, and to prevent his office ever becoming "parliamentary." "What he *wishes*," the

Queen wrote in her diary, "is not to be kicked out by these violent radicals, who have made such *attacks* on him. I assured him that would not be. He was ready to resign, but could not allow himself to be turned out, and his last words were: 'I place myself in your hands.' " A few days later H.R.H. went to Windsor and the Queen was surprised to find him "firmly resolved not to resign although H.M. pointed out that resignation would be advisable on every ground. H.R.H. repeated previous arguments as to yielding to popular clamour, his capacity for work etc. . . . To go now would be to show 'the white feather' . . . The Queen told Colonel Bigge she could not have said more to H.R.H. without being rude."" The Duke was in too great perplexity to be consistent, and he was buffeted round the four points of the compass by contradictory advice, most of it admittedly of his own seeking.

Lady Geraldine was at first inclined to think that he ought to resign at once, "and retire with dignity, and not wait to be kicked out by those yelping curs." But she agreed with what the Duke told Campbell-Bannerman about the need for a royal prince at the head of the Army. They stand quite "aloof from politics and keep quite out of intrigues of *all* sorts (that is! *he* certainly has!!) whereas suppose you had Lord Roberts as the head of the Army, *every man* of Wolseley's following would be tabooed and kept down, and if Wolseley was at the head, ditto ditto would be the case with all Robert's following! And so all the way through." The Duke of Richmond, however, "most strongly and positively advised and urged him not to resign," and Lady Geraldine, anxious that H.R.H. should "not play into the Queen and Prince's hands," seems to have come to the view that it would be best to "leave it to them, if they can behave so infamously, after all his long services, 'to kick him out like a dog!' ""

The Queen discussed the problem with Rosebery on May 9, and although she told him: "I did not agree with the whole affair, and the haste exhibited," she could not but see the force of the Prime Minister's argument that "there was a feeling abroad that George was too old, though he was extremely popular; and that it was not only a few Radicals, but also the opposition, which would not support the Government in defending George's position." If other officers had to retire at sixty-seven, it was asked, how could it be right for H.R.H. to remain in office at seventy-six? On May 16 the Queen saw the Secretary for War after luncheon, "who was very kind and sensible. He believed that, if George C. were to resign about November, there would be a great demonstration in his favour, and that things would be so arranged that he would leave regretted by the whole nation. Should he, however, cling to office it might lead to regrettable unpleasantness. Mr. C.-Bannerman spoke with great kindness and affection of George, saying that he felt a filial affection for him. . . . Saw George C., which was a trying and painful interview. He was quite calm, but would not see the reason for resigning, so that our interview led to nothing, which is very despairing."

Campbell-Bannerman, who acted throughout these melancholy proceedings with tact and consideration, saw H.R.H. the day after his visit to Windsor. Although the Duke resisted the idea of resigning, it appeared that he was willing to "place himself in the Queen's hands." The distinction involved showed, in the War Minister's phrase, "a refinement worthy of the Schoolmen," but he believed it advisable to humour the Duke. Campbell-Bannerman, describing the interview to Bigge, said that the Duke was "as always most kindly and extremely frank. He gave an explanation of his position which for the first time made me clearly understand the distinction he draws between the resignation of his office, and placing himself in the Queen's hands. By resignation he thinks it would be implied that he took some blame to himself, that he admitted the argument of age, that he confessed failure, that he gave way to vulgar attacks. If he was not conscious of failure, why should he resign? On the other hand, if he places himself in H.M.'s hands, what he means is that he is ready to do whatever, on the advice of her Ministers, she desires. And by way of illustrating what he meant, he recited to me the letter which H.M. would probably write to him. Her Majesty, he thought, would say, 'Since I saw you, I have considered the matter, and I find that my Ministers are of opinion that an altered organization should be given to the administration of the Army: that this alteration involves a considerable change in the duties of your office and cannot be carried out while you hold it, and therefore I think it best that you should,' etc. etc. I really think there is force in the distinction H.R.H. draws: he will not resign, but if the Queen asks him to do so, he will give up his office.'"

The Prince of Wales misguidedly attempted to ease the situation. He was "sorry that the Queen should have to go through such an ordeal with the Duke," and he decided to do what he could on his own to impress upon his uncle that he should retire. His method of broaching so delicate a subject was clumsy and injudicious. While driving to Kempton Park races with the Duke, "à deux in his carriage, suddenly says to him 'Oh! *by the by* (!!!!!!!!!) I have a message for you from the Queen reflecting upon it all round and weighing it, she is convinced that the only plan is for you to resign'!!! proceeding to explain that the sooner the better! certainly before the end of the year. And kindly suggesting 'You might go to India!!! to make a break! *as you would miss it at first.*' "" "It is such disgusting, filthy ingratitude," wrote Lady Geraldine on May 19, "after all he has endured and swallowed and fought and struggled for all but forty years for the Queen's sake, who has never manfully and honestly supported him! The whole thing is intrigue, it is perfectly clear, between the Prince, and Lord Rosebery, two beastly opportunists! Lord Rosebery thinking to avoid difficulties for his government is ready to throw the Duke as a sop to the radical wolves."

The Duke, on May 19, "had a lengthened conversation with Campbell-Bannerman on a wish expressed that I should, before the end of this year, retire from my command of the Army with a view to great changes being made at the War Office. This decision has filled me with the very deepest sorrow as I still feel quite equal to the performance of my duties, and never anticipated such a decision being come to without my willing consent, but I must submit as best I can to the inevitable, but I own that I am disgusted with this, to my mind, most unjustifiable proceeding, though Mr. C.-B. was most amiable in all he said." On the same day he received a letter from the Queen saying that she had reluctantly decided upon his resignation. The city of refuge, to which in the last resort he had ever turned for succour, had pulled up the drawbridge and refused him admittance. "My dear George," ran the letter, "since seeing you on Thursday I have given much anxious thought to the question of your tenure of the office of Commander-in-Chief. I quite appreciate the reasons which make you reluctant to resign the Office which you have so long held with the greatest advantage to the Army, and with my most entire confidence and approbation. I have, however, come to the conclusion, on the advice of my Ministers, that considerable changes in the distribution of duties among the Headquarters of my Army are desirable. These alterations cannot be effected without reconstituting the particular duties assigned to the Commander-in-Chief, and therefore, though with much pain, I have arrived at the decision that, for your own sake as well as in the public interest, it is inexpedient that you should much longer retain that position, from which I think you should be relieved at the close of your Autumn duties. This necessary change will be as painful to me as it is to you, but I am sure it is best so. Believe me, always your very affectionate Cousin and Friend, Victoria R. & I."[n]

"My dear Cousin," replied the Duke the following day, "It was with great pain and deep sorrow that I read the letter you sent me yesterday, for, although I was fully aware that a change was contemplated which would result in my being called upon to relinquish my high position as head of your Majesty's Army, it certainly did not occur to me that the change had been so far prepared that it would be necessary for you to come to an immediate decision. To me therefore it has come like a surprise in this respect, but of course I accept the inevitable, though I deeply regret it, not alone or even chiefly on personal grounds, but for the interests of the Crown and Army, so seriously involved in any changes in the direction indicated. I have now only to express the hope, that after a service to your Majesty of fifty-eight years, thirty-nine of which as your Commander-in-Chief, my feelings may be spared every mortification that may be avoidable in making so great an alteration in my future position; and feeling assured that I have done my utmost to perform my duties absolutely for the interests of the Crown, the Country, and the Army, I remain, my dear cousin, Your most dutiful cousin, George.'"

The Duke, by remaining deaf to hints, had forced the Queen to be blunt, even brutal, but, as he saw it, she had surrendered to her Ministers and betrayed him in the process. Sir Redvers Buller, the Adjutant General, "thought the Duke had been clumsily dealt with. H.R.H. said he came to Windsor, saw the Queen, who apparently quite understood he would not resign, returned satisfied and then two days later got a letter which he thought was not a kind one, virtually giving him the 'sack' as H.R.H. termed it." The Duke was "bitterly hurt with the Queen," and regarded himself as the victim of a "court intrigue." Unaccustomed to keeping his indignation to himself, he complained of his ill-treatment to Princess Edward of Saxe-Weimar. As a result, Lady Geraldine was deeply annoyed and disturbed "to hear the *dreadful* indiscretion of Princess Edward *repeating* everything the Duke has told her and been saying to her all this week at Kew! and to note, what I alas, know too well, the dire effects of *his* indiscretion in speaking so *terribly* openly and fully to *everybody*, to and before *every* sort and kind of person! It is too disastrous.'"

Sir Arthur Bigge was told early in June by Sir Reginald Gipps that "he never remembered any important subject having been kept so secret," and as Sir Arthur, very wisely, was anxious "that the outside world should not know that H.R.H. is holding out," Princess Edward's chatter was especially unfortunate.

Although the Commander-in-Chief had no choice but to resign, he determined to fight a strenuous rear guard over the exact date of his retirement. Lord Rosebery nearly cracked under the strain of battle. He sent Bigge a telegram in cypher: "The Duke, I am afraid, gets worse and worse." The Prime Minister had a long-standing engagement to dine at Gloucester House. But he had "had a somewhat painful correspondence with the Duke of Cambridge," and the dinner was scheduled for the day after Campbell-Bannerman was to announce the resignation. The Prime Minister therefore was "most anxious to get off this engagement. Would it be possible for Lord Rosebery to be commanded to Windsor that night?"

Wherever the Duke went, he made no attempt to disguise his sorrow and scarcely bothered to pretend that he had consented to retire. At the Staff College, on his last annual visit, "standing with his back to the anteroom fire, in full regalia, in the familiar attitude, hands clasped behind his back, the head thrust slightly forward, shoulders a little rounded, he closed his usual address, summing up the merits and imperfections of the outgoing class, with the words, 'Gentlemen, I have been told that I am now a fifth wheel to the coach, and that it is time that I made way for a man who is younger and more closely in touch with the military requirements of the present day.' His voice broke as he made the announcement, and he gruffly continued in soldierly fashion, in spite of obvious emotion, to explain the high principles of loyalty, honour, and affection for the Army which had inspired him in his life's work. There was not one there, however imbued as he might be with the new doctrine, who did not share the sadness with which the old Duke, their real friend, told of his imminent severance from the command of the Army he loved so well." Even more distressing was the Duke's farewell to his staff on October 31. "My last day at the office. It is also dearest Louisa's [Mrs. FitzGeorge's] birthday, once so happy, now a sad anniversary. I drove early to Kensal Green, where I found everything as it should be, but very sad. On my return had luncheon at home. Mildmay with us. I then drove to the old Horse Guards . . . From there went to the Pall Mall office and at four thirty took leave of all the officers of my own department . . . where a very large number attended. I made them a farewell address which I believe was good though extremely painful and distressing to me. In the evening I had a dinner at home, a farewell to all my Horse Guards staff . . . It is a sad moment to me and I feel it intensely, the general feeling of regret at my departure and sympathy with me as well as appreciation of my long service being my only consolation." Sir Henry Wilson, in his diary, described the last leave-taking at the Horse Guards. "At four o'clock all the H.Q. Staff assembled in the Military Secretary's room, and the old Duke of Cambridge came in and bid us goodbye. The poor old man broke down."[n]

The Duke's resignation was announced on June 21, and the day after, Lady Geraldine saw him at Gloucester House. "We went downstairs for a little refreshment. I was able to say one quarter of a word to him of my regret and grief, when he came, kind and dear, to ask if I would not have some tea. He touched his head and with a *laugh!!* said 'kicked out!!' More sad than words can express!!" To the end of his life, H.R.H. maintained that he had been ill treated. On February 12, 1904, a month before he died, "he spoke of the way beastly Rosebery's Government *kicked him out* after forty years' service and how abominably badly they behaved to him!" Writing to his friend Lady Dorothy Nevill to thank her for a kind note of sympathy, he made it quite clear that his retirement had not been voluntary. "I never resigned nor even contemplated resignation," he informed her, "but when told that these proposed changes were to be carried out, I had no choice left but that of not offering any resistance in my person and thus it has, alas! come about. It simply amounts to my being most summarily *turned* out, and at the shortest notice without my retirement being awarded to me!! *Strong order this I think!!!* after thirty-nine years in my present high position. It is *very* sad, but my friends are *most kind.*" On September 27 he made a speech at Edinburgh in which he told his audience that "he believed that he could have gone on much longer at his post, but it had been thought advisable that others should follow him. He only hoped that his successors would have at the end of their career as much sentiment respecting their office as he experienced at that moment. . . . In conclusion his Royal Highness, who had spoken with considerable emotion, declared that he would withdraw from public life with the conviction that he had endeavoured always to do his duty."

It was a splendid tribute to Campbell-Bannerman that it never seems to have occurred to the Duke to blame him for what had happened. Bigge complimented the Secretary for War on acting "throughout these painful negotiations . . . with the greatest tact and kindliness of heart." The Queen invested him at Windsor with a G.C.B. "It is specially meant," he told a friend, "as a mark of her approval of my conduct of the negotiations about the poor old Duke of Cambridge. She has repeatedly told me that no one except myself could have managed it. That is a little strong, but she is very effusive about it." The negotiations left him "quite worn out. I carried the Queen with me throughout and most of her family. She was in fact most interested and anxious. The difficulty was the poor old dear himself, and I am thankful to say he is still most friendly and grateful to me for the way I have managed the whole business, and we have never been other than friends. Such a result I am very proud of, and I can now rest on my laurels."

333

Campbell-Bannerman escaped censure, but the Duke was not disposed to be so charitable toward the Queen, the Prince of Wales, and Lord Rosebery. "A little before seven came the Duke!" wrote Lady Geraldine on June 24. "He had tea. Much depressed and disgusted with the whole thing! . . . We discussed the whole miserable affair. *All* had behaved so badly! and treated him so shamefully! Rosebery a regular cur! The worst of all the Queen! who bowls him over altogether! Utterly selfish, without a particle of consideration for him! who has so long and so gallantly fought her battles for her. She and the Prince only excel each other in opportunism! and are besides too stupid in their short-sightedness, ever more and more submitting to become nothing but the most contemptible of figureheads!"

Lady Geraldine was passionately indignant at the way Queen Victoria had treated the Duke, allowing him to be "sent away like a footman in disgrace." "Happily dear heart! the universal expressions of appreciation and regret of most of the press, his many friends, and the Army are 'very flattering' and soothing to him." "It does make my blood boil," she wrote on July 16, "how abominably she behaves to him! She [the Queen] is such a coward, for when she was likely to see him at last Saturday's review, she had it conveyed to him not to allude to her to the subject, she did not wish to discuss it." A week later she complained: "It is too *abominable,* too *infamous* of the Queen! rouses all my fiercest bitterest indignation against her!! The other day when she had him to dine and sleep at Windsor *she never* made the *most distant allusion* to his losing the command, by a single word!!!"

On the evening of June 21, Campbell-Bannerman announced the news of the Duke's impending retirement, and later that same night the Government was defeated in the House of Commons. The Conservatives moved a surprise vote of censure against the Secretary for War, on the Army's reserves of cordite. It was carried by a majority of seven; Rosebery at once resigned, and Lord Salisbury returned to power. For a moment the Duke thought that he might after all retain his post, but Lord Lansdowne, the new War Minister, soon disappointed such hopes. One consequence of the change of Government was that Wolseley was appointed to succeed H.R.H., rather than Sir Redvers Buller, the Liberals' candidate for the office. "It sets my brain on fire," wrote Lady Geraldine, "the way they behave. Lord Lansdowne!!! whom I have so erroneously believed to be a *gentleman!* The insolence of him, when the Duke was discussing with him the question of some fitting title to be given him to preserve *some* connection with the Army and give him status, (which *probably*, if they were *men* and not sneaks, *ought* to be Honorary Commander-in-Chief for life, of course, and spontaneously conferred, without query!!!). He had the insolence to answer: 'Yes! but then it must be clearly understood *that* you do not interfere in Army matters, there must be no interference with the Army!' God!! How my blood boils to write it!! The insolence of the word 'interfere'! Beastly little whippersnapper. In no one thing has he shown a spark of good feeling!'"

The Duke himself, when Lansdowne was appointed Secretary for War, described him, on July 1, after their first official interview, as "very nice as he is always and a great gentleman." Evidently he did not altogether share Lady Geraldine's vehement emotions, but he did regard his retirement as "a terrible blow and I think most ungenerous and unfair, particularly as to the manner in which it was brought about." The Conservative Government, which he had hoped might reverse Rosebery's decision, very soon made it clear that it would "do nothing to mitigate the painful position I am placed in, which greatly distresses me.'"

Wolseley, who had long plotted and preached the Duke's retirement, and who was now himself to become Commander-in-Chief, with greatly reduced powers, felt a certain chivalrous sympathy for his vanquished enemy.

He wrote him a generous letter on his resignation. "I know," he told his wife, "the old gentleman likes and dislikes me by turns, just as I do him. But he is down on his luck."" The Duke was consoled by the condolences he received and the affection and regrets displayed. "Was alone in my room," he wrote on the first day of 1896, "thinking of all my dear friends in various parts of the world. Thus closed a year of sad reminiscences, as with it has closed my active service, very unexpectedly to myself, though very flattering to me from the great feeling of sympathy and regret expressed to me in all manners and ways by the whole Army and by the Nation at large." Writing to General Harrison in November 1895, the Duke told him how comforted he was by the regard the Army had shown him. "It is very gratifying to me," he declared, "to know and feel that the whole Army regrets my departure from the Chief Command of a noble service of which I have always felt proud, and which I believe to be in as efficient a condition as it is possible that it could have been made during the period I have had to control it. I withdraw with the deepest sorrow and regret, and the feelings of my heart and all my interest in life will continue with and for the Army till the end of my days.""

The Queen, despite scepticism felt in certain quarters, was anxious to do whatever she could to mitigate her cousin's sorrow. She appointed him her first personal Aide-de-Camp and promised to continue to consult him on Army affairs and to support him in his struggle with the Government over his retiring pension. It is true that H.R.H. in the end received no sort of a grant, that he was seldom referred to on military matters, and that the duties of first personal Aide-de-Camp, as defined in the letter appointing him to the position, were, on Wolseley's insistence, transferred to the new Commander-in-Chief. But the Queen was sincere in her gratitude and in her desire to be considerate. "It is with great and much pain," she told H.R.H., "that I see you leave the high, important and responsible office which you have held so worthily for nearly forty years.

Accept also my sincerest thanks for the great services you have rendered to the Country, to the Army and myself, which will ever be most gratefully remembered. Believe me that I feel deeply for you in this severance of a *tie* which existed so long between you and the Army. It is not, however, a *real* severance, for you are a Field Marshal and Colonel of many Regiments. I need not either say that I shall be glad to have your opinion on affairs of importance connected with the Army. I shall gladly support anything which the Government may feel able to propose for you. With renewed expressions of my affection and friendship. Believe me always, Your very affectionate Cousin and Friend." The Princess of Wales, always considerate and full of good feeling, sent him a telegram: "My thoughts are much with you, dear Uncle George, through all this most trying time. I share your sorrow from my heart; it is very hard for you, and will be regretted by all. Best love from here. Alix."

Of all the hundreds of letters he received, he was particularly touched by one from Florence Nightingale. As a sharp critic of military affairs, she could easily have remained silent. She wrote out of no sense of formal politeness, but from personal knowledge and appreciation. "Will you allow me to offer to Y.R.H., at the close of nearly forty years work for the Army, something more than the sympathy of silence on your retirement? My excuse for intrusion at such a time as this, is the honour of having been allowed to work with the Army and for it in days gone by. It has endowed my life with interests, occupations, and friendships that have enabled me to follow and to understand more fully than would have been otherwise possible the advance made since then in the health, comfort, and general well-being of our soldiers. Very few now living can know how much of that advance is owing to the patient personal efforts of Y.R.H., which date back to the times when by far the most serious dangers to the soldiers in peace or war were bad food, insufficient accommodation

337

for man and horse, and an absolute neglect of sanitary measures . . . It requires one who, to some extent at least, has been an official, to realize that nothing less than many years of minute attention to matters of detail, each of which brought its own special contribution to the soldier's welfare, could have made his position and profession what it is to-day. To transform the fashions of a profession is harder than to succeed in a hundred campaigns, for it requires an enthusiasm for the drudgery of detail of which the public have no knowledge, and for which, therefore, they gave no thanks. But rewarded work has never been so good as thankless work, and if known work has been the admiration of the world, it is the unknown work that is its salvation."[*]

The early weeks of the Duke's retirement were so filled with farewell dinners that he had scarcely time to brood over the events of the past months. The enthusiasm shown was exhilarating. "*All* say, everywhere, that *never* was cheering heard like the cheers that greet him, at all times! They told also, of the Mansion House dinner last night, Lord James of Hereford said in his life he had never heard such a noise as the Duke's name was received with! Again and again renewed, a perfect *storm* of cheers! adding 'I know *I* broke two plates with my fork, in trying to add to the noise'! The Duke spoke of how gratifying to him the unanimity of good feeling shown him is! With tears in his dear eyes! saying 'I am going through in my life what occurs to most after their death!' Only it is not many 'who come so well off! but it is really as though I were dead, and shown what is said of me after it!' "[**]

End of an Era

AFTER fifty-eight years as a serving officer, the Duke clung to every opportunity to preserve his associations with the Army. As first personal Aide-de-Camp to the Queen, he had, in her own words, "the right of attending me on all military occasions, and of holding the Parade on my birthday." The appointment had been made to enable H.R.H. to keep up his connection with the Army, "who are deeply attached to you."ⁿ The pleasure he derived from being in uniform again, and taking a parade, touchingly evinced his passionate fondness for the world of soldiering. As the old gentlemen at Henley Regatta pathetically renew their youth by sporting Edwardian blazers and Leander caps perched on their grey heads, so the retired Commander-in-Chief momentarily revived the glory of former days: mounted on a specially exercised charger, he took the salute, dressed in his Field Marshal's uniform.

But despite the Queen's promise that the Duke should take the birthday parade, Wolseley insisted on doing so himself. "Would not any man who had a spark of decent feeling," commented Lady Geraldine, "say to his predecessor who so shortly ago was his superior officer and had been for a *lifetime*, it were a *pleasure* to see him for an hour in his old position!" The Duke and Duchess of York were hotly indignant when they heard that Uncle George was being elbowed out by Wolseley and declared it was too outrageous to be allowed."

As had been predicted, the Queen capitulated, and her first A.D.C., who by her own suggestion was entitled to the salute on her birthday, was invited as a mere spectator to watch Wolseley take the parade. Lady Geraldine was almost choked by her "unutterable wrath and boiling indignation." Wolseley was described as a "sneak," "snob," and a "dirty dog devoid of one single feeling of a gentleman." When the Queen went "back from her word," and "positively allows and agrees that the mongrel shall take the salute . . . there are no words to express the outrage it is." For Lady Geraldine to have exhausted the vocabulary of obloquy, and found "no words" to express her rancour, the provocation must have been singular indeed. The diarist, however, did not remain deprived of invective for long. "When instead of standing by him as she should have done," the account continues, the Queen "so *shamefully* threw the Duke over and forced him to resign, she herself wrote to him by way of a sop, *such* a sop!! that she made him her first A.D.C.!! and that at her Birthday Parade he should *always take the salute,* a perfectly spontaneous suggestion of her own, unsought, unasked, and now because this beastly snob has the vulgar insolence to announce he does not choose it shall be, she throws her prerogative to the winds, does away with the faint *myth* of it being *her* Army, succumbs and kowtows and *dares* not say she will have it! In this which is purely a compliment, a mere civil acknowledgement that her cousin for forty years faithfully administered 'her' Army. It is too sickening, and makes me so angry it makes me quite ill! I have no words and no language for it, and cannot write about it, it is such a burning shame."[n]

The Duke, with considerable foresight, had bought properties in the Coombe and Kingston districts at a time when they were entirely rural. Their values greatly increased as London spread—which made him a rich man. But, although not without resources of his own, H.R.H. believed that, after so many years of service, he was entitled to a pension. The Queen declared the idea was "preposterous," Campbell-Bannerman opposed it, and eventually the Cabinet decided it was out of the question. Lord Lansdowne, while negotiations were still in progress, suggested that anticipated opposition might be disarmed if as a "small concession" H.R.H. were to give permission, as Ranger of the Royal Parks, for the troops to drill in Hyde Park on the grass in front of Knightsbridge Barracks, and for the volunteers to hold field days in Richmond Park. While the Duke was wintering at Cannes in 1896, the familiar telegrams, letters, and memoranda sped back and forth. The Queen, Bigge, the Prince of Wales, Lord Salisbury, Lord Lansdowne, all agreed that the Duke's request for a pension could not be met, and in the end he abandoned the idea himself, but not without an added sense of ingratitude and injustice. He told Lady Geraldine, on April 1, 1896, that he had decided it would be "impossible to submit himself to the ordeal of an annual allowance voted yearly in each successive estimates with yearly insult and insolence from the curs of the House of Commons!! But it diminishes his income by £4,500 per annum." Within a year, he had been turned out of office, had been refused a pension, and had not even been permitted the privilege of taking the salute on Horse Guards Parade. After over half a century of holding the Queen's commission, he had hoped for more than abrupt dismissal. But England has seldom lavished gratitude on its public servants, and they may consider themselves fortunate if after a lifetime of service they are permitted to languish in destitute obscurity.

It took the Duke a considerable time to accustom himself to the leisure of retirement. His inner resources were few. He read very little and he was becoming too infirm to spend an entire day shooting. He craved companionship, but had outlived most of his friends. The pleasures that remained to him were the company of his sons and grandchildren, Mrs. Vyner and her circle, winters at Cannes, summers in Germany, and long conversations about the past, his family, and the Army.

In the last years of his life he was able to give more time to the numerous charities he had always supported. While he was a young man, it had been discovered that he was a persuasive speaker and generous with his help, and consequently he had been appointed a governor of several schools and hospitals. Even in his days as Commanding-in-Chief, he had never believed in remote patronage and had regularly attended board meetings at Christ's Hospital, Wellington College, service associations, and a dozen other institutions from the Royal Soldiers' Daughters' Home to the Victoria Hospital, Kingston-on-Thames. In all of these he took a deep personal interest and to all gave more than his name and a donation. But however ingeniously he devised occupations, they were at best inadequate substitutes for the work and routine which a lifetime of habit had made part of his existence. He particulary missed receiving official dispatches, and felt like a "fish out of water," getting only scraps of news, instead of full information.

The Queen's Diamond Jubilee celebrations in 1897 crowded London with envoys, princes, and foreign relations. The round of parades and reviews and commemoration days which filled the end of June delighted the Duke. His imperial pride swelled at the sight of troops from Canada, Africa, and India, and the ceremonies of Jubilee Day itself, June 22, he described as the "most glorious and notable" he ever attended. "The effect will, I think, be prodigious for good throughout the world, and especially for this Empire." The morning was a glorious one, "not too bright, but mild air . . . I was up early, and all my guests arrived in good time. About a hundred or more were in my rooms. I drove to the Royal Mews at nine forty-five where I mounted my Chestnut Horse 'Rifleman' which carried me most admirably all through the day. The procession started punctually at eleven fifteen. I rode on the left hand of the Queen's carriage. All the arrangements including the 'turn out' were perfect, the behaviour of the people magnificent, the decorations lovely." That evening H.R.H. attended a state banquet at the palace and a reception afterwards. He was seventy-eight at the time, but expressed surprise when he returned to Gloucester House to find that he was more than ready for sleep.

Four days later, dressed in his Trinity House uniform, he joined the royal train to Portsmouth for the great Naval review. "Embarked at the Dockyard with the Prince [of Wales] and Princess and all the Royalties and special Ambassadors in the Royal Yacht *Victoria and Albert*. We were thirty-one. The day cleared up beautifully, and the afternoon was perfect for this special occasion. Steamed out to Spithead, where the grand fleet of one hundred and sixty-six vessels was anchored in four long lines, each extending a mile. It was a grand and noble sight of wealth and strength and very heart-stirring. We steamed up and down the lines and anchored in the very centre abreast the flagship . . . whilst the foreign Admirals and their Flag Captains, as well as our own, came on board to be received by the Prince of Wales. We then proceeded back into harbour . . . I stayed at Government House . . . After dinner had a magnificent sight of the Fleet, brilliantly illuminated with electric light—a truly heart-stirring sight and a sign of the development of the Empire over the Seas. The Prince and Princess steamed out in the Royal Yacht, and as they left the Lines to return to harbour, the entire Fleet fired a simultaneous salute of twenty-one guns, which produced a grand effect." The next evening the Duke gave a dinner at Gloucester House, "in plain clothes" to the Prince of Wales and "all the Royal Princes and special Ambassadors for the Jubilee." The food was excellent— the Duke's chef was one of the best in London—the plate looked "charming," and the band of the Grenadiers melodiously punctuated the conversation. On July 1, yet another "perfect day," H.R.H. joined the Prince of Wales's train for the review at Aldershot. On arrival at Farnborough, he rode over to the encampment with the Duke of York. Augustus FitzGeorge was put in charge of the Grand Duchess and Princess Mary, for whom the Duke had sent down carriages for the occasion. "The luncheon was very well done, the Royalties at a large table, and the suites and others in a tent to the number of eighty. The Prince and we all then rode quietly to the Parade Ground . . . which was green and fresh to look at and the road well watered, so we had no dust. The Queen arrived at four thirty. The crowd on the ground and in the stands erected was very great . . . The Duke of Connaught commanded, and made all the arrangements, which were quite perfect and not a hitch or accident took place. The Queen was much pleased, and well she might be! I never saw a finer parade at Aldershot."

The Duchess of Teck's visit to the Jubilee Review was one of her last public appearances. Earlier in the year she had been taken seriously ill in the night and had been saved by immediate surgery, but her recovery was only temporary, and at three a.m. on the morning of October 27, after a second emergency operation, her heart failed. The Duke at the time was staying at Sandringham, and on receiving "a most painful and unexpected telegram from poor Teck, announcing to me the afflicting news of the sudden death of my dear sister Mary," he and the Prince of Wales started at once for London; the Duke of York joined them at Cambridge. After luncheon they set out for White Lodge, Richmond, where Nelson, dipping his finger in port, had drawn on the tablecloth the plan of the battle of Trafalgar, and where for many years past the Teck family had lived and entertained beyond their means. On arrival at White Lodge, H.R.H. found the place thronged with agitated relations. "Saw dearest Mary on her deathbed. She reminded me so very much of the countenance of my dearest Mother. Heard all the details

of Mary's last moments. The operation had been successfully performed. She came to, and spoke a few words,
then fell into a comatose state, the heart having given
way from the shock to the system, and she expired very
quietly at three o'clock in the morning . . . Am overwhelmed with letters and telegrams of condolence . . .
from all parts at home and abroad."

The funeral was held on November 3 at St. George's
Chapel, Windsor. "We were in plain clothes, but there was
a dignity and real devotion about it, which was most impressive and gratifying and the hymns and singing of the
choir were perfect." At a Memorial Service held at White
Lodge on October 31, the Duke had been unable to hear
the prayers and psalms, which distressed him very much,
so the service at Windsor, sad though it was, consoled him
at least by being audible. Even before his wife's death,
Prince Teck's mind had been failing, he had been given
to fits of unaccountable laughter, and his conversation had
become incoherent. The Duke for a time visited his brother-
in-law after his sister's death, but found him "daily growing worse" and "much more confused in his mind and
very difficult to understand." When Teck died in 1900 it
was a relief to his family, for his mind had gone, and for
two years he had been kept completely secluded at White
Lodge, surrounded by attendants and not even seeing his
children.

The last years of the Duke's life were constantly sad-
dened by deaths. Even Gladstone's end he regretted. "Mr.
Gladstone died this morning," he wrote on May 29, 1898,
"calmly and peacefully, a great man less in the world,
after a most remarkable career. Personally he was always
very amiable to me, though a dangerous politician with a
most remarkable intellect." On December 16 of the same
year, Christopher Sykes, the Prince of Wales's long-
suffering companion and a close friend of the Duke, succumbed after a brief illness. "I am deeply grieved," wrote
H.R.H., "though not surprised. He was always a most

345

loyal friend to me and I shall greatly miss him, poor dear fellow." On March 15, 1901, Charles Fairbrother died. The Duke previously had deplored that he saw so little of him, "but he seems to prefer a solitary life." Then, while at Cannes, a telegram came to say that "Charles died last night at eleven thirty. Poor fellow, a happy release of a very unhappy man, as he would have no friends and specially avoided all the members of his family. He never came near my house since Christmas year, which is too sad." But accustomed as the Duke grew to such losses, there was one departed friend he never forgot. "Deposited a wreath on poor Mrs. Beauclerk's grave as tomorrow was the day of her death twenty years ago. How time flies, I could hardly believe it, also visited my dear Louisa's grave."

The outbreak of the Boer War in 1899, which H.R.H. followed with professional interest, gave him a new lease of life. He even went to Waterloo Station to see Sir Redvers Buller off to the front, and he eagerly inspected regiments going out to South Africa. The French at Cannes were pro-Boer, and this so incensed H.R.H. that he wintered instead at Monte Carlo, which he hated, and where he missed his friends of the Château. His last visit to the Queen, on December 4, 1900, was taken up with discussing the war. "I found her fairly well, though much distressed . . . at the state of military affairs generally."

In the New Year, on January 19, the Duke set out for Monte Carlo. Before leaving, he had read depressing accounts of the Queen's health in the newspapers, but the Duchess of York advised him to start as intended. At Paris the reports were so gloomy that he decided to return to England. "On reaching Charing Cross at seven forty-five, heard that the dear Queen had passed away quietly and calmly surrounded by her children and grandchildren . . . It is a fearful blow and great catastrophe not only for England but for the world at large." The Duke shared in the universal feeling that it was almost impossible to conceive of England without the Queen. "Parliaments," as Gladstone had once observed, "and Ministers pass, but she abides in lifelong duty, and she is to them as the oak in the forest is to the annual harvest in the field."

The next day, at two o'clock, the Duke was summoned to St. James's to attend a Privy Council. He was received by the Prince of Wales "most graciously and kindly and with great dignity and affection." The Prince "accepted the Throne under the title of Edward VII in an extremely well expressed address." That evening he "dined with the Duke of York to meet the King." The Queen's funeral was held on February 2. "Fortunately the day was dry, though cold and dreary. I drove to Victoria Station with Prince Edward and Dolly, now in waiting, and there joined all the Kings and Royalties, whence I rode with the King and Emperor behind the hearse. The Royal train with the Queen's body arrived at eleven, and then we all started. I drove in the fourth carriage with Edward Weimar and Lord Wolseley. The crowds were very enormous, but their demeanour magnificent, solemn and silent. Got to Paddington at one, and left for Windsor by train at a few minutes afterwards. At Windsor Station there was a sad delay by the Artillery horse in the shaft of the gun carriage kicking violently. Fortunately no injury resulted; the horses were taken out, and the Guard of Honour of Bluejackets put in their place and dragged the remains up to St. George's Chapel. We walked through the town, following in procession, and I managed to get through it, leaning on Dolly's arm. The Church was crowded, the Archbishop of Canterbury and the Bishop of Winchester officiating; the service was choral. We then walked back to the castle where lunch was served to us in the usual dining room . . . After that I returned to London by seven o'clock, being dead beat, and I just crawled into bed."

H.R.H., who was very much broken by the Queen's death, discussed it with the Duke of Grafton, whom he met after the service at Windsor. " 'I shall go soon myself,'

347

he groaned, and to cheer him up the Duke of Grafton said he was nearly as old himself, upon which the old Duke said almost cheerfully, 'Ah! We will both go together.' "[n] H.R.H. was so fatigued by the funeral that the following day he "rested and slept alternately," a procedure he followed after Edward VII's coronation in August, the last great ceremony he ever attended. Apart from the Grand Duchess, he was the only surviving member of the Royal Family who could recall Queen Victoria's coronation, and his advice on precedent was anxiously sought.

In August 1903 the Duke paid a visit to Germany, but his strength was gradually failing, and he was forced more and more to withdraw from public life. "I keep on going," he said, "for I notice that when men give up their ordinary pursuits and do nothing they generally die very soon." On October 6 he abandoned his diary: "Age tells so much now upon me that I have no alternative. I give it up with reluctance and great regret." Early in 1904 his final illness began. There was no fight left in him. At the beginning of the year the office of Commander-in-Chief had been abolished. Nearly all his friends were dead. His sister Augusta, his sons, Lady Geraldine, the King, Queen Alexandra, the Wales', and Mrs. Vyner were all that were left of his once crowded world. He no longer had anything to live for, and so "prayed God to take him, he is so *weary* of waiting." "He [Augustus FitzGeorge] tells me," wrote Lady Geraldine on March 8, "the Duke speaks mostly of old, old far away days; of his early days, not wandering, quite all there, but thinking, asking, nothing or very little of the present, full of recollections of the Past!" On March 17, only a few days before his eighty-fifth birthday, he passed peacefully away in the presence of Mrs. Hamilton and his three sons.

"With profound regret," said *The Times* the following morning, "we have to announce that His Royal Highness the Duke of Cambridge died at Gloucester House, Piccadilly, yesterday morning shortly after half-past-ten o'clock. Soon after two o'clock in the morning His Royal Highness was seized with another attack of haemorrhage of the stomach and became restless, and about daybreak there was a recurrence of the haemorrhage. At nine o'clock a messenger was despatched to His Royal Highness's domestic chaplain, the Reverend Doctor Sheppard, Sub-Dean of the Chapels Royal, who arrived promptly at Gloucester House and read prayers at the bedside. The bulletin issued at nine o'clock clearly indicated that the end was approaching. It was as follows: 'The Duke of Cambridge passed a restless night. There has been a recurrence of haemorrhage this morning. His Royal Highness is now in a condition of profound exhaustion.' From this time onwards, the Duke, greatly weakened by loss of blood, became rapidly worse, and the end was so painless and peaceful that those at the bedside hardly realized the actual passing."

The newspapers were smothered in obituaries, portraying a man moving in a royal world of aldermen, red carpets, brass bands, silver trowels, and illuminated addresses; a world of grandeur, decorations, epaulettes, orders, field marshals' batons, and resounding titles. But although the Duke had wrung many a mayor by the hand, and although his own sister was the Grand Duchess of Mecklenburg-Strelitz, there was a world elsewhere: the world of Chesham Street, of Queen Street, of Horley, and of Kensal Green. The newspapers thought of the Duke of Cambridge as the first grandson to be born to George III and the last to die. Hardly anyone living recalled H.R.H. as a young man: the youthful Commander-in-Chief, the scourge of Sir George Brown, the handsome husband of an enchanting bride. He was remembered as a crippled old gentleman shuffling down Piccadilly, leaning heavily on his son's arm. But even this faded image of an active man commanded affection and respect.

In the House of Commons, the Prime Minister, Mr. Balfour, spoke of the Duke's services to England, both in the field and in the office of Commander-in-Chief. "Although I suppose it would be too much to hope," he said, "that at any time of our political history questions connected with the War Office should be outside the pale of controversy, there is one thing in which every man will agree—namely, that the Duke of Cambridge devoted to his great office his whole time, his whole energy, his whole strength, and that he was intimately and profoundly acquainted with every question that affected the British Army, and that throughout his whole career he possessed the confidence of both officers and men." Campbell-Bannerman, speaking for the Opposition, described the Duke as "the true friend of all his friends," whose "personal charm drew to him everyone with whom he came in contact." "The Duke of Cambridge," he declared, "was devoted with an intensity of devotion beyond description to the Army of which he was Commander-in-Chief for many years."

At his own desire the Duke was buried at Kensal Green, but the King ordered that the first part of the service should be held in Westminster Abbey. Princess Augusta, writing to her niece, the Princess of Wales, regretted that "he will not be laid to rest in the family vault at Windsor, and is to be taken to a strange resting place, so far away from us all!" The day before the funeral, fixed for March 22, a short service was held at Gloucester House. The Duke's body rested in a polished oak coffin exactly like that chosen for Queen Victoria. Above it were placed the crossed batons of a field marshal, surmounted with a coronet of a Prince of the Blood Royal. Edward VII, Queen Alexandra, the Prince and Princess of Wales, the Teck boys (the eldest of whom in 1917 was created Marquess of Cambridge), Mrs. Hamilton, the FitzGeorges, Lady Geraldine, and the Duke's servants assembled in the state dining room for prayers.

The day of the funeral was bright, with a hint of spring —a detail which in any other circumstance the Duke himself would have noted in his diary. The south transept of the Abbey, reserved for military mourners, was a mass of scarlet and glinting light. The coffin was wrapped in the Union Jack with the Royal Standard draped over it. Rear

Admiral Adolphus FitzGeorge and Colonel Augustus Fitz-
George, upon whom the very next day the King conferred
the K.C.V.O., although they had been relegated to the ninth
carriage in the procession to the Abbey, were permitted to
stand by their father's remains. Colonel George FitzGeorge
sat in a private pew with his son. He had recently suffered
from a stroke and was unable to appear in uniform. The
Abbey was packed with representatives of Emperors and
Kings, with Ministers, Members of both Houses, and a vast
company of officers. Among the pall-bearers were Lord
Wolseley, Lord Roberts, Sir Evelyn Wood, Sir Redvers
Buller, and Sir John French. There were representatives of
Trinity House, the Royal Parks, several hospitals, charities,
and a variety of institutions with which the Duke had been
associated. While the congregation assembled, a march
was played which Purcell had composed for the funeral of
Queen Mary and which had been used at his own burial
service.

As the mourners left the Abbey, the Guards' Massed
Bands struck up the Dead March from *Saul* and the sound
of guns fired from St. James's Park heralded the funeral
procession. The five-mile-long route was lined with dense
masses of people who stood in the brilliant sunshine in
absolute silence. As the coffin passed, the soldiers lining the
road presented arms, afterwards resting on reversed arms
until the cortège had gone by. Princess May described it as
"the most impressive and beautiful sight . . . I have ever
seen, too upsetting for words, and I cried floods all the time
Aunt Alix [the Queen] was so feeling and dear to me
. . . she feels Uncle's death very much indeed." In the
procession, Lord Roberts and Lord Wolseley were put into
the same carriage. For years they had not spoken to each
other. About the only thing they had in common was that
they were both successors of the Duke as Commander-in-
Chief." Finally at Kensal Green there was another short
service and a hymn was sung by the choir of the Chapels
Royal. As the coffin of the Duke was placed in the vault

beside that of Mrs. FitzGeorge, three volleys were fired by men of the Grenadier Guards and a bugler sounded the "Last Post."

Had the Duke of Cambridge been born the son of a country squire instead of a grandson of George III, he would have been fortunate to figure in some regimental history; but being a Prince of the Blood, he had "greatness thrust upon him." As Commander-in-Chief he performed the duties of his office to the complete satisfaction of the Army—except for a handful of progressive officers who were exasperated by his obstruction of reform. His rough and forthright manner, his affection for those under his command, his enviable grasp of the details of his profession, his endless industry, his constant defence of regimental traditions, and his repeated struggles to prevent reductions won him the regard of both officers and men. The frustration of successive Secretaries for War was a measure of the success he achieved in defending the soldier's interests. No other Commander-in-Chief ever held office so long or was so loved by the rank and file. For all Wolseley's brilliance and for all his achievements, he never even momentarily challenged the Duke in the Army's affection.

The Duke's conservatism has been represented as destructive of all improvement. The truth is that many of the reforms he resisted were ignorantly conceived, were opposed by some of the shrewdest officers in the Army, and were often inspired by political, not military, necessity. Although as Commander-in-Chief he may have grown excessively sceptical of the merits of changes enthusiastically advocated by successive Secretaries of State, it need not be assumed that every proposal described by its exponents as a "reform" was invariably a change for the better. Indeed, improvements whose merits are not in dispute may be ill timed and ill devised. General Harman in 1888 told Ponsonby: "The Duke is the best friend the Army has, and knows its requirements better than any living man, and were it not for what many are pleased to call 'his obstruction' to the reforms that are so constantly being advanced, the Service instead of being the popular profession it is would soon become quite the reverse."[*]

The Duke's reluctance to countenance alterations, which he maintained unsettled the Army, involved him in repeated collisions both with War Ministers and with a group of officers led by Wolseley. From the clash of their opposing views emerged a number of moderate and necessary changes. "Providence, with a curiously perpetual regard for England, seems to have sent her this diametrically opposed pair [H.R.H. and Wolseley]: one to save her from being caught unawares entangled in the cobwebs of antiquity, and the other to temper the remorseless blast of revolution to the healthy breeze of evolution."[*]

The Duke's opponents, although relatively few in numbers, were energetic publicists. H.R.H. had frequent occasion to deplore their subversive speeches and controversial newspaper articles. They made a great noise and, because they attacked established things, were able to accuse of bigotry anyone who dissented from their views. They distorted intricate issues so that they appeared simple, and they did scant justice to their opponents' views. They represented themselves as fearless and enlightened reformers, while they portrayed the Horse Guards officials as uncritical retrogrades. They painted the conflict as a struggle between new and old, between modern methods based on the lessons of contemporary war, and outdated traditions deriving from Napoleonic times. It was a battle between Wolseley, "the very model of a modern Major General," and an old-fashioned Crimean soldier who had forgotten nothing and learnt nothing. Such were the simple terms to which the argument was reduced. Subsequent writers, attracted by the loud and compelling clamour of Wolseley and his disciples, have overlooked his opponents' views. Cardwell and Childers have been accepted at their own exalted estimates, and although some reluctance has been shown to swallow all that Wolseley said about himself by way of congratulation, his opinions about the Duke of Cambridge have been handed from history book to history book as if they were holy lore which it would be blasphemy to dispute.

The Duke's conservatism was more an attitude of mind than a political creed. As Commander-in-Chief he officially strove to avoid commitment to party, but his sympathy for Tory imperialism was widely known. Once, while listening to a debate in the House of Commons he so far forgot himself as to cheer Disraeli for denouncing Liberal reforms. When Gladstone was Prime Minister, H.R.H. would audibly criticize Government measures in a stage whisper to some neighbouring peer in the House of Lords, or would sit "in the centre of the front gallery of the House of Commons, whence he could observe the Treasury bench and look down upon the Premier with a face that did not speak unbounded trust. Who knows? Perhaps the Liberal leader in his view was a dangerous person who ought, if he had his deserts, to be dragged off and summarily tried by a drum-head court-martial . . . At the dinner to Lord Roberts at the Mansion House in 1893 for instance, when Home Rule was the absorbing topic of political discussion, he spoke of the *United* Kingdom with such a marked stress on the first of those two words that the City Tories cheered vociferously."[n]

At one of his last functions as Commander-in-Chief, he addressed his military colleagues: "Gentlemen, there have been great changes in my time—great changes. But I can say this. Every change has been made at the right time, and the right time is when you cannot help it." At a luncheon at the Mansion House, he told his audience: "Everybody nowadays is asking for change; they want to change this and they want to change that; in fact, they want to change everything. I don't see any good in changing everything. We have done very well as we are, and I don't see that any change is needed. I'm quite satisfied with things as they are."[n]

The Duke's satisfaction with "things as they are" made him insensitive to hallowed abuses. "He seems to have believed, quite honestly, that the Army as he had found it, created by such a master of war as the Duke of Wellington, must be the best for all time, and he had not realized the changes which had since taken place in the armies of Europe." Sir William Robertson has told how H.R.H. once took the chair at a lecture given to officers of the Aldershot garrison on the subject of foreign cavalry, "when he proved to be a veritable Balaam in commending the lecturer to the audience. 'Why should we want to know anything about foreign cavalry?' he asked. 'We have better cavalry of our own. I fear, gentlemen, that the Army is in danger of becoming a mere debating society.' "[n]

Writing in his diary on November 5, 1881, the anniversary of Inkerman Day, the Duke remarked: "What glorious recollections are connected with that memorable day and how things have changed since then, too sad and I prefer the *past* to the present." Breakfasting with Sir Almeric Fitzroy some time after Queen Victoria's death, the Duke was "very outspoken, as ever, and regretted the indifference to old-time usages" which marked Edwardian times. When the Duchess of Cambridge died, he kept the house and grounds of Kew Cottage exactly as they were in her lifetime. Not a picture was changed or a stick of furniture moved. Indeed, when it was realized that the piano in the library had been placed out of position, Mrs. Mold, the housekeeper, had it immediately turned round "and put as it was when Princess Mary used to play to Prince Teck." Kew Cottage, at least, was a province where no busybody could meddle with the past.

Some of the Duke's resistance to innovations in the Army proceeded from his conviction that change should be gradual. He was quite capable of appreciating the need for "modifications to bring matters about to modern requirements," but he believed it was "far more advantageous" to introduce reforms "slowly and gradually . . .

355

and to give time for reflection on trial." "The Army," he told Wolseley in 1890, "has of late years had more changes than enough, and wants absolute *rest* from constant surprises . . . I am afraid you don't believe in *sentiment,* but I do so *strongly,* especially in military matters . . . I am old-fashioned, you will say; but I don't think I can be accused of having sacrificed any real efficiency to old-fashioned notions of the past."" The Duke's military experience led him to conclude that the spirit of an army depended upon tradition, regimental pride, and trust between officers and men. As the woodman's axe in a matter of hours can destroy the growth of centuries, so rash reforms could overnight annihilate the morale of the Queen's Army. Rational reforms, however efficient in themselves, if they diminished the soldier's will to fight, if they deprived him of a sense of patriotism and history, or made him careless of the honour of his regiment, were a liability rather than an asset.

Sometimes the Duke's resistance to change hardened into unthinking habit, and encouraged him to condemn what he had not troubled to understand. During the manoeuvres of 1871, H.R.H. had remarked that "outpost duties of Infantry still require much study." Accepting the hint, Hamley, the Commandant of the Staff College, examined the subject and evolved a new system. In the autumn of 1876, "he applied for an opportunity of testing his new methods by putting them into practice with troops from Aldershot . . . The Duke signified a desire to be present . . . The day was a vile one, the troops hazy as to what was required of them, and their officers little inclined to enthusiasm over the experiment . . . The Duke, accompanied by Airey, who was on the eve of relinquishing the appointment of Adjutant General, rode round the outpost line. He had been puzzled at the preliminary explanation he received, and mystification grew as he listened to the answers to questions he put to regimental officers he encountered. One thing was sufficiently clear to him: that here was a complete reversal of the existing system. He turned to Airey and exclaimed, 'If this is right, Airey, what we have been doing all our lives is wrong!' Airey assented. The Duke called for the assembly of all officers. Hamley and his students were there, the General Officer Commanding-in-Chief, Aldershot Command, and his staff, hanging on the words of the Army's Chief. Without inviting the umpires' comments the Duke gave his criticism. He roundly condemned the new system, and mercilessly lashed Hamley with vigorous destructive sarcasm in front of all. Nor would he listen then or later to any submission by Hamley to the effect that the experiment, as staged, was an unfair one, on unsuitable ground, by troops who had no opportunity of grasping the parts they were playing before an audience who had taken no trouble to discover what they were to see, nor to read his pamphlet on the subject."[n]

Although Hamley's schemes did not commend themselves to the Commander-in-Chief, he often expressed interest in novelties. When Colonel Burnaby crossed the Channel by balloon in 1882, he was sent to report himself to the Duke on his return from what had been an unauthorized expedition. Instead of a stinging rebuke, the Colonel found himself subjected to a cross-examination about flying. H.R.H. "was much interested in the enterprise, and admired Burnaby's pluck, and said he would like to go up in a balloon himself with Burnaby, only he feared 'there would be such a hullabaloo.' "[n]

The Duke was fascinated by the invention of the phonograph, and a recording he made on one of the earliest machines is still in existence. He was the first member of the royal family "to make a practical trial of the motorcar in the early stage of its legal existence." While H.R.H. was staying with Sir Berkeley Digby Sheffield in January 1897 at Normanby Park in Lincolnshire, one of the other guests took him for a drive in his Bollée car, despite the fact that

357

snow lay thick on the ground. "After the mechanism had been thoroughly explained his Royal Highness took his seat as a passenger and made a prolonged tour in the park. The going was heavy on account of the snow, and some slight ascents were slowly negotiated, but the Bollée acquitted herself most satisfactorily. At the end of the trip the Duke not only expressed his delight with the novel sport, but mounting into the chauffeur's seat, he made some little runs on his own account, to test his powers of steering and controlling motorcars.'" When Edward VII took the Duke on a drive on August 25, 1901, H.R.H. observed: "We went most steadily and safely and without dust, but I cannot say I like the mode of conveyance and prefer carriages *with* horses."

At no time was the Duke unaware that his critics thought him reactionary and obstructive. When discussing his career with Colonel Verner, appointed to write his official military biography, he concluded an interview by saying: "You can let them know that I am not quite such a damned old fool as some of them say." In a speech delivered at Edinburgh in 1895, just before he gave up office, he said that he had sometimes been "twitted" with the statement that age had made him very loath to carry out changes. "A man could not pass through life as long as he had without having seen some very remarkable changes in every sphere, and as science advanced and intelligence increased, change must find its way into every condition of life and into every profession. Therefore to say that he had objected to changes was simply ridiculous. He should not be in the position which he had held for thirty-nine years if such had been the case, but he had always felt that changes must be effected with much prudence and consideration. If they made changes for change's sake, he thought they were doing a most dangerous thing indeed. If, on the other hand, they made changes for the sake of improving and advancing, not only would they be beneficial in themselves, but they were essential in order to keep pace with the world at large. Therefore he could not understand how anyone in his position could put his face against changes which must come. He had never hindered these changes, but had accepted them and supported them, and led them to a great extent."ⁿ

Many of the Secretaries for War with whom the Duke worked paid tribute to the loyal way in which he carried out decisions, once they had been reached. While he was Commander-in-Chief, the Army was utterly transformed from top to bottom, and not always in accordance with his ideas. "Only when those transformations can be viewed from some distance of time in their true perspective," wrote Fortescue in his great *History of the British Army,* "can justice be done to the unfailing loyalty and tact with which the Duke discharged his most difficult and trying duties."ⁿ

Even the Commander-in-Chief's most ferocious critics could hardly pretend that he did not possess an extraordinary knowledge of military affairs. Gathorne-Hardy, when he went to the War Office, was greatly impressed by the Duke's familiarity with "all the minutest details of the work of his high office." H.R.H.'s grasp of his duties was assisted by an enviable memory. Once Princess Augusta was looking in her room for *John Gilpin,* "on which the Duke set forth and recited to us the whole poem straight off!! I should think it is a hundred years since he heard, or thought of it!!" "The Duke's mastery of the working of the whole complex machinery of the Army was phenomenal," wrote Lord Redesdale. "Still more extraordinary was his knowledge of its officers. This was due to the fact that during the whole time of his tenure of office no promotion to any rank above that of captain was made without his personal investigation and sanction. In this way, being gifted with a singularly retentive memory, he had an intimate acquaintance with the careers and capabilities of all the senior officers."ⁿ

Randolph Churchill in 1887 presided over a Committee of Enquiry into Army Finance. One of the Committee members was a Lancashire M.P. called Jennings, who boasted that he would expose the Duke's incompetence by ruthless cross-examination, and was amazed to find himself come off worst in the encounter. Jennings pressed the Commander-in-Chief to tell him how many guns and how much ammunition the Army had available in an emergency. " 'I cannot tell you,' said the Duke. 'I fear I must insist on an answer,' said Jennings, and appealed to the Chairman for support, which he received. 'If you don't know your duty, sir, I know mine,' said the Duke, 'and that is not to tender our official secrets to the whole of Europe, as you propose. I won't answer.' Jennings, after his illustrious opponent had left the chair, said to me admiringly: 'That old man knows as much about his business as the very best store-keeper does about his shop.' "[n]

The high opinion which Jennings formed of the Commander-in-Chief was shared by many whose expert knowledge entitled them to speak with more authority. General Dillon, an experienced and able officer, delighted the Duchess of Cambridge by his appreciation of her son. "General Dillon came," wrote Lady Geraldine on September 5, 1880. "He began speaking of the Duke and it did one's heart *good* to hear in what terms!! The immensely high opinions of him, of his nobility and greatness of character, his worth, his high qualities, abilities and merits! Most touching and gratifying to hear his honest and most genuine admiration for him! He told us that one day he was speaking with Sir Charles Yorke of the Duke's *marvellous* knowledge of the Army and every individual in it and Sir Charles enlarging on his great qualities, said: 'With his extraordinary powers of memory, his quickness of perception, his wonderful precision of judgement, he does not at all realize how *great* he is!' As Dillon said, impossible to condense a character more correctly and accurately! He talked of his excellent speeches, how well expressed and never missing a point, bringing everything in! And said what a misfortune they had not all been cut out and collected. He spoke of his great and extraordinary industry, the *amount* of work he does! That at the office everything is in his own handwriting, how he reads and signs everything! Every promotion, every nomination his own doing, *his* own decision; how his own first thought, *his* judgement always proves the best, 'He could buy and sell us all!' How able and clear and concise his writings are, always hitting the point! He told us he had just read such a *clever, able, admirable* paper from him upon Kandahar and all the Afghanistan question! which is to go to the Queen and the Cabinet and Lord Ripon, quite admirable and again his taste and tact and judgement in such a paper as he had to write to Wolseley at the Cape, in fact a reprimand! but so *ably* and judiciously done and with such good feeling, that he, Wolseley, could not but feel it as such, yet it was *impossible* he *could* take exception to it, or resent it! He told us how all the Army felt *no one* but he could hold his position! And how he Dillon was talking with someone the other day of how remarkable it is in the length of time he has been in that prominent responsible position how *little* that is ill natured or nasty has ever been said against him, how the ill disposed have been unable to find anything to fasten upon! Of his excellence and kindliness of heart and consideration for others! Of his *great* and perfect honesty, that can evince no suspicion; his *total* absence of vanity!"

Nearly all attacks on the Duke may be traced to Wolseley and his "press gang." "The dear old Bumble-bee," he told his wife in 1890, "is to me now thank God as far removed as the dodo is from the thoughts of a modern ornithologist— what a huge mass of humbug he is and what a swindle upon the public. Drawing a very large sum annually from the State and remaining on to injure our Army still further as much as he can. It would have paid the nation, hand over hand to have given him an extra £20,000 a year twenty years ago to leave the Army. Had he done so, we should now have had an Army.'"

It is not always easy to know what Wolseley really thought or believed. His letters to his wife were intended principally to amuse her, and in order to be entertaining he exaggerated, as Irishmen will. The Duke only too often exasperated him and frustrated his plans. Consequently, it relieved him to say behind the old man's back what he could not say to his face. In Wolseley's autobiography, intended for the world and written when the flames of controversy had turned to ashes, he described the Duke of Cambridge as "a very clever Prince, who knew the Army thoroughly, and was looked up to and most justly liked by all ranks in it. Educated to believe in the Army as he found it, because it had been made by the Great Duke of Wellington, he honestly and firmly believed that what had been created by such a master of war must be the best for all time. He had not, apparently, fully taken in the great changes which the system of universal military service had produced in European armies. He refused to believe in an Army Reserve, and honestly looked upon our endeavour to create one here as not only a mad folly, but as a crime against the State. No more loyal and devoted Englishman ever wore a red coat, but nothing would or could convince him than an Army Reserve in this country would be forthcoming when wanted. Recent experience, however, has proved how absolutely wrong the old school of officers were upon this point, and no man more than His Royal Highness has ever been thoroughly converted to modern ideas on this point. I have mentioned this about a Royal Personage under whom I was long privileged to work, because I liked him more and more the better I knew him. Indeed no one who served for so many years on his staff could fail to love his amiable qualities, or to admire his manliness of feeling. His honesty of purpose, loyalty to the Army, devotion to duty, sincere patriotism and deep and real attachment to his Queen and country pervaded all he did. I rejoice to have this opportunity for thus expressing my feelings regarding so great a Personage, because in the course of our long intimacy I had often to differ materially from his views upon Army matters and to propose changes in which, at the time, he did not always concur.'''

Wolseley, despite many notable conflicts with the Duke, was chivalrous to him in his old age, and used to visit him until the end. "Lord Wolseley came at twelve," wrote the Duke on July 8, 1903, "and we had a long talk together over most of the events of the present day, which was most interesting to me. He is always most agreeable." After the Duke's death, Sir Adolphus FitzGeorge wrote to Wolseley consulting him on the advisability of presenting his father's papers to the Royal United Service Institution. Wolseley replied that the idea was an admirable one. He continued his letter by saying that, although he often differed from the Duke's views upon Army matters, "I always had a great respect for His opinions. They were invariably honest and straightforward, and coming from a Soldier of very long experience in our Army, they always deserved—and met with from me—the most serious consideration. At all times and upon all occasions, even when we differed most, I never for a moment forgot that He was a member of our Royal Family, and I have reason to know that he fully recognized that fact. He was usually outspoken in His views upon men and measures, but He never 'hit below the belt.' He was a very good friend and a strong hater. Unfortunately for Him, He often had about Him flatterers who were bad counsellors and who led Him astray, that is, according to my poor judgement. His weak point was—I thought—listening to them, and I was, perhaps, too much behind the scenes to remain silent when, as I thought, they misled Him. Had He been left to exercise his own judgement, he would, I felt, have avoided much of the trouble he had with some of the Secretaries of State for War whom He was called upon to deal with. This was my opinion, because He certainly was a man of great ability.'"

One of the most frequent duties of the Commander-in-Chief was making speeches. As the Duke supported many charities, and as he was the obvious person to propose the toast of the Army on almost any occasion, he was overwhelmed with requests and invitations. "He was a capital after-dinner speaker," wrote Lord Redesdale. "His downright, honest periods, given out with that sonorous and beautiful voice for which the descendants of George the Third are famous, went straight home to the hearts of his audience." "As a speaker of a certain kind," said a soldier who had often heard him, "the Duke was certainly second to none in the Kingdom. H.R.H. came down to inspect the regiment at Aldershot before it sailed for India somewhere in the Nineties. I was present on the occasion as a guest of the regiment. At the end of the inspection, the Duke formed the regiment up in quarter-column and made a speech which lasted some ten minutes. At the end of that time I will not say that there was not a dry eye in the regiment, but I will certainly say that a number of the N.C.O.'s and men were very visibly affected. It was a very wonderful speech, manly and vigorous, but at the same time intensely pathetic. The Duke was at that time an old man, and the speech was in the nature of a lasting farewell to a regiment which he loved.'"

The Army's affection for the Duke was partly inspired by the trouble he always took over individuals. Every soldier, no matter what his rank, knew he could go to the Duke "and that he would spare neither time nor trouble to redress any genuine injustice." Sir Harry Johnston described H.R.H. as "one of the kindest and most considerate persons I ever encountered: far more patient and painstaking as a listener and a setter-right than his colleague Lord Wolseley—infinitely more so than a Kitchener or a

Buller." It was one of the principal reasons that the Duke "won something that Wolseley with his faultless efficiency, never won; the deep, universal affection of his Army." The Duke's papers abound with letters in which he concerned himself with the plight of individuals. An officer's widow, Mrs. Harriet Middleton, whose husband died in service in India, sent the Duke a copy of the last letter she received from him. "I feel," he told his wife, "that my work here has in many ways affected my health, but I have worked honestly for the good of my regiment and country and for my dear and good master the Duke of Cambridge. He will I know assist you with the darling boys and you may go to him with perfect confidence that he will treat you kindly for my sake. Tell him what I say and I should like him to know how grateful I am to him for all his many favours and personal kindness to me."[n] What form the Duke's help took is not related, but a letter of gratitude shows that the appeal was not unavailing.

The position of the Commander-in-Chief was in some ways patriarchal. He knew almost every officer by sight and name, and he felt particularly responsible for Army Cadets. His frequent visits to Woolwich and Sandhurst made him familiar with the rising generation of soldiers. When necessity demanded, H.R.H. upbraided the young gentlemen for a variety of shortcomings. "The Duke goes to Woolwich," wrote Lady Geraldine on July 23, 1886. "He was not pleased! The report of the Cadets, as to conduct was *excellent*, but as to their studies very bad indeed! so that he had to pitch into them tremendously, he did not wish to do so before the reporters, for it to go forth to the whole world, so he made them a speech in public, pro bono publico! and then sent them all into another room and there in private pitched into them finely!!"

The Duke's immense correspondence with generals all over the globe reveals the detailed interest and knowledge he showed in their campaigns, in their personal welfare, and in the troops under their command. Lord Napier, to mention a single example, never forgot the "generous support" H.R.H. afforded him in Abyssinia in 1868. Often the Commander-in-Chief would sit up late into the night, writing letters full of advice and encouragement and news from England, to catch the Indian mail. He was no remote figurehead, supreme and unapproachable, but a genial ever-present chief, easily moved to wrath, but with a heart full of compassion. Lady Jephson relates that her brother "was once walking behind two soldiers when the Duke drove past. 'There goes *dear* old Garge,' said one, 'long life to him!' "⁷¹

Those who knew the Duke intimately, officers immediately under him in the Horse Guards or his A.D.C.s, found him a thoughtful and delightful companion. Airey, just before retiring from the office of Adjutant General, told the Duchess of Cambridge that "in all the fifteen years I have been connected with H.R.H. *never once* have I had an angry, impatient fretful word from him!" Edmond Mildmay, an A.D.C. since Crimean days, declared that the Duke was "without exception the most *charming* travelling companion anyone ever travelled with!! Always cheery, bright, taking everything well, facilitating everything, so that Edmond always feels the Duke is travelling with him, not he with the Duke!"⁷²

Outside the War Office, in the middle of the road, stands a statue of the Duke of Cambridge, looking down Whitehall toward the Cenotaph. It was Edward VII who suggested that the memorial should take the form of a "big man on a big horse." Lady Geraldine, who visited the sculptor, Captain Jones, in his studio, thought his work "a very fine and noble thing." At the present time not many people notice it, as they hurry by, and those inquisitive enough to give it a second glance wonder who on earth the Duke of Cambridge was, and what he did to earn so prominent a position. The answer is simple. He devoted his entire life to the service of his Queen and country—ideals which in Vic-

torian days required neither apology nor justification—
and for almost forty years, in an age of revolutionary
change, preserved, despite repeated assaults, those customs and traditions which are the life and soul of an army.
He preferred sentiment to calculation and men to measures; and he knew from the roots of his being what many
of his adversaries never fully appreciated: that British
soldiers were not figures in a ledger but creatures of flesh
and blood, "mortal men," who needed to be cajoled, hu-
moured, and, in supreme moments, inspired. No army
could have sustained those feats of endurance and courage
which become almost commonplaces of Victorian achievement, unless possessed by a living sense of past glories and
triumphs. We owe it to the Duke of Cambridge that, despite
the reorganization of every regiment in the Kingdom, old
customs endured, old traditions flourished, and old loyalties
survived. That this was so was no mere indulgence of the
reactionary whim of a royal retrograde: it was the salvation
of the Queen's Army.

The Duke of Cambridge's Contemporaries 1856–1895

Prime Ministers	Secretaries of State for War	Adjutants General
1856 Palmerston	Panmure	Sir G. Wetherall
1858 Derby	1858 General Peel	1860 Sir J. Y. Scarlett
1859 Palmerston	1859 Sidney Herbert	1865 Lord William
1865 Russell	1861 Sir G. Lewis	Paulet
1866 Derby	1863 Earl de Grey	1870 Sir R. Airey
1868 Disraeli	(Marquis	1876 Sir C. Ellice
1868 Gladstone	of Ripon)	1882 Sir G. Wolseley
1874 Beaconsfield	1866 Hartington	1882 Sir. R. Taylor
1880 Gladstone	1866 General Peel	1882 Lord Wolseley
1885 Salisbury	1867 Sir J. Pakington	1885 Sir A. Alison
1886 Gladstone	1868 Cardwell	1885 Viscount
1886 Salisbury	1874 Gathorne-Hardy	Wolseley
1892 Gladstone	(Earl of	1890 Sir R. Buller
1894 Rosebery	Cranbrook)	
1895 Salisbury	1878 Col. Stanley	
	(Earl of	
	Derby)	
	1880 Childers	
	1882 Hartington	
	1885 W. H. Smith	
	1886 Campbell-Bannerman	
	1886 W. H. Smith	
	1887 Stanhope	
	1892 Campbell-Bannerman	
	1895 Lansdowne	

Note on Sources

THERE ARE TWO MAIN MANUSCRIPT SOURCES for the life of H.R.H. the Duke of Cambridge. The first is the Royal Archives at Windsor Castle, and the second the papers in the possession of the FitzGeorge family. In addition to these, there are papers in the political collections of the British Museum, the Public Record Office, and in the library of the Royal United Service Institution.

The material in the Royal Archives falls into five categories. First, there are the Duke's own papers, as yet uncatalogued, kept in the Diary Room. Second, there are the papers of the Cambridge family, including Queen Mary's papers. Third, there are a miscellany of royal manuscripts (e.g., the Queen's diary, the Queen's letters, the Duke of Connaught's papers, etc.). Fourth, there is a huge section devoted to Army affairs; and, finally, there is Lady Geraldine Somerset's diary.

The FitzGeorge collection consists mainly of letters of H.R.H. and Mrs. FitzGeorge, letters between the Fitz-George sons and their parents, letters to H.R.H. from the Queen, and the Duke's diaries. Some of these, which were available to the official biographers soon after H.R.H.'s death, have since been lost.

The principal printed sources are Sheppard's *Memoir* and Verner's *Military Life of H.R.H. the Duke of Cambridge* —both in two volumes.

A large number of other manuscripts and books have been consulted. Reference to the Notes on Chapters will give further details of some of the material on which this biography is based.

Notes for Chapters

THE FOLLOWING NOTES are designed to give the sources of information upon which the chapters are based. I have used the abbreviation R.A. for the Royal Archives at Windsor. I have not given references in the text: (i) To the source of extracts which the text itself reveals. For example, a dated diary entry has been left to speak for itself. Where the name of an author is omitted, it may be presumed to be the Duke. The Note on Sources indicates where letters, diaries, etc. may be consulted. (ii) To letters, etc., in the FitzGeorge collection, which is uncatalogued and not generally available. Reference is only made to the FitzGeorge collection where the text omits information, such as the date of a letter or who it is from. (iii) To brief quotations from reasonably obvious or unimportant sources.

It is not to be presumed that an extract for which a manuscript source is given has therefore never appeared in print. I have read both in manuscript and in manuscript copies, published collections, and books quoting such collections, extracts, for example, from Queen Victoria's letters or Cardwell's papers. References made in these notes to such extracts have been ascribed indiscriminately to the original document, to published collected papers, or to secondary sources. The inconsistency involved seemed preferable to the overwhelming labour of eliminating it.

NOTES FOR CHAPTER I

p. 3, *l.* 19　*The Complete Peerage.* Edited by the Hon. Vicary Gibbs. St. Catherine Press. 1912. Vol. II. pp. 496–7.

p. 3, *l.* 25　*A Short Memoir of His Late Royal Highness Adolphus*

Duke of Cambridge. Lt.-Gen. Sir James Reynett. A pamphlet. 1858. p. 28.

p. 4, l. 34 *Queen Adelaide.* Mark Hopkirk. Murray. 1946. p. 10.

p. 6, l. 3 *H.R.H. George Duke of Cambridge.* Edgar Sheppard. Longmans. 1906. Vol. I. p. 5.

p. 6, l. 19 *The Journal of Mrs. Arbuthnot.* Edited by Francis Bamford and the Duke of Wellington. Macmillan. 1950. Vol. II. pp. 252–3.

p. 6, l. 36 *The Life and Letters of The Fourth Earl of Clarendon.* Sir H. Maxwell. Arnold. 1913. Vol. I. p. 48.

p. 7, l. 34 *Correspondence of Sarah Spencer Lady Lyttelton 1787–1870.* Edited by the Hon. Mrs. Hugh Wyndham. Murray. 1912. p. 294.

p. 9, l. 8 *Gossip of the Century.* Byrne. Ward and Downey. 1892. Vol. I. pp. 67–9.

p. 9, l. 29 *A Memoir of Her Royal Highness Princess Mary Adelaide Duchess of Teck.* C. Kinloch Cooke. Murray. 1900. Vol. I. p. 24.

p. 10, l. 1 *Memories.* Lord Redesdale. Hutchinson. 1915. Vol. II. p. 703.

p. 10, l. 22 Ella Taylor's Reminiscences. R.A. Addl. Mss. A/8. 390.

p. 11, l. 8 *A Memoir of Her Royal Highness Princess Mary Adelaide Duchess of Teck.* C. Kinloch Cooke. Murray. 1900. Vol. I. pp. 26–7.

p. 11, l. 28 Lady Geraldine Somerset's Diary. 11 November 1886. R.A.

p. 14, l. 3 *H.R.H. George Duke of Cambridge.* Edgar Sheppard. Longmans. 1906. Vol. I. pp. 9–10.

p. 14, l. 26 *Letters of Dorothea Princess Lieven.* Edited by Lionel G. Robinson. Longmans. 1902. p. 373.

p. 15, l. 20 Diary of Queen Adelaide. R.A. Georgian Addl. Mss. 21/7.

p. 16, l. 8 *Bygone Years. Recollections.* Leveson Gower. Murray. 1905. p. 4.

p. 16, l. 19 *Lord James of Hereford.* Lord Askwith. Bevin. 1930. p. 213.

p. 16, l. 23 Diary of Queen Adelaide. Preface. R.A. Georgian Addl. Mss. 21/7.

p. 17, l. 8 Lady Geraldine Somerset's Diary. 25 December 1886. R.A.

p. 17, l. 14 *Glimpses of King William IV and Queen Adelaide.* Cecil White. Brimley Johnson. 1902. pp. 33–4.

p. 20, *l.* 13   H.R.H. *George Duke of Cambridge.* Edgar Sheppard. Longmans. 1906. Vol. I. p. 26.

p. 24, *l.* 33   H.R.H. *George Duke of Cambridge.* Edgar Sheppard. Longmans. 1906. Vol. I. pp. 39–40.

p. 26, *l.* 10   The Queen's Diary. 16 May 1838. R.A.

p. 31, *l.* 21   H.R.H. *George Duke of Cambridge.* Edgar Sheppard. Longmans. 1906. Vol. I. pp. 56–7.

p. 32, *l.* 3   *Military Life of H.R.H. The Duke of Cambridge.* Willoughby Verner. Murray. 1905. Vol. I. pp. 23–4.

p. 33, *l.* 3   Prince Albert to His Father. 6 March 1838. R.A. Addl. Mss. A/14.

p. 34, *l.* 6   *Henry Ponsonby, His Life and Letters.* Arthur Ponsonby. Macmillan. 1953. p. 92.

p. 35, *l.* 19   *Under Five Reigns.* Lady Dorothy Nevill. Methuen. 1910. p. 262. *Dramatic Reminiscences.* G. Vandenhoff. Thomas W. Cooper. 1860. p. 90. *The World.* 22 January 1890.

p. 37, *l.* 3   *Memoirs.* Sir Almeric Fitzroy. Hutchinson. 1925. pp. 299–300.

p. 38, *l.* 12   Duke of Cambridge to the Queen. 21 April 1889. R.A. L.2.111.

p. 38, *l.* 25   Duke of Cambridge to Adolphus FitzGeorge. 11 September and 29 October 1869. FitzGeorge Papers.

p. 39, *l.* 24   Queen to Duke of Connaught. 11 October 1882. R.A. Addl. Mss. A/15. 3785.

p. 39, *l.* 31   *Famous Morganatic Marriages.* Kingston. Stanley Paul. 1919. p. 157.

p. 41, *l.* 18   *Famous Morganatic Marriages.* Kingston. Stanley Paul. 1919. p. 160.

NOTES FOR CHAPTER 2

p. 45, *l.* 16   *The Greville Memoirs.* Edited by Lytton Strachey and Roger Fulford. Macmillan. 1938. Vol. 5. pp. 49–50, 77–9.

p. 45, *l.* 32   Lady Geraldine Somerset's Diary. 7 April 1884. R.A.

p. 46, *l.* 4   *Military Life of H.R.H. The Duke of Cambridge.* Willoughby Verner. Murray. 1905. Vol. I. p. 26.

p. 46, *l.* 25   H.R.H. *George Duke of Cambridge.* Edgar Sheppard. Longmans. 1906. Vol. I. p. 85.

p. 46, *l.* 25   H.R.H. *George Duke of Cambridge.* Edgar Sheppard. Longmans. 1906. Vol. I. p. 88.

p. 47, *l.* 31   Duke of Cambridge to W. F. Forster. 5 January and June 1848. Duke's Papers. R.A.

p. 48, *l.* 2   Duke of Cambridge to W. F. Forster. 21 December 1849. Duke's Papers. R.A.

p. 48, *l.* 23   *The Letters of Queen Victoria.* Edited by G. E. Buckle. Murray. 1926. Second series. Vol. II. p. 151.

p. 49, *l.* 17   *H.R.H. George Duke of Cambridge.* Edgar Sheppard. Longmans. 1906. Vol. I. pp. 88–9.

p. 49, *l.* 27   Memorandum, April 1849. Dublin. FitzGeorge Papers.

p. 50, *l.* 3   *H.R.H. George Duke of Cambridge.* Edgar Sheppard. Longmans. 1906. Vol. I. p. 94.

p. 51, *l.* 33   *A Memoir of Her Royal Highness Princess Mary Adelaide Duchess of Teck.* C. Kinloch Cooke. Murray. 1900. Vol. I. p. 116.

p. 52, *l.* 12   Memorandum of Prince Albert. R.A. L.23.19.

p. 52, *l.* 15   The Queen to Lord John Russell. 1850. R.A. L.23, 20 and 21.

p. 52, *l.* 30   Prince Albert to Duke of Saxe-Coburg. R.A. Add. A/14.96.

p. 53, *l.* 7   Memorandum of Prince Albert. 1850. R.A. L.23.32.

p. 53, *l.* 27   FitzGeorge Papers.

p. 54, *l.* 12   *A Memoir of Her Royal Highness Princess Mary Adelaide Duchess of Teck.* C. Kinloch Cooke. Murray. 1900. Vol. I. pp. 131–2.

p. 54, *l.* 20   The Queen to Duke of Cambridge. 18 November 1852. FitzGeorge Papers.

p. 55, *l.* 5   Memorandum of Prince Albert. September 1852. R.A. E2.L4.

p. 55, *l.* 30   *The War Office Past and Present.* Owen Wheeler. Methuen. 1914. pp. 135–6.

p. 57, *l.* 17   Mrs. FitzGeorge to Duke of Cambridge. December. Undated. Duke of Cambridge to Mrs. FitzGeorge. 6 October 1850 and 29 January 1851. FitzGeorge Papers.

p. 57, *l.* 29   Mrs. FitzGeorge to Duke of Cambridge. Undated. Duke of Cambridge to Mrs. FitzGeorge. 26 June 1848. FitzGeorge Papers.

p. 59, *l.* 16   *A History of the British Army.* J. W. Fortescue. Macmillan. 1899–1930. Vol. XIII. p. 534.

p. 59, *l.* 37   *The War Office.* Hampden Gordon. Putnam. 1935. p. 35.

p. 60, *l.* 12   *The Military Forces of the Crown.* Charles Clode. Murray. 1869. Vol. I. p. 263.

p. 61, *l.* 23   *Story of a Soldier's Life.* Wolseley. Constable. 1903. Vol. I. p. 53.

p. 62, *l.* 6   *Parliament and the Army.* Lt.-Col. Omond. Cambridge University Press. 1933. p. 82.

p. 62, *l.* 32   *The Staff and the Staff College.* A. R. Godwin-Austen. Constable. 1927. p. 86.

p. 64, *l.* 16   Lord Wolseley to the Duke of Cambridge. 11 December 1884. Duke's Papers. R.A.

p. 65, *l.* 1   *The Destruction of Lord Raglan.* Christopher Hibbert. Longmans. 1961. p. 8.

NOTES FOR CHAPTER 3

p. 71, *l.* 23   *H.R.H. George Duke of Cambridge.* Sheppard. Longmans. 1906. Vol. I. p. 121.

p. 72, *l.* 8   *Military Life of H.R.H. The Duke of Cambridge.* Verner. Murray. 1905. Vol. I. p. 66.

p. 72, *l.* 37   Colonel Seymour to Colonel Phipps. Scutari. 27 May 1854. R.A. F.1.11.

p. 73, *l.* 2   Prince Edward of Saxe-Weimar to the Queen. 8 July 1854. R.A. F.1.17.

p. 73, *l.* 8   *Seventy-one Years of a Guardsman's Life.* General Sir George Higginson. Smith, Elder and Co. 1916. p. 129.

p. 74, *l.* 33   Mrs. FitzGeorge to the Duke of Cambridge. 11 September 1854. FitzGeorge Papers.

p. 77, *l.* 13   *This for Remembrance.* Lord Coleridge. Fisher Unwin. 1925. p. 89.

p. 80, *l.* 33   Mrs. FitzGeorge to the Duke of Cambridge. 20 September, 5 June, and 30 June 1854. FitzGeorge Papers.

p. 81, *l.* 6   Duke of Cambridge to Mrs. FitzGeorge. 28 June 1854. FitzGeorge Papers.

p. 82, *l.* 2   Mrs. FitzGeorge to the Duke of Cambridge. 16 October, 1 and 14 June, 6 July 1854. FitzGeorge Papers.

p. 82, *l.* 24   Lord Wolseley to the Duke of Cambridge. 9 November 1894. Duke's Papers. R.A.

p. 83, *l.* 28   Mrs. FitzGeorge to the Duke of Cambridge. 1 June, 24 May 1854. Duke of Cambridge to Mrs. FitzGeorge. 18 June 1854. FitzGeorge Papers.

p. 87, *l.* 19   *The Destruction of Lord Raglan.* Hibbert. Longmans. 1961. p. 181.

p. 87, *l.* 37   Captain Gordon. 6 December 1854. R.A. F.1.35.

p. 88, *l.* 9   Duke of Newcastle to Lord Raglan. 27 November 1854. Public Record Office. W.O. 6/70. p. 50.

p. 88, *l.* 15   *The Three Sergeants.* Morris. Quoted in Verner Vol. I. p. 83.

p. 88, *l.* 22   Prince of Wales. Memorandum. 1856. R.A. T.1.110.

p. 88, *l.* 26   *The Correspondence of Priscilla, Countess of Westmorland.* Edited by Lady Weigall. Murray. 1909. p. 247.

p. 89, *l.* 34   *Richard Cobden. The International Man.* J. A. Hobson. Fisher Unwin. 1918. p. 115.

p. 91, *l.* 4   Duke of Cambridge to Duchess of Cambridge. 18 November. R.A. Addl. Mss. 8/8. 208.

p. 91, *l.* 18   Duke of Cambridge to Mrs. FitzGeorge. 14 and 22 November 1854. FitzGeorge Papers.

p. 91, *l.* 35   Prince Edward of Saxe-Weimar to the Queen. 28 November 1854. R.A. G.20.29.

p. 92, *l.* 9   Duke of Cambridge to Mrs. FitzGeorge. 29 November 1854. FitzGeorge Papers.

p. 92, *l.* 25   Queen to Duke of Cambridge. 15 December 1854. R.A. G.20.128.

p. 93, *l.* 18   *The Life of Florence Nightingale.* Sir E. Cook. Macmillan. 1914. Vol. I. pp. 384–5.

p. 93, *l.* 26   Lord W. Paulet to the Duke of Cambridge. 26 March 1855. Duke's Papers. R.A.

p. 97, *l.* 29   Duke of Cambridge to Duchess of Cambridge. 8 November 1854, 1 January 1855, 30 November 1854, 18 December 1854, 7 January 1855, 22 January 1855. R.A. G.18.119. Addl. Mss. A/8, 175, 172, 194, 176, 180.

p. 97, *l.* 37   The Queen to Lord Raglan. 1 January 1855. R.A. G.21.65.

p. 98, *l.* 16   The Queen to the Duke of Cambridge. 19 January 1855. R.A. G.22.59.

p. 98, *l.* 20   The Queen to Lord Raglan. 18 February 1855. R.A. G.24.73.

p. 99, *l.* 15   The Duke of Cambridge to the Queen. 24 November 1854. R.A. G.20.31.

p. 99, *l.* 30   *The Invasion of the Crimea.* A. W. Kinglake. Blackwood. 1863–1887. Vol. III. pp. 132–3.

p. 100, *l.* 12   Lord Wolseley to His Wife. 10 November 1884, 12 August 1887, 26 September 1884. Library of Royal United Service Institution.

p. 100, *l.* 24   Colonel Gordon to General Grey. 7 November 1854. Lord James Murray to Sir George Couper. 16 December 1854. Colonel Phipps to the Queen. Undated. R.A. G.18.112, G.20.129, F1.85.

p. 101, *l.* 12   *Louis Napoleon and the Recovery of France.* Simpson. Longmans. 1923. p. 270. Footnote 3.

p. 103, *l.* 27   Duke of Cambridge to Lord Hardinge. 4 February 1856. Duke's Papers. R.A.

p. 104, *l.* 5   *The Panmure Papers.* Edited by Sir G. Douglas. Hodder and Stoughton. 1908. Vol. I. p. 112.

p. 105, *l.* 4   *The Panmure Papers.* Edited by Sir G. Douglas. Hodder and Stoughton. 1908. Vol. I. pp. 282, 227–8, 379, 380.

p. 106, *l.* 26   A History of the British Army. J. W. Fortescue. 1899–1930. Vol. XIII. p. 140.

p. 106, *l.* 31   Sir G. Cornwall Lewis to Duke of Cambridge. 28 January 1863. Duke's Papers. R.A.

p. 107, *l.* 6   Sir George Brown to Duke of Cambridge. 4 February 1864. Duke's Papers. R.A.

p. 107, *l.* 29   The Duke of Cambridge to De Lacy Evans. 4 February 1864. Duke's Papers. R.A.

p. 108, *l.* 21   De Lacy Evans to the Duke of Cambridge. 7 February 1864. Duke's Papers. R.A.

p. 108, *l.* 114   Lord Clyde to the Duke of Cambridge. 11 February 1864. Duke's Papers. R.A.

p. 109, *l.* 14   Sir George Brown to the Duke of Cambridge. 11 February 1864. Duke's Papers. R.A.

p. 110, *l.* 7   *The Panmure Papers.* Edited by Sir G. Douglas. Hodder and Stoughton. 1908. Vol. I. p. 152.

p. 110, *l.* 30   *The Destruction of Lord Raglan.* Hibbert. Longmans. 1961. pp. 232–3.

NOTES FOR CHAPTER 4

p. 114, *l.* 2   *The Letters of Queen Victoria.* Ed. Benson and Esher. Murray. 1907. First Series. Vol. III. pp. 252–3.

p. 115, *l.* 34   *H.R.H. George Duke of Cambridge.* Sheppard. Longmans. 1906. Vol. I. pp. 177–8, 179.

p. 116, *l.* 4   Mrs. FitzGeorge to the Duke of Cambridge. 28 September 1856. FitzGeorge Papers.

p. 117, *l.* 31   *The Panmure Papers.* Ed. Sir G. Douglas. Hodder and Stoughton. 1908. Vol. I. pp. 86, 126.

p. 118, *l.* 5   *The Life of H.R.H. The Prince Consort.* Sir T. Martin. Smith, Elder and Co. 1874–1880. Vol. II. p. 255.

p. 118, *l.* 9   *The Life of Lord Roberts.* David James. Hollis and Carter. 1954. p. 224.

p. 118, *l.* 25   *A History of the British Army.* J. W. Fortescue. Macmillan. 1899–1930. Vol. XIII. p. 539.

p. 119, *l.* 27   Duke of Cambridge to Sir Hope Grant. 3 December 1859. Duke's Papers. R.A.

p. 121, *l.* 7   Duke of Cambridge to Sir Colin Campbell. 10 December 1857. Duke's Papers. R.A.

p. 122, *l.* 26   *Military Life of H.R.H. The Duke of Cambridge.* Verner. Murray. 1905. Vol. I. p. 170.

p. 122, *l.* 7   Duke of Cambridge to Sir Colin Campbell. 10 December 1857. Duke's Papers. R.A.

p. 122, *l.* 26   *Military Life of H.R.H. The Duke of Cambridge.* Verner. Murray. 1905. Vol. I. pp. 215, 271.

p. 123, *l.* 11   The Duke of Cambridge to Lord Mansfield. 27 November 1865. Duke's Papers. R.A.

p. 123, *l.* 32   Queen to Lord Palmerston. 19 July 1857. Lord Palmerston to the Queen. 18 July 1857. R.A. E.9.81 and 80.

p. 124, *l.* 14   *The Monarchy in Politics.* J. A. Farrer. Fisher and Unwin. 1917. pp. 288–93.

p. 124, *l.* 36   *Military Life of H.R.H. The Duke of Cambridge.* Verner. Murray. 1905. Vol. I. p. 269.

p. 126, *l.* 23   Sir George Lewis to Duke of Cambridge. 8 October 1861. Duke of Cambridge to Sir George Lewis. 8 October 1861. Duke's Papers. R.A.

p. 126, *l.* 35   *The Life of Lord Wolseley.* Sir F. Maurice and Sir G. Arthur. Heinemann. 1924. p. 236.

p. 127, *l.* 12   *The Staff and the Staff College.* A. R. Godwin-Austen. Constable. 1927. pp. 225, 155.

p. 127, *l.* 29   *Stray Recollections.* Sir C. Callwell. Arnold. 1923. Vol. I. p. 289.

p. 127, *l.* 37   *The Staff and the Staff College.* A. R. Godwin-Austen. Constable. 1927. pp. 117–18.

p. 128, *l.* 13   *The Panmure Papers.* Ed. Sir G. Douglas. Hodder and Stoughton. 1908. Vol. I. pp. 283, 288.

p. 129, *l.* 26   *The Staff and the Staff College.* A. R. Godwin-Austen. Constable. 1927. p. 74.

p. 130, *l.* 27   *Stray Recollections.* Sir C. Callwell. Arnold. 1923. Vol. I. pp. 287–8.

p. 131, *l.* 27   *Records and Reactions.* Earl of Midleton. Murray. 1939. pp. 81–2.

p. 131, *l.* 31   *Notes of a Nomad.* Lady Jephson. Hutchinson. 1918. pp. 177–8.

p. 132, *l.* 32   *Sixty Years of a Soldier's Life.* Sir A. Turner. Methuen. 1912. pp. 30–1.

p. 133, *l.* 30   Duke of Cambridge to Sir Colin Campbell. 25 May 1858. 26 December 1857. Duke's Papers. R.A.

p. 133, *l.* 34   Duchess of Gloucester to Princess Mary Adelaide. 28 November 1851. R.A. Addl. Mss. A/8. L.342.

p. 134, *l.* 17   *A Memoir of Her Royal Highness Princess Mary Adelaide Duchess of Teck.* C. Kinloch Cooke. Murray. 1900. Vol. I. p. 89.

p. 137, *l.* 19   *H.R.H. George Duke of Cambridge.* Sheppard. Longmans. 1906. Vol. I. pp. 221–2.

p. 138, *l.* 12   The Queen to the King of the Belgians. 23 July 1863. R.A. Addl. Mss. Y.110.4.

p. 138, *l.* 29   *H.R.H. George Duke of Cambridge.* Sheppard. Longmans. 1906. Vol. I. p. 226.

p. 139, *l.* 6   Queen to King Leopold of the Belgians. Windsor, 9 June 1863. R.A. Addl. Mss. Y.109.34.

p. 140, *l.* 24   Duke of Cambridge to Lord de Grey. 8 March 1864. Duke's Papers. R.A. *Military Life of H.R.H. The Duke of Cambridge.* Verner. Murray. 1905. Vol. I. pp. 297–8.

p. 141, *l.* 12   Duke of Cambridge to Sir Donald Rose. 5 April 1883. Duke's Papers. R.A.

p. 141, *l.* 19   *The War Office Past and Present.* Wheeler. Methuen. 1914. p. 169.

p. 141, *l.* 29   Duke of Cambridge to Queen. 31 December 1860. R.A. E.12.109.

p. 142, *l.* 11   Duke of Cambridge to Mrs. FitzGeorge. 4 August 1858. Duke's Diary. 5 May 1866. FitzGeorge Papers.

p. 142, *l.* 22   Duke of Cambridge to Adolphus FitzGeorge. 29 October 1868. FitzGeorge Papers.

p. 143, *l.* 34   Duke of Cambridge to Adolphus FitzGeorge. 31 October, 17 October 1865. FitzGeorge Papers.

p. 144, *l.* 14   Duke of Cambridge to Adolphus FitzGeorge. 18 May, 3 December 1866, 27 March 1867. FitzGeorge Papers.

p. 144, *l.* 31   Duke of Cambridge to Mrs. FitzGeorge. 1 October 1857. FitzGeorge Papers.

p. 145, *l.* 4   Duke of Cambridge to Mrs. FitzGeorge. 31 August 1856. FitzGeorge Papers.

p. 145, *l.* 20   Duke's Diary. 3 April 1867. FitzGeorge Papers.

p. 145, *l.* 35   Duke of Cambridge to Mrs. FitzGeorge. 2 August 1867. FitzGeorge Papers.

NOTES FOR CHAPTER 5

p. 147, *l.* 25   The Duke of Cambridge to Sir W. Mansfield. 10 December 1868. Duke's Papers. R.A.

p. 148, *l.* 29   *Lord Cardwell at the War Office.* Sir R. Biddulph. Murray. 1904. Appendix 1. pp. 249–54.

p. 150, *l.* 28   *Military Life of H.R.H. The Duke of Cambridge.* Verner. Murray. 1905. Vol. I. pp. 409, 416.

p. 151, *l.* 16   *Lord Haliburton.* Atlay. Smith, Elder & Co. 1909. p. 16.

p. 151, *l.* 32   Duke of Cambridge to General Forster. 31 August 1871. Duke's Papers. R.A.

p. 152, *l.* 32   *Military Life of H.R.H. The Duke of Cambridge.*

Verner. Murray. 1905. Vol. I. p. 401. *The Reign of Queen Victoria.* Hector Bolitho. Collins. 1949. p. 268.

p. 153, *l.* 3   Lord Airey to the Duke of Cambridge. 20 August 1870. Duke's Papers. R.A.

p. 153, *l.* 17   Duke of Cambridge to Cardwell. 29 July 1870. 28 December 1869. Public Record Office. GD. 48. 3/14 and 12.

p. 154, *l.* 34   *Military Life of H.R.H. The Duke of Cambridge.* Verner. Murray. 1905. Vol. I. pp. 392, 399.

p. 155, *l.* 37   *The Life of Lord Wolseley.* Sir F. Maurice and Sir G. Arthur. Heinemann. 1924. p. xx.

p. 156, *l.* 26   Lord Lansdowne to Sir F. Knollys. 8 June 1897. R.A. T.10.63.

p. 157, *l.* 3   Queen's Diary. 2 August, 24 February 1871. R.A.

p. 157, *l.* 15   *Concerning Queen Victoria and Her Son.* Sir G. Arthur. Robert Hale. 1953. p. 153.

p. 158, *l.* 24   Lord A. Loftus to Duke of Cambridge. 21 July, 23 July, 30 July 1870. Duke's Papers. R.A.

p. 158, *l.* 31   *Queen Mary.* James Pope-Hennessy. Allen and Unwin. 1959. p. 101.

p. 159, *l.* 6   *Life of Lord Kitchener.* Sir G. Arthur. Macmillan. 1920. Vol. I. pp. 10–11.

p. 159, *l.* 31   *Letters of Field-Marshal Lord Napier of Magdala.* Ed. Lt.-Col. H. D. Napier. Jarrold and Sons. 1936. pp. 28–9.

p. 160, *l.* 25   *From Wellington to Wavel.* Sir G. Arthur. Hutchinson. 1942. p. 72.

p. 161, *l.* 12   *The Life of Lord Roberts.*   David James. Hollis and Carter. 1954. pp. 170–1.

p. 162, *l.* 17   *Hansard.* 21 February 1871.

p. 163, *l.* 2   *Letters of Queen Victoria.* Ed. G. E. Buckle. Murray. 1928. Second Series. Vol. II. pp. 162–3.

p. 163, *l.* 21   *Money or Merit.* de Fonblanque. Charles J. Skeet. 1857. p. 12.

p. 164, *l.* 2   *Punch.* 5 August 1871.

p. 165, *l.* 11   *A Letter on Army Reform.* M. J. Higgins. Varty. 1855. pp. 3–4, 8.

p. 165, *l.* 33   *Lord Cardwell at the War Office.* Sir R. Biddulph. Murray. 1904. pp. 76, 78, 116.

p. 166, *l.* 23   "Edward T. Cardwell: Peelite." *Transactions of the American Philosophical Society.* Arvel Erickson. New Series. Vol. 49, part 2. 1959. p. 81. *Lord Cardwell at the War Office.* Sir R. Biddulph. Murray. 1904. pp. 116–17.

p. 166, *l.* 31   *Military Life of H.R.H. The Duke of Cambridge.* Verner. Murray. 1905. Vol. II. pp. 6–7.

p. 167, *l.* 35   *A Personal History of the Horse Guards.* J. H. Stocqueler. Hurst and Blackett. 1873. pp. 153–4.

p. 168, *l.* 2   *Military Forces of the Crown.* Charles Clode. Murray. 1869. Vol. II. p. 86.

p. 168, *l.* 18   *Parliament and the Army.* Lt.-Col. Omond. Cambridge University Press. 1933. pp. 120–1. *Panmure Papers.* Ed. Sir G. Douglas. Hodder and Stoughton. 1908. Vol. II. p. 492.

p. 170, *l.* 5   Cardwell to Duke of Cambridge. 3 June 1871. Duke of Cambridge to Cardwell. 3 June 1871. Public Record Office. GD. 48. 4/15.

p. 171, *l.* 3   Duke of Cambridge to the Queen. 6 and 12 July 1871. Duke's Papers. R.A.

p. 171, *l.* 28   Queen to Gladstone (copy). 8 July 1871. Duke's Papers. R.A.

p. 172, *l.* 4   *The Letters of Queen Victoria.* Ed. G. E. Buckle. Murray. 1928. Second Series. Vol. II. p. 143.

p. 173, *l.* 26   *A Personal History of the Horse Guards.* J. H. Stocqueler. Hurst and Blackett. 1873. p. 285.

p. 177, *l.* 25   *Henry Ponsonby. His Life from His Letters.* A. Ponsonby. Macmillan. 1943. pp. 99–100.

p. 177, *l.* 30   *Under Five Reigns.* Lady Dorothy Nevill. Methuen. 1910. pp. 204–5.

p. 178, *l.* 7   *King Edward VII.* Sir S. Lee. Macmillan. 1925, Vol. I. pp. 13–14.

p. 178, *l.* 20   Queen to Duke of Connaught. 25 July 1875. R.A. Z.207.3.

p. 180, *l.* 17   Queen to Duke of Cambridge. 17 April 1873. Fitz-George Papers.

NOTES FOR CHAPTER 6

p. 184, *l.* 22   *Gathorne-Hardy, First Earl of Cranbrook. A Memoir.* Ed. A. E. Gathorne-Hardy. Longmans. 1910. Vol. I. p. 343.

p. 187, *l.* 28   *The Life of Lord Wolseley.* Sir F. Maurice and Sir G. Arthur. Heinemann. 1924. pp. 254, 284. Wolseley to Lady Wolseley. 7 July 1886. Royal United Service Institution.

p. 190, *l.* 17   *Before the Lamps Went Out.* Wingfield-Stratford. Hodder and Stoughton. 1945. pp. 21–3.

p. 190, *l.* 35   *From Wellington to Wavell.* Sir G. Arthur. Hutchinson. 1942. p. 74.

p. 191, *l.* 7   *Military Life of H.R.H. The Duke of Cambridge.* Verner. Murray. 1906. Vol. II. pp. 148–9.

p. 193, *l.* 9   *Military Life of H.R.H. The Duke of Cambridge.* Verner. Murray. 1906. Vol. II. pp. 159–60, 160–1.

p. 196, *l.* 4 *Letters of Field-Marshal Lord Napier.* Ed. Lt.-Col. H. D. Napier. Harrold and Sons. 1936. p. 101.

p. 198, *l.* 13 Queen to Duke of Cambridge. 20 July 1879. Duke's Papers. R.A.

p. 200, *l.* 8 *Military Life of H.R.H. The Duke of Cambridge.* Verner. Murray. 1906. Vol. II. pp. 156–7.

p. 200, *l.* 28 Christine V de Aros to Duke of Cambridge. 11 August 1879. Duke's Papers. R.A.

p. 201, *l.* 10 Duke of Cambridge to Sir C. Campbell. 10 October, 24 November 1857. Duke's Papers. R.A.

p. 202, *l.* 25 *The Life of Lord Wolseley.* Sir F. Maurice and Sir G. Arthur. Heinemann. 1924. p. 236.

p. 202 *l.* 34 *Life of Lord Roberts.* David James. Hollis and Carter. 1954. p. 212.

p. 204, *l.* 30 *Military Life of H.R.H. The Duke of Cambridge.* Verner. Murray. 1906. Vol. II. pp. 159, 165, 170–1, 172–3.

p. 205, *l.* 20 *The Life of Lord Wolseley.* Sir F. Maurice and Sir G. Arthur. Heinemann. 1924. p. 213.

p. 206, *l.* 8 Duke of Cambridge to Sir E. Johnson. 17 April 1879. Duke of Cambridge to Colonel Stanley. 31 May 1879. Duke's Papers. R.A.

p. 208, *l.* 30 Lord Wolseley to Lady Wolseley. 11 April 1880. Royal United Service Institution.

p. 209, *l.* 21 Duke of Cambridge to the Queen. February 1886. R.A. C.37.285.

p. 209, *l.* 33 *The Life and Correspondence of the Right Hon. Hugh C. E. Childers.* Lt.-Col. Spencer Childers. Murray. 1901. Vol. II. p. 53.

p. 210, *l.* 2 *The Life of Sir Charles Dilke.* Gwyn and Tuckwell. Murray. 1917. Vol. I. p. 472.

p. 210, *l.* 19 *The Life and Correspondence of the Right Hon. Hugh C. E. Childers.* Lt.-Col. Spencer Childers. Murray. 1901. Vol. II. p. 57.

p. 212, *l.* 19 Sir C. Phipps to Prince Consort. 5 June 1858. R.A. E.10.82.

p. 215, *l.* 7 *The Life of Lord Wolseley.* Sir F. Maurice and Sir G. Arthur. Heinemann. 1924. p. 140.

p. 215, *l.* 25 *Letters of Field-Marshal Lord Napier of Magdala.* Ed. Lt.-Col. H. D. Napier. Jarrold & Sons. 1936. pp. 111, 114.

p. 216, *l.* 25 Lord Cranbrook to Duke of Cambridge. 24 November 1881. General Steele to Duke of Cambridge. 13 November 1881. Duke's Papers. R.A.

p. 219, *l.* 11 *The Life of Lord Wolseley.* Sir F. Maurice and Sir G. Arthur. Heinemann. 1924. pp. 231–2.

p. 220, *l.* 15   Duke of Cambridge to Lord Hartington. 28 September 1881. Duke's Papers. R.A.

p. 220, *l.* 22   Lady Geraldine Somerset's Diary. 8 August 1855. R.A.

p. 221, *l.* 32   Right Hon. Hugh Childers to Duke of Cambridge. 13 September 1881. Duke's Papers. R.A.

p. 233, *l.* 5   Duke of Cambridge to the Queen. 17 October 1881. Duke's Papers. R.A.

p. 224, *l.* 2   *The Life of Sir William Harcourt.* Constable. 1923. Vol. I. p. 41.

p. 227, *l.* 21   Sir H. Ponsonby to Duke of Cambridge. 7 November 1881. Duke of Cambridge to Queen. 10 November 1881. FitzGeorge Papers.

p. 228, *l.* 20   Prince of Wales to Duke of Cambridge. 28 November 1881. FitzGeorge Papers.

NOTES FOR CHAPTER 7

p. 230, *l.* 24   *Military Life of H.R.H. The Duke of Cambridge.* Verner. Murray. 1905. Vol. II. pp. 202, 204–5.

p. 231, *l.* 37   Duke of Cambridge to Ponsonby. 21 December 1880. Duke of Cambridge to the Queen. 27 December 1880. Duke's Papers. R.A.

p. 232, *l.* 14   *Letters of Field-Marshal Lord Napier of Magdala.* Ed. Lt.-Col. H. D. Napier. Jarrold & Sons. 1936. p. 95.

p. 233, *l.* 28   Lord Wolseley to Lady Wolseley. 3 September 1882. Royal United Service Institution.

p. 234, *l.* 8   Lady Geraldine Somerset's Diary. 16 November 1882. R.A.

p. 234, *l.* 22   Lady Geraldine Somerset's Diary. 14 March 1882. R.A.

p. 234, *l.* 26   Prince George to Duke of Cambridge. 19 August 1833. R.A. Addl. Mss. A/8. 501.

p. 235, *l.* 19   *The Staff and the Staff College.* A. R. Godwin-Austen. Constable. 1927. p. 184.

p. 236, *l.* 2   *Military Life of H.R.H. the Duke of Cambridge.* Verner. Murray. 1905. Vol. II. p. 251.

p. 236, *l.* 29   Duke of Cambridge to Sir E. Wood. 27 April 1883. Duke's Papers. R.A.

p. 237, *l.* 23   Duke of Cambridge to Sir Donald Stewart. 30 May, 6 June, 4 July 1884. Duke's Papers. R.A.

p. 238, *l.* 22   *Military Life of H.R.H. The Duke of Cambridge.* Verner. Murray. 1905. Vol. II. p. 270.

p. 239, *l.* 22   *The Staff and the Staff College.* A. R. Godwin-Austen. Constable. 1927. p. 207.

p. 240, *l.* 7   Lord Wolseley to Duke of Cambridge. 4 April 1885. Duke's Papers. R.A.

p. 241, *l.* 13   Lord Wolseley to Duke of Cambridge. 23 October 1884. Duke's Papers. R.A.

p. 241, *l.* 28   *Military Life of H.R.H. The Duke of Cambridge.* Verner. Murray. 1905. Vol. II. p. 299.

p. 242, *l.* 27   *The Life of Lord Wolseley.* Sir F. Maurice and Sir G. Arthur. Heinemann. 1924. p. 252.

p. 242, *l.* 32   Lord Wolseley to Lady Wolseley. 1 February 1887. Royal United Service Institution.

p. 243, *l.* 11   Lord Wolseley to Lady Wolseley. 20 September 1884. 1 February 1887. Royal United Service Institution.

p. 243, *l.* 15   *Records and Reactions.* Earl of Midleton. Murray. 1939. p. 82.

p. 243, *l.* 32   *The Life of Lord Wolseley.* Sir F. Maurice and Sir G. Arthur. Heinemann. 1924. p. 253.

p. 244, *l.* 28   Lord Wolseley to Lady Wolseley. 8 December 1855. 21 September 1882. Royal United Service Institution. Lady Geraldine Somerset's Diary. 3 April 1883. R.A.

p. 245, *l.* 8   *The Letters of Disraeli to Lady Bradford and Lady Chesterfield.* Ed. Marquis of Zetland. Ernest Benn. 1929. Vol. II. p. 254.

p. 245, *l.* 25   *The Life of the Right Hon. Sir Henry Campbell-Bannerman.* J. A. Spender. Hodder and Stoughton. 1923. Vol. I. p. 99.

p. 247, *l.* 2   Duke's Diary. 8 January 1887. FitzGeorge Papers.

p. 247, *l.* 29   *Military Life of H.R.H. The Duke of Cambridge.* Verner. Murray. 1905. Vol. II. pp. 335–6.

p. 249, *l.* 31   Gathorne-Hardy to Duke of Cambridge. 6 February 1877. Colonel Stanley to Duke of Cambridge. 2 February 1879. Duke's Papers. R.A.

p. 250, *l.* 15   *Military Life of H.R.H. The Duke of Cambridge.* Verner. Murray. 1905. Vol. II. p. 313. Lady Geraldine Somerset's Diary. 16 February 1881. R.A.

p. 250, *l.* 33   Lady Geraldine Somerset's Diary. 22 January 1887. R.A.

NOTES FOR CHAPTER 8

p. 260, *l.* 9   Lord Wolseley to Lady Wolseley. 31 August 1890. Royal United Service Institution.

p. 261, *l.* 17   Duke of Cambridge to Prince of Wales. 26 and 29 November 1881. R.A. Addl. Mss. A/5. 28 and 29.

p. 261, *l.* 23   Lord Wolseley to Lady Wolseley. 9 April 1882 [misdated]. Royal United Service Institution.

p. 262, *l.* 5   Lady Geraldine Somerset's Diary. 14 February 1884. R.A.

p. 263, *l.* 20   Duke of Connaught to the Queen. 11 January 1883. Queen to Duke of Connaught. 13 January 1883. R.A. Addl. Mss. A/15. 3886, 3891. Queen to Sir T. Biddulph. R.A. Addl. Mss. A/22. 306.

p. 263, *l.* 24   Lady Geraldine Somerset's Diary. 15 January 1883. 25 May 1884. R.A.

p. 267, *l.* 17   Lady Geraldine Somerset's Diary. 3, 7 January 1883. R.A.

p. 267, *l.* 28   Lady Geraldine Somerset's Diary. 14 January 1883. R.A.

p. 268, *l.* 7   Lady Geraldine Somerset's Diary. 10 August 1883. R.A.

p. 269, *l.* 36   *Under Five Reigns.* Lady Dorothy Nevill. Methuen. 1910. p. 263.

p. 273, *l.* 22   Lady Geraldine Somerset's Diary. 11 January, 10 January 1883. R.A.

p. 276, *l.* 33   Duke of Cambridge to Adolphus FitzGeorge. 16, 19 September 1875. FitzGeorge Papers.

p. 280, *l.* 18   Duke of Cambridge to Adolphus FitzGeorge. 13 March 1893. FitzGeorge Papers.

p. 280, *l.* 30   Lady Geraldine Somerset's Diary. 17 November 1880. 16 December 1879. R.A.

p. 281, *l.* 9   Lady Geraldine Somerset's Diary. 21 October 1879. 15 July 1883. 8 December 1878. R.A.

p. 281, *l.* 26   Lady Geraldine Somerset's Diary. 30 January 1883. 7 April 1878. R.A.

p. 282, *l.* 12   *When I Was at Court.* Lord Ormathwaite. Hutchinson. 1937. pp. 54–5.

p. 283, *l.* 10   Lady Geraldine Somerset's Diary. 8 August 1878. 25 July 1886. R.A.

p. 283, *l.* 28   Lady Geraldine Somerset's Diary. 14 March 1886. R.A.

p. 284, *l.* 16   Lady Geraldine Somerset's Diary. 28 December 1879. 18 February 1879. 26 September 1882. R.A.

p. 285, *l.* 4   Lady Geraldine Somerset's Diary. 25 September 1885. R.A.

p. 285, *l.* 14   Lady Geraldine Somerset's Diary. 11 March 1882. 28 December 1877. R.A.

p. 286, *l.* 3   Lord Wolseley to Lady Wolseley. 31 July 1880. 28 September 1882. Royal United Service Institution.

p. 286, *l.* 31   Lady Geraldine Somerset's Diary. 15, 26 January, 12 February 1884. R.A.

p. 289, *l.* 13   Lady Geraldine Somerset's Diary. 30 January 1882. R.A.

p. 290, *l.* 2   Lady Geraldine Somerset's Diary. 18, 28 January 1887. R.A.

p. 291, *l.* 6   *H.R.H. George Duke of Cambridge.* Sheppard. Longmans. 1906. Vol. II. p. 200.

p. 292, *l.* 6   *Memoirs.* Sir A. Fitzroy. Hutchinson. 1925. p. 300.

p. 294, *l.* 22   Duke of Cambridge to the Queen. 18 January 1890. R.A. Z.72.22.

p. 298, *l.* 9   Lady Geraldine Somerset's Diary. 14 May 1884. 19 August 1886. R.A.

NOTES FOR CHAPTER 9

p. 301, *l.* 5   Lady Geraldine Somerset's Diary. 14 October 1887. R.A.

p. 302, *l.* 18   Lady Geraldine Somerset's Diary. 2 May 1888. R.A.

p. 303, *l.* 5   Lord Wolseley to Lady Wolseley. 9 April 1888. 25 June 1895. Royal United Service Institution. Lord Wolseley to Sir H. Ponsonby. 5 May 1890. R.A. W.12.66.

p. 304, *l.* 25   *The Letters of Queen Victoria.* Ed. G. E. Buckle. Murray. 1926. Third Series. Vol. I. p. 411.

p. 305, *l.* 15   Queen to Sir H. Ponsonby. March 1890. R.A. W.12.14.

p. 305, *l.* 35   F. Edwards to Sir H. Ponsonby. 19 March 1890. R.A. W.12.21. Queen to Sir H. Ponsonby. 20 March 1890. R.A. W.12.22. *The Letters of Queen Victoria.* Ed. G. E. Buckle. Murray. 1926. Third Series. Vol. I. p. 599.

p. 306, *l.* 14   Duke of Cambridge to Sir H. Ponsonby. 3 April 1890. R.A. W.12.26. Sir H. Ponsonby to Duke of Cambridge. 5 April 1890. R.A. W.12.29.

p. 306, *l.* 21   Sir H. Ponsonby to Prince of Wales. 12 August 1890. R.A. W.12.93.

p. 306, *l.* 27   Lord Wolseley to Sir H. Ponsonby. 10 April 1890. R.A. W.12.31.

p. 309, *l.* 1   *The Letters of Queen Victoria.* Ed. G. E. Buckle. Murray. 1926. Third Series. Vol. I. pp. 625, 627–9.

p. 309, *l.* 16   *The Letters of Queen Victoria.* Ed. G. E. Buckle. Murray. 1926. Third Series. Vol. I. p. 630.

p. 309, *l.* 32   Queen to Duke of Cambridge. 29 December 1891. R.A. Z.72.31.

p. 310, *l.* 33 Lord Wolseley to Lady Wolseley. 19 August 1890. Royal United Service Institution.

p. 310, *l.* 35 *Henry Ponsonby. Queen Victoria's Private Secretary.* Ed. A. Ponsonby. Macmillan. 1942. p. 108.

p. 311, *l.* 12 Lord Coventry to Sir Redvers Buller. 4 February 1891. FitzGeorge Papers.

p. 311, *l.* 34 Sir Redvers Buller to the Queen. Sir Redvers Buller to the Duke of Cambridge. 13 February 1891. FitzGeorge Papers.

p. 312, *l.* 26 Prince of Wales to Duke of Cambridge. 13 February 1891. FitzGeorge Papers.

p. 312, *l.* 36 Memorandum of Prince of Wales. Undated. [1891]. FitzGeorge Papers.

p. 313, *l.* 15 Sir F. Knollys to Duke of Cambridge. 13 February 1891. FitzGeorge Papers.

p. 313, *l.* 24 Duke of Fife to Duke of Cambridge. 13 June 1891. FitzGeorge Papers.

p. 313, *l.* 31 Sir F. Knollys to Sir H. Ponsonby. 15 February 1891. R.A. Y.182.11.

p. 314, *l.* 7 *Life and Adventures.* Frank Harris. Richards Press. 1947. p. 455.

p. 316, *l.* 30 *An Autobiography.* Elizabeth Butler. Constable. 1922. pp. 218–19.

p. 317, *l.* 20 Lady Geraldine Somerset's Diary. 15 December 1893. R.A.

p. 318, *l.* 5 *The Life of Lord Roberts.* David James. Hollis and Carter. 1954. p. 381.

p. 319, *l.* 3 Lady Geraldine Somerset's Diary. 18 May 1893. 30 December 1895. R.A.

p. 319, *l.* 14 *The Life of Lord Wolseley.* Sir F. Maurice and Sir G. Arthur. Heinemann. 1924. p. 225.

p. 319, *l.* 21 Lord Wolseley to Lady Wolseley. 25 August 1889. Royal United Service Institution.

p. 319, *l.* 37 Prince of Wales to Sir H. Ponsonby. R.A. W.10.88.

p. 321, *l.* 26 *Embassies of Other Days and Further Recollections* Lady Paget. Hutchinson. 1923. Vol. II. p. 413.

p. 322, *l.* 2 *Labby.* Hesketh Pearson. Hamish Hamilton. 1936. p. 250.

p. 323, *l.* 2 Lady Geraldine Somerset's Diary. 19 January, 5 November 1885. 30 January 1887. R.A.

p. 324, *l.* 5 Lady Geraldine Somerset's Diary. 20 April 1895. 21 May, 27 July 1894. R.A.

p. 324, *l.* 32 Lady Geraldine Somerset's Diary. 7 July 1893. R.A.

p. 325, *l.* 12 Lady Geraldine Somerset's Diary. 17 July 1892. R.A. Duke of Cambridge to the Queen. February 1886. R.A. C.37.285.

p. 325, *l.* 33   Memoranda. Sir A. Bigge. R.A. E.41.28 and 47. Sir F. Knollys to Sir A. Bigge. 1 June 1895. R.A. E.41.71.

p. 326, *l.* 13   Memorandum. Sir A. Bigge. 16 May 1895. R.A. E.41.49.

p. 326, *l.* 34   Lady Geraldine Somerset's Diary. 7 May, 18 May 1895. R.A.

p. 328, *l.* 13   *The Life of the Right Hon. Sir H. Campbell-Bannerman.* J. A. Spender. Hodder and Stoughton. 1923. Vol. I. pp. 149–50.

p. 328, *l.* 27   Sir F. Knollys to Sir A. Bigge. 12 May 1895. R.A. E.41.26. Lady Geraldine Somerset's Diary. 18 May 1895. R.A.

p. 329, *l.* 33   *Military Life of H.R.H. The Duke of Cambridge.* Verner. Murray. 1905. Vol. II. pp. 395–6.

p. 330, *l.* 17   *The Letters of Queen Victoria.* Ed. G. E. Buckle. Murray. 1926. Third Series. Vol. II. p. 513.

p. 330, *l.* 37   Memorandum of Sir A. Bigge. R.A. E.41.129. Lady Geraldine Somerset's Diary, 10 June 1895.

p. 331, *l.* 19   Lord Rosebery to Sir A. Bigge. 19 June 1895. R.A. E.41.104.

p. 332, *l.* 22   *The Staff and the Staff College.* Godwin-Austen. Constable. 1927. p. 222. *Field-Marshal Sir Henry Wilson.* Sir C. E. Callwell. Cassell. 1927. Vol. I. p. 19.

p. 333, *l.* 8   *The Life and Letters of Lady Dorothy Nevill.* R. Nevill. Methuen. 1919. p. 136.

p. 333, *l.* 23   Memorandum. Sir A. Bigge. 20 May 1895. R.A. E.41.57.

p. 333, *l.* 36   *The Life of the Rt. Hon. Sir Henry Campbell-Bannerman.* J. A. Spender. Hodder and Stoughton. 1923. Vol. I. p. 157.

p. 335, *l.* 22   Lady Geraldine Somerset's Diary. 20 October 1895. R.A.

p. 335, *l.* 33   Duke's Diary. 20 June, 16 August 1895. FitzGeorge Papers.

p. 336, *l.* 3   Lord Wolseley to Lady Wolseley. 23 August 1895. Royal United Service Institution.

p. 336, *l.* 22   *Recollections of a Life in the British Army.* Sir R. Harrison. Smith, Elder and Co. 1908. pp. 326–7.

p. 338, *l.* 14   *Military Life of H.R.H. The Duke of Cambridge.* Verner. Murray. 1905. Vol. II. pp. 404–5, 403, 402–3.

p. 338, *l.* 30   Lady Geraldine Somerset's Diary. 10 November 1895. R.A.

NOTES FOR CHAPTER 10

p. 339, *l.* 8   *Military Life of H.R.H. The Duke of Cambridge.* Verner. Murray. 1905. Vol. II. p. 399.

p. 339, *l.* 26   Lady Geraldine Somerset's Diary. 2 May, 15 February 1896. R.A.

p. 340, *l.* 30   Lady Geraldine Somerset's Diary. 8 May 1896. R.A.

p. 348, *l.* 3   *Memoirs.* Sir Almeric Fitzroy. Hutchinson. 1925. Vol. I. p. 45.

p. 350, *l.* 21   *Queen Mary.* J. Pope-Hennessy. Allen and Unwin. 1959. p. 388.

p. 351, *l.* 35   *Queen Mary.* J. Pope-Hennessy. Allen and Unwin. 1959. p. 388. *A Picture of Life.* Mersey. Murray. 1941. p. 208.

p. 353, *l.* 5   *Henry Ponsonby. His Life from His Letters.* A. Ponsonby. Macmillan. 1943. p. 93.

p. 353, *l.* 16   *The Staff and the Staff College.* A. R. Godwin-Austen. Constable. 1927. p. 226.

p. 354, *l.* 25   *Fifty Years of Fleet Street.* Sir J. Robinson. Macmillan. 1904. pp. 299–300.

p. 354, *l.* 37   *The Life of Lord Wolseley.* Sir F. Maurice and Sir G. Arthur. Heinemann. 1924. p. 234. *Victorians, Edwardians and Georgians.* J. Boon. Hutchinson. 1928. p. 233.

p. 355, *l.* 14   *From Private to Field Marshal.* Sir W. Robertson. Constable. 1921. p. 17.

p. 356, *l.* 8   *Military Life of H.R.H. The Duke of Cambridge.* Verner. Murray. 1905. Vol. II. p. 363.

p. 357, *l.* 17   *The Staff and the Staff College.* A. R. Godwin-Austen. Constable. 1927. pp. 179–80.

p. 357, *l.* 28   *Memoirs Discreet and Indiscreet.* Herbert Jenkins. 1917. p. 55.

p. 358, *l.* 10   *Motoring Annual and Motorist's Year Book.* 1903.

p. 359, *l.* 5   *The Times.* 27 September 1895.

p. 359, *l.* 15   *A History of the British Army.* J. W. Fortescue. Macmillan. 1899–1930. Vol. XIII. p. 557.

p. 359, *l.* 35   *Gathorne-Hardy, First Earl of Cranbrook.* A. Gathorne-Hardy. Longmans. 1910. Vol. I. p. 343. Lady Geraldine Somerset's Diary. 19 April 1885. R.A. *Memories.* Lord Redesdale. Hutchinson. 1915. Vol. II. p. 700.

p. 360, *l.* 15   *Records and Reactions.* Lord Midleton. Murray. 1939. pp. 82–3.

p. 362, *l.* 3   Lord Wolseley to Lady Wolseley. 9 October 1890. Royal United Service Institution.

p. 363, *l.* 7   *The Story of a Soldier's Life.* Wolseley. Constable. 1903. Vol. II. pp. 234–5.

p. 364, *l.* 3   Lord Wolseley to Sir A. FitzGeorge. December 1906. FitzGeorge Papers.

p. 364, *l.* 27   *Memories.* Lord Redesdale. Hutchinson. 1915. p. 700. *Forty Years On.* Lord E. Hamilton. Hodder and Stoughton. 1922. p. 185.

p. 365, *l.* 16   *The Story of My Life.* Sir H. Johnston. Chatto and Windus. 1923. p. 153. Mrs. Middleton to the Duke of Cambridge. 29 April 1875. Duke's Papers. R.A.

p. 366, *l.* 10   *Notes of a Nomad.* Lady Jephson. Hutchinson. 1918. p. 177.

p. 366, *l.* 24   Lady Geraldine Somerset's Diary. 5 August 1876. 31 October 1884. R.A.

Select Bibliography

Arthur, Sir George: *From Wellington to Wavell*. Hutchinson. 1942.

Bamford, Francis, Ed.: *The Journal of Mrs. Arbuthnot*. Macmillan. 1950.

Biddulph, General Sir Robert: *Lord Cardwell at the War Office*. Murray. 1904.

Bond, Brian: "The Retirement of the Duke of Cambridge." *Journal of the Royal United Service Institution*, No. 624 (1961).

Buckle, G. E., Ed.: *The Letters of Queen Victoria*. Murray. 1926.

Childers, Lt.-Col. Spencer: *The Life and Correspondence of the Rt. Hon. Hugh C. E. Childers*. Murray. 1901.

Clode, Charles: *The Military Forces of the Crown; Their Administration and Government*. Murray. 1869.

Douglas, Sir George, Ed.: *The Panmure Papers*. Hodder and Stoughton. 1908.

Duff, Ethel M.: *The Life Story of H.R.H. The Duke of Cambridge*. Stanley Paul. 1938.

Erickson, Arvel: "Edward T. Cardwell: Peelite." *Transactions of the American Philosophical Society*, N.S. Vol. 49, part 2 (1959). American Philosophical Society.

Farrer, J. A.: *The Monarchy in Politics*. Fisher and Unwin. 1917.

Fortescue, J. W.: *A History of the British Army*. 13 Volumes. Macmillan. 1899–1930.

Gathorne-Hardy, A. E., Ed.: *Gathorne-Hardy, First Earl of Cranbrook. A Memoir*. Longmans. 1910.

Godwin-Austen, A. R.: *The Staff and the Staff College*. Constable. 1927.

Gordon, Hampden. *The War Office*. Putnam. 1935.

Hibbert, Christopher: *The Destruction of Lord Raglan*. Longmans. 1961.

James, David: *The Life of Lord Roberts*. Hollis and Carter. 1954.

Kinglake, A. W.: *The Invasion of the Crimea*. 8 Volumes. Blackwood. 1863–1887.

Kingston, Charles: *Famous Morganatic Marriages*. Stanley Paul. 1919.

Kinlock Cooke, Charles: *A Memoir of Her Royal Highness Princess Mary Adelaide Duchess of Teck*. 2 Volumes. Murray. 1900.

Lee, Sir Sidney: *King Edward VII—A Biography*. 2 Volumes. Macmillan. 1925.

Martin, Sir T.: *The Life of H.R.H. The Prince Consort.* 5 Volumes. Smith, Elder and Co. 1874–1880.

Maurice, Sir F., and Arthur, Sir G.: *The Life of Lord Wolseley.* Heinemann. 1924.

Maxwell, Sir H.: *The Life and Letters of the Fourth Earl of Clarendon.* 2 Volumes. Arnold. 1913.

Napier, Lt.-Col. H.D., Ed.: *Letters of Field-Marshal Lord Napier of Magdala.* Jarrold & Sons. 1936.

Omond, Lt.-Col. J. S.: *Parliament and the Army.* Cambridge University Press. 1933.

Ponsonby, A.: *Henry Ponsonby, Queen Victoria's Private Secretary, His Life from His Letters.* Macmillan. 1943.

Pope-Hennessy, James: *Queen Mary.* Allen and Unwin. 1959.

Robertson, Sir William: *From Private to Field-Marshal.* Constable. 1921.

Sandars, Mary: *The Life and Times of Queen Adelaide.* Stanley Paul. 1915.

Sheppard, Edgar: *H.R.H. George Duke of Cambridge.* 2 Volumes. Longmans. 1906.

Spender, J. A.: *The Life of the Right Hon. Sir Henry Campbell-Bannerman.* 2 Volumes. Hodder and Stoughton. 1923.

Stocqueler, J. H.: *A Personal History of the Horse Guards from 1750 to 1872.* Hurst and Blackett. 1873.

Strachey, Lytton, and Fulford, Roger, Ed.: *The Greville Memoirs.* Macmillan. 1938.

Verner, Willoughby: *Military Life of H.R.H. The Duke of Cambridge.* 2 Volumes. Murray. 1905.

Wheeler, Captain Owen: *The War Office Past and Present.* Methuen. 1914.

Wolseley, Field-Marshal Viscount: *The Story of a Soldier's Life.* Constable. 1903.

Wyndham, Mrs. Hugh, Ed.: *Correspondence of Sarah Spencer Lady Lyttelton 1787–1870.* Murray, 1912.

Index

A

Aberdeen, 324

Abu Klea, Battle of, 242

Abyssinia, 366

Adelaide, Queen: takes George under her wing in England, 11–20; George's confirmation, 20–3; death of William IV, 23–5

Afghanistan, 191, 361

Africa, South, 152, 190–7, 200, 207, 346

Airey, Lord, 100, 109, 110, 152, 169, 356, 366

Albany, H.R.H. Duke of, 234

Aldershot, 112, 173, 187, 191, 210–11, 319, 322, 344, 355, 356, 357

Alexandra of Denmark, Princess, *see* Wales, Princess of

Alexandra, Queen, *see* Wales, Princess of

Alexandria, 316

Alma, Battle of, 76–80, 85, 87, 106–7, 109, 200–1, 319, 322

Almacks, 260

America, 140

Amherst, Lord, 117

Anne, Queen, 3

Anson, Gen., 133

Arabi, 233

Army: reforms, 58–65; Commander-in-Chief's functions, 115–17; state of, 118; Duke's letters and reforms, 119; Kneller Hall, 120; estimates and Commissariat, 120; in-

Army (*cont.*)
adequacy of defence, 121–2; expenditure, 122–3; Indian army, 122–3; Sir John Burgoyne's pamphlet, 125; Duke's low opinion of Staff College, 126–9; staff training, 127–32; Staff College reconstituted, 128–32; reforms under Cardwell, 148–56; Army Enlistment Act, 160; abolition of purchase, 163–73; territorial system, 230–2; khaki uniform, 234–6; Camel Corps, 240; military expenditure, 249–50; Hartington Report, 304–9

Army and Navy Gazette, 142, 215

Athens, 32

Augusta, Princess, 18, 22, 51, 70, 158, 182, 252, 271, 290, 324, 343, 348, 349

Australia, 142, 275

B

baccarat, 310

Baden-Baden, 253

Bagot, Sir Charles, 6

Balaclava, Battle of, 85–6, 87, 89, 90–1

Balfour, Arthur, 349

Balmoral, 222, 223, 228, 256

Baring, Rosa, 274

Baring, Sir Evelyn, 241

Bateson, 295

Bath and Wells, Bishop of, 28

Bayswater Gate, 271

i

Index

Cambridge, Duke of (*cont.*)
18; censures sister, 318; last year in office, 320; "The Cambridge Constitution," 320; very stout, 321; shooting ducks on the Serpentine, 321; engagement and death of Duke of Clarence, 323; marriage of Princess May, 324; resignation, 326–38; letter from Queen and reply, 329–30; grievances, 332–3; government defeat, 334; Wolseley Commander-in-Chief, 335; condolences, 336; Aide-de-Camp to Queen, 336, 339; no pension, 336–7, 340–1; retirement, 338, 340–1; properties, 340–1; companionship of family, 341; charities, 342; Diamond Jubilee celebrations, 342–4; death of Duke and Duchess of Teck, 344–6; death of friends, 345; Boer War, 346; last visit to Queen, 346; death of Queen, 346–8; Edward VII's coronation, 348; death, 348; obituaries and funeral, 349–52; summing up, 352–67; speeches, 364; affection of Army, 364; correspondence, 365–6; statue, 366

Cambridge, Princess Augusta, Duchess of: marriage and birth of a son (George), 5; interest in politics, music and theatre, 10; description of, 10; grief when George leaves Hanover, 13–14; George's confirmation, 20–2; leaves Hanover, 25; Victoria's coronation, 26–8; George's marriage, 35–7;

Cambridge, Duke of (*cont.*)
death of Duke, 50–2; sealed letter from George, 67–8; opposition to George's return home from Crimea, 94; correspondence, 95–7; welcome home, 101; review of troops at Aldershot, 112; George Commander-in-Chief, 113–14; death of Duchess of Gloucester, 133–4; death of Prince Consort, 135–8; abhorrence of Prince Consort, 138; marriage of Princess Mary Adelaide, 139–40; grudge against Prussia, 158–9; stroke, 182; George discusses Wolseley, 193; Wolseley "A firebrand," 220; Egypt parade, 233; Gladstone, 245–6; Randolph Churchill's resignation, 248; Golden Jubilee, 250; Naval Review, 252; garden party and Gladstone, 253; George's anniversary, 256–7; death of Louisa Beauclerk, 262; Louisa Beauclerk a delightful person, 263; tales of Louisa Beauclerk, 267; George reads old letters, 268; meets grandsons, 273; Adolphus's marriage, 276–7; George's imitations and music, 280–1; Christmas party, 282; gossip about Queen, 285–6; recollections of old days, 286–7; interest in foreign affairs, 287–8; illness and death, 290

Cambridge, Marquess of, 350
Camel Corps, 240
Campbell, Sir Colin, 67, 77–8, 108, 122, 132–3, 201
Campbell-Bannerman, Mr., 245, 324, 326, 327, 331, 333, 334, 350
Canada, 342

v

A NOTE ON THE TYPE

THE TEXT of this book was set in a typeface called *Primer*, designed by RUDOLPH RUZICKA for the Mergenthaler Linotype Company and first made available in 1949. Primer, a modified modern face based on Century broadface, was designed with a view to greatest legibility in the use of today's methods of composition and printing.

Primer is Ruzicka's third typeface. In 1940 he designed Fairfield, and in 1947 Fairfield Medium, both for the Mergenthaler Linotype Company.

Ruzicka was born in Bohemia in 1883 and came to the United States at the age of eleven. He attended public schools in Chicago and later the Chicago Art Institute. During his long career he has been a wood engraver, etcher, cartographer, and book designer. For many years he was associated with Daniel Berkeley Updike and produced the annual keepsakes for The Merrymount Press from 1911 until 1941.

Ruzicka has been honored by many distinguished organizations, and in 1936 he was awarded the gold medal of the American Institute of Graphic Arts. From his home in New Hampshire, Ruzicka continues to be active in the graphic arts.

Typography and binding design by
WARREN CHAPPELL